Angel Sanctuary

story and art by Kaori Yuki
vol.4

Angel Sanctuary

Vol. 4
Shôjo Edition

STORY AND ART BY KAORI YUKI

Translation/JN Productions
English Adaptation/Marv Wolfman
Touch-up & Lettering/James Hudnall
Cover, Graphics & Design/Izumi Evers
Editor/William Flanagan
Supervising Editor/Frances E. Wall

Managing Editor/Annette Roman
Editorial Director/Alvin Lu
Director of Production/Noboru Watanabe
Sr. Director of Licensing & Acquisitions/Rika Inouye
Vice President of Sales/Joe Morici
Vice President of Marketing/Liza Coppola
Executive Vice President/Hyoe Narita
Publisher/Seiji Horibuchi

Published by VIZ, LLC
P.O. Box 77010
San Francisco, CA 94107

Shôjo Edition
10 9 8 7 8 5 4 3 2 1
First printing, September 2004

Angel Sanctuary ™

story and art by **Kaori Yuki**   vol.4

The Story Thus Far

High school boy Setsuna Mudo has just destroyed the world. He's always been a troublemaker, but his worst sin was falling incestuously in love with his beautiful sister Sara. However, his troubles were foreordained; he is the reincarnation of an angel, the Lady Alexiel, who rebelled against Heaven and led the demons of hell, the Evils, in a revolt. Her punishment was to be reborn into tragic life after tragic life. This time, her life is Setsuna.

But these days, God does not reign in heaven, and the rule of the highest angels, child-like Metatron, and strict dictator Sevothtarte is shaky. Through the forbidden use of innocent human lives, the cherubim Katan has resurrected the high angel Rosiel from slumber and banishment on Earth. Rosiel, no longer quite sane, does not at once ascend to heaven to reclaim his position as most favored of God, but instead sets his servants, Katan and the selfish young female angel, Kirie, to attack Setsuna and somehow reawaken the dormant Alexiel within him.

Kurai and Arachne, two Evils—Alexiel's followers from the revolt—do what they can to help Setsuna, as does Setsuna's mysterious immortal friend Kira. They succeed in giving Setsuna a few days of true happiness with Sara, but the price is Kira's freedom when he is arrested and charged with murder. Hearing this on the news, Setsuna and Sara return to Tokyo to try to help Kira, but before they can meet with him, a disguised Kirie meets them at the bus station and leads them into the trap. Sara throws herself between Setsuna and the murderous Kirie only to take the attack herself and die.

Sara's death forces Alexiel to reawaken from within Setsuna, and the power of the reawakening destroys Tokyo and threatens to destroy the world.

Contents

Characters

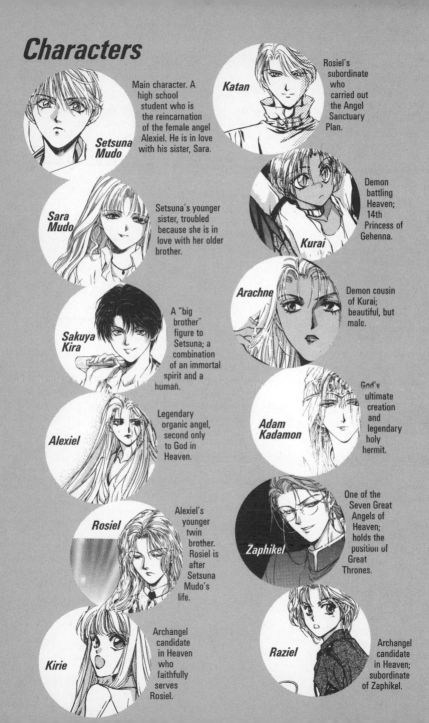

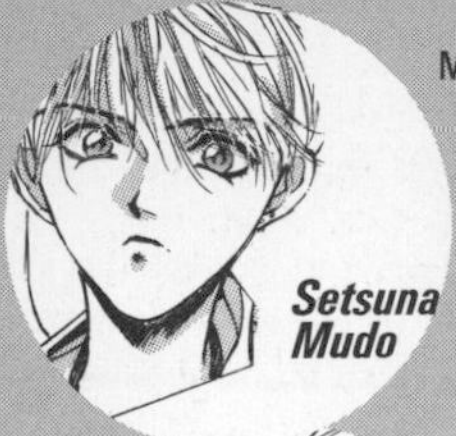
Setsuna Mudo

Main character. A high school student who is the reincarnation of the female angel Alexiel. He is in love with his sister, Sara.

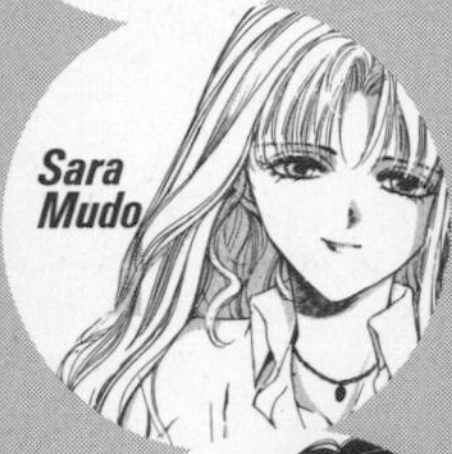
Sara Mudo

Setsuna's younger sister, troubled because she is in love with her older brother.

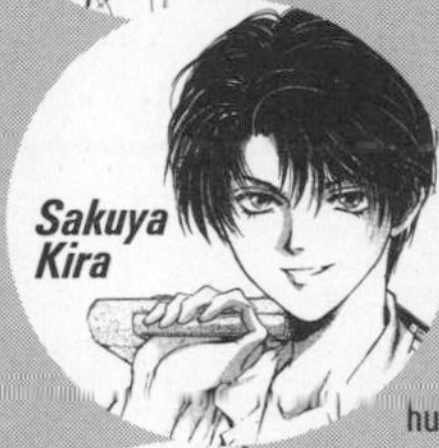
Sakuya Kira

A "big brother" figure to Setsuna; a combination of an immortal spirit and a human.

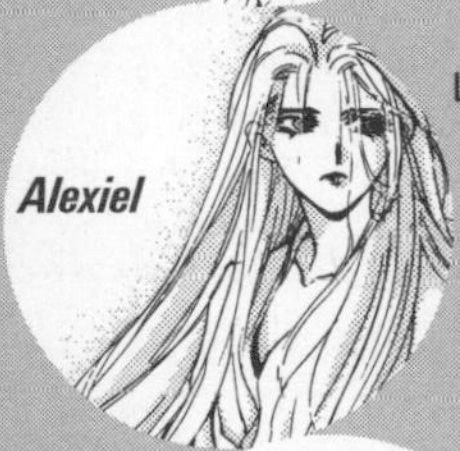
Alexiel

Legendary organic angel, second only to God in Heaven.

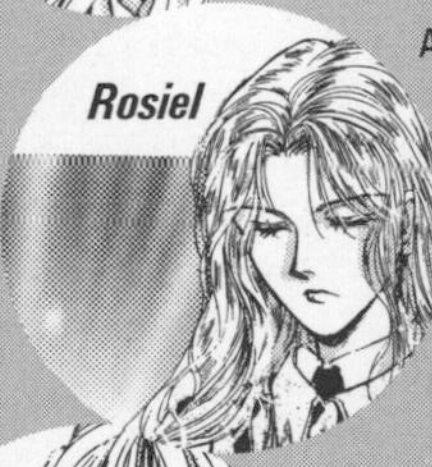
Rosiel

Alexiel's younger twin brother. Rosiel is after Setsuna Mudo's life.

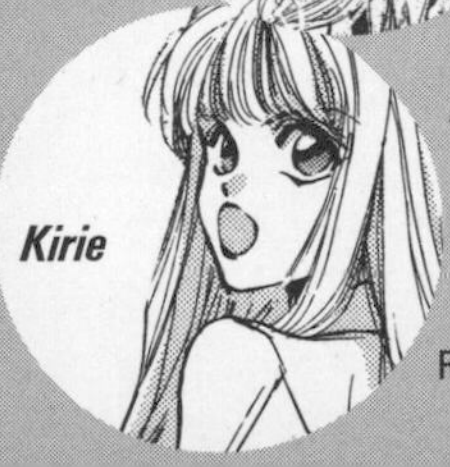
Kirie

Archangel candidate in Heaven who faithfully serves Rosiel.

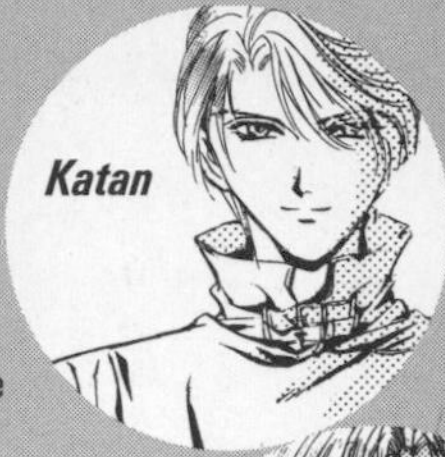
Katan

Rosiel's subordinate who carried out the Angel Sanctuary Plan.

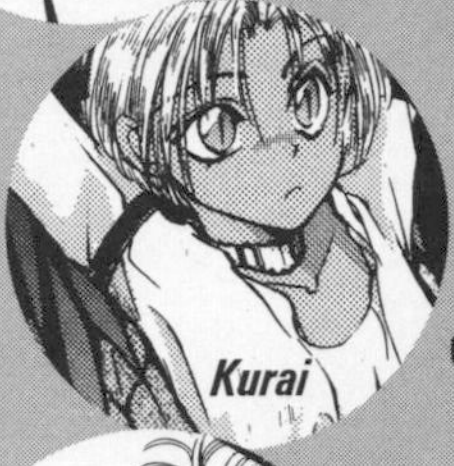
Kurai

Demon battling Heaven; 14th Princess of Gehenna.

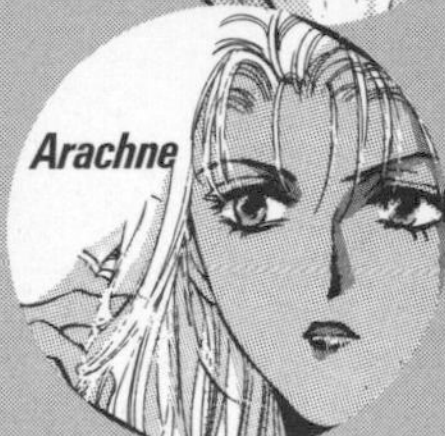
Arachne

Demon cousin of Kurai; beautiful, but male.

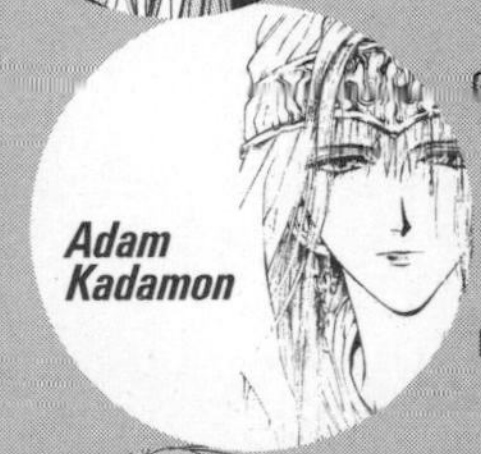
Adam Kadamon

God's ultimate creation and legendary holy hermit.

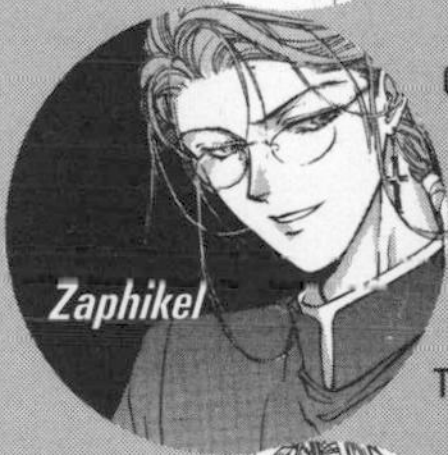
Zaphikel

One of the Seven Great Angels of Heaven; holds the position of Great Thrones.

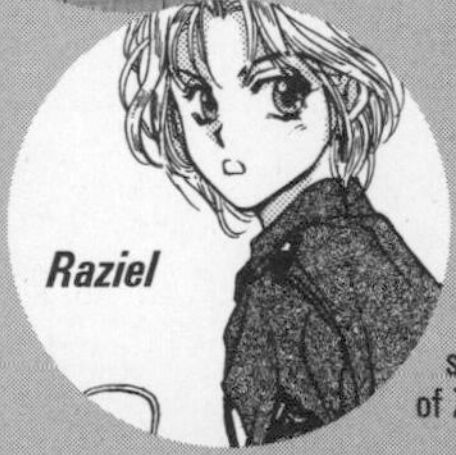
Raziel

Archangel candidate in Heaven; subordinate of Zaphikel.

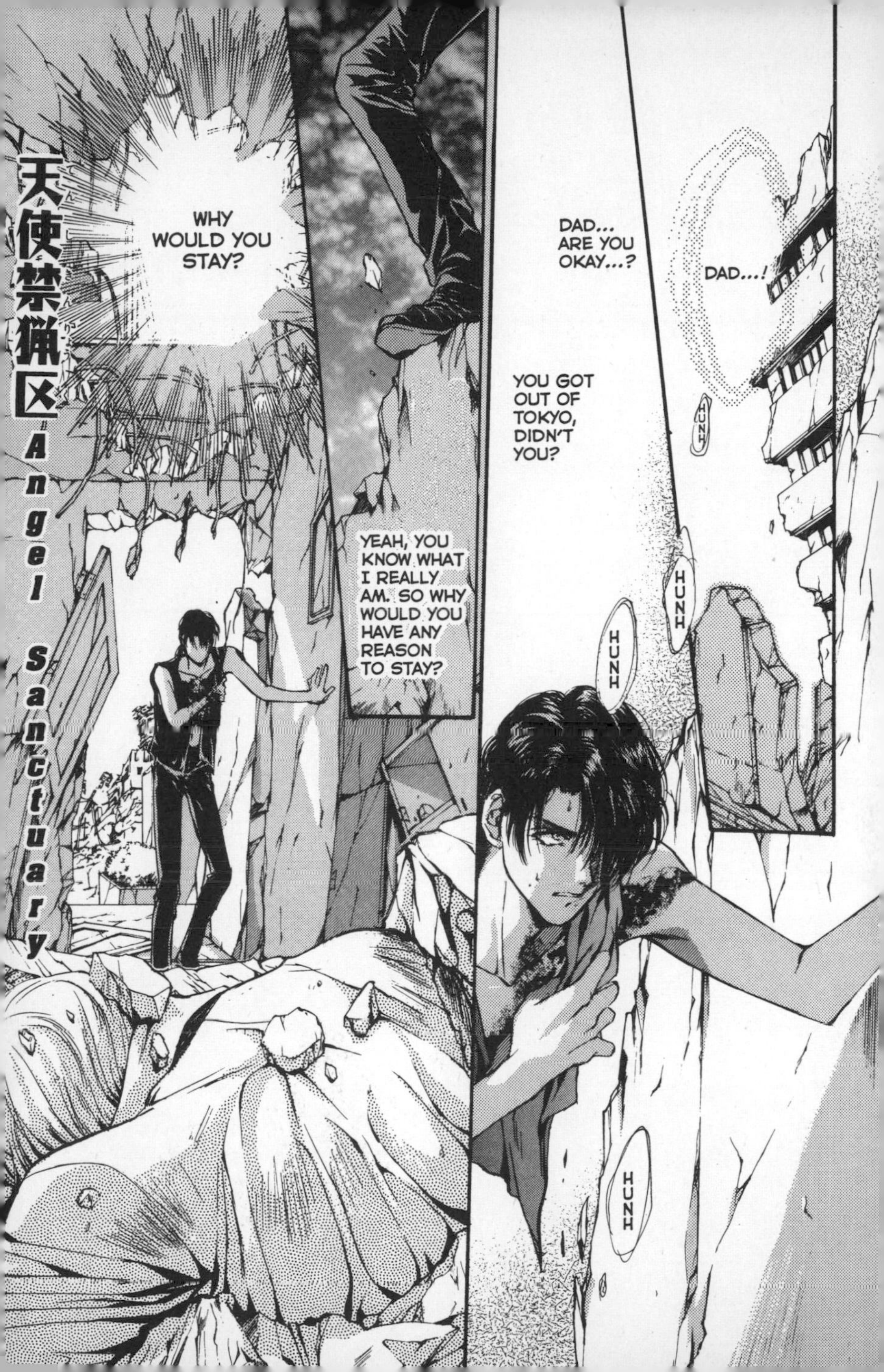
DAD...!
HUNH
HUNH
HUNH
HUNH
DAD... ARE YOU OKAY...?
YOU GOT OUT OF TOKYO, DIDN'T YOU?
YEAH, YOU KNOW WHAT I REALLY AM. SO WHY WOULD YOU HAVE ANY REASON TO STAY?
WHY WOULD YOU STAY?
天使禁猟区
Angel Sanctuary

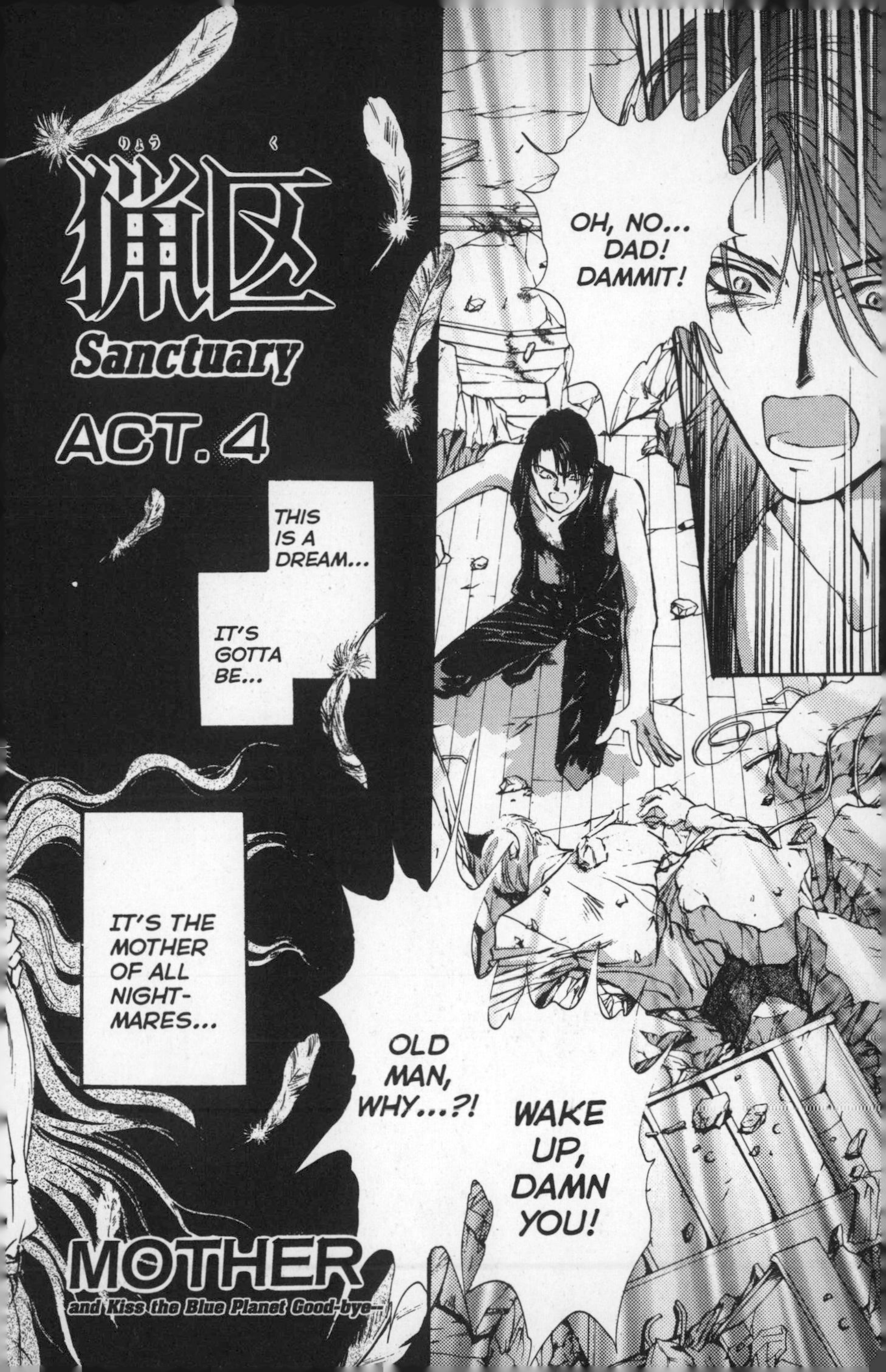
OH, NO... DAD! DAMMIT!
OLD MAN, WHY...?!
WAKE UP, DAMN YOU!
猟区（りょうく）
Sanctuary
ACT. 4
THIS IS A DREAM...
IT'S GOTTA BE...
IT'S THE MOTHER OF ALL NIGHT-MARES...
MOTHER
and Kiss the Blue Planet Good-bye--

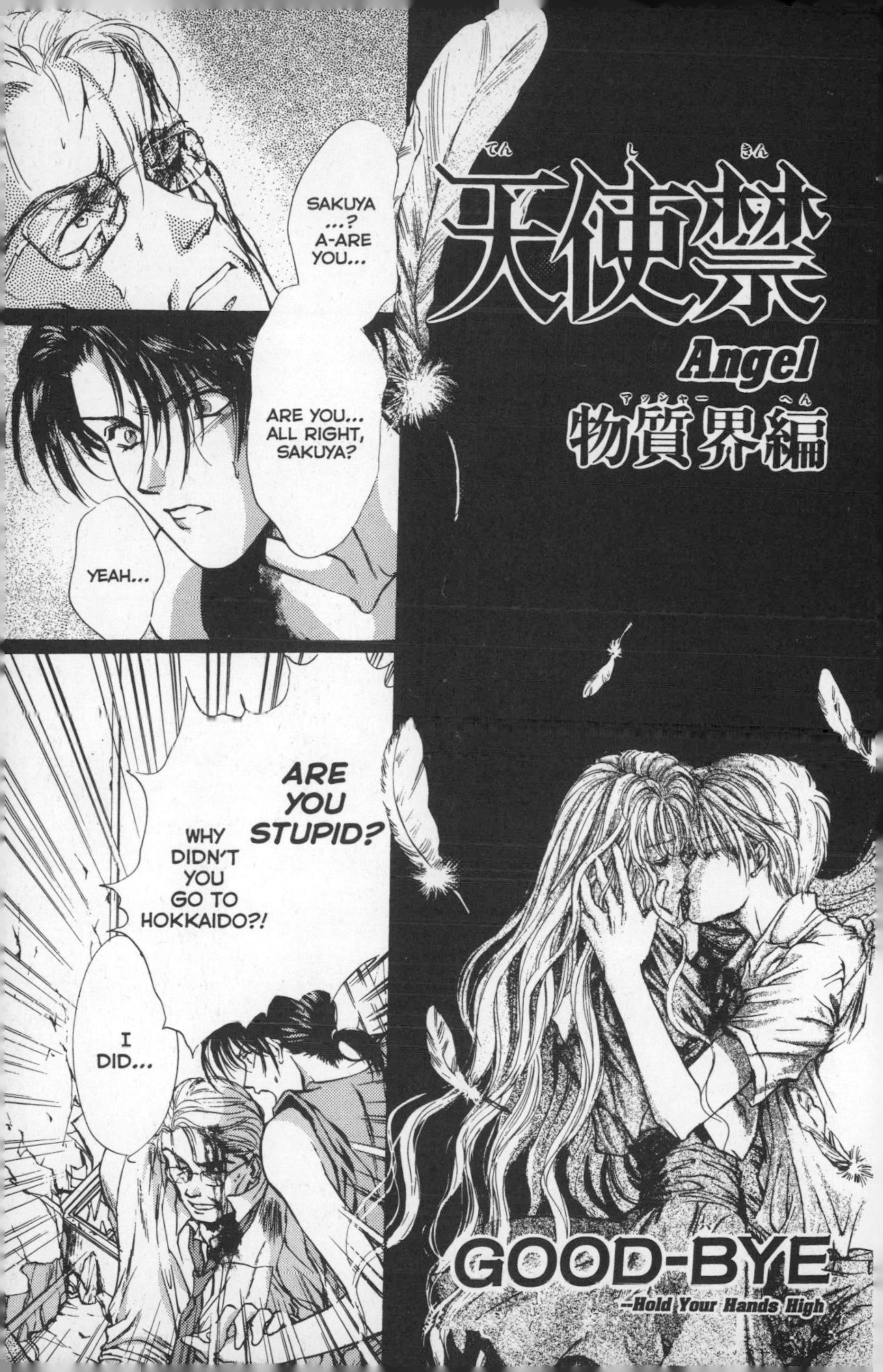
天使禁
てんしきん
Angel
物質界編
アッシャーへん
GOOD-BYE
--Hold Your Hands High
SAKUYA ...? A-ARE YOU...
ARE YOU... ALL RIGHT, SAKUYA?
YEAH...
ARE YOU STUPID?
WHY DIDN'T YOU GO TO HOKKAIDO?!
I DID...

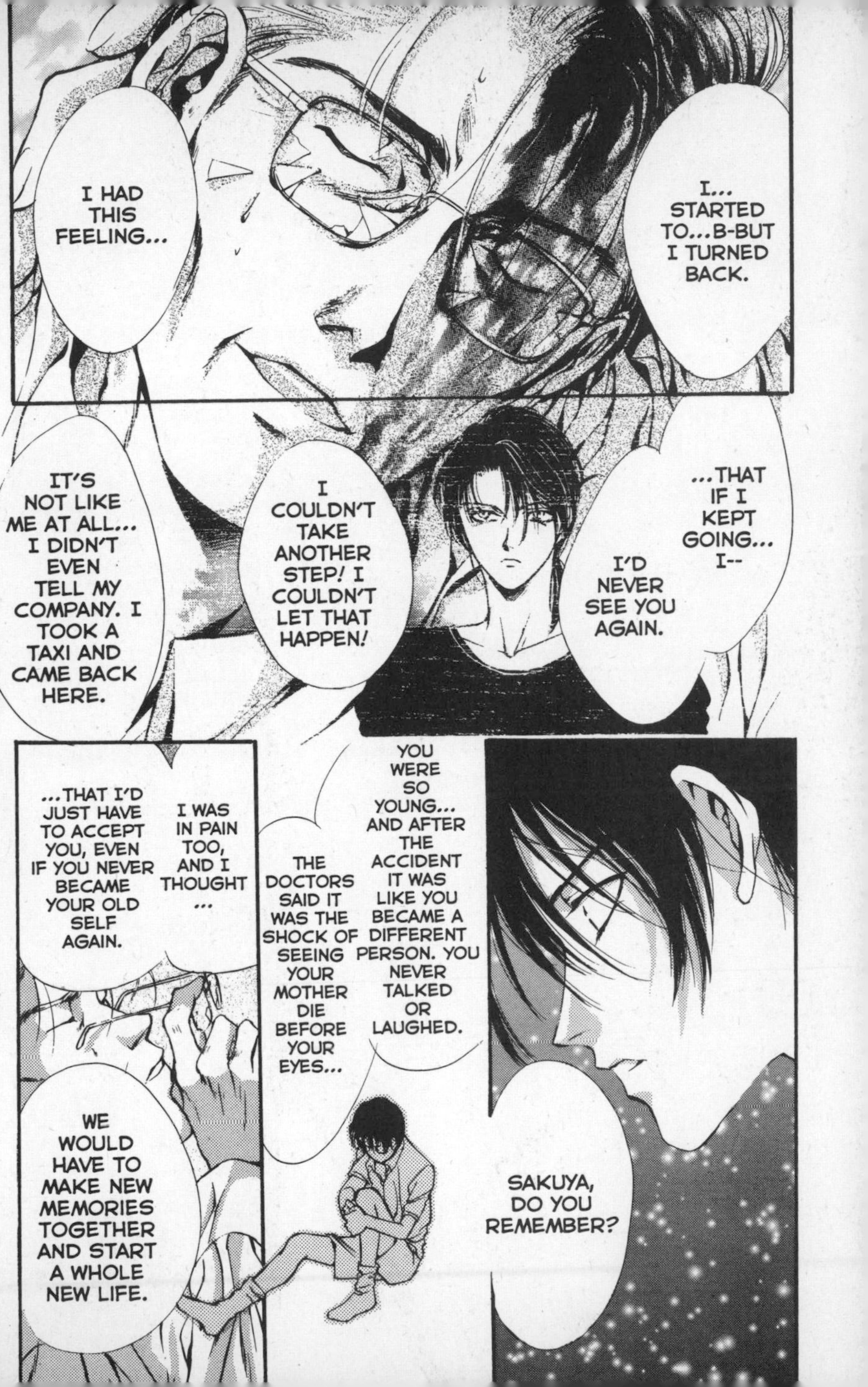
I... STARTED TO...B-BUT I TURNED BACK.
I HAD THIS FEELING...
...THAT IF I KEPT GOING... I--
I'D NEVER SEE YOU AGAIN.
I COULDN'T TAKE ANOTHER STEP! I COULDN'T LET THAT HAPPEN!
IT'S NOT LIKE ME AT ALL... I DIDN'T EVEN TELL MY COMPANY. I TOOK A TAXI AND CAME BACK HERE.
SAKUYA, DO YOU REMEMBER?
YOU WERE SO YOUNG... AND AFTER THE ACCIDENT IT WAS LIKE YOU BECAME A DIFFERENT PERSON. YOU NEVER TALKED OR LAUGHED.
THE DOCTORS SAID IT WAS THE SHOCK OF SEEING YOUR MOTHER DIE BEFORE YOUR EYES...
I WAS IN PAIN TOO, AND I THOUGHT ...
...THAT I'D JUST HAVE TO ACCEPT YOU, EVEN IF YOU NEVER BECAME YOUR OLD SELF AGAIN.
WE WOULD HAVE TO MAKE NEW MEMORIES TOGETHER AND START A WHOLE NEW LIFE.

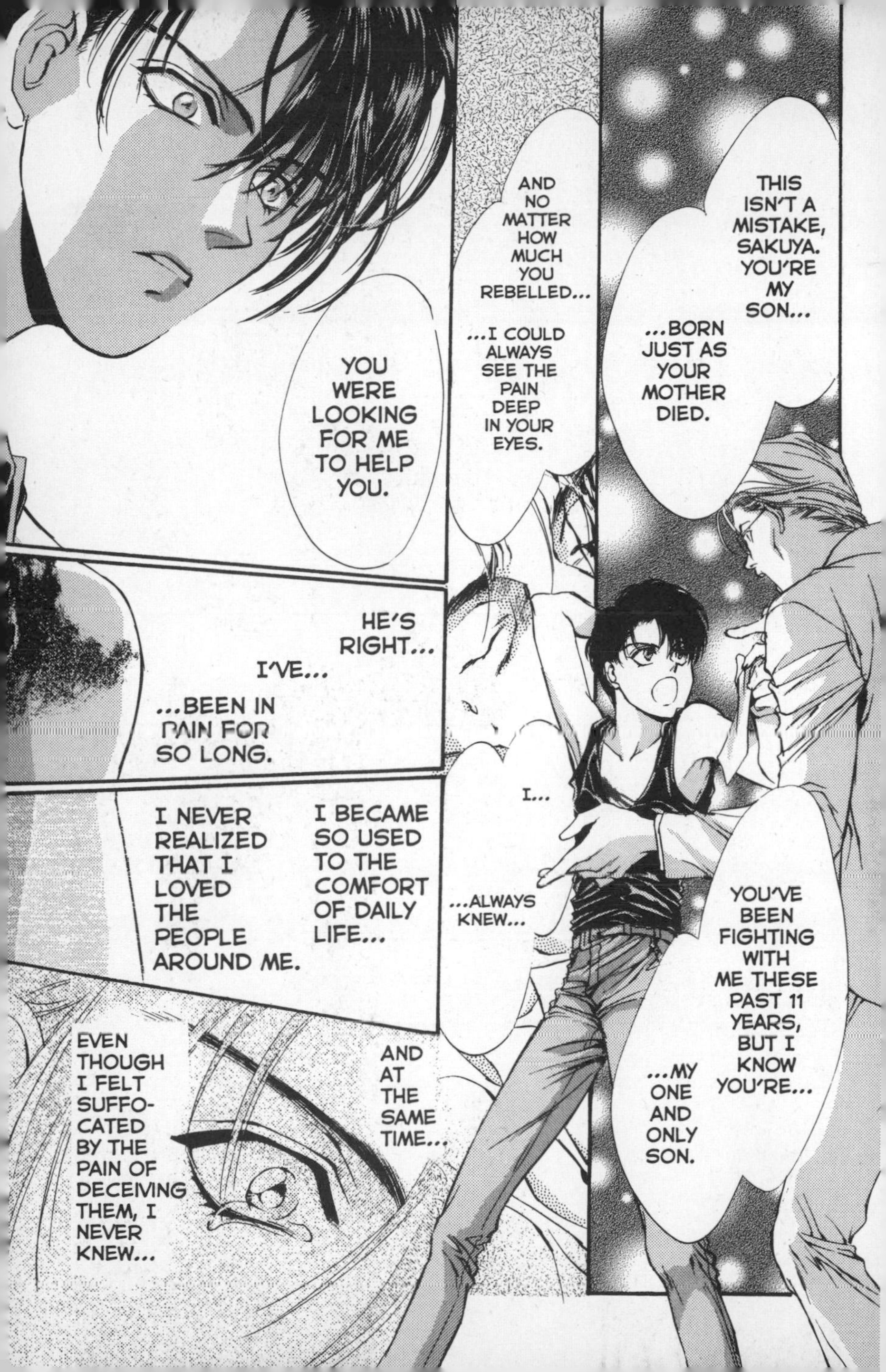
THIS ISN'T A MISTAKE, SAKUYA. YOU'RE MY SON...
...BORN JUST AS YOUR MOTHER DIED.
AND NO MATTER HOW MUCH YOU REBELLED...
...I COULD ALWAYS SEE THE PAIN DEEP IN YOUR EYES.
YOU'VE BEEN FIGHTING WITH ME THESE PAST 11 YEARS, BUT I KNOW YOU'RE...
...MY ONE AND ONLY SON.
I...
...ALWAYS KNEW...
YOU WERE LOOKING FOR ME TO HELP YOU.
HE'S RIGHT...
I'VE...
...BEEN IN PAIN FOR SO LONG.
I BECAME SO USED TO THE COMFORT OF DAILY LIFE...
I NEVER REALIZED THAT I LOVED THE PEOPLE AROUND ME.
AND AT THE SAME TIME...
EVEN THOUGH I FELT SUFFOCATED BY THE PAIN OF DECEIVING THEM, I NEVER KNEW...

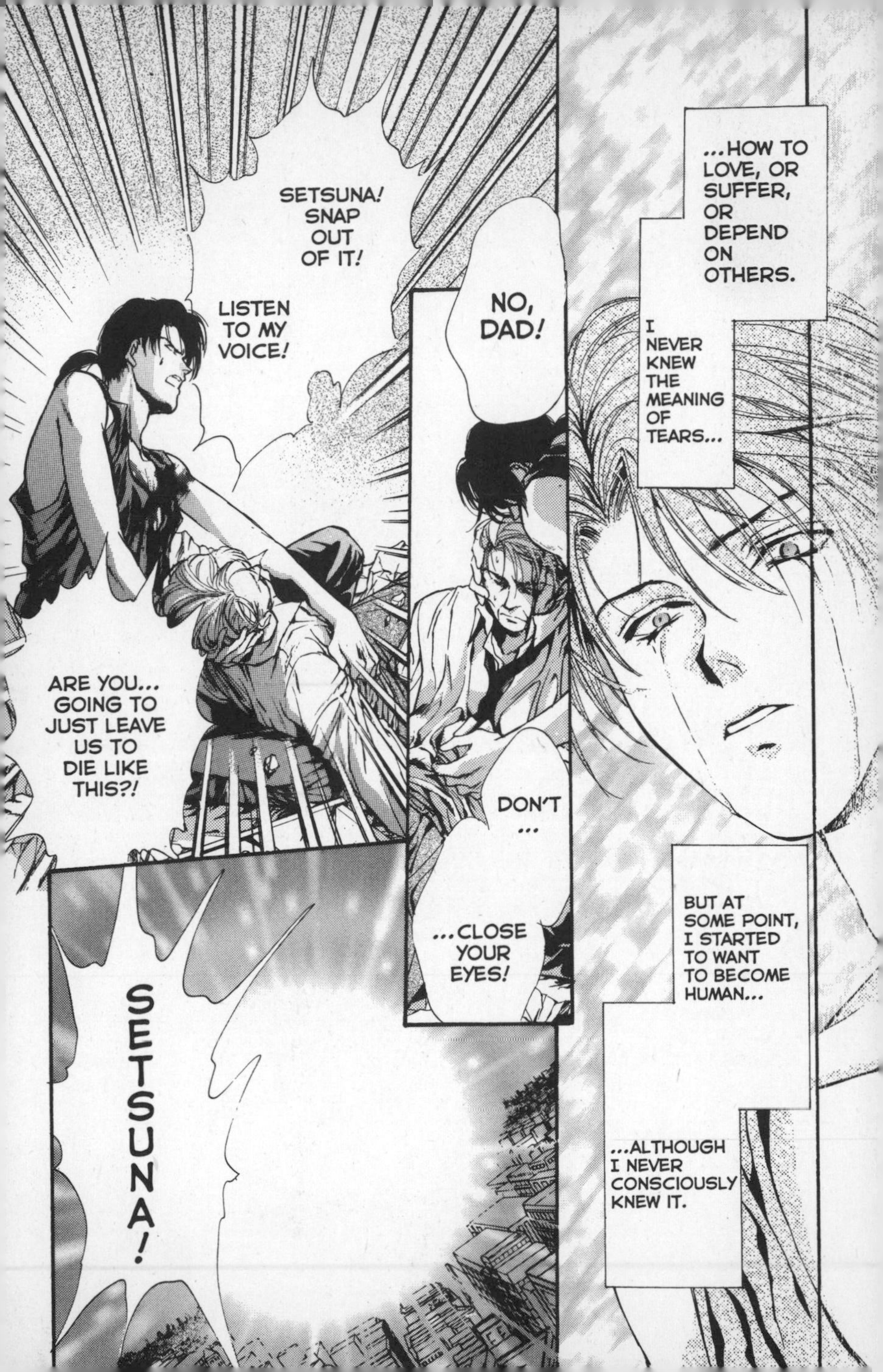
...HOW TO LOVE, OR SUFFER, OR DEPEND ON OTHERS.
I NEVER KNEW THE MEANING OF TEARS...
BUT AT SOME POINT, I STARTED TO WANT TO BECOME HUMAN...
...ALTHOUGH I NEVER CONSCIOUSLY KNEW IT.
SETSUNA! SNAP OUT OF IT!
LISTEN TO MY VOICE!
ARE YOU... GOING TO JUST LEAVE US TO DIE LIKE THIS?!
NO, DAD!
DON'T ...
...CLOSE YOUR EYES!
SETSUNA!

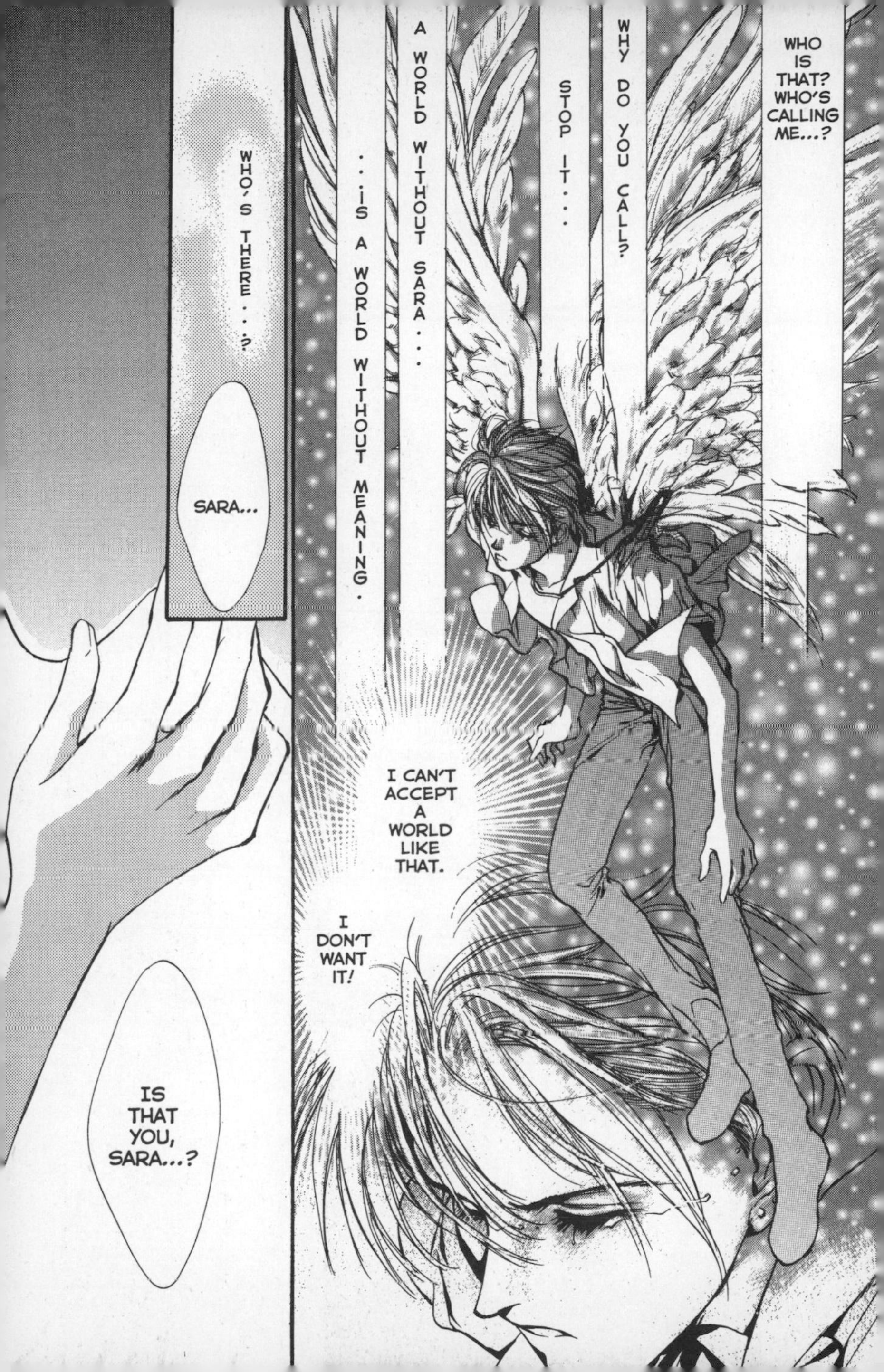
WHO IS THAT? WHO'S CALLING ME...?
WHY DO YOU CALL?
STOP IT...
A WORLD WITHOUT SARA...
...IS A WORLD WITHOUT MEANING.
I CAN'T ACCEPT A WORLD LIKE THAT.
I DON'T WANT IT!
WHO'S THERE...?
SARA...
IS THAT YOU, SARA...?

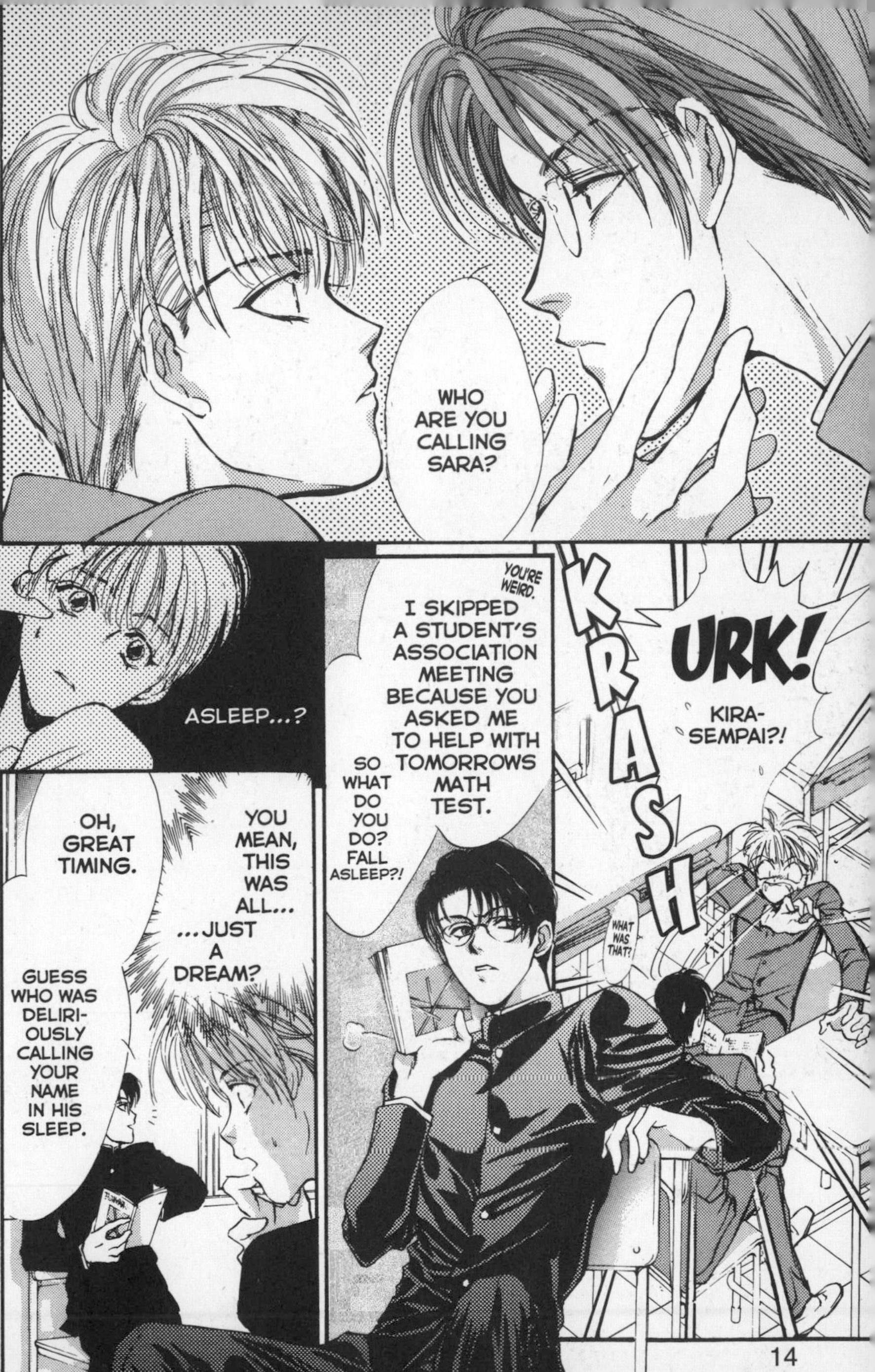

WHO ARE YOU CALLING SARA?
URK!
KRASH
KIRA-SEMPAI?!
WHAT WAS THAT?
YOU'RE WEIRD.
I SKIPPED A STUDENT'S ASSOCIATION MEETING BECAUSE YOU ASKED ME TO HELP WITH TOMORROWS MATH TEST.
SO WHAT DO YOU DO? FALL ASLEEP?!
ASLEEP...?
YOU MEAN, THIS WAS ALL...
...JUST A DREAM?
OH, GREAT TIMING.
GUESS WHO WAS DELIRI-OUSLY CALLING YOUR NAME IN HIS SLEEP.

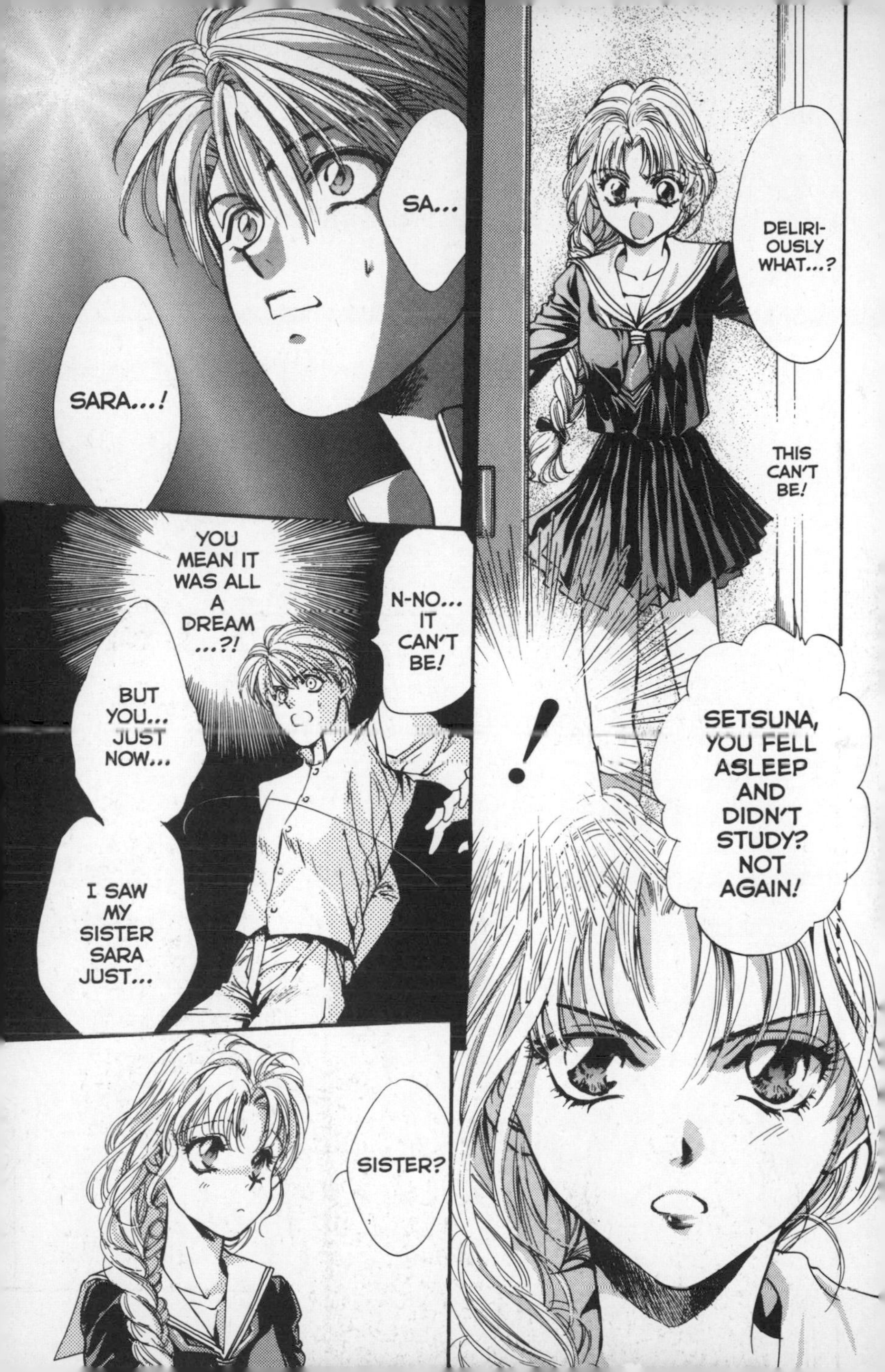
DELIRI-OUSLY WHAT...?
THIS CAN'T BE!
!
SETSUNA, YOU FELL ASLEEP AND DIDN'T STUDY? NOT AGAIN!
SA...
SARA...!
N-NO... IT CAN'T BE!
YOU MEAN IT WAS ALL A DREAM ...?!
BUT YOU... JUST NOW...
I SAW MY SISTER SARA JUST...
SISTER?

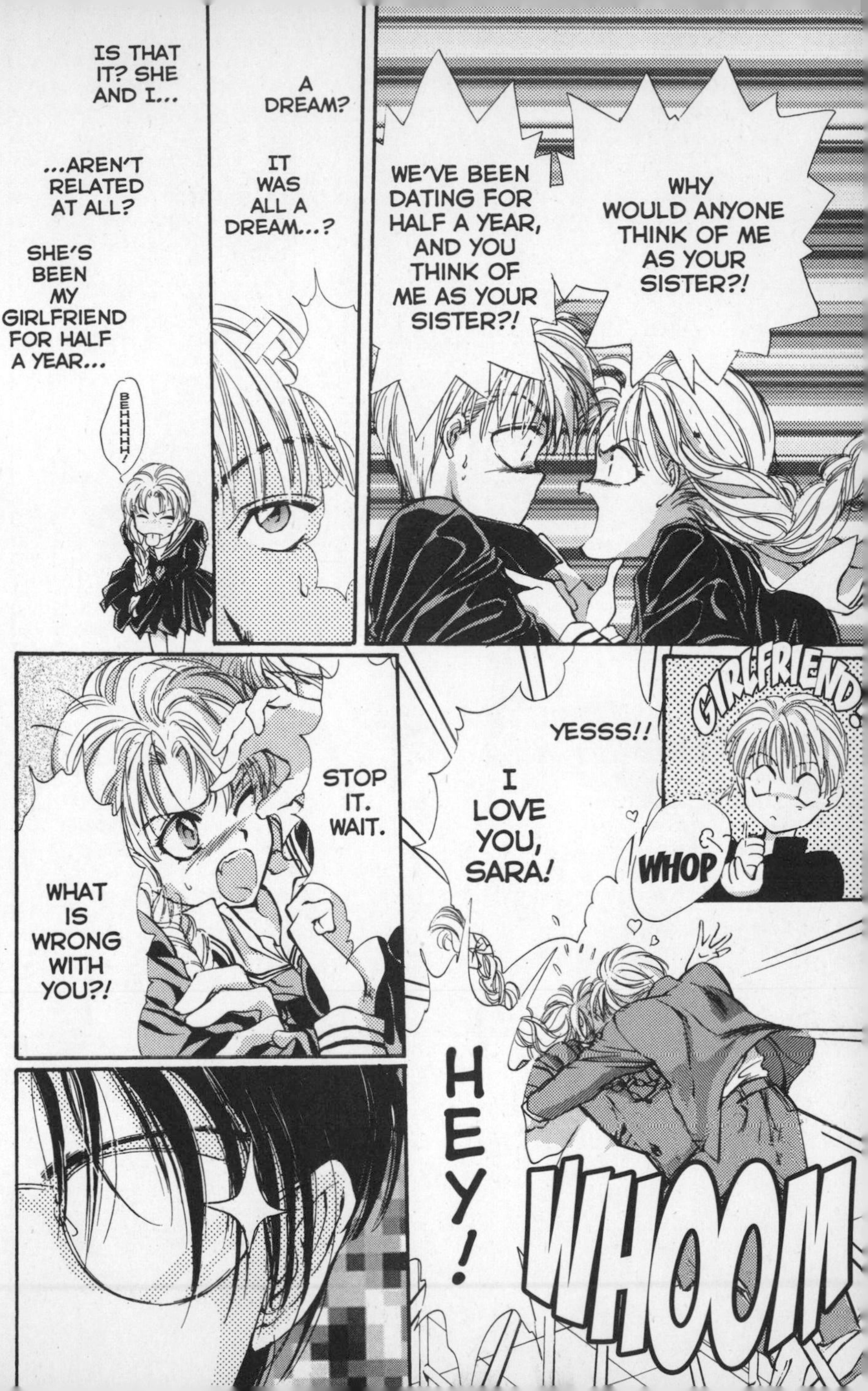
WHY WOULD ANYONE THINK OF ME AS YOUR SISTER?!
WE'VE BEEN DATING FOR HALF A YEAR, AND YOU THINK OF ME AS YOUR SISTER?!
A DREAM?
IT WAS ALL A DREAM...?
IS THAT IT? SHE AND I...
...AREN'T RELATED AT ALL?
SHE'S BEEN MY GIRLFRIEND FOR HALF A YEAR...
BEHHHHH!
GIRLFRIEND
WHOP
YESSS!!
I LOVE YOU, SARA!
WHOOM
HEY!
STOP IT. WAIT.
WHAT IS WRONG WITH YOU?!

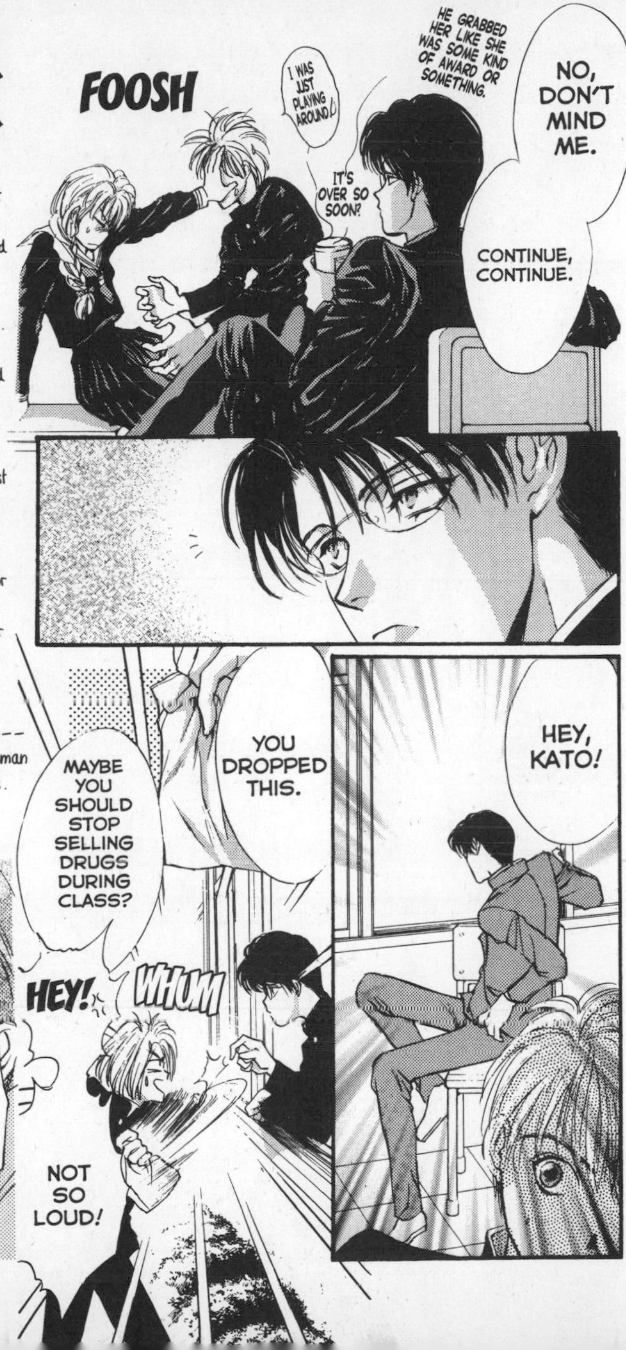
NO, DON'T MIND ME.
HE GRABBED HER LIKE SHE WAS SOME KIND OF AWARD OR SOMETHING.
I WAS JUST PLAYING AROUND
CONTINUE, CONTINUE.
IT'S OVER SO SOON?
FOOSH
HEY, KATO!
YOU DROPPED THIS.
MAYBE YOU SHOULD STOP SELLING DRUGS DURING CLASS?
WHUM
HEY!
NOT SO LOUD!

Hi there! Angel Sanctuary is at volume four at last

Or should I say "already"?

It seems like so long, and yet such a short time. "Assiah--The Material World" reaches its climax. This particular episode is one I was looking forward to for quite some time. In explaining the plot to my editor, this rather impressionable manga artist became so overly involved with the main character's situation that she almost burst into tears. My editor simply nodded without a word, but boy was I ever embarrassed! What was I doing, crying over a story I wrote?! It wasn't that I was moved, or anything--it's just that I'm a woman with very loose tear ducts.

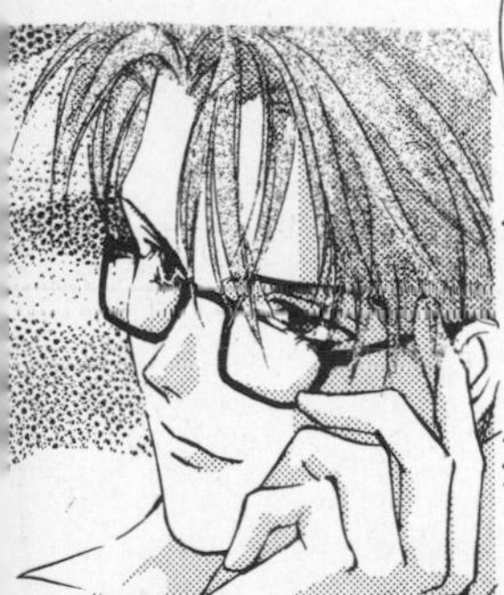

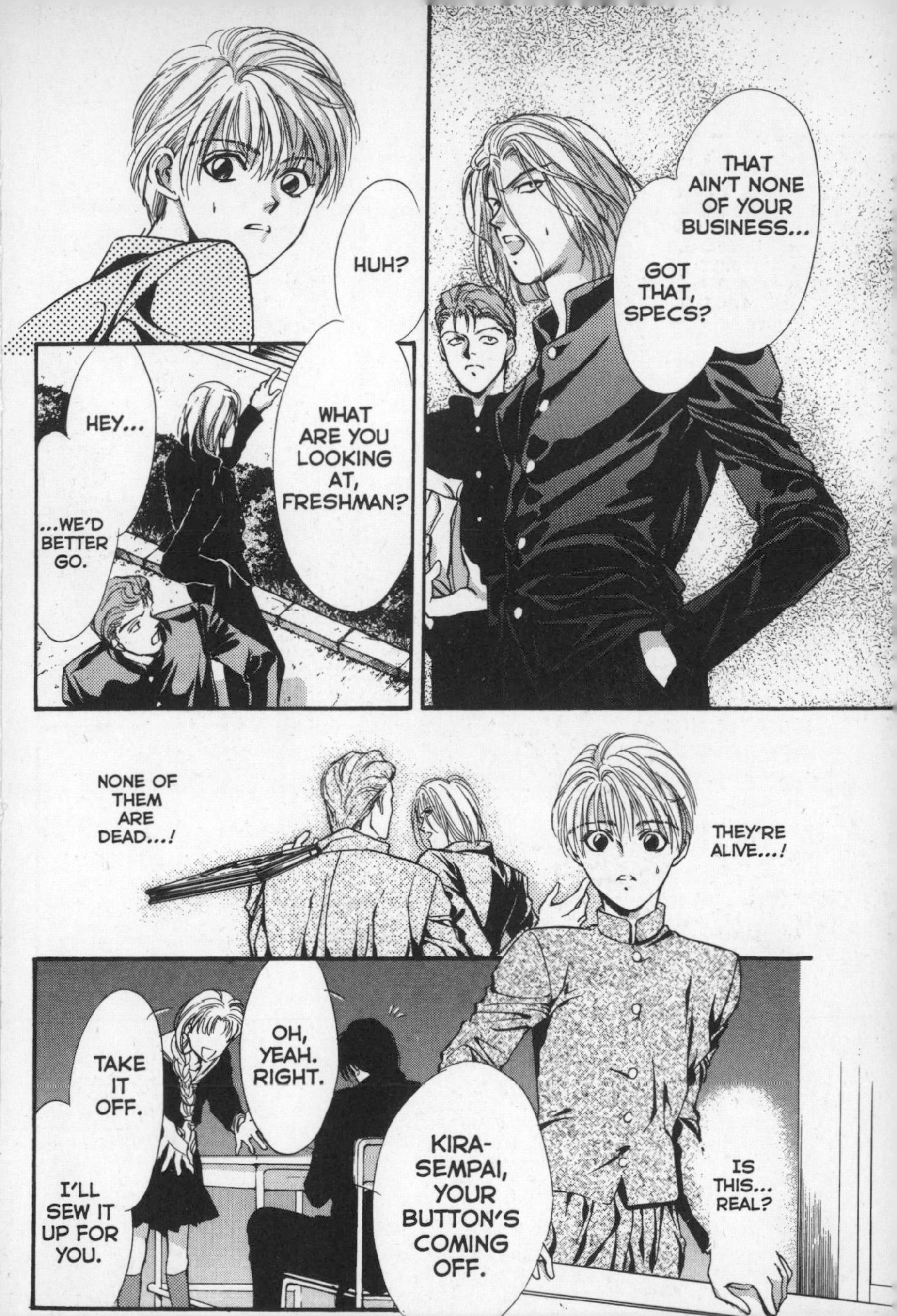
THAT AIN'T NONE OF YOUR BUSINESS...
GOT THAT, SPECS?
HUH?
WHAT ARE YOU LOOKING AT, FRESHMAN?
HEY...
...WE'D BETTER GO.
THEY'RE ALIVE...!
NONE OF THEM ARE DEAD...!
IS THIS... REAL?
KIRA-SEMPAI, YOUR BUTTON'S COMING OFF.
OH, YEAH. RIGHT.
TAKE IT OFF.
I'LL SEW IT UP FOR YOU.

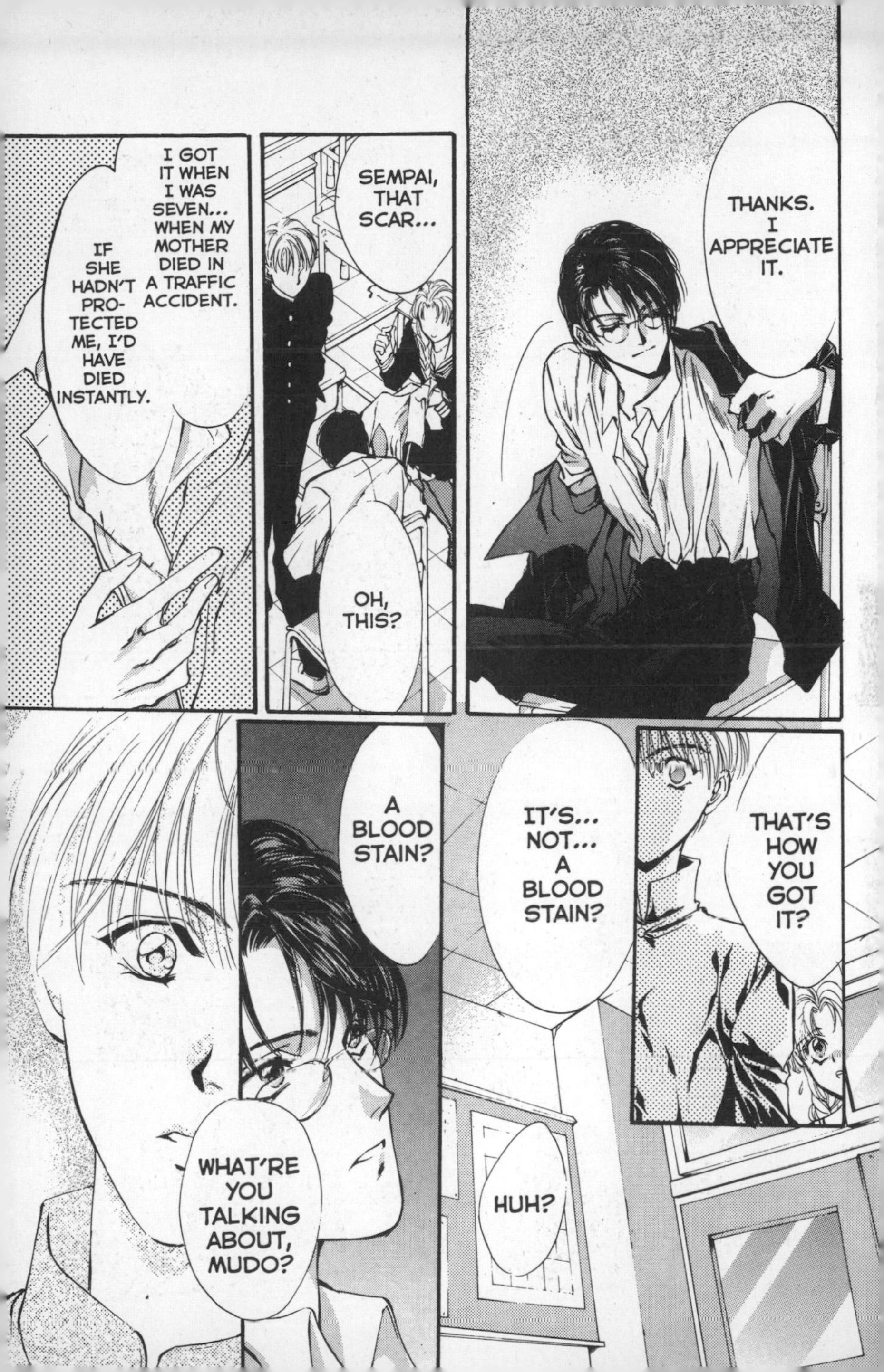
THANKS. I APPRECIATE IT.
SEMPAI, THAT SCAR...
OH, THIS?
I GOT IT WHEN I WAS SEVEN... WHEN MY MOTHER DIED IN A TRAFFIC ACCIDENT.
IF SHE HADN'T PRO-TECTED ME, I'D HAVE DIED INSTANTLY.
THAT'S HOW YOU GOT IT?
IT'S... NOT... A BLOOD STAIN?
HUH?
A BLOOD STAIN?
WHAT'RE YOU TALKING ABOUT, MUDO?

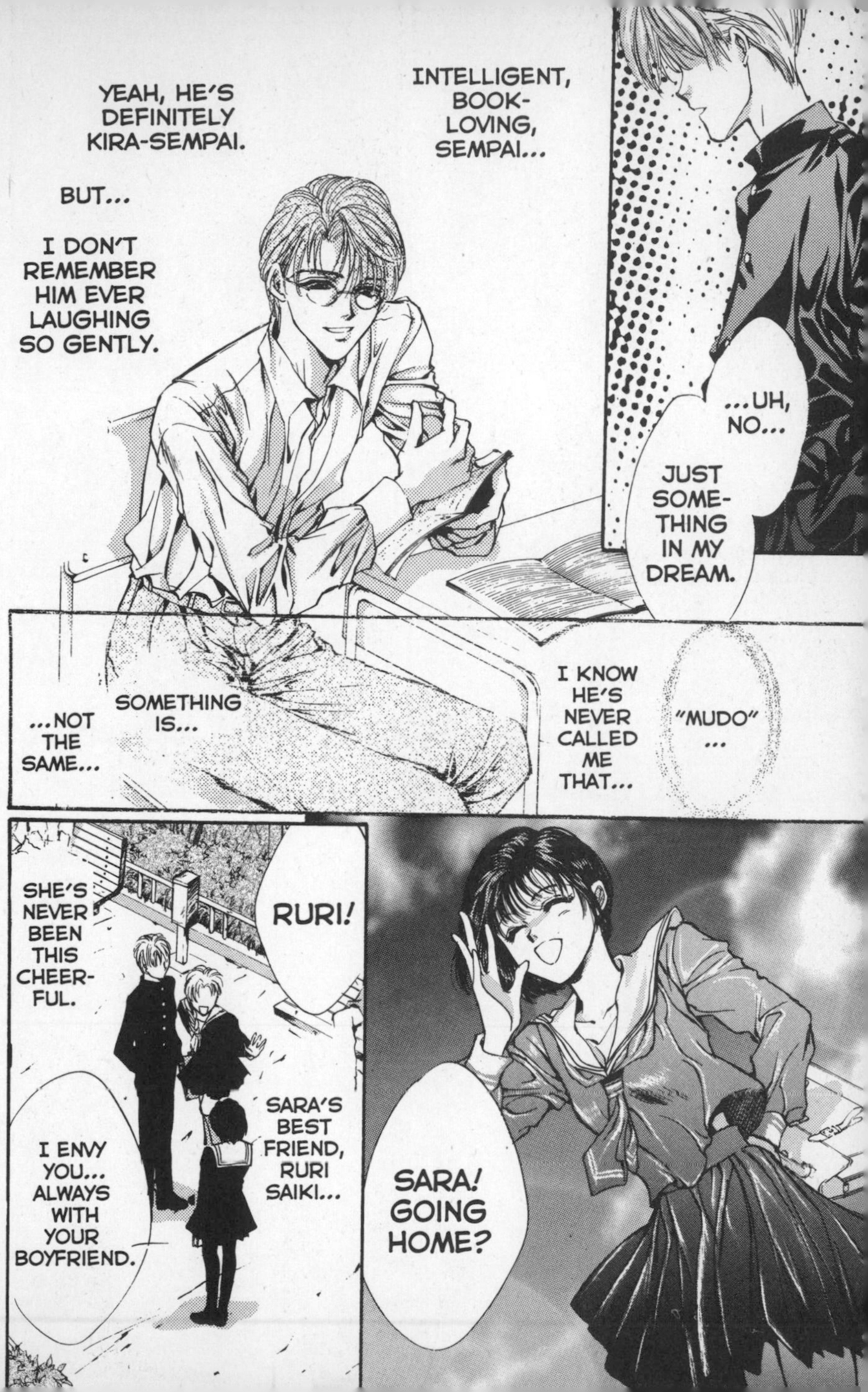
...UH, NO... JUST SOMETHING IN MY DREAM.
INTELLIGENT, BOOK-LOVING, SEMPAI...
YEAH, HE'S DEFINITELY KIRA-SEMPAI.
BUT...
I DON'T REMEMBER HIM EVER LAUGHING SO GENTLY.
"MUDO" ...
I KNOW HE'S NEVER CALLED ME THAT...
SOMETHING IS...
...NOT THE SAME...
SARA! GOING HOME?
RURI!
SHE'S NEVER BEEN THIS CHEERFUL.
SARA'S BEST FRIEND, RURI SAIKI...
I ENVY YOU... ALWAYS WITH YOUR BOYFRIEND.

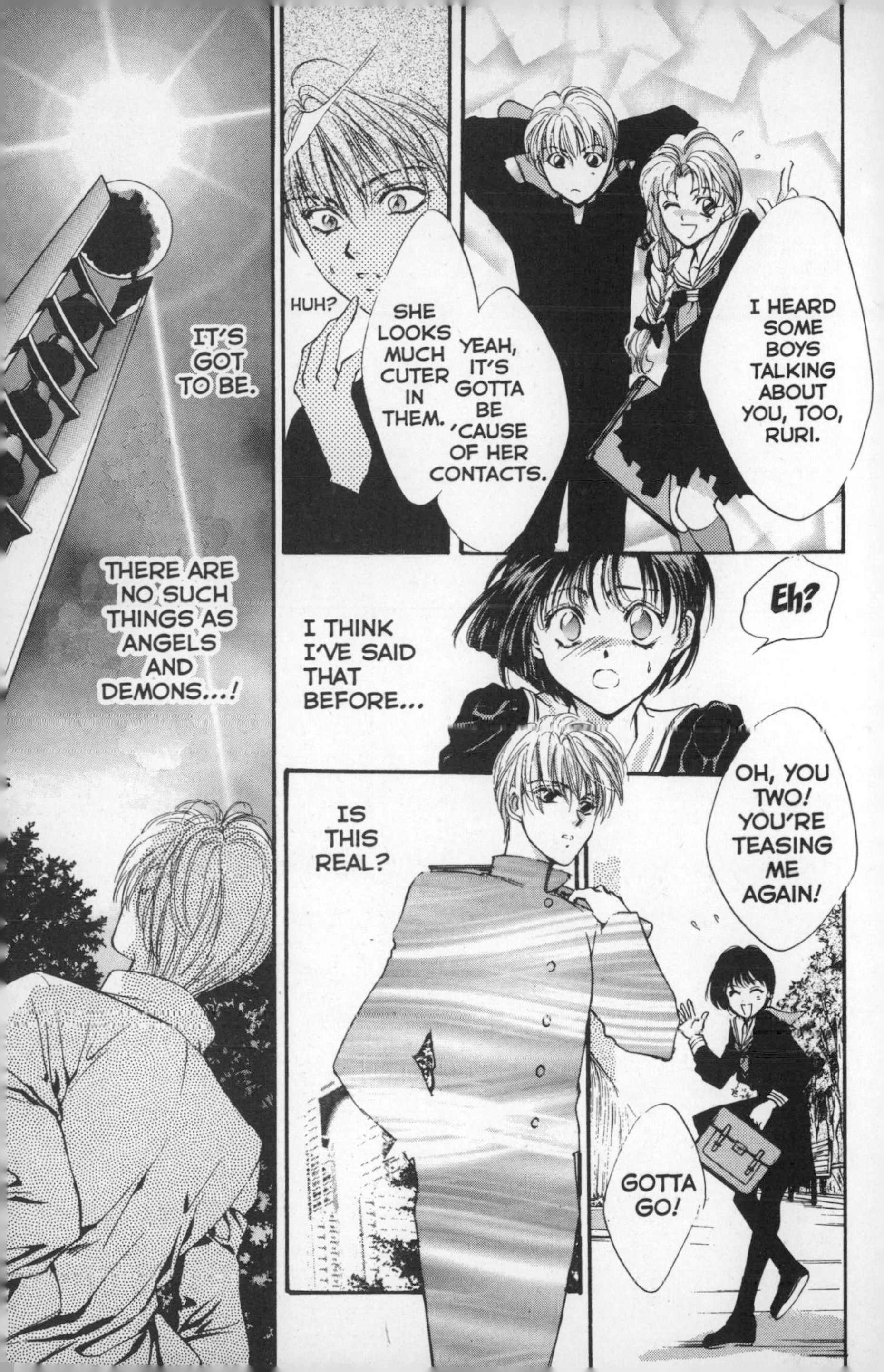
I HEARD SOME BOYS TALKING ABOUT YOU, TOO, RURI.
YEAH, IT'S GOTTA BE 'CAUSE OF HER CONTACTS.
SHE LOOKS MUCH CUTER IN THEM.
HUH?
Eh?
I THINK I'VE SAID THAT BEFORE...
OH, YOU TWO! YOU'RE TEASING ME AGAIN!
GOTTA GO!
IS THIS REAL?
IT'S GOT TO BE.
THERE ARE NO SUCH THINGS AS ANGELS AND DEMONS...!

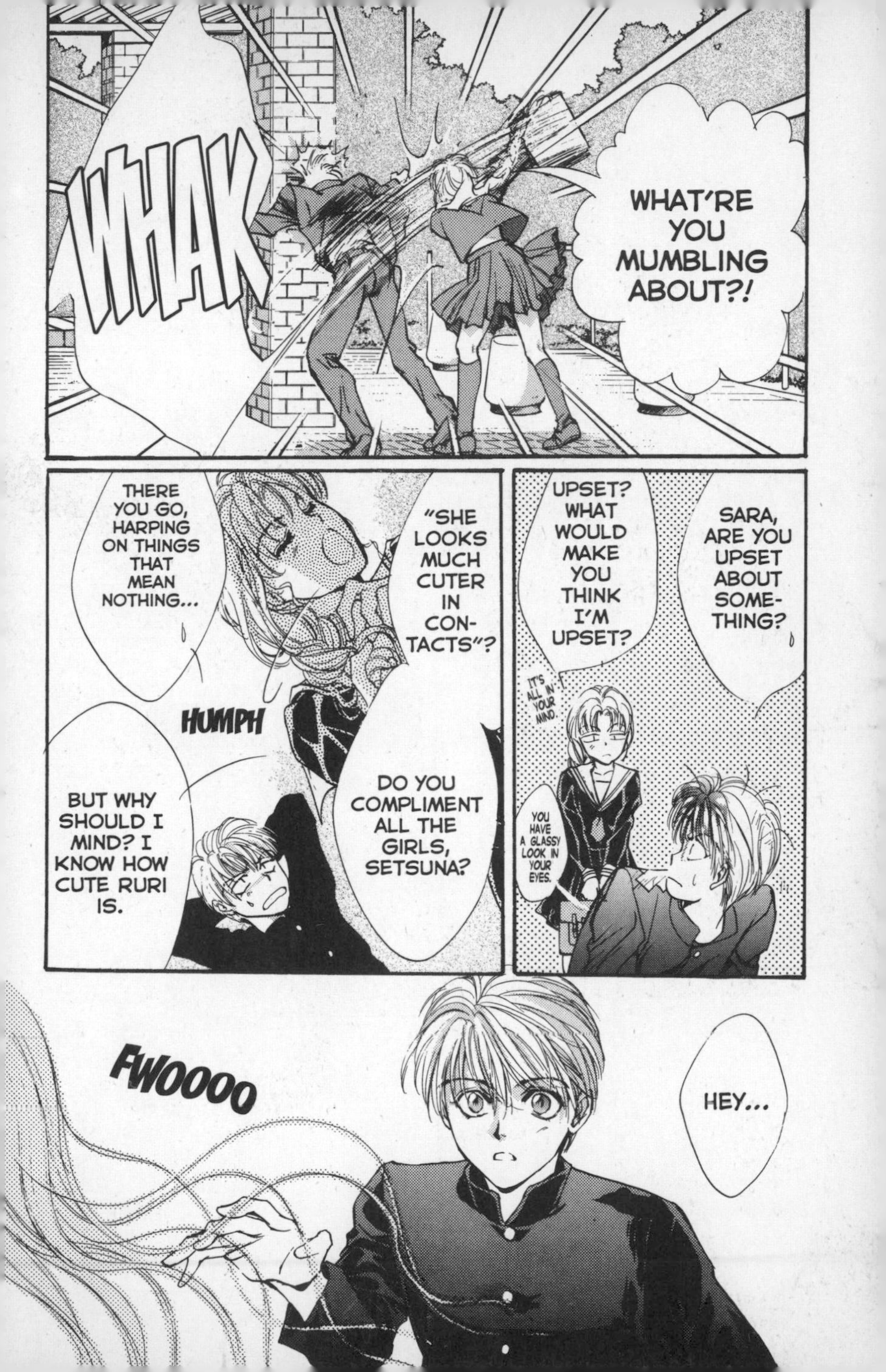

WHAT'RE YOU MUMBLING ABOUT?!
WHAK
SARA, ARE YOU UPSET ABOUT SOME-THING?
UPSET? WHAT WOULD MAKE YOU THINK I'M UPSET?
IT'S ALL IN YOUR MIND.
YOU HAVE A GLASSY LOOK IN YOUR EYES.
"SHE LOOKS MUCH CUTER IN CON-TACTS"?
THERE YOU GO, HARPING ON THINGS THAT MEAN NOTHING...
HUMPH
DO YOU COMPLIMENT ALL THE GIRLS, SETSUNA?
BUT WHY SHOULD I MIND? I KNOW HOW CUTE RURI IS.
HEY...
FWOOOO

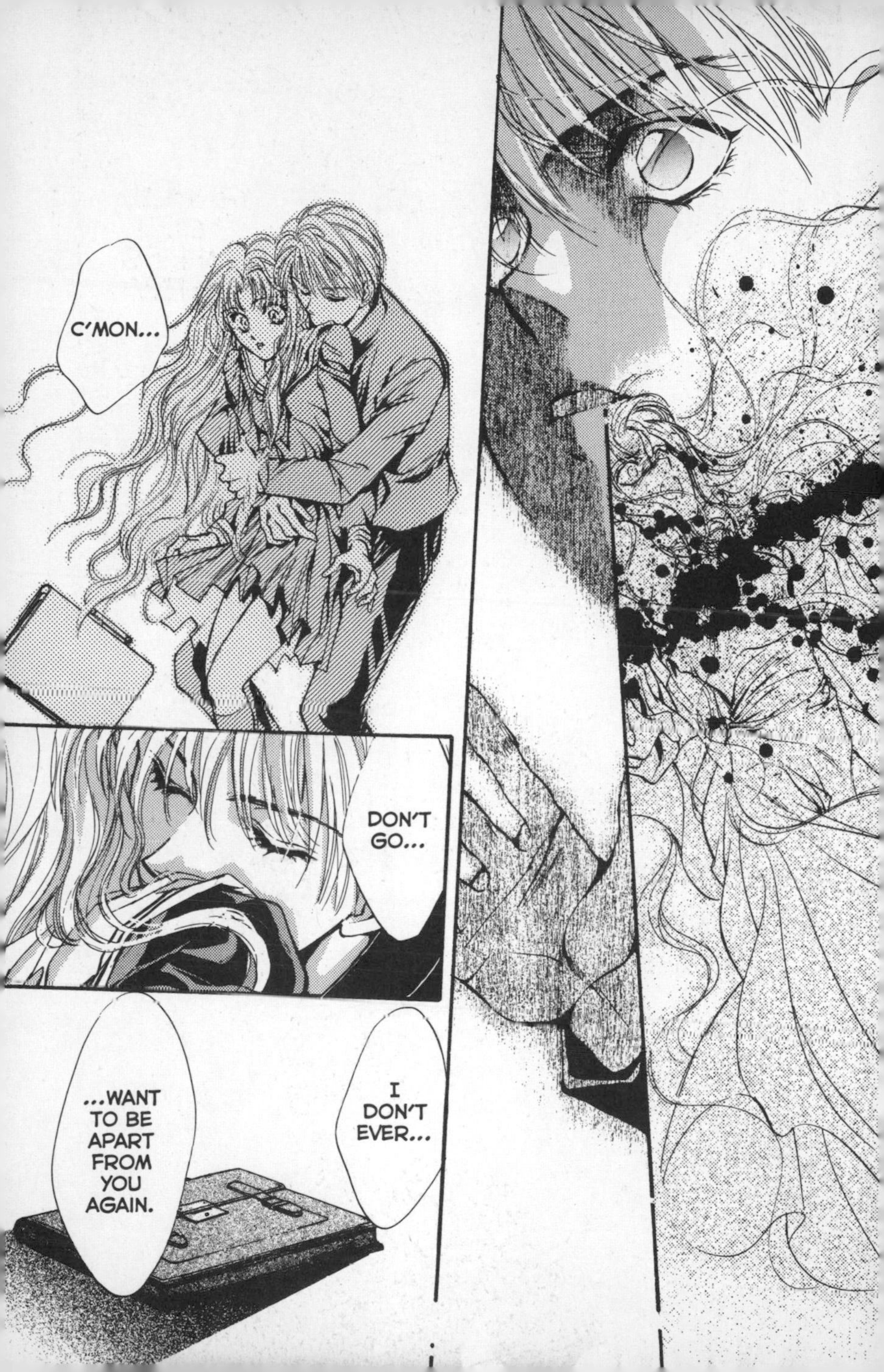
C'MON...
DON'T GO...
I DON'T EVER...
...WANT TO BE APART FROM YOU AGAIN.

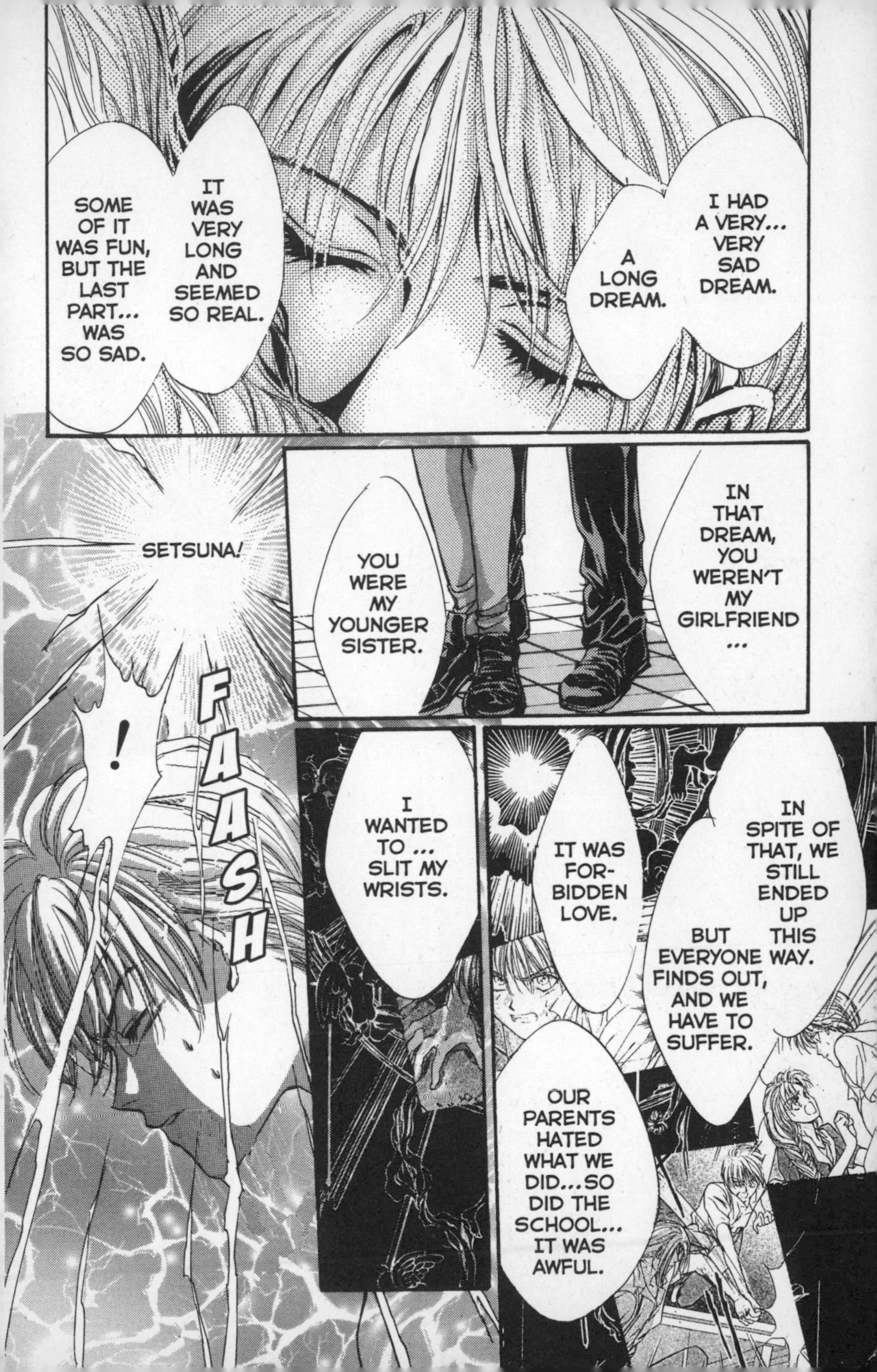
I HAD A VERY... VERY SAD DREAM.
A LONG DREAM.
IT WAS VERY LONG AND SEEMED SO REAL.
SOME OF IT WAS FUN, BUT THE LAST PART... WAS SO SAD.
IN THAT DREAM, YOU WEREN'T MY GIRLFRIEND ...
YOU WERE MY YOUNGER SISTER.
IT WAS FOR-BIDDEN LOVE.
IN SPITE OF THAT, WE STILL ENDED UP THIS WAY.
BUT EVERYONE FINDS OUT, AND WE HAVE TO SUFFER.
OUR PARENTS HATED WHAT WE DID...SO DID THE SCHOOL... IT WAS AWFUL.
I WANTED TO ... SLIT MY WRISTS.
SETSUNA!
FAASH
!

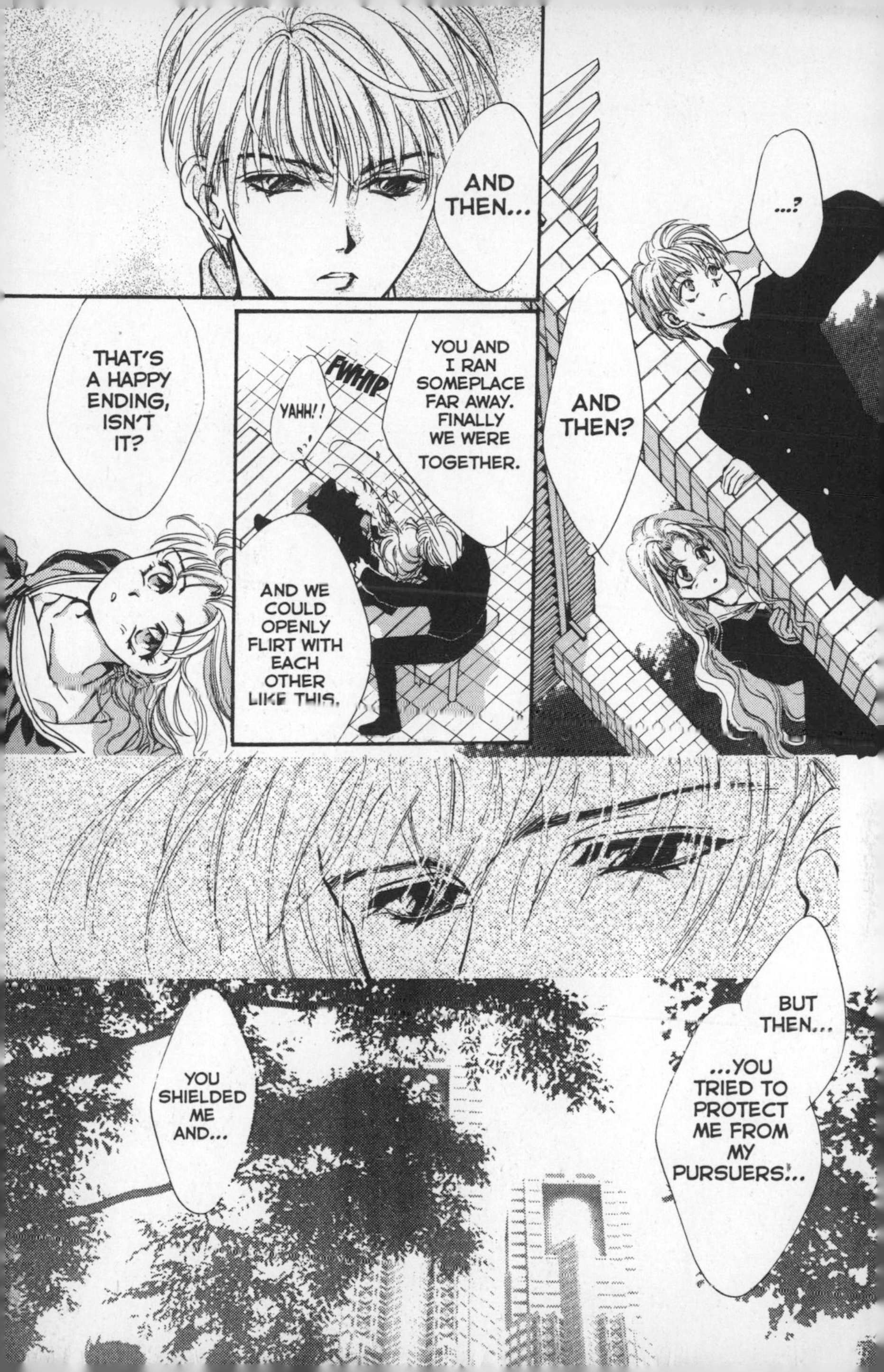
...?
AND THEN?
AND THEN...
YOU AND I RAN SOMEPLACE FAR AWAY. FINALLY WE WERE TOGETHER.
FWHIP
YAHH!!
AND WE COULD OPENLY FLIRT WITH EACH OTHER LIKE THIS.
THAT'S A HAPPY ENDING, ISN'T IT?
BUT THEN...
...YOU TRIED TO PROTECT ME FROM MY PURSUERS!...
YOU SHIELDED ME AND...

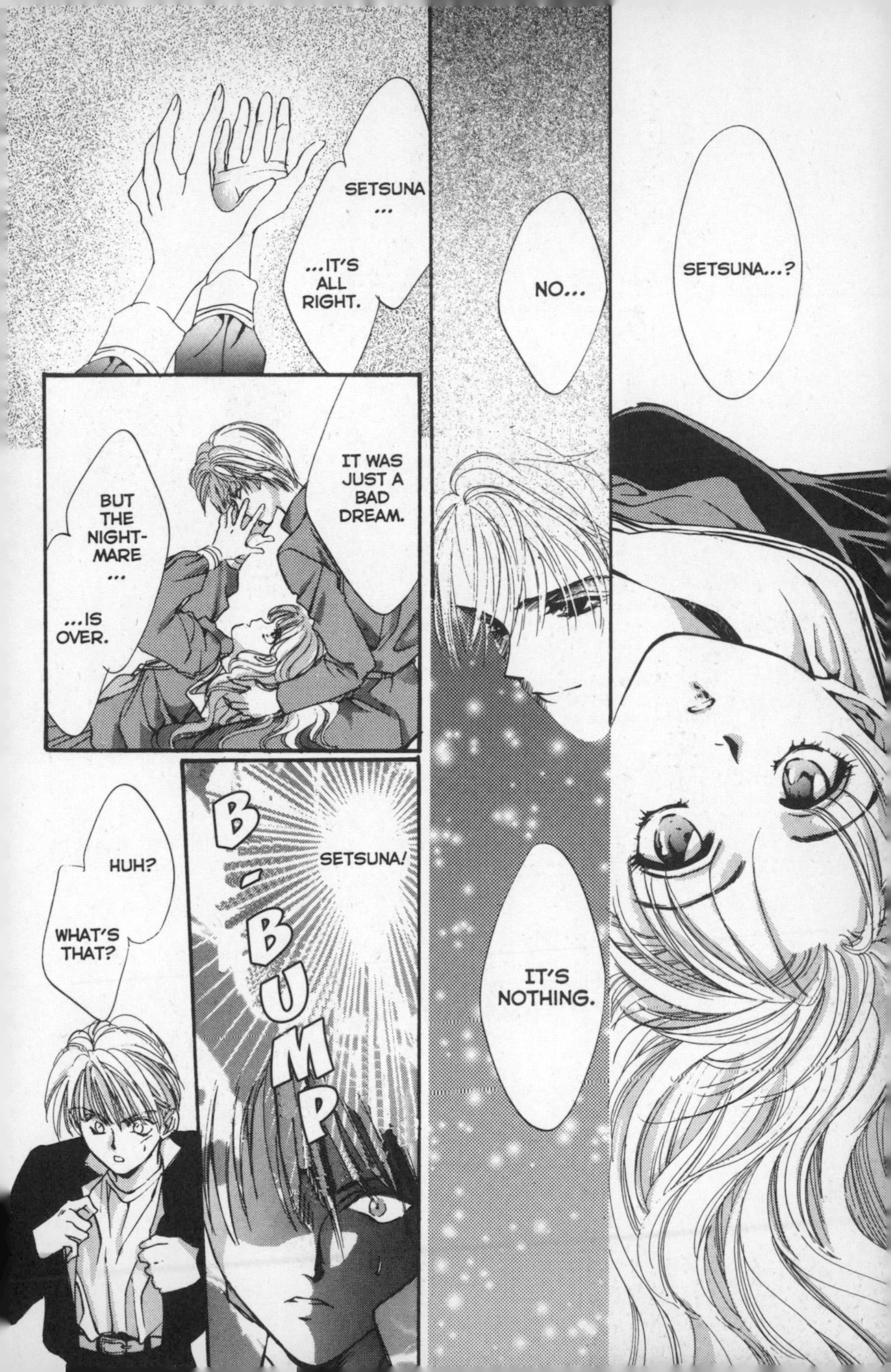
SETSUNA...?
NO...
IT'S NOTHING.
SETSUNA...
...IT'S ALL RIGHT.
IT WAS JUST A BAD DREAM.
BUT THE NIGHT-MARE...
...IS OVER.
SETSUNA!
B-BUMP
HUH?
WHAT'S THAT?

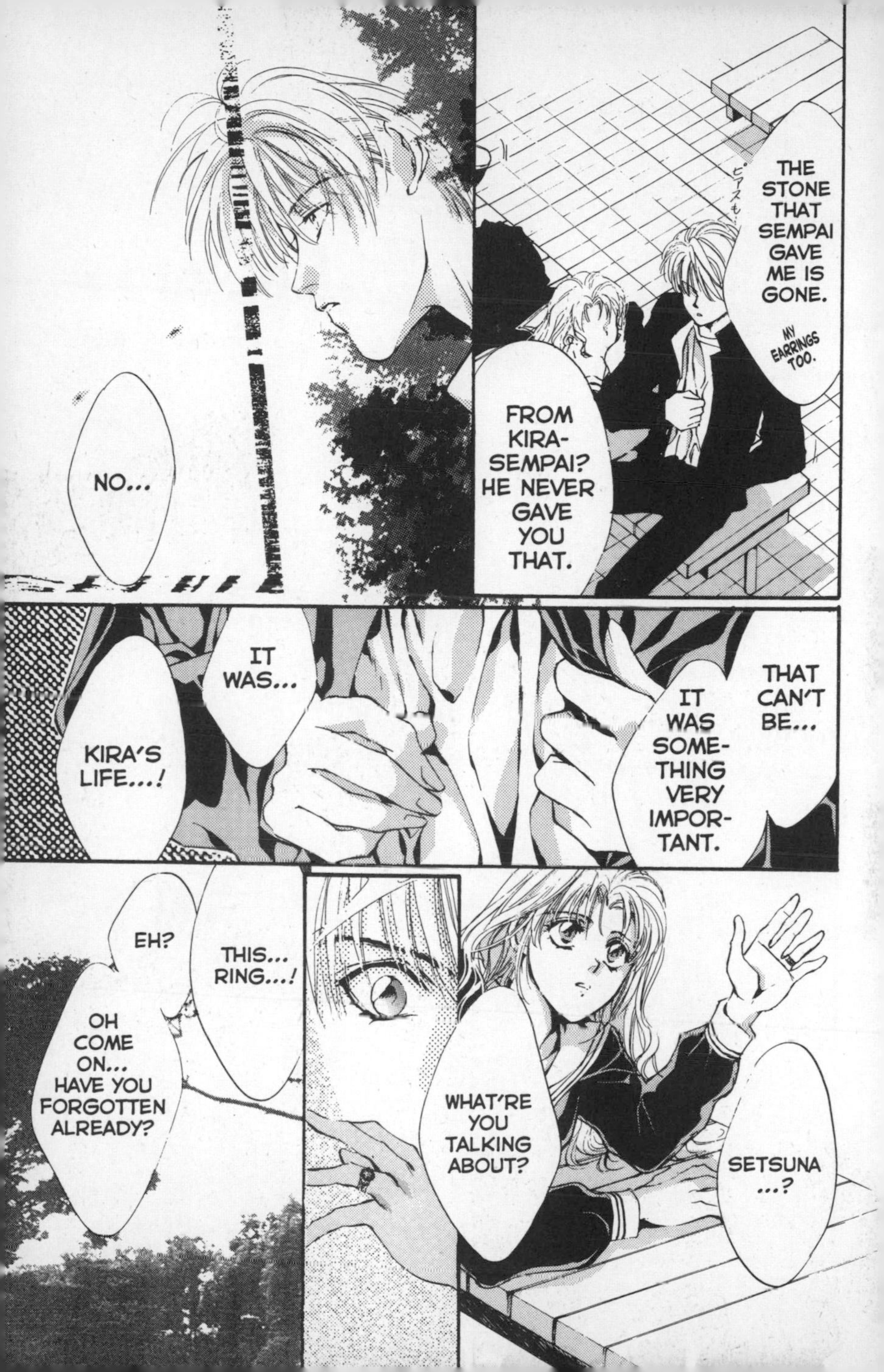
THE STONE THAT SEMPAI GAVE ME IS GONE.
ピアスも…
MY EARRINGS TOO.
FROM KIRA-SEMPAI? HE NEVER GAVE YOU THAT.
NO...
THAT CAN'T BE...
IT WAS SOMETHING VERY IMPORTANT.
IT WAS...
KIRA'S LIFE...!
SETSUNA ...?
WHAT'RE YOU TALKING ABOUT?
THIS... RING...!
EH?
OH COME ON... HAVE YOU FORGOTTEN ALREADY?

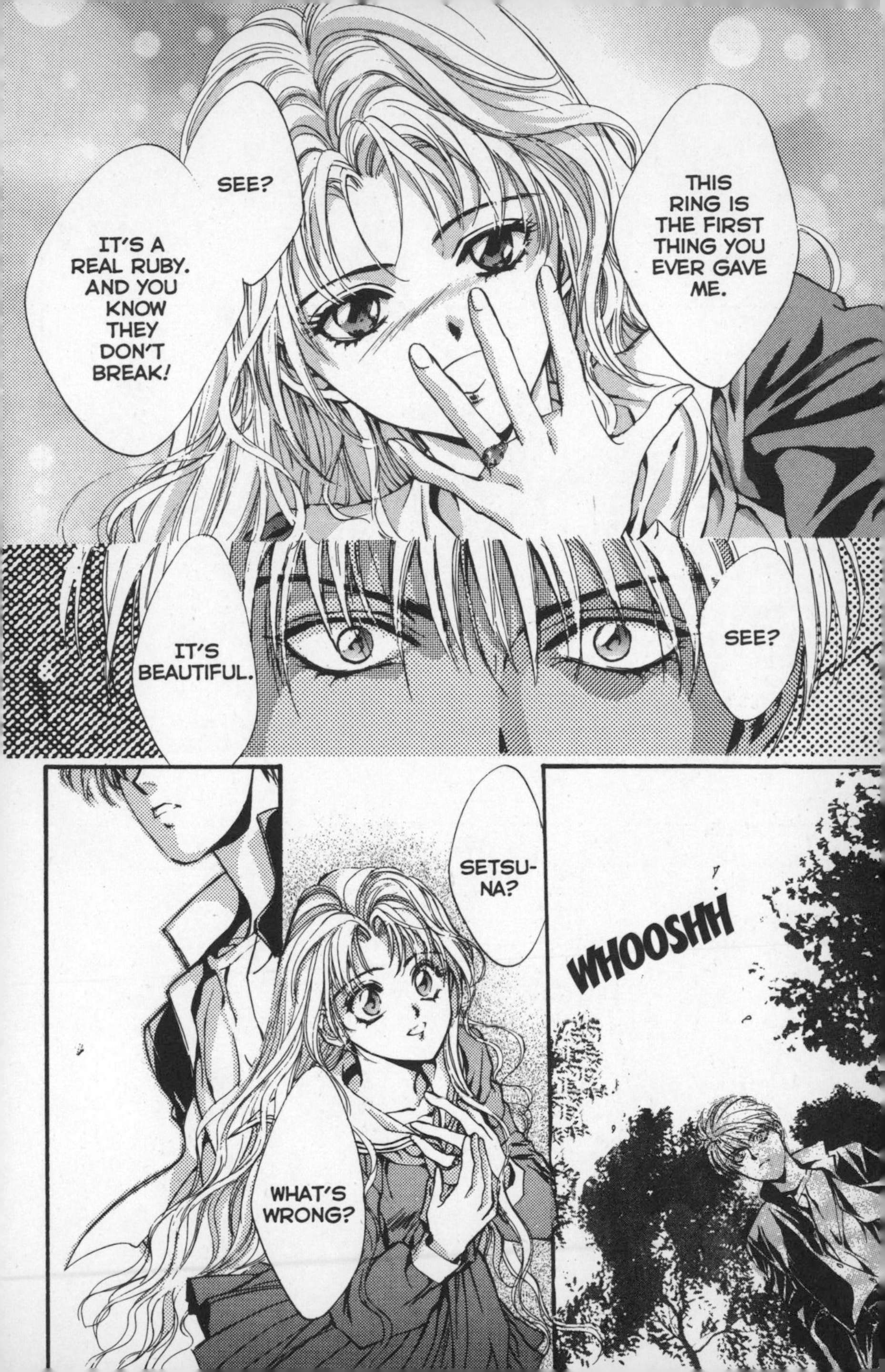
THIS RING IS THE FIRST THING YOU EVER GAVE ME.
SEE?
IT'S A REAL RUBY. AND YOU KNOW THEY DON'T BREAK!
SEE?
IT'S BEAUTIFUL.
WHOOSHH
SETSU-NA?
WHAT'S WRONG?

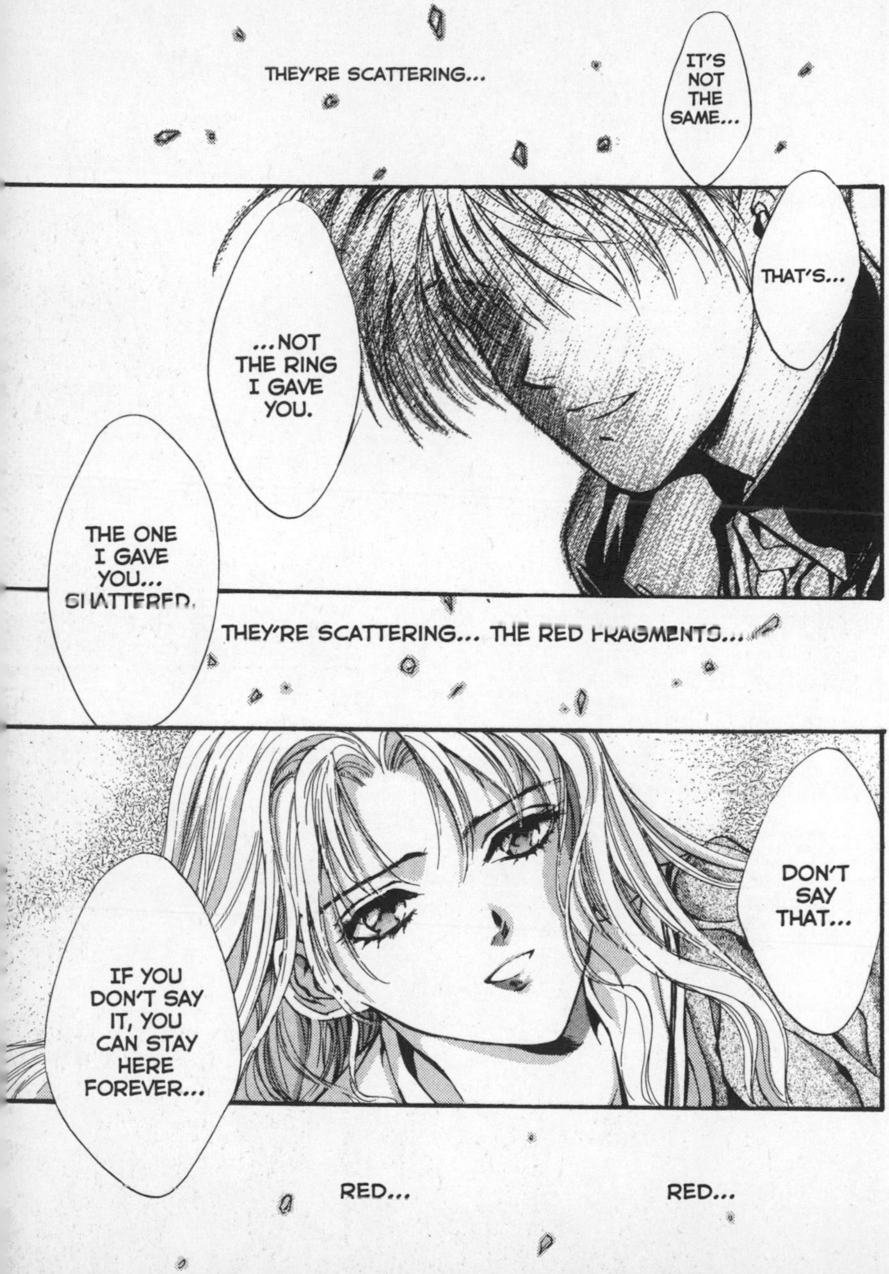
IT'S NOT THE SAME...
THEY'RE SCATTERING...
THAT'S...
...NOT THE RING I GAVE YOU.
THE ONE I GAVE YOU... SHATTERED.
THEY'RE SCATTERING... THE RED FRAGMENTS...
DON'T SAY THAT...
IF YOU DON'T SAY IT, YOU CAN STAY HERE FOREVER...
RED...
RED...

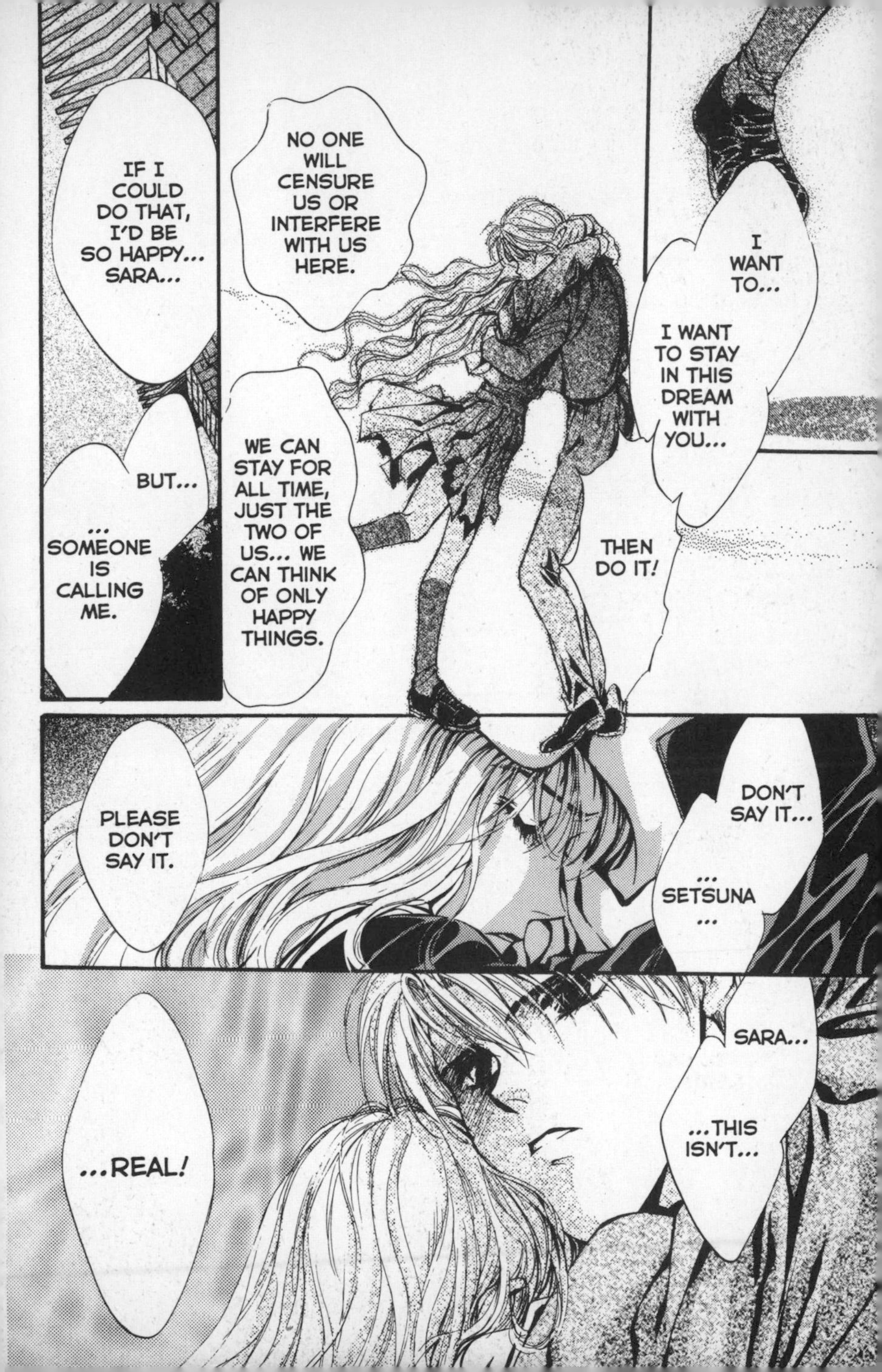
I WANT TO...
I WANT TO STAY IN THIS DREAM WITH YOU...
THEN DO IT!
NO ONE WILL CENSURE US OR INTERFERE WITH US HERE.
WE CAN STAY FOR ALL TIME, JUST THE TWO OF US... WE CAN THINK OF ONLY HAPPY THINGS.
IF I COULD DO THAT, I'D BE SO HAPPY... SARA...
BUT...
... SOMEONE IS CALLING ME.
DON'T SAY IT...
... SETSUNA ...
PLEASE DON'T SAY IT.
SARA...
...THIS ISN'T...
...REAL!

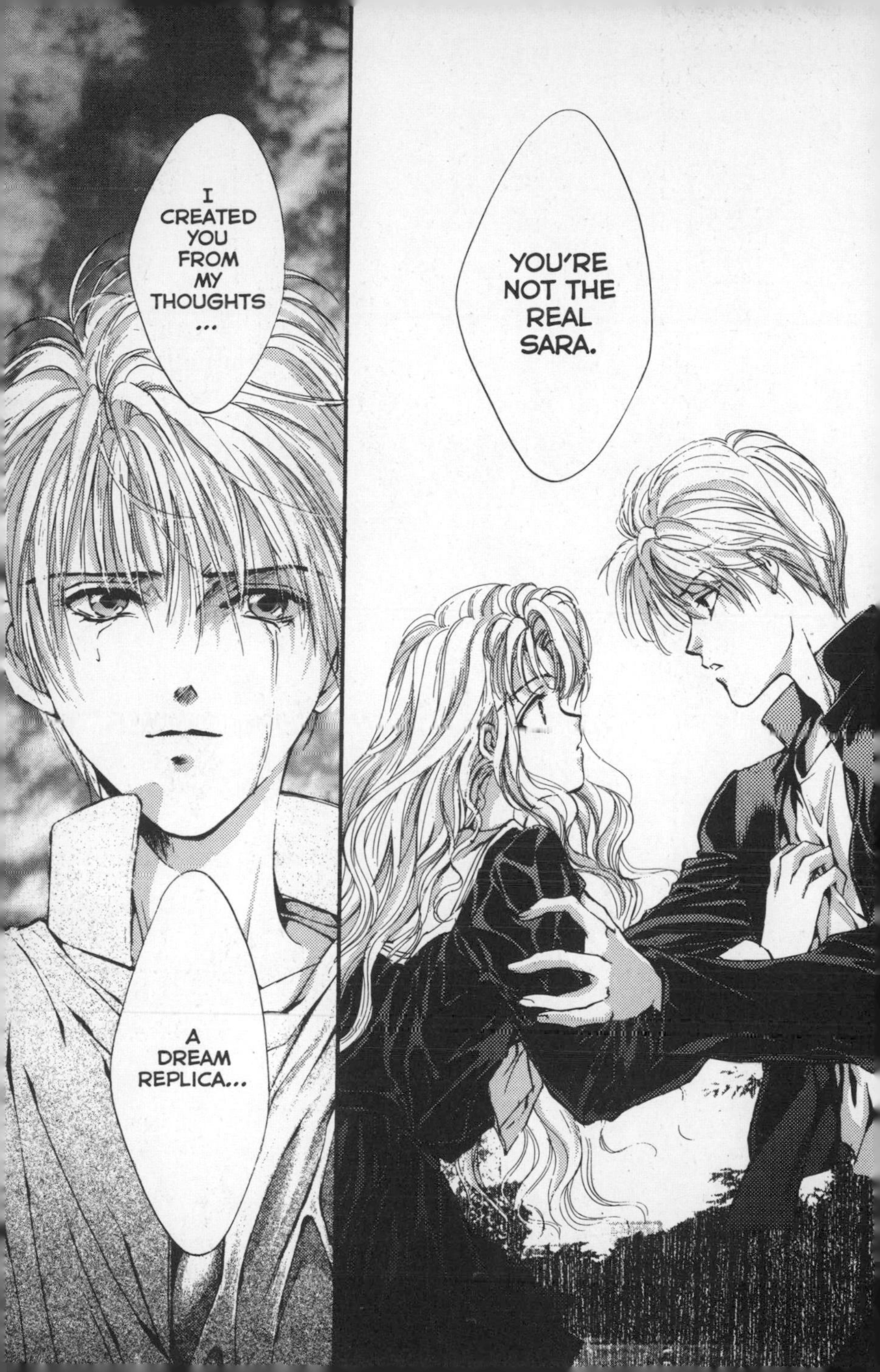
YOU'RE NOT THE REAL SARA.
I CREATED YOU FROM MY THOUGHTS...
A DREAM REPLICA...

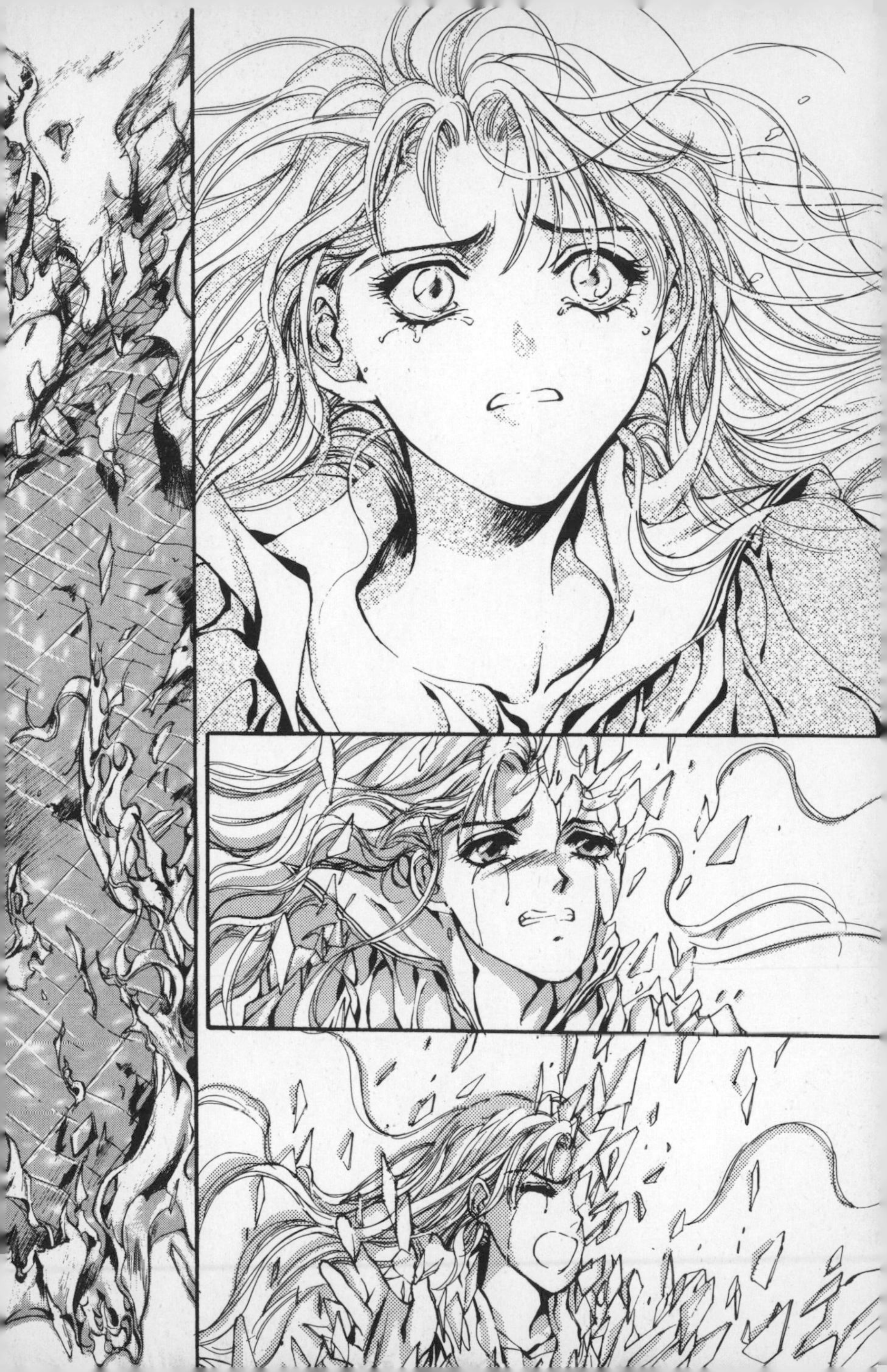

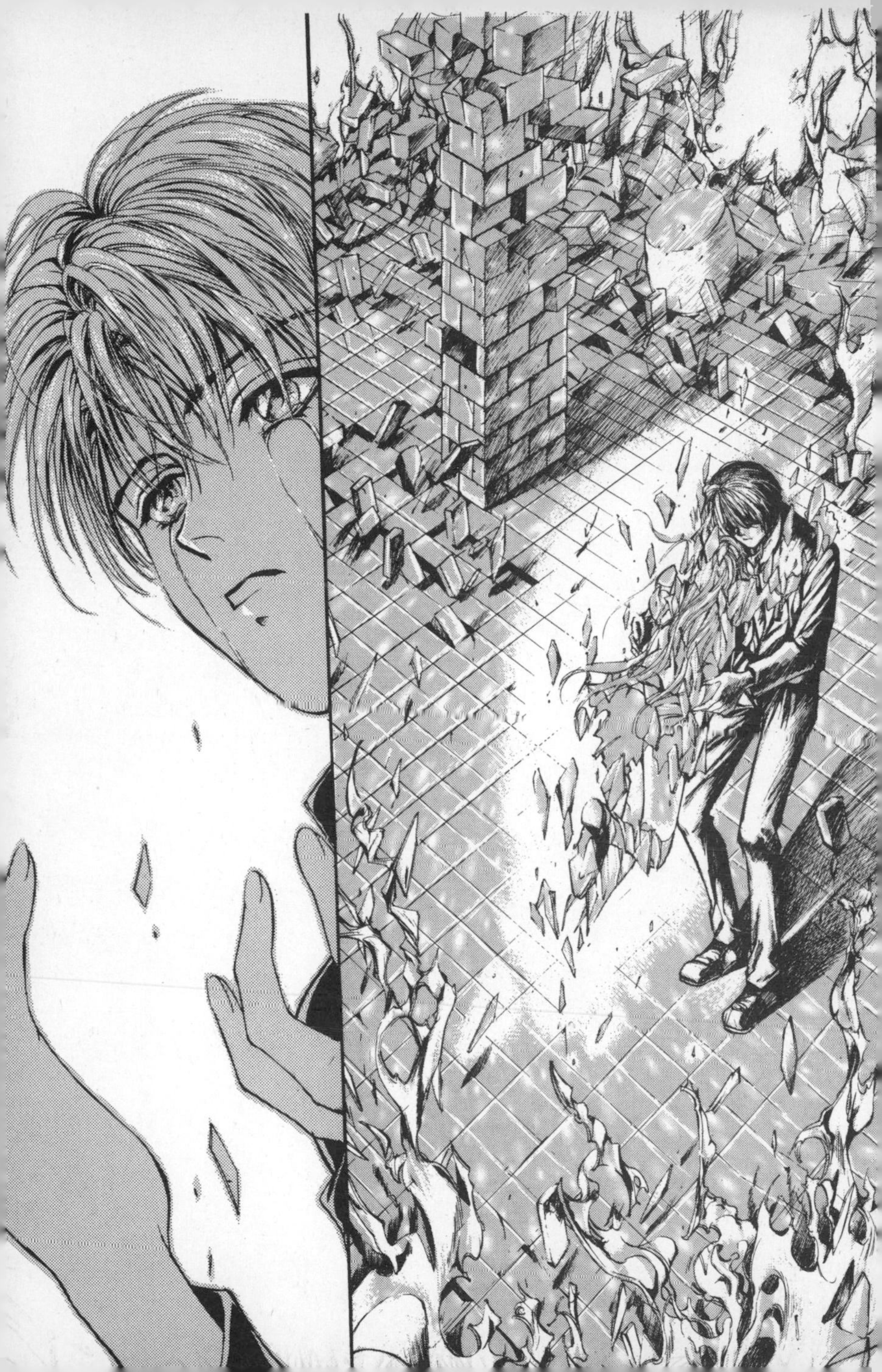

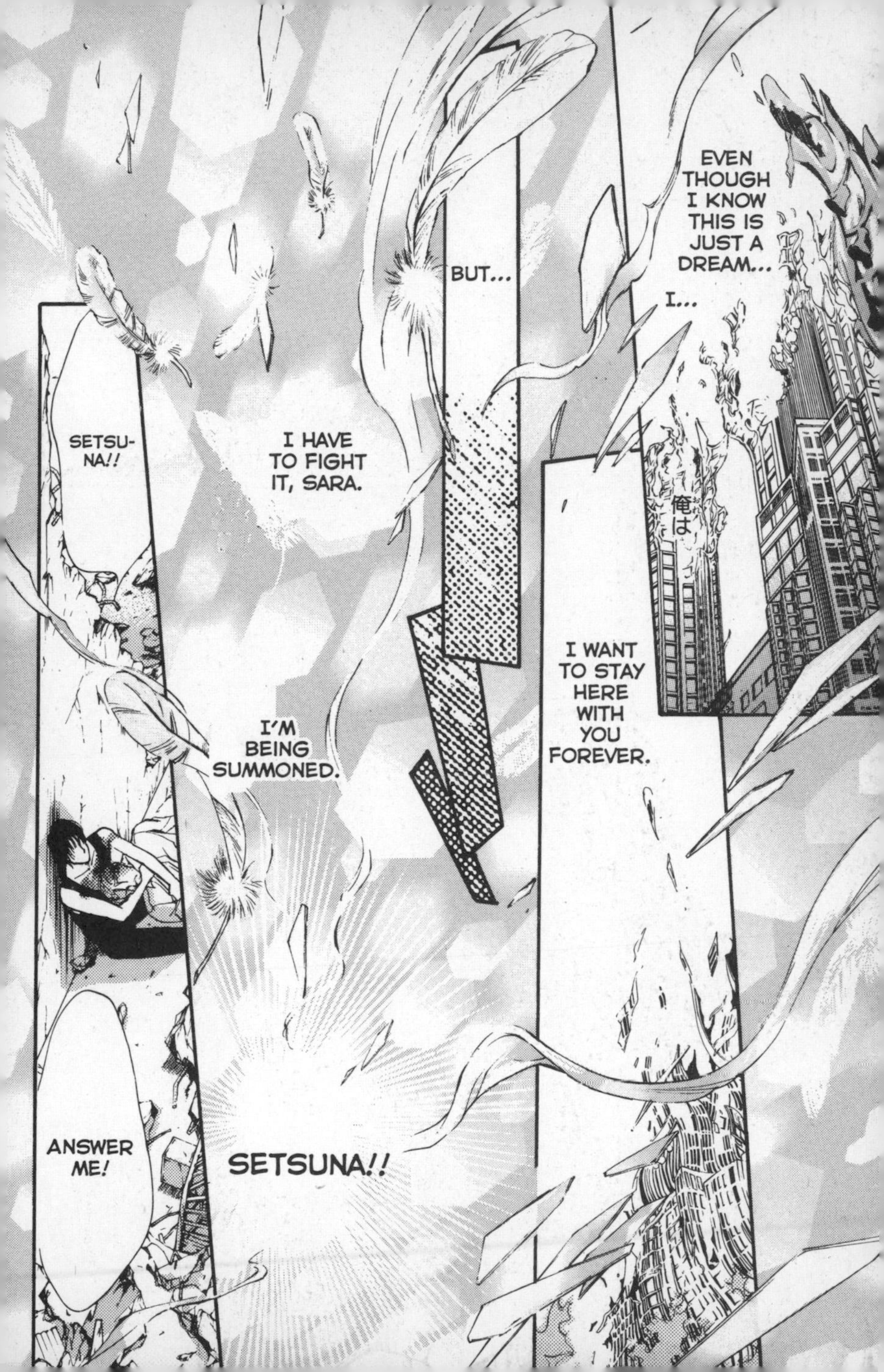
EVEN THOUGH I KNOW THIS IS JUST A DREAM...
I...
俺は
I WANT TO STAY HERE WITH YOU FOREVER.
BUT...
I HAVE TO FIGHT IT, SARA.
I'M BEING SUMMONED.
SETSU-NA!!
ANSWER ME!
SETSUNA!!

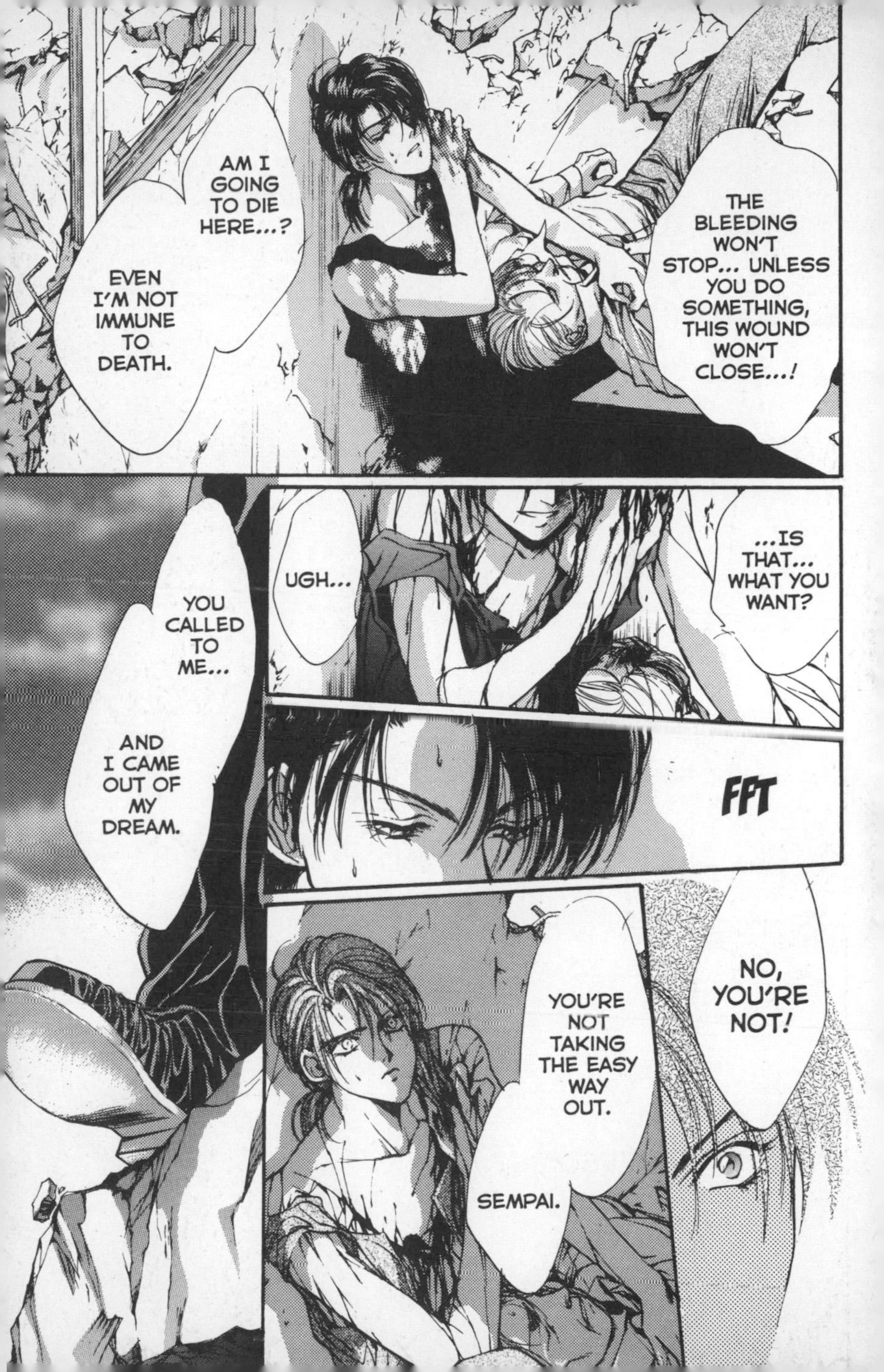
THE BLEEDING WON'T STOP... UNLESS YOU DO SOMETHING, THIS WOUND WON'T CLOSE...!
AM I GOING TO DIE HERE...?
EVEN I'M NOT IMMUNE TO DEATH.
...IS THAT... WHAT YOU WANT?
UGH...
FFT
NO, YOU'RE NOT!
YOU'RE NOT TAKING THE EASY WAY OUT.
SEMPAI.
YOU CALLED TO ME...
AND I CAME OUT OF MY DREAM.

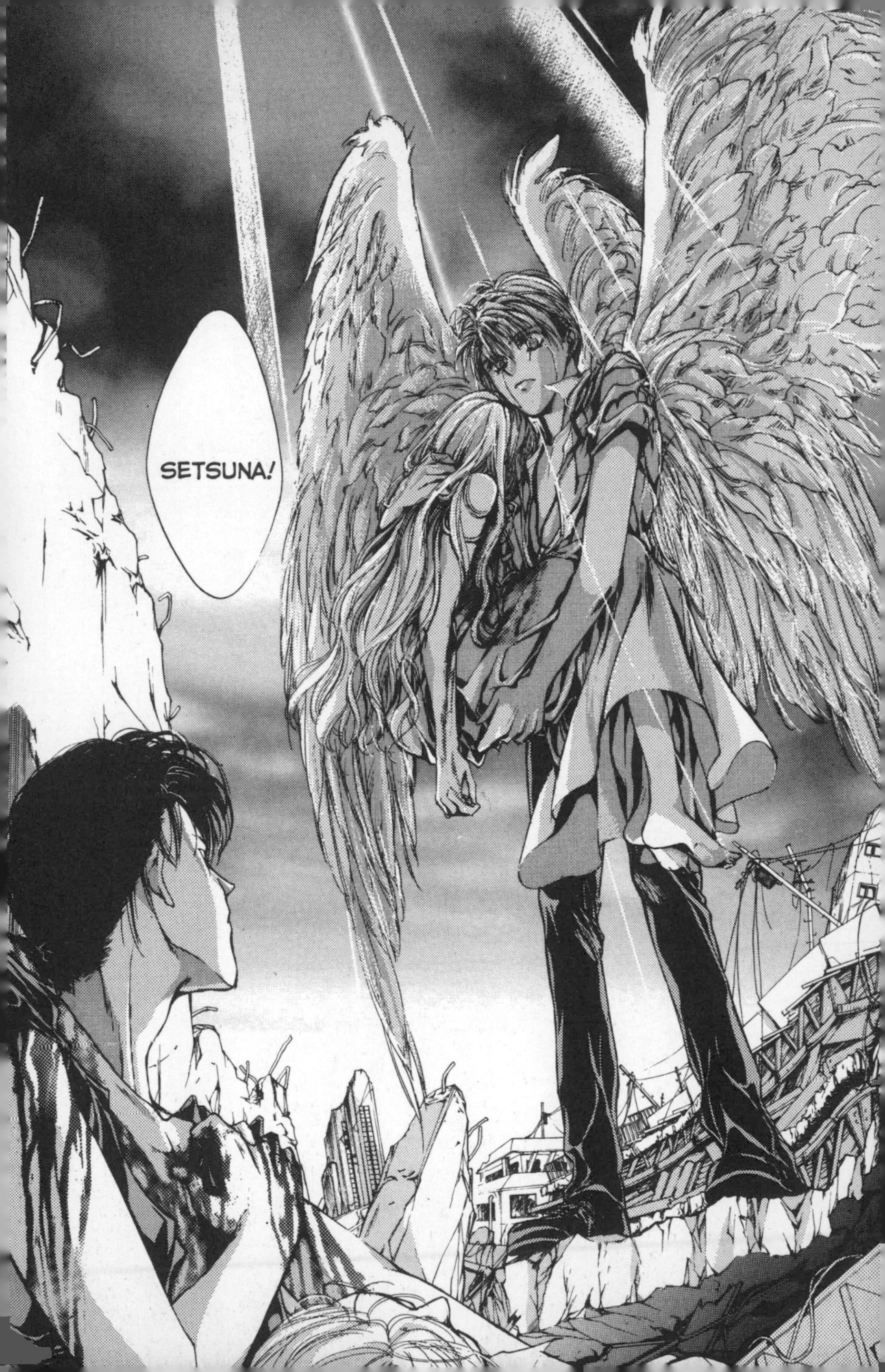
SETSUNA!

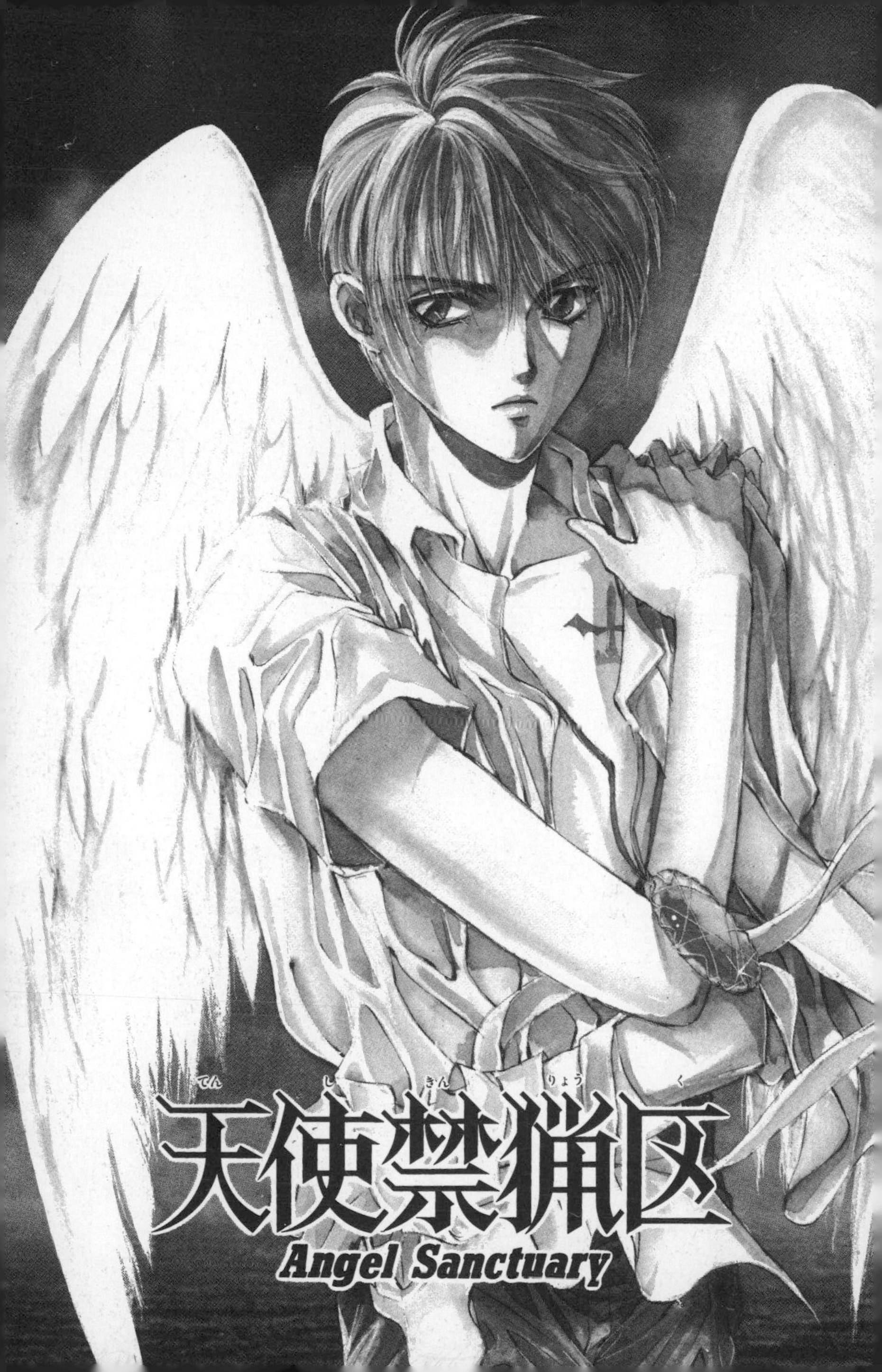
てん し きん りょう く
天使禁猟区
Angel Sanctuary

did you end your life in peace?

did you die in pain? were you afraid?

your palms have gone cold in a tightly clenched fist.

your red lips and hair that blew in the wind;
made me wonder whether this might all have been a dream.

kill me with the pain you felt;
with your final good-bye.

take me with you.

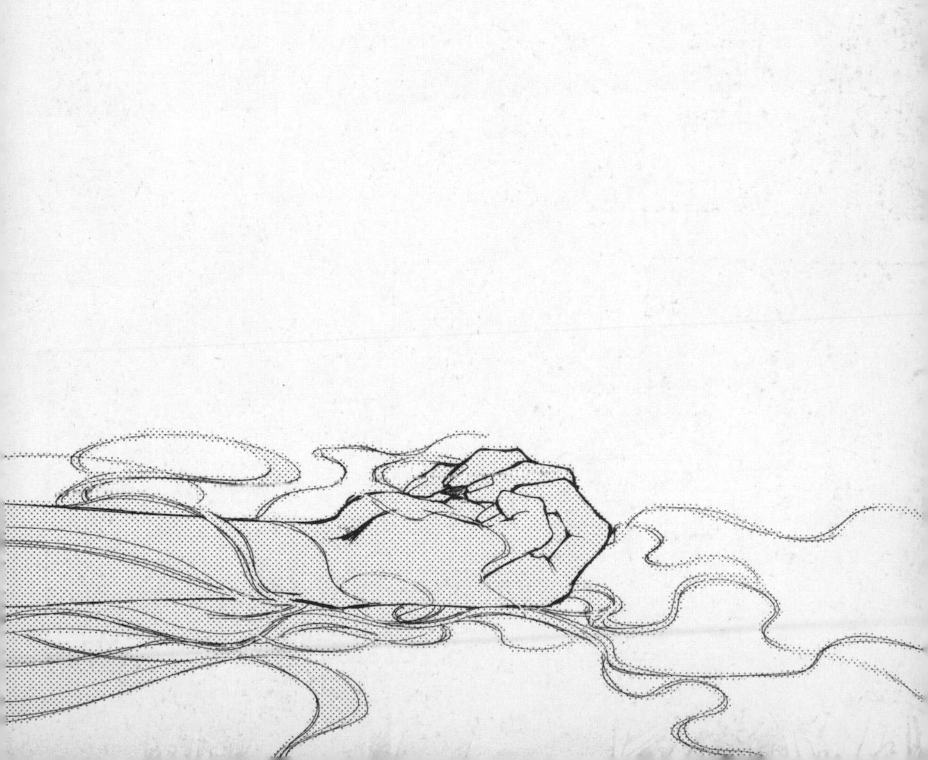

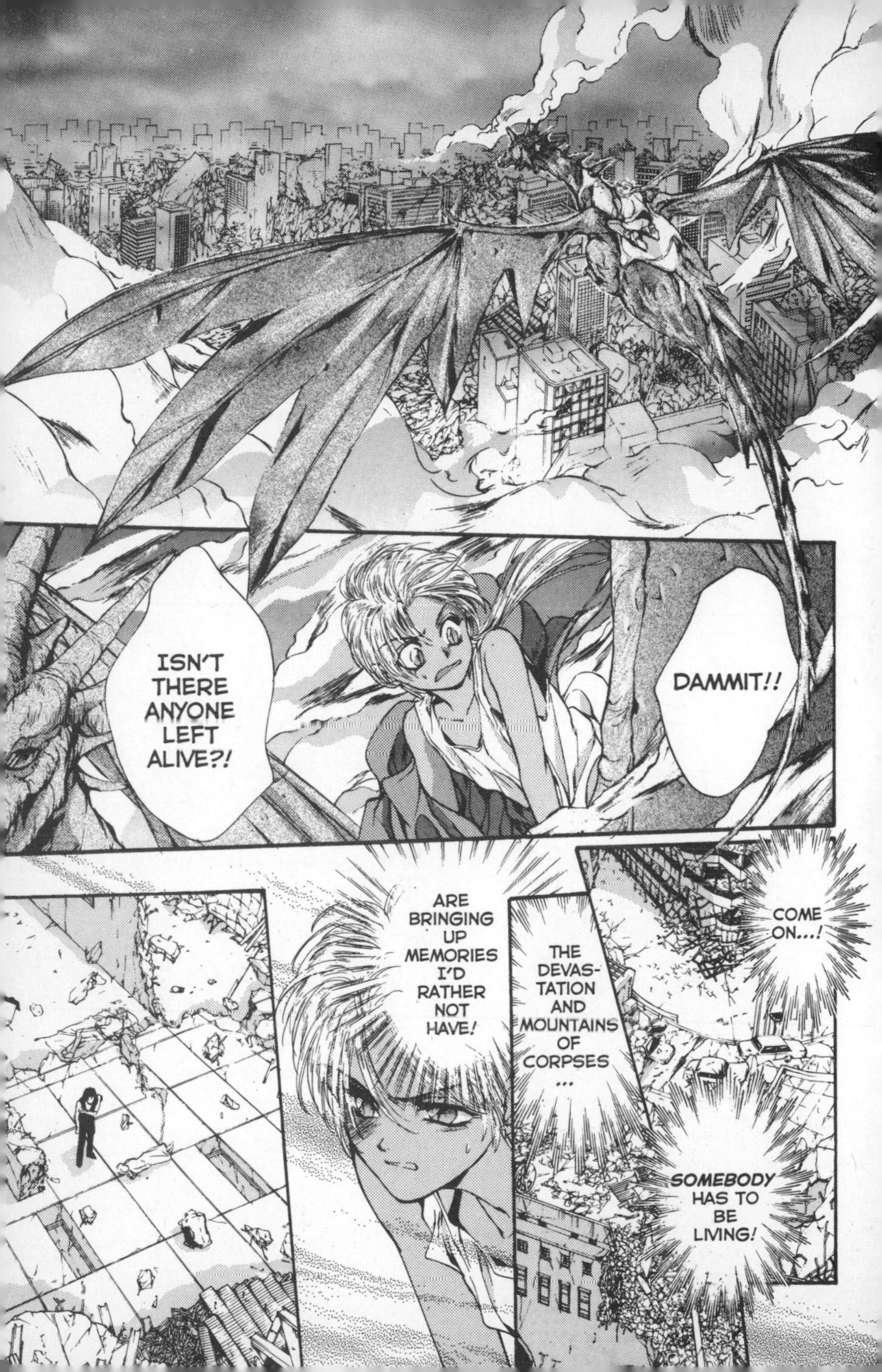
DAMMIT!!
ISN'T THERE ANYONE LEFT ALIVE?!
COME ON...!
SOMEBODY HAS TO BE LIVING!
THE DEVAS-TATION AND MOUNTAINS OF CORPSES ...
ARE BRINGING UP MEMORIES I'D RATHER NOT HAVE!

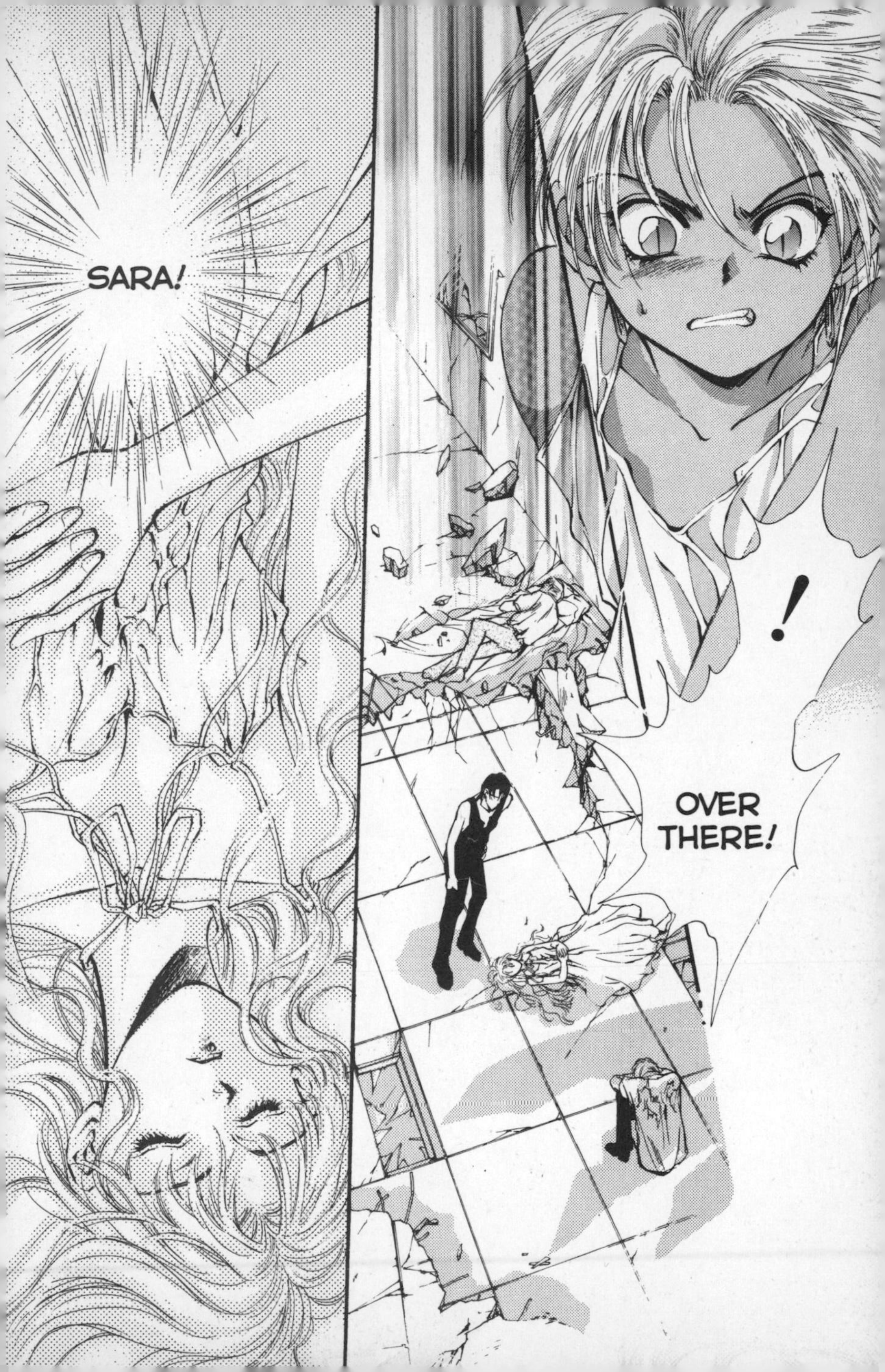
!
OVER THERE!
SARA!

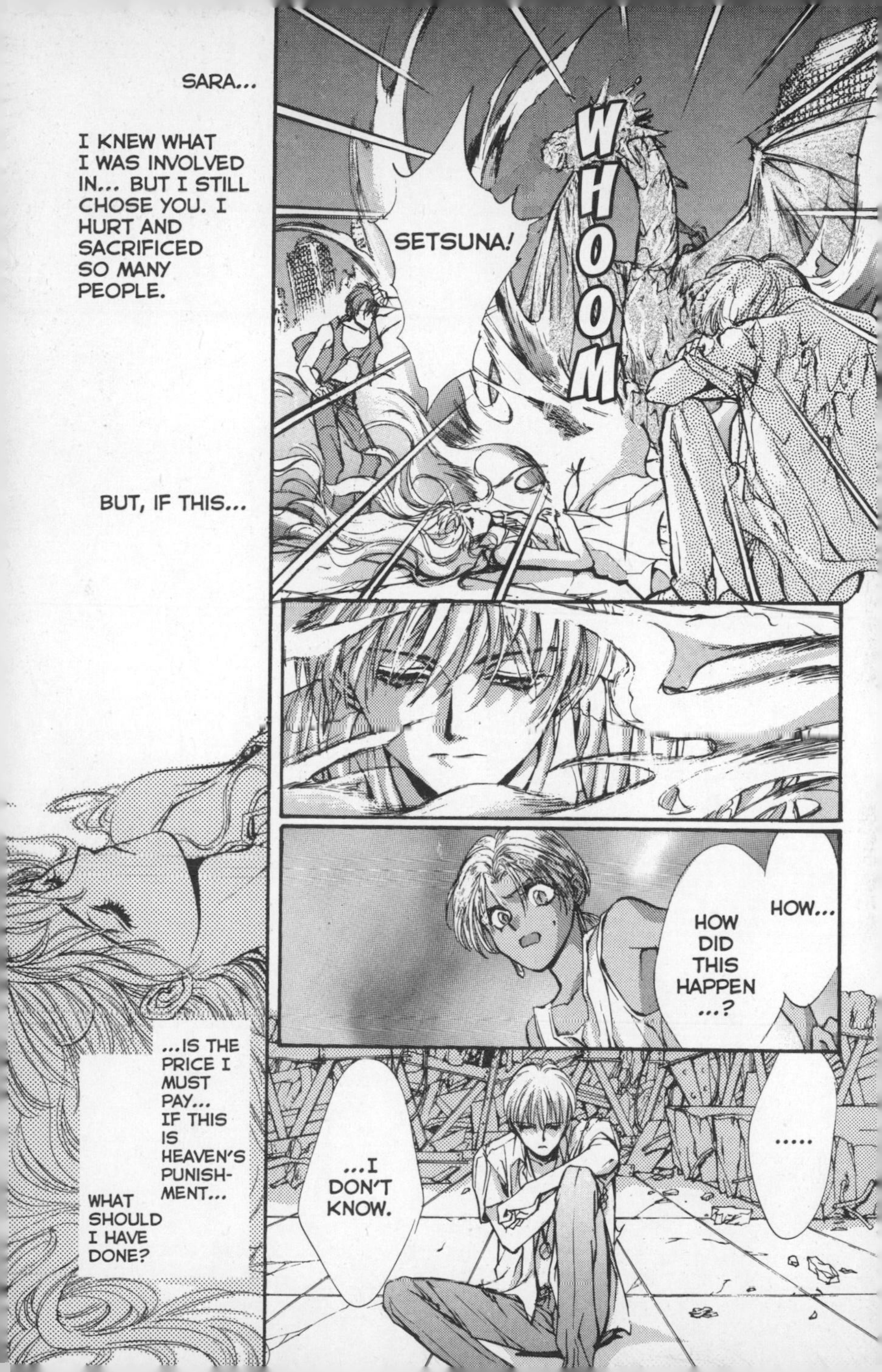
WHOOM
SETSUNA!
HOW...
HOW DID THIS HAPPEN ...?
.....
...I DON'T KNOW.
SARA...
I KNEW WHAT I WAS INVOLVED IN... BUT I STILL CHOSE YOU. I HURT AND SACRIFICED SO MANY PEOPLE.
BUT, IF THIS...
...IS THE PRICE I MUST PAY... IF THIS IS HEAVEN'S PUNISH-MENT...
WHAT SHOULD I HAVE DONE?

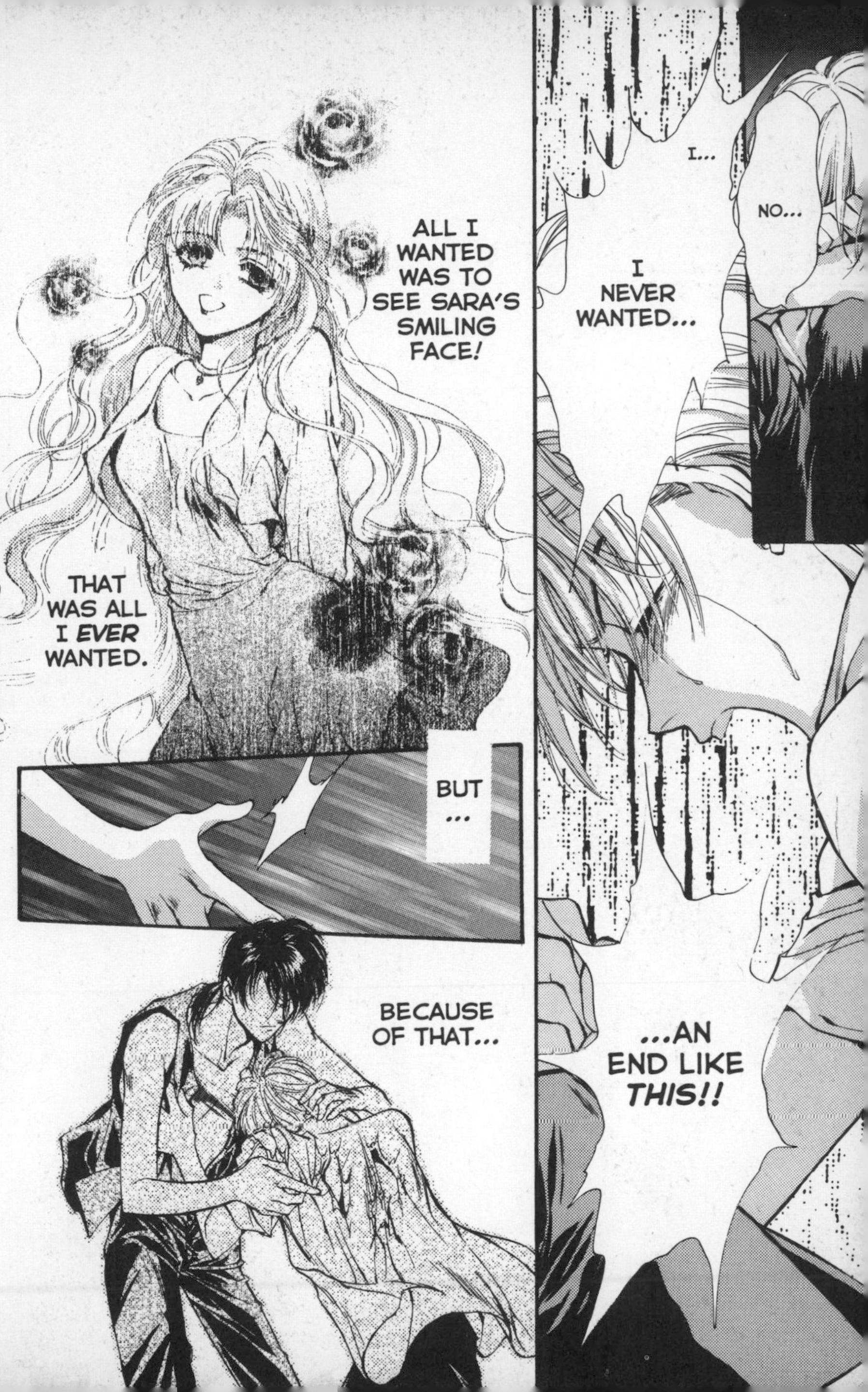
I...
NO...
I NEVER WANTED...
...AN END LIKE *THIS!!*
ALL I WANTED WAS TO SEE SARA'S SMILING FACE!
THAT WAS ALL I *EVER* WANTED.
BUT ...
BECAUSE OF THAT...

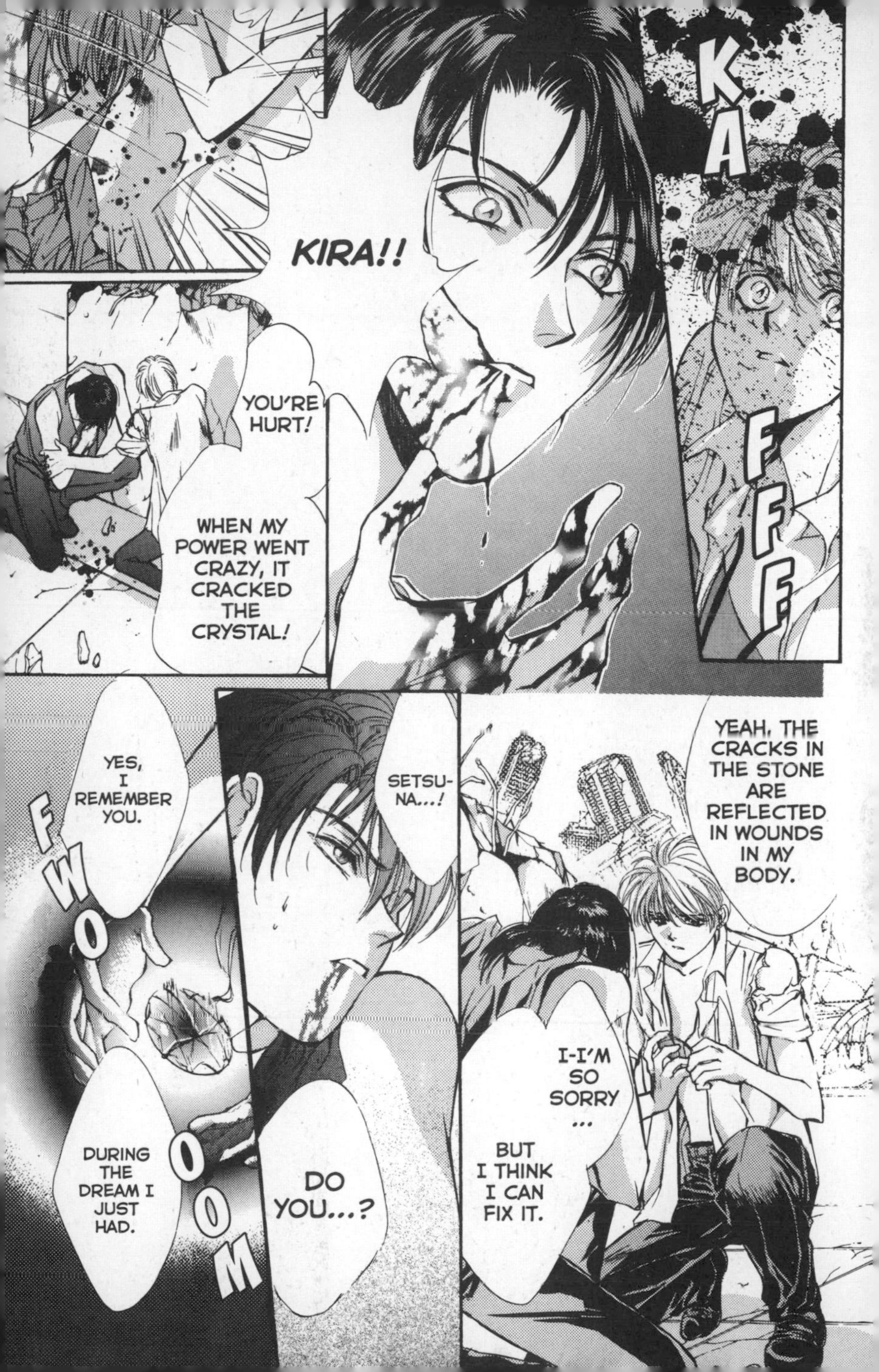
KA
FFF
KIRA!!
YOU'RE HURT!
WHEN MY POWER WENT CRAZY, IT CRACKED THE CRYSTAL!
YEAH, THE CRACKS IN THE STONE ARE REFLECTED IN WOUNDS IN MY BODY.
I-I'M SO SORRY...
BUT I THINK I CAN FIX IT.
SETSU-NA...!
DO YOU...?
YES, I REMEMBER YOU.
FWOOOOM
DURING THE DREAM I JUST HAD.

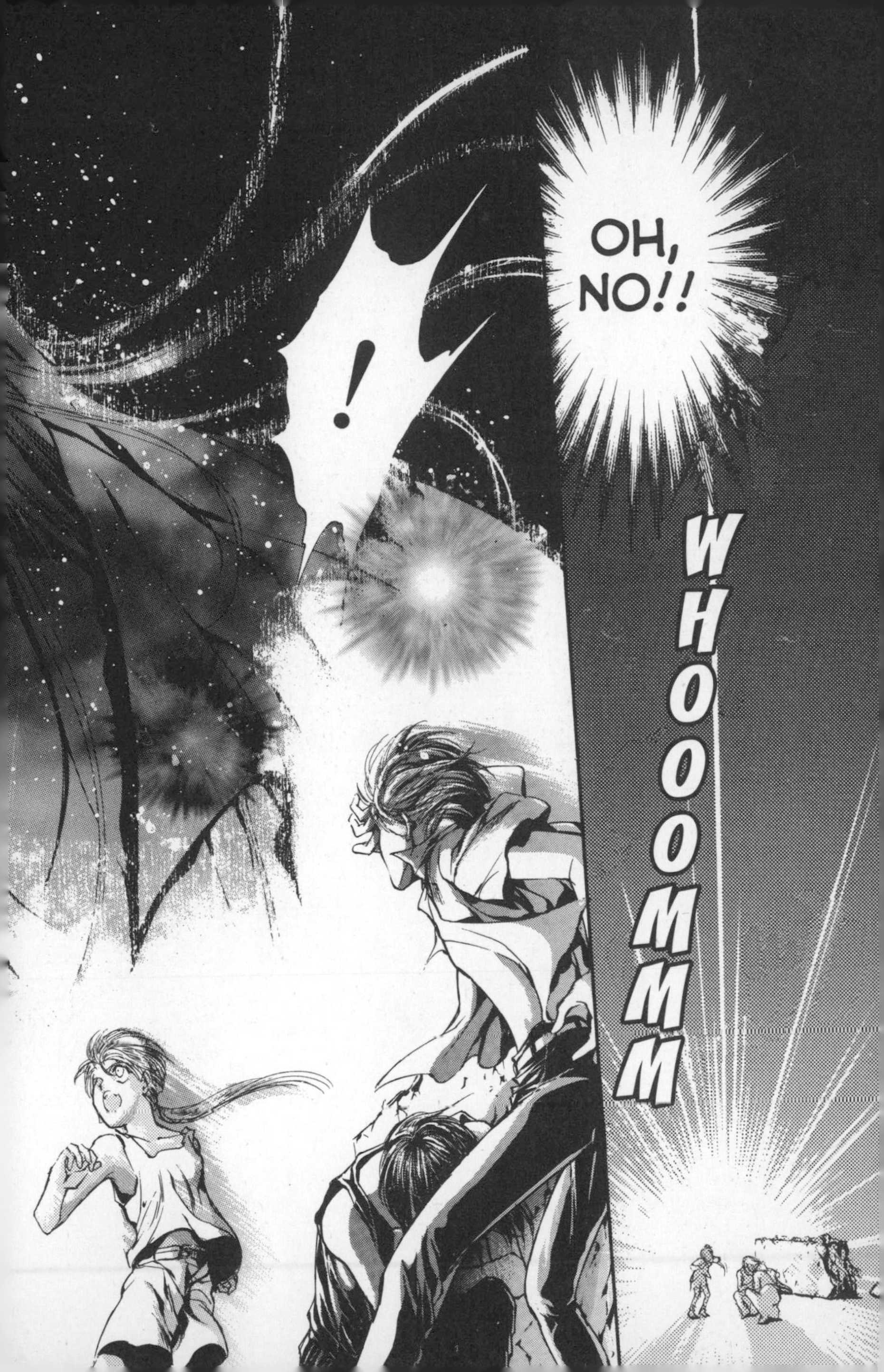
OH, NO!!
WHOOOOMMM
!

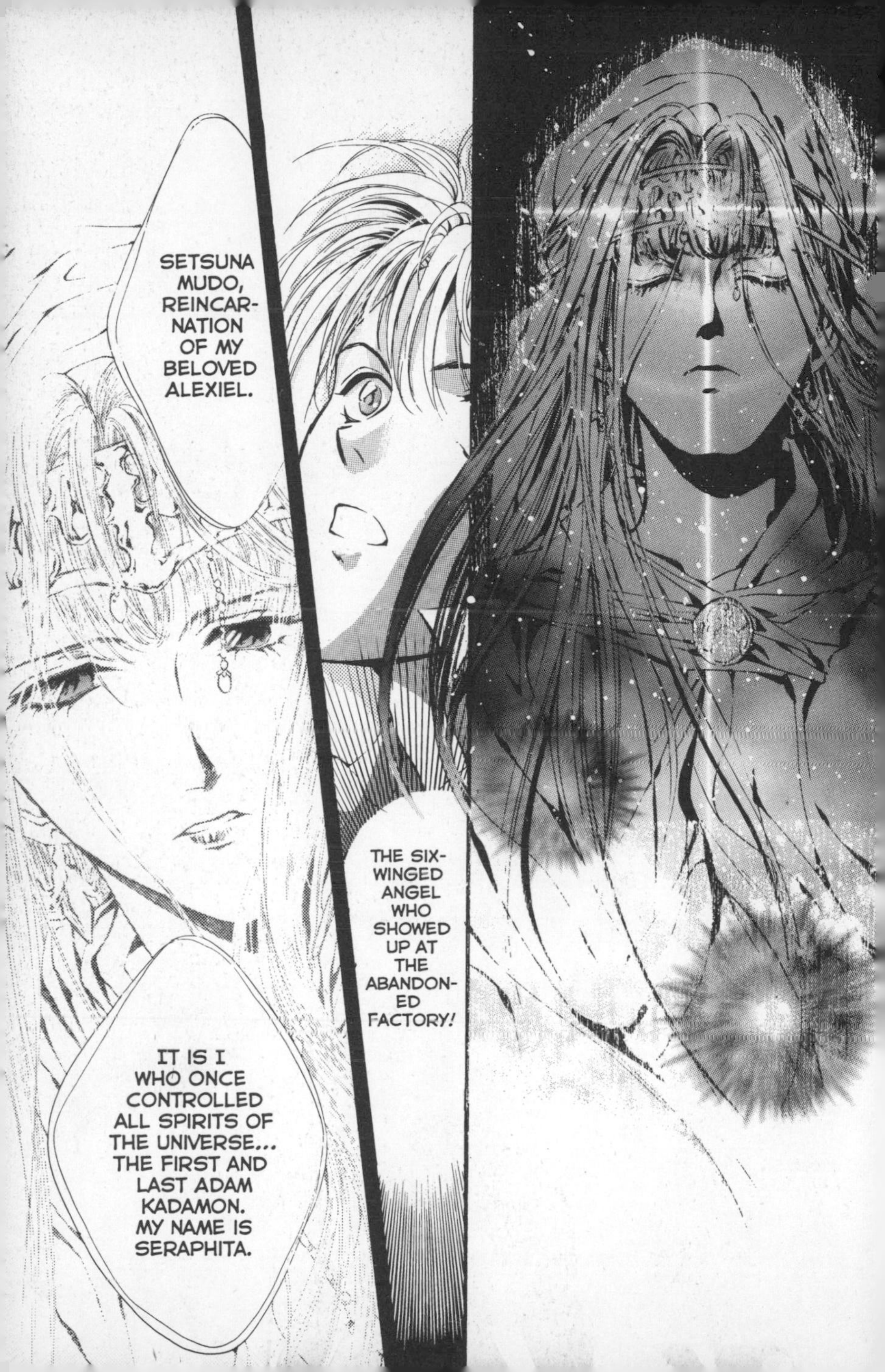
THE SIX-WINGED ANGEL WHO SHOWED UP AT THE ABANDONED FACTORY!
SETSUNA MUDO, REINCARNATION OF MY BELOVED ALEXIEL.
IT IS I WHO ONCE CONTROLLED ALL SPIRITS OF THE UNIVERSE... THE FIRST AND LAST ADAM KADAMON. MY NAME IS SERAPHITA.

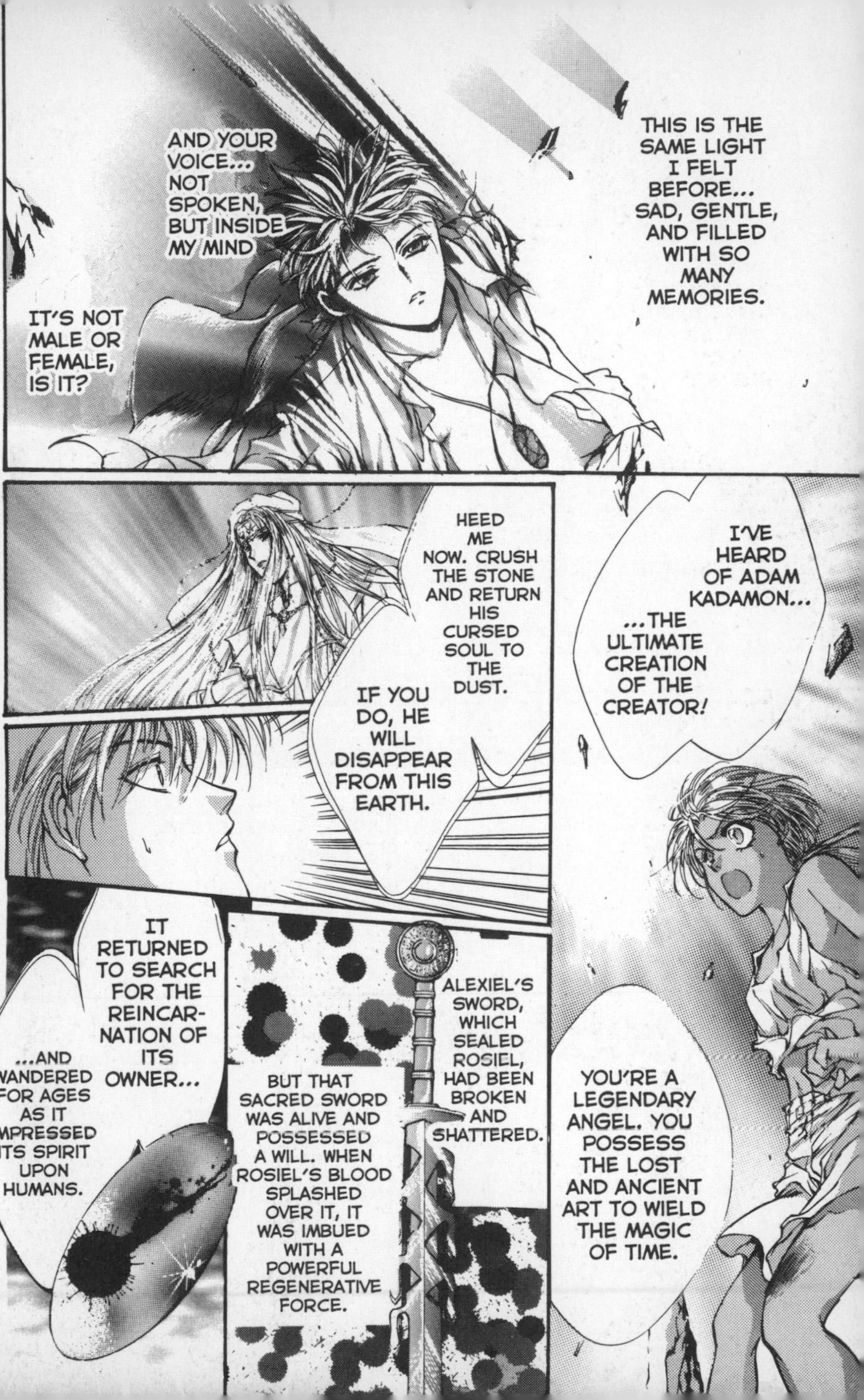
THIS IS THE SAME LIGHT I FELT BEFORE... SAD, GENTLE, AND FILLED WITH SO MANY MEMORIES.
AND YOUR VOICE... NOT SPOKEN, BUT INSIDE MY MIND
IT'S NOT MALE OR FEMALE, IS IT?
I'VE HEARD OF ADAM KADAMON...
...THE ULTIMATE CREATION OF THE CREATOR!
YOU'RE A LEGENDARY ANGEL. YOU POSSESS THE LOST AND ANCIENT ART TO WIELD THE MAGIC OF TIME.
HEED ME NOW. CRUSH THE STONE AND RETURN HIS CURSED SOUL TO THE DUST.
IF YOU DO, HE WILL DISAPPEAR FROM THIS EARTH.
ALEXIEL'S SWORD, WHICH SEALED ROSIEL, HAD BEEN BROKEN AND SHATTERED.
BUT THAT SACRED SWORD WAS ALIVE AND POSSESSED A WILL. WHEN ROSIEL'S BLOOD SPLASHED OVER IT, IT WAS IMBUED WITH A POWERFUL REGENERATIVE FORCE.
IT RETURNED TO SEARCH FOR THE REINCAR-NATION OF ITS OWNER...
...AND WANDERED FOR AGES AS IT IMPRESSED ITS SPIRIT UPON HUMANS.

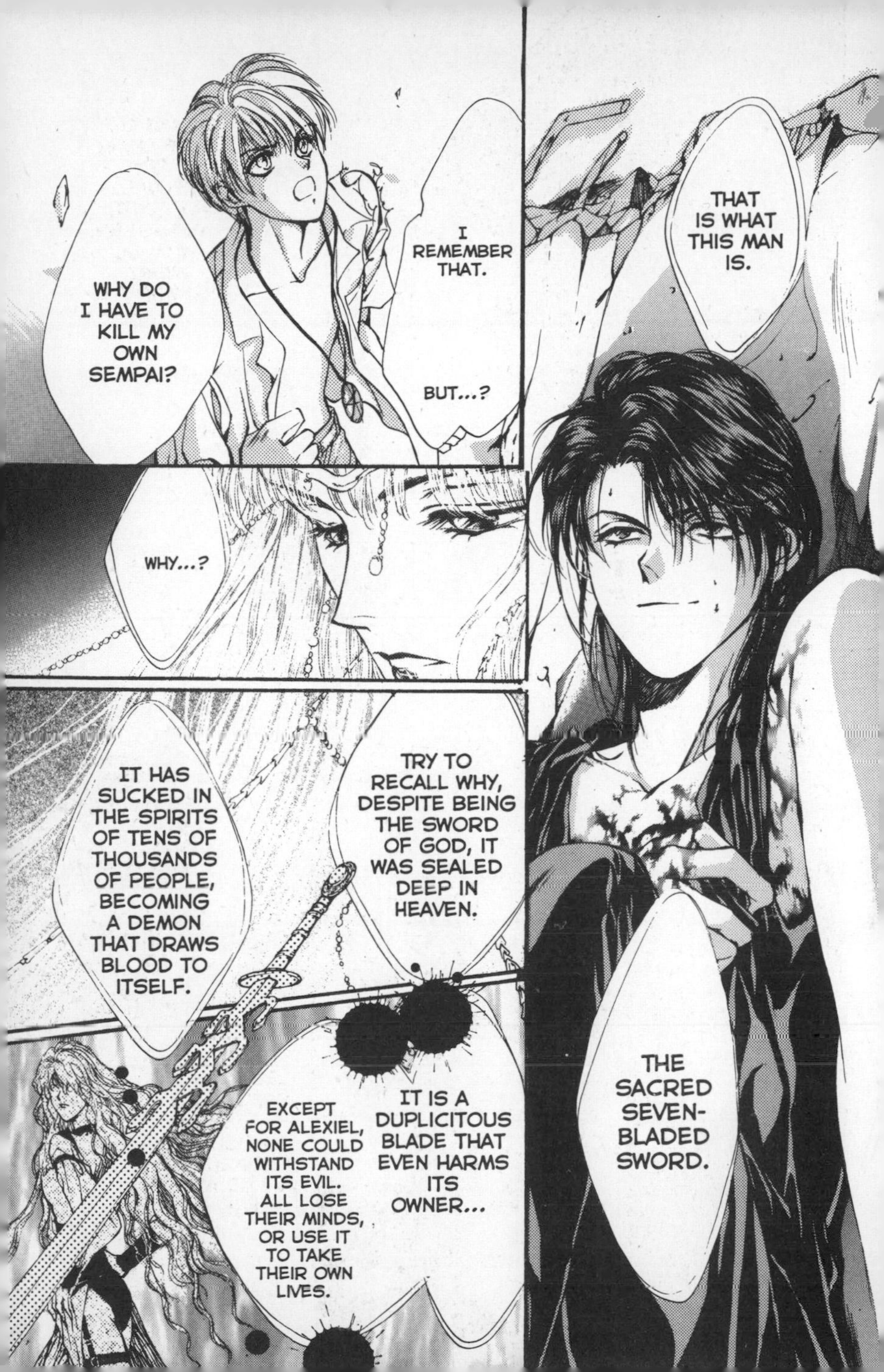
THAT IS WHAT THIS MAN IS.
THE SACRED SEVEN-BLADED SWORD.
I REMEMBER THAT.
BUT...?
WHY DO I HAVE TO KILL MY OWN SEMPAI?
WHY...?
TRY TO RECALL WHY, DESPITE BEING THE SWORD OF GOD, IT WAS SEALED DEEP IN HEAVEN.
IT HAS SUCKED IN THE SPIRITS OF TENS OF THOUSANDS OF PEOPLE, BECOMING A DEMON THAT DRAWS BLOOD TO ITSELF.
IT IS A DUPLICITOUS BLADE THAT EVEN HARMS ITS OWNER...
EXCEPT FOR ALEXIEL, NONE COULD WITHSTAND ITS EVIL. ALL LOSE THEIR MINDS, OR USE IT TO TAKE THEIR OWN LIVES.

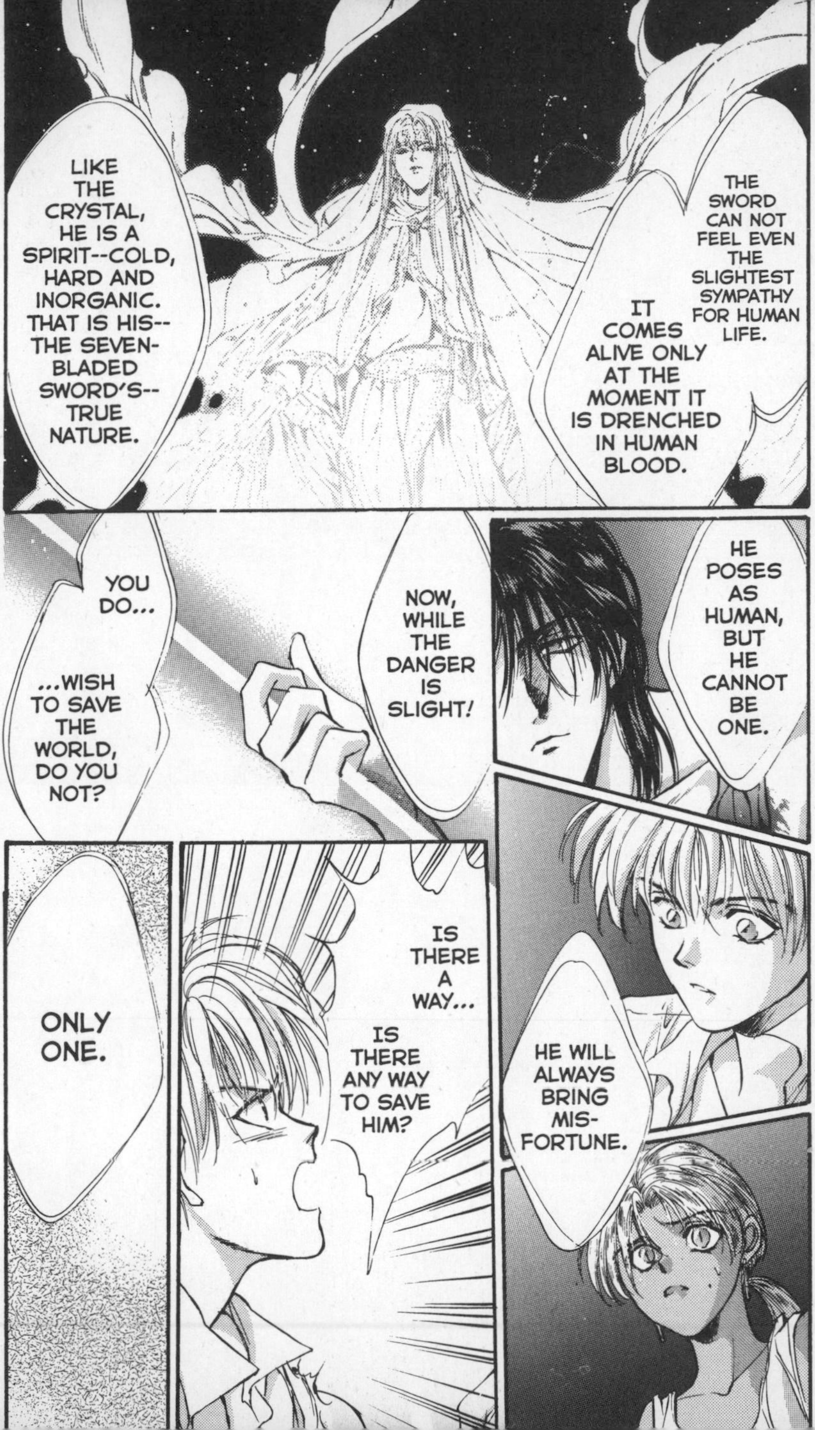
THE SWORD CAN NOT FEEL EVEN THE SLIGHTEST SYMPATHY FOR HUMAN LIFE.
IT COMES ALIVE ONLY AT THE MOMENT IT IS DRENCHED IN HUMAN BLOOD.
LIKE THE CRYSTAL, HE IS A SPIRIT--COLD, HARD AND INORGANIC. THAT IS HIS--THE SEVEN-BLADED SWORD'S--TRUE NATURE.
HE POSES AS HUMAN, BUT HE CANNOT BE ONE.
NOW, WHILE THE DANGER IS SLIGHT!
YOU DO...
...WISH TO SAVE THE WORLD, DO YOU NOT?
HE WILL ALWAYS BRING MIS-FORTUNE.
IS THERE A WAY...
IS THERE ANY WAY TO SAVE HIM?
ONLY ONE.

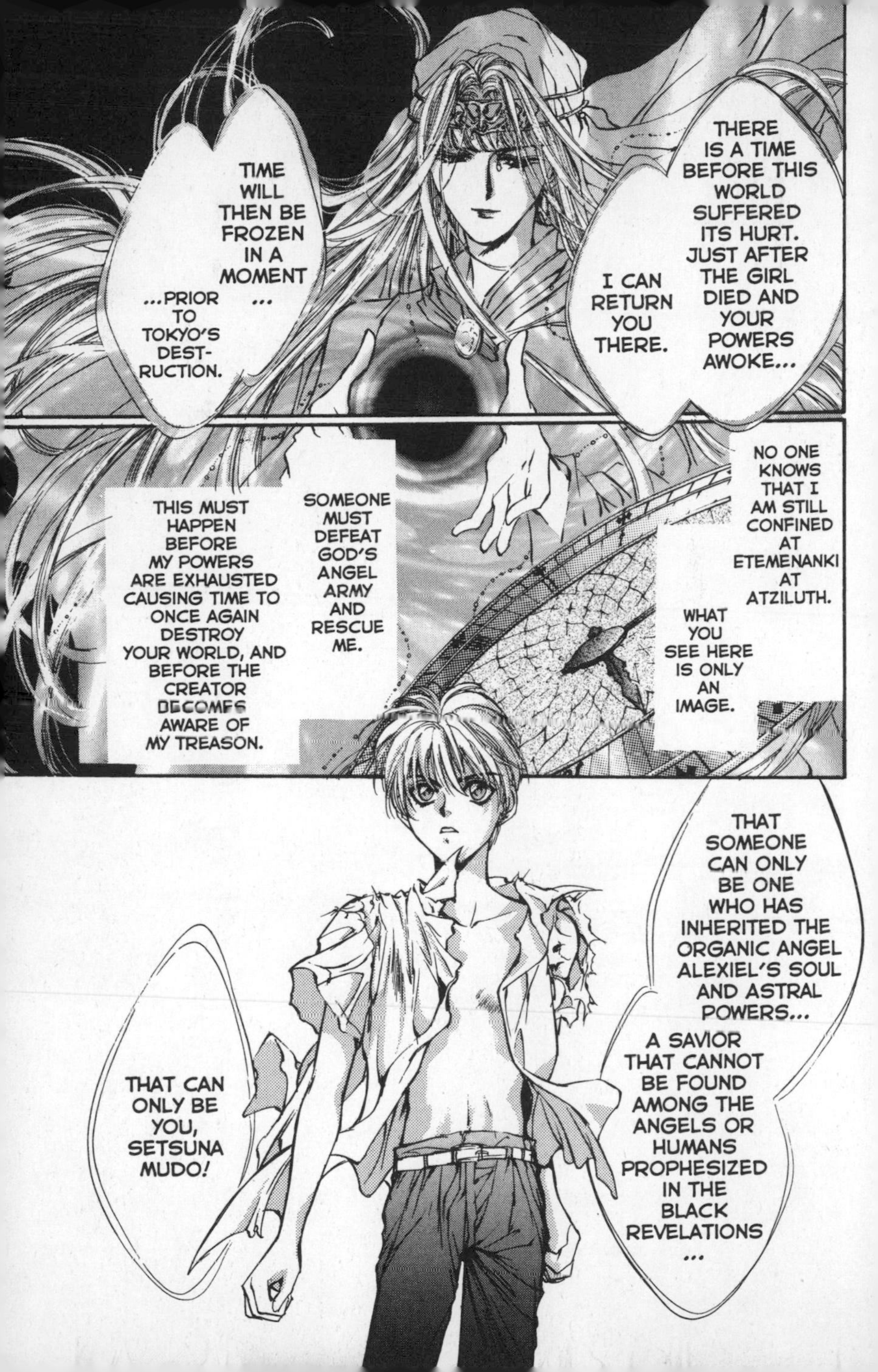
THERE IS A TIME BEFORE THIS WORLD SUFFERED ITS HURT. JUST AFTER THE GIRL DIED AND YOUR POWERS AWOKE...
I CAN RETURN YOU THERE.
TIME WILL THEN BE FROZEN IN A MOMENT ...
...PRIOR TO TOKYO'S DEST-RUCTION.
NO ONE KNOWS THAT I AM STILL CONFINED AT ETEMENANKI AT ATZILUTH.
WHAT YOU SEE HERE IS ONLY AN IMAGE.
SOMEONE MUST DEFEAT GOD'S ANGEL ARMY AND RESCUE ME.
THIS MUST HAPPEN BEFORE MY POWERS ARE EXHAUSTED CAUSING TIME TO ONCE AGAIN DESTROY YOUR WORLD, AND BEFORE THE CREATOR BECOMES AWARE OF MY TREASON.
THAT SOMEONE CAN ONLY BE ONE WHO HAS INHERITED THE ORGANIC ANGEL ALEXIEL'S SOUL AND ASTRAL POWERS...
A SAVIOR THAT CANNOT BE FOUND AMONG THE ANGELS OR HUMANS PROPHESIZED IN THE BLACK REVELATIONS ...
THAT CAN ONLY BE YOU, SETSUNA MUDO!

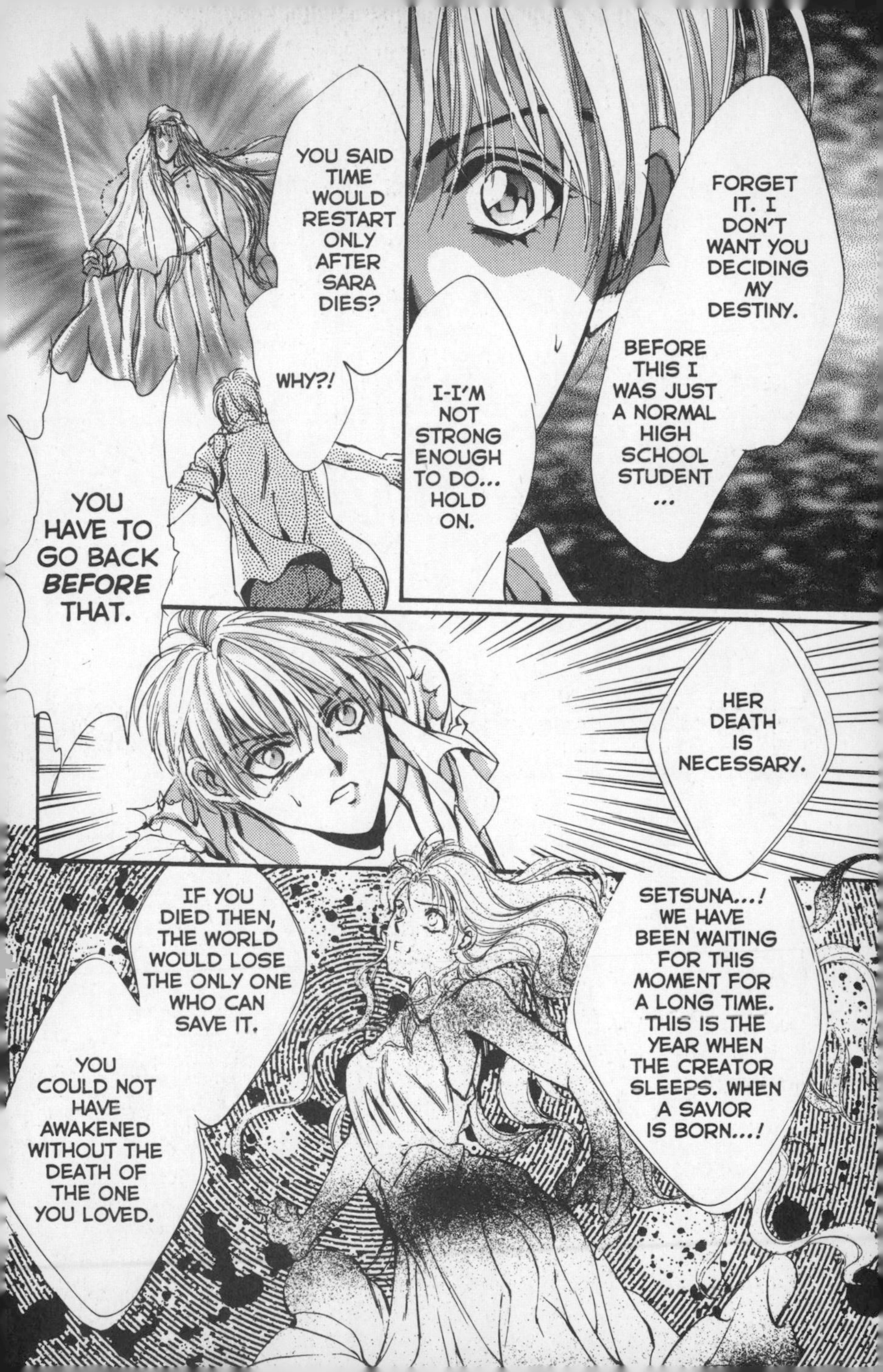
FORGET IT. I DON'T WANT YOU DECIDING MY DESTINY.
BEFORE THIS I WAS JUST A NORMAL HIGH SCHOOL STUDENT ...
I-I'M NOT STRONG ENOUGH TO DO... HOLD ON.
YOU SAID TIME WOULD RESTART ONLY AFTER SARA DIES?
WHY?!
YOU HAVE TO GO BACK *BEFORE* THAT.
HER DEATH IS NECESSARY.
SETSUNA...! WE HAVE BEEN WAITING FOR THIS MOMENT FOR A LONG TIME. THIS IS THE YEAR WHEN THE CREATOR SLEEPS. WHEN A SAVIOR IS BORN...!
IF YOU DIED THEN, THE WORLD WOULD LOSE THE ONLY ONE WHO CAN SAVE IT.
YOU COULD NOT HAVE AWAKENED WITHOUT THE DEATH OF THE ONE YOU LOVED.

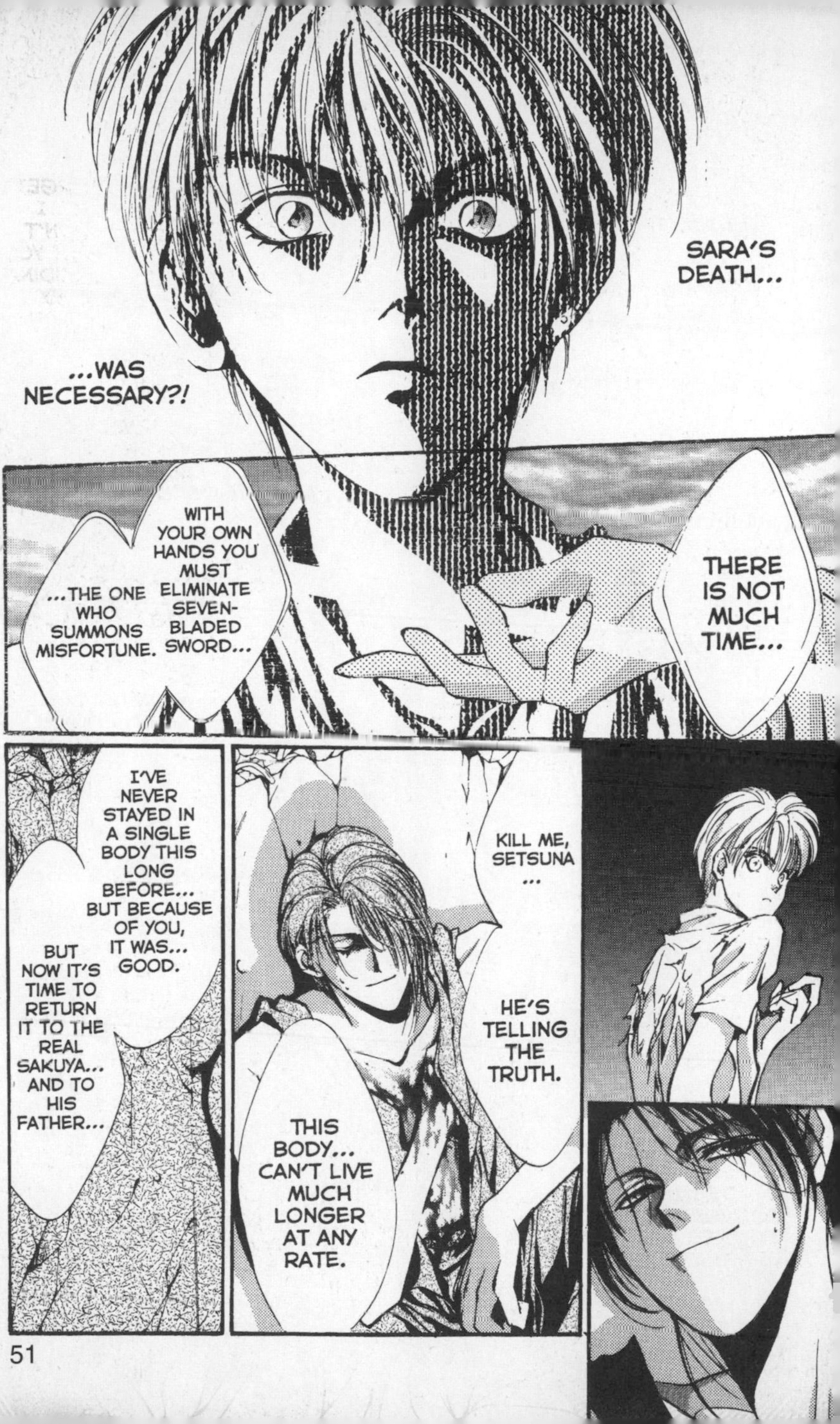
SARA'S DEATH...
...WAS NECESSARY?!
THERE IS NOT MUCH TIME...
WITH YOUR OWN HANDS YOU MUST ELIMINATE SEVEN-BLADED SWORD...
...THE ONE WHO SUMMONS MISFORTUNE.
KILL ME, SETSUNA ...
HE'S TELLING THE TRUTH.
THIS BODY... CAN'T LIVE MUCH LONGER AT ANY RATE.
I'VE NEVER STAYED IN A SINGLE BODY THIS LONG BEFORE... BUT BECAUSE OF YOU, IT WAS... GOOD.
BUT NOW IT'S TIME TO RETURN IT TO THE REAL SAKUYA... AND TO HIS FATHER...

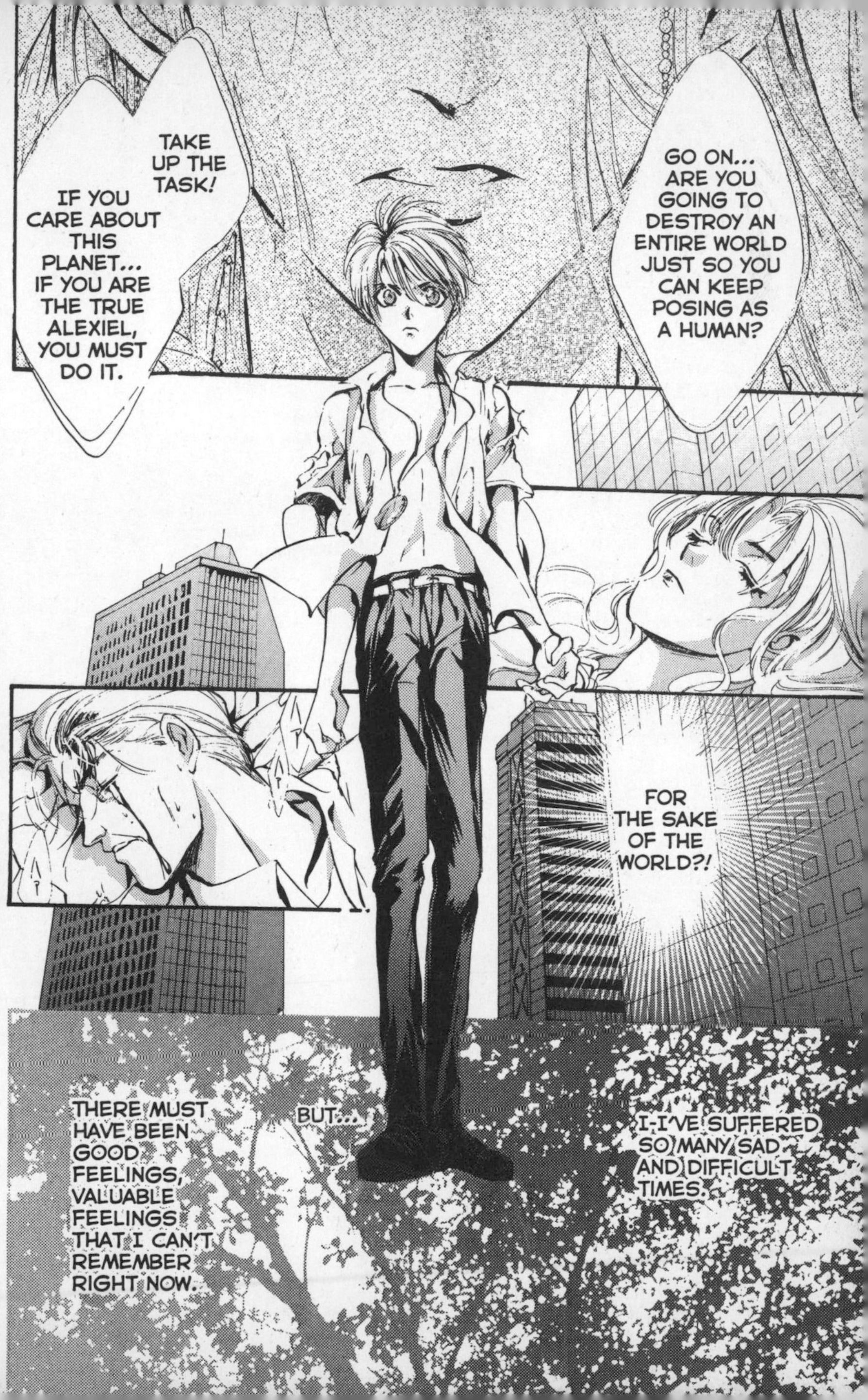
GO ON... ARE YOU GOING TO DESTROY AN ENTIRE WORLD JUST SO YOU CAN KEEP POSING AS A HUMAN?
TAKE UP THE TASK!
IF YOU CARE ABOUT THIS PLANET... IF YOU ARE THE TRUE ALEXIEL, YOU MUST DO IT.
FOR THE SAKE OF THE WORLD?!
I-I'VE SUFFERED SO MANY SAD AND DIFFICULT TIMES.
BUT...
THERE MUST HAVE BEEN GOOD FEELINGS, VALUABLE FEELINGS THAT I CAN'T REMEMBER RIGHT NOW.

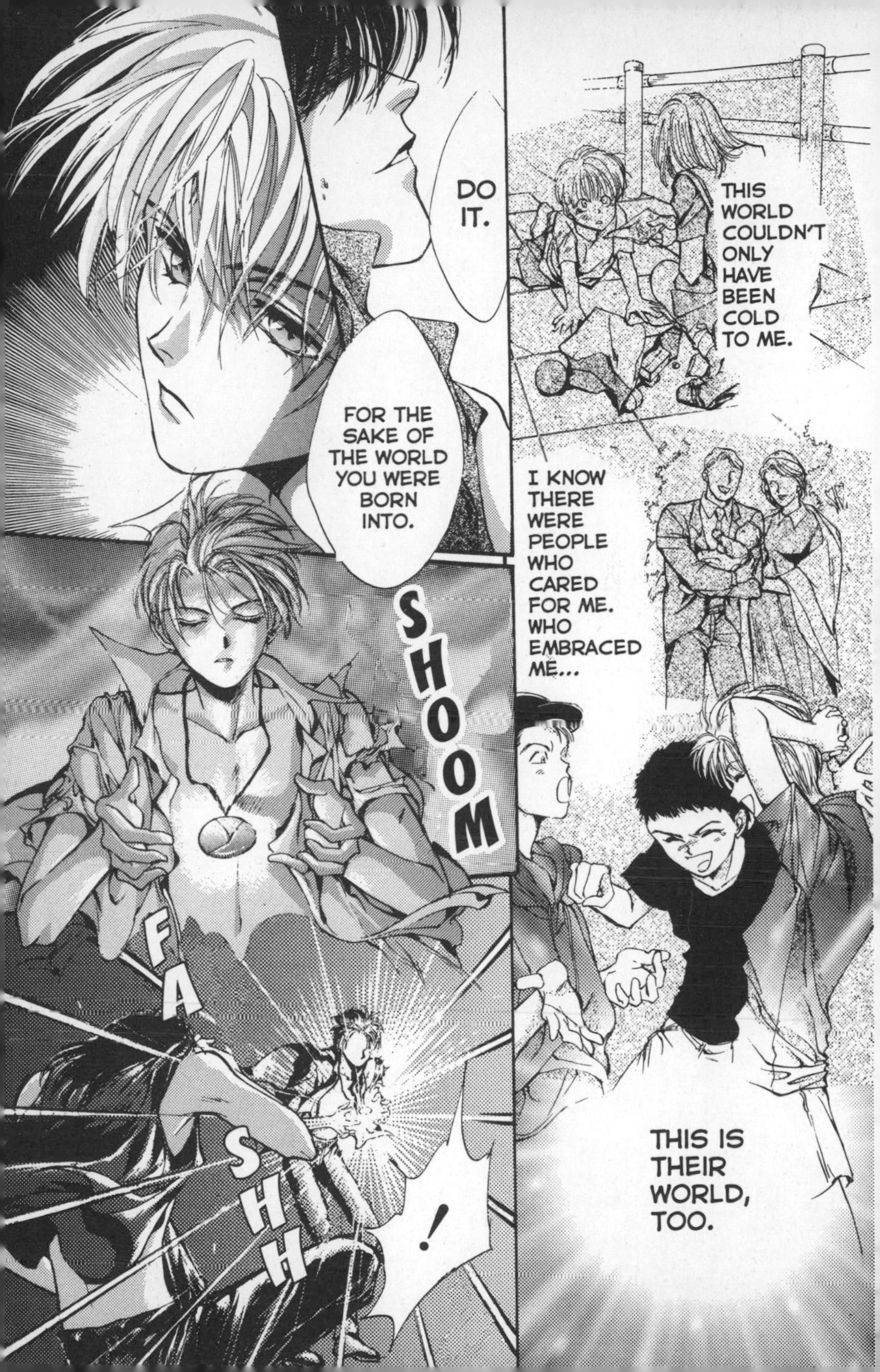
THIS WORLD COULDN'T ONLY HAVE BEEN COLD TO ME.
I KNOW THERE WERE PEOPLE WHO CARED FOR ME. WHO EMBRACED ME...
THIS IS THEIR WORLD, TOO.
DO IT.
FOR THE SAKE OF THE WORLD YOU WERE BORN INTO.
SHOOM
FA
SHH
!

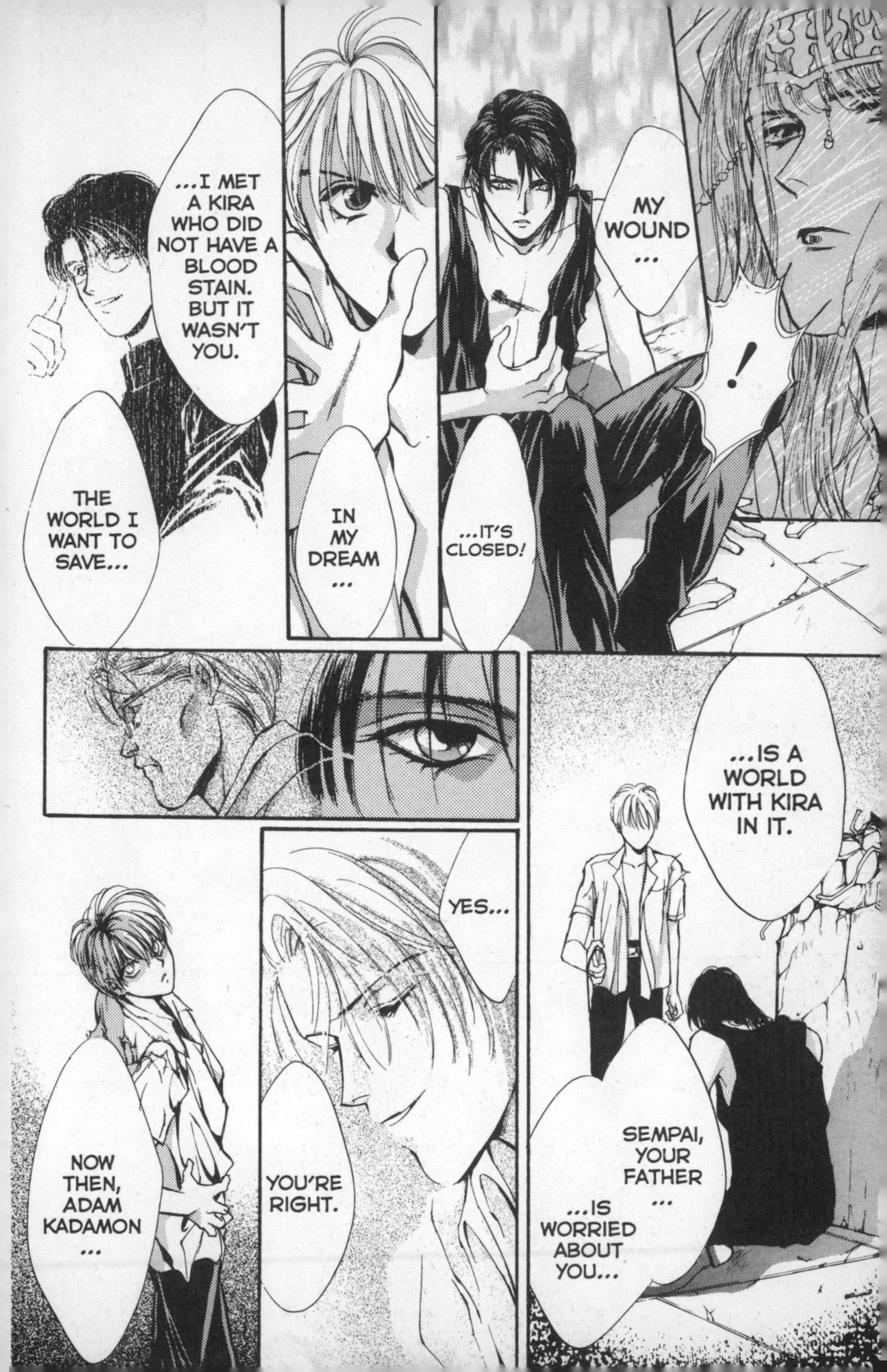
!
MY WOUND ...
...IT'S CLOSED!
IN MY DREAM ...
...I MET A KIRA WHO DID NOT HAVE A BLOOD STAIN. BUT IT WASN'T YOU.
THE WORLD I WANT TO SAVE...
...IS A WORLD WITH KIRA IN IT.
SEMPAI, YOUR FATHER ...
...IS WORRIED ABOUT YOU...
YES...
YOU'RE RIGHT.
NOW THEN, ADAM KADAMON ...

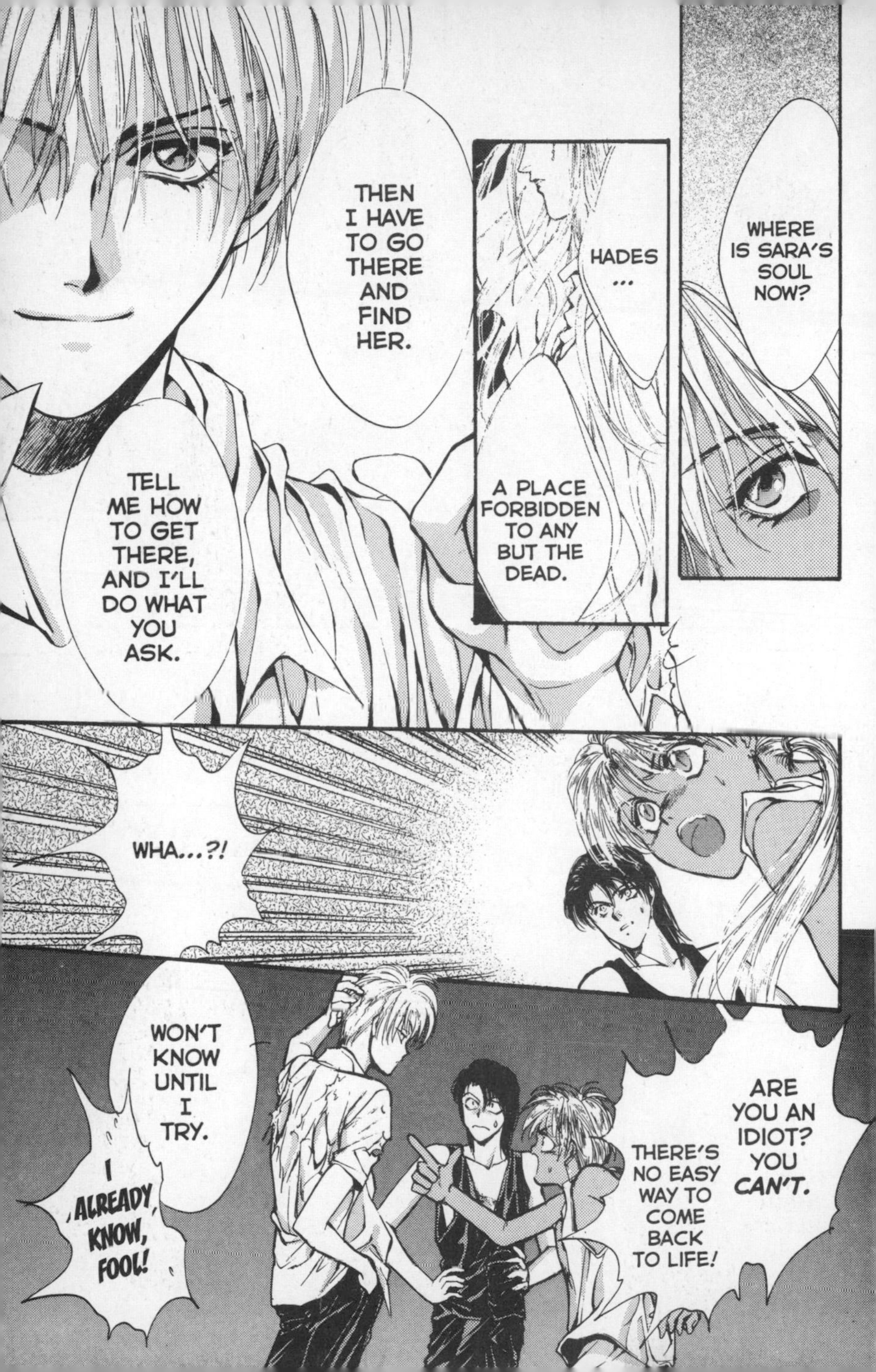
WHERE IS SARA'S SOUL NOW?
HADES...
A PLACE FORBIDDEN TO ANY BUT THE DEAD.
THEN I HAVE TO GO THERE AND FIND HER.
TELL ME HOW TO GET THERE, AND I'LL DO WHAT YOU ASK.
WHA...?!
ARE YOU AN IDIOT? YOU CAN'T.
THERE'S NO EASY WAY TO COME BACK TO LIFE!
WON'T KNOW UNTIL I TRY.
I ALREADY KNOW, FOOL!

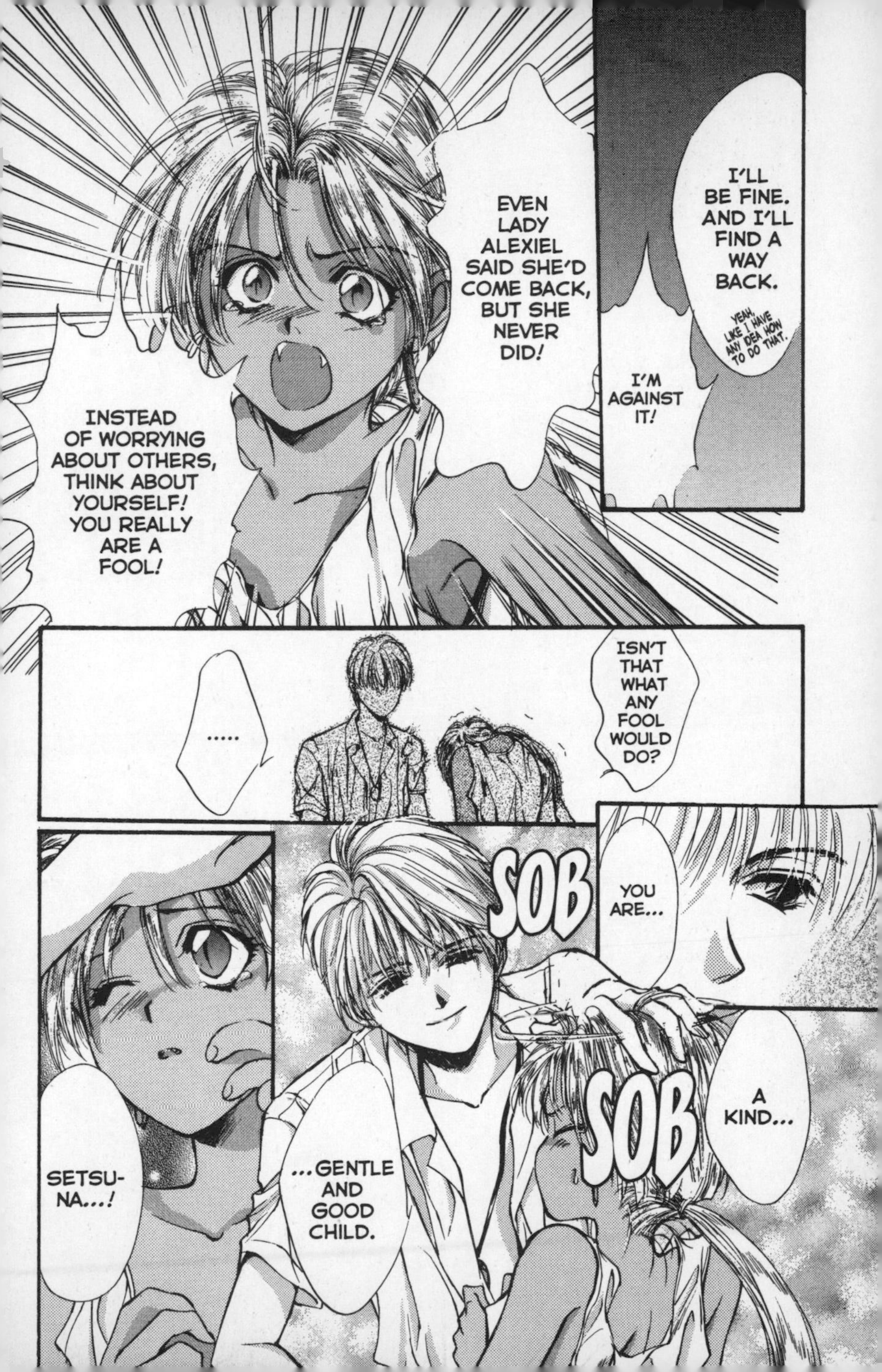
I'LL BE FINE. AND I'LL FIND A WAY BACK.
YEAH, LIKE I HAVE ANY IDEA HOW TO DO THAT.
I'M AGAINST IT!
EVEN LADY ALEXIEL SAID SHE'D COME BACK, BUT SHE NEVER DID!
INSTEAD OF WORRYING ABOUT OTHERS, THINK ABOUT YOURSELF! YOU REALLY ARE A FOOL!
ISN'T THAT WHAT ANY FOOL WOULD DO?
.....
YOU ARE...
SOB
A KIND...
SOB
...GENTLE AND GOOD CHILD.
SETSU-NA...!

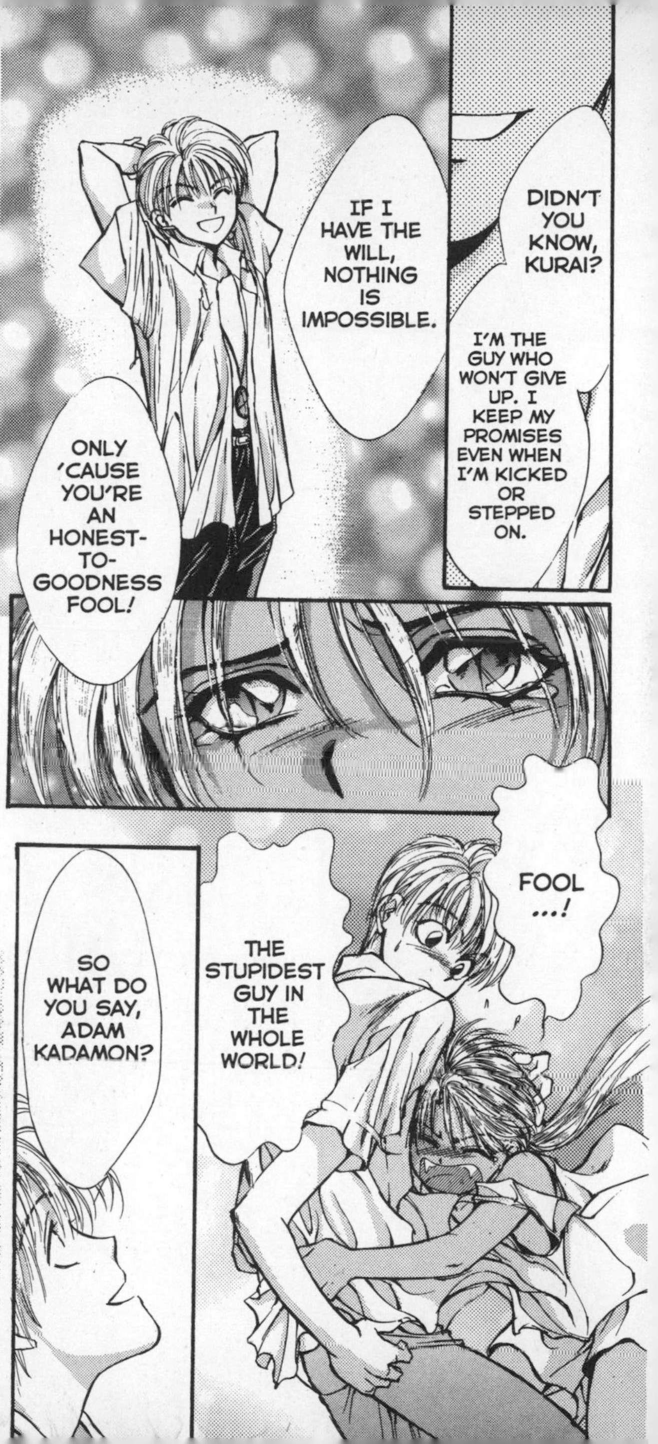
DIDN'T YOU KNOW, KURAI?
I'M THE GUY WHO WON'T GIVE UP. I KEEP MY PROMISES EVEN WHEN I'M KICKED OR STEPPED ON.
IF I HAVE THE WILL, NOTHING IS IMPOSSIBLE.
ONLY 'CAUSE YOU'RE AN HONEST-TO-GOODNESS FOOL!
FOOL ...!
THE STUPIDEST GUY IN THE WHOLE WORLD!
SO WHAT DO YOU SAY, ADAM KADAMON?

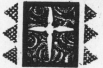

And so we've come to the final episode of the Book of the Material World. Just for this episode, I was allowed ten extra pages. I'm glad. I ouldn't have gotten it all in the normal 30 pages. Adam Kadamon, making an appearance for the first time in quite a while, was a difficult character to draw. I was finally able to reveal Kira's true identity. And then there's Sara's death, which, though shocking, was inevitable for the story's sake. Occasionally, I heard opinions asking about what happened to Katan (and also to Kirie) (Poor Sara ! 0)
And so (?), the Rosiel scenes that follow are ones I've wanted to do for quite some time. It turned out to be a scene I have a bit of a soft spot for.

Aah ♪
there I go, feeling sentimental again
This is embarrassing!

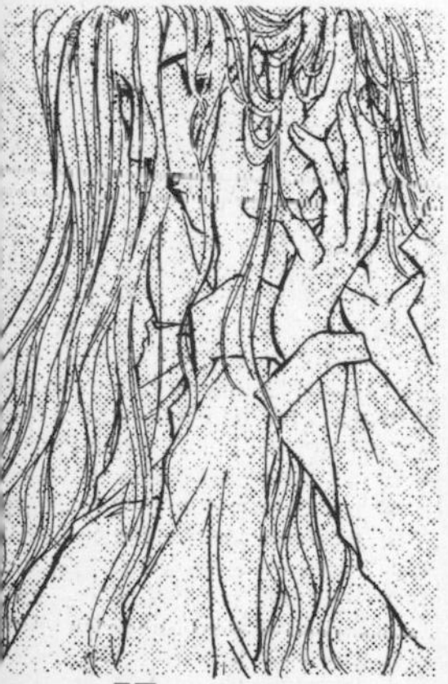

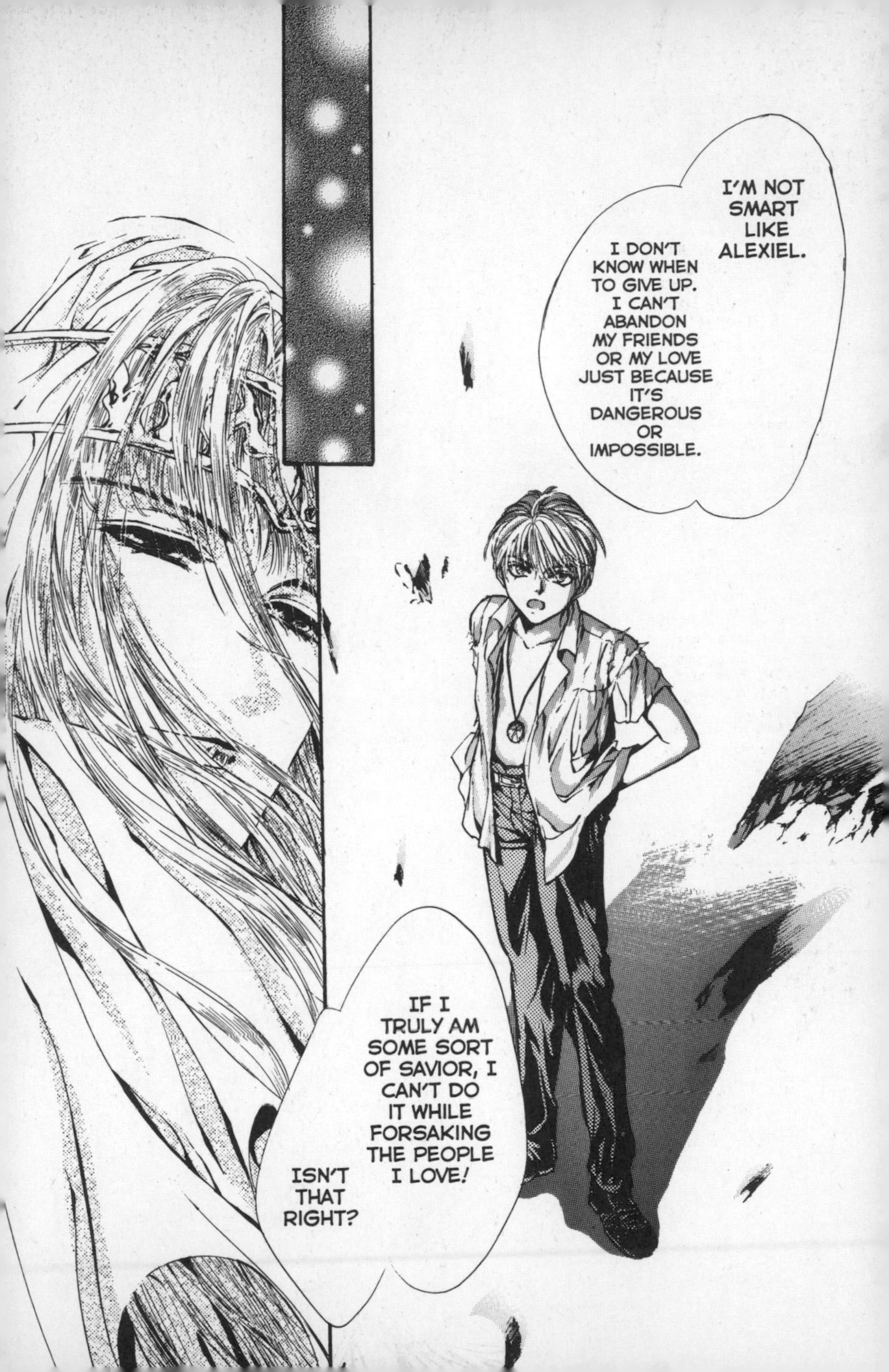
I'M NOT SMART LIKE ALEXIEL.
I DON'T KNOW WHEN TO GIVE UP. I CAN'T ABANDON MY FRIENDS OR MY LOVE JUST BECAUSE IT'S DANGEROUS OR IMPOSSIBLE.
IF I TRULY AM SOME SORT OF SAVIOR, I CAN'T DO IT WHILE FORSAKING THE PEOPLE I LOVE!
ISN'T THAT RIGHT?

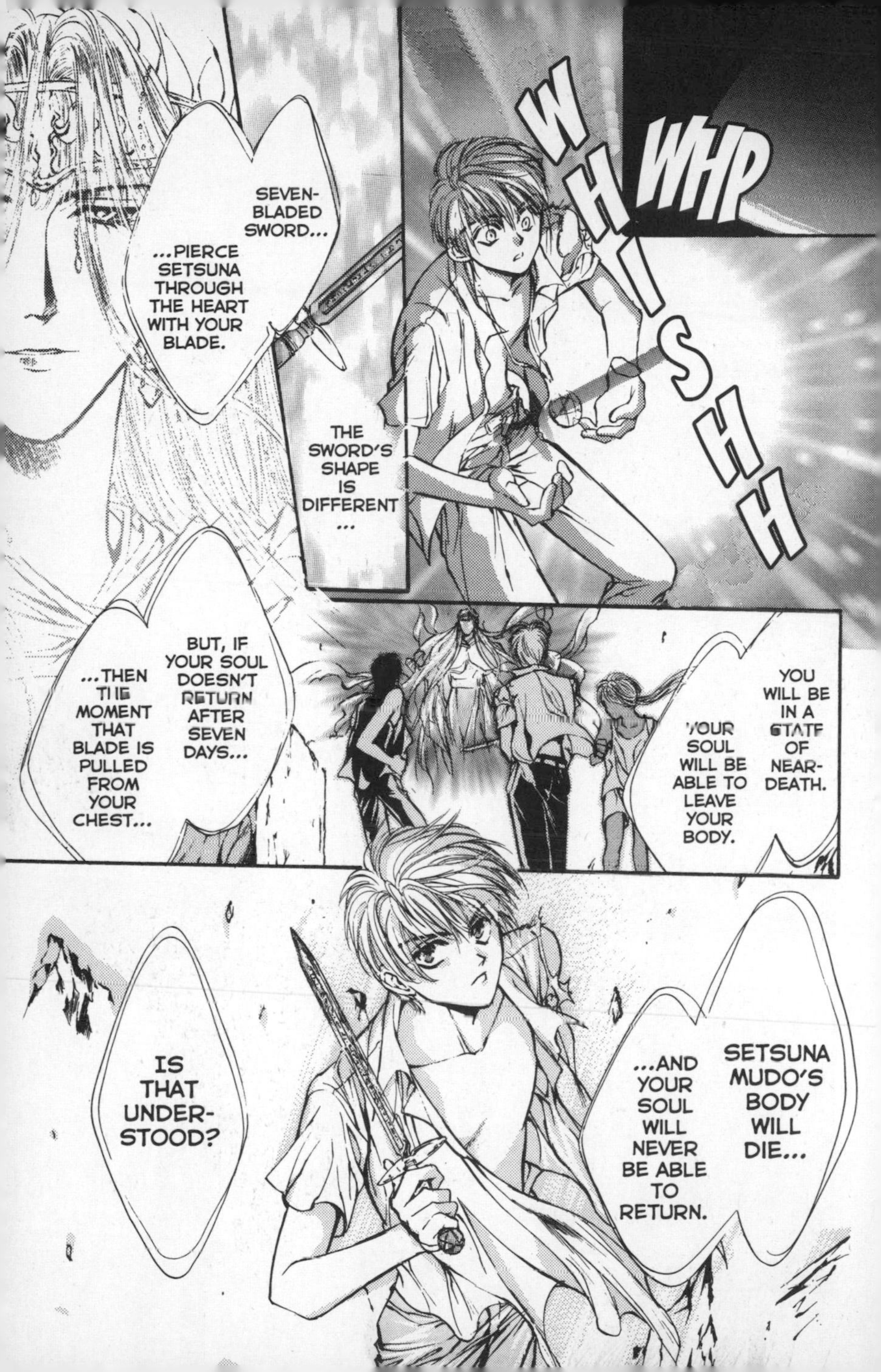
SEVEN-BLADED SWORD...
...PIERCE SETSUNA THROUGH THE HEART WITH YOUR BLADE.
WHP
WHISHHH
THE SWORD'S SHAPE IS DIFFERENT...
YOU WILL BE IN A STATE OF NEAR-DEATH.
YOUR SOUL WILL BE ABLE TO LEAVE YOUR BODY.
BUT, IF YOUR SOUL DOESN'T RETURN AFTER SEVEN DAYS...
...THEN THE MOMENT THAT BLADE IS PULLED FROM YOUR CHEST...
SETSUNA MUDO'S BODY WILL DIE...
...AND YOUR SOUL WILL NEVER BE ABLE TO RETURN.
IS THAT UNDERSTOOD?

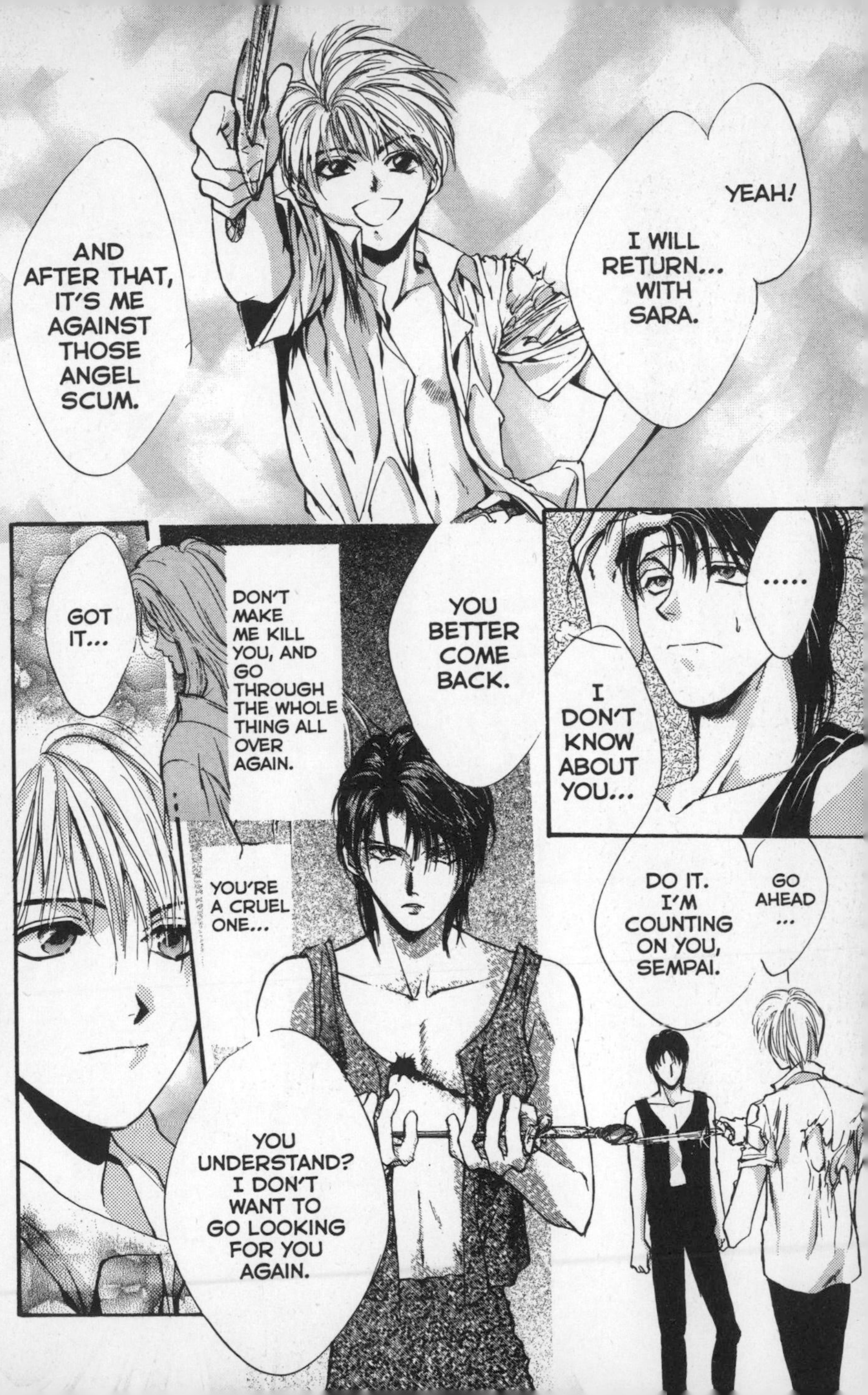
YEAH!
I WILL RETURN... WITH SARA.
AND AFTER THAT, IT'S ME AGAINST THOSE ANGEL SCUM.
.....
I DON'T KNOW ABOUT YOU...
GO AHEAD...
DO IT. I'M COUNTING ON YOU, SEMPAI.
YOU BETTER COME BACK.
DON'T MAKE ME KILL YOU, AND GO THROUGH THE WHOLE THING ALL OVER AGAIN.
GOT IT...
YOU'RE A CRUEL ONE...
YOU UNDERSTAND? I DON'T WANT TO GO LOOKING FOR YOU AGAIN.

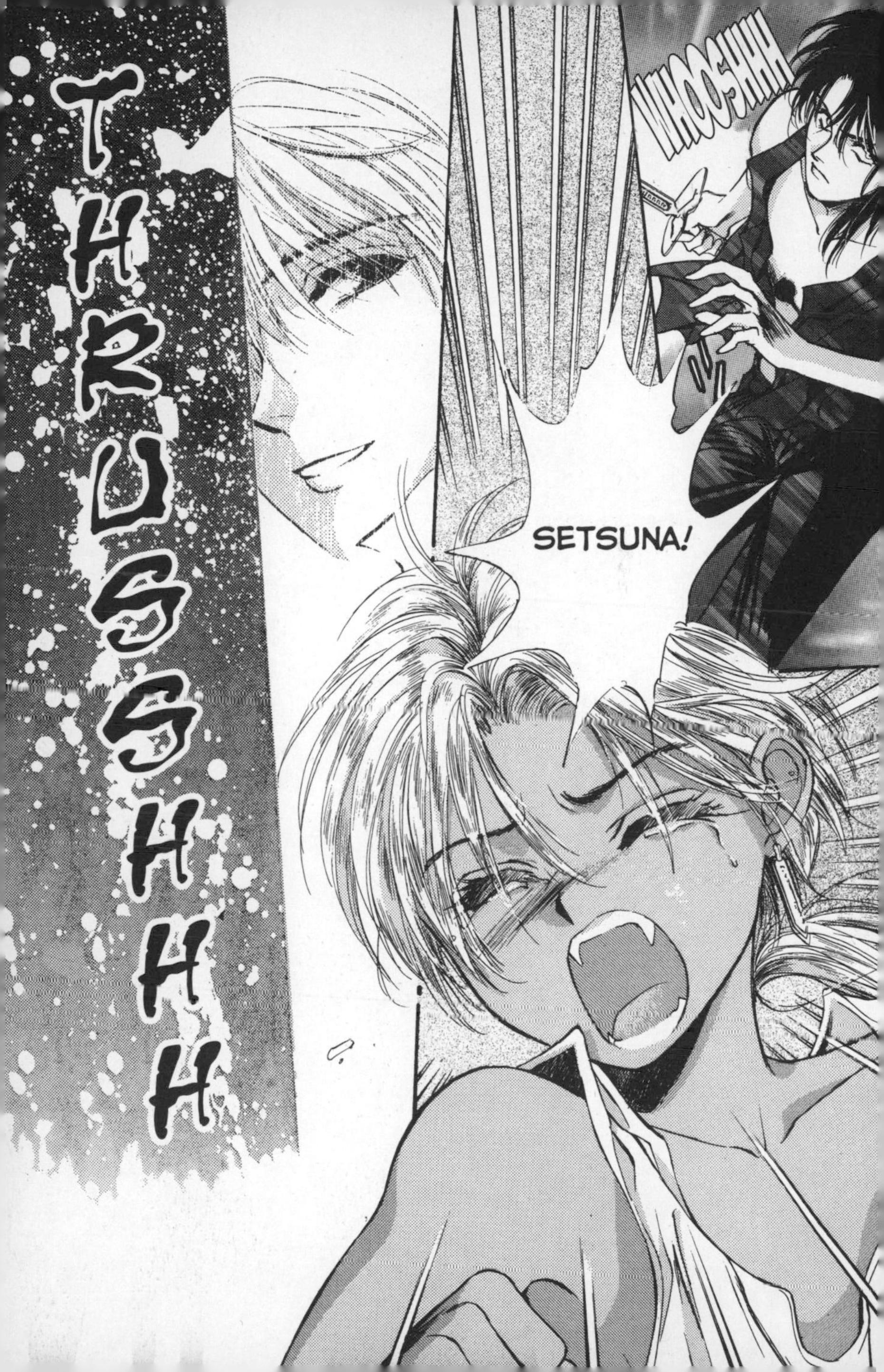
WHOOSHHH
SETSUNA!
THRUSSHHH

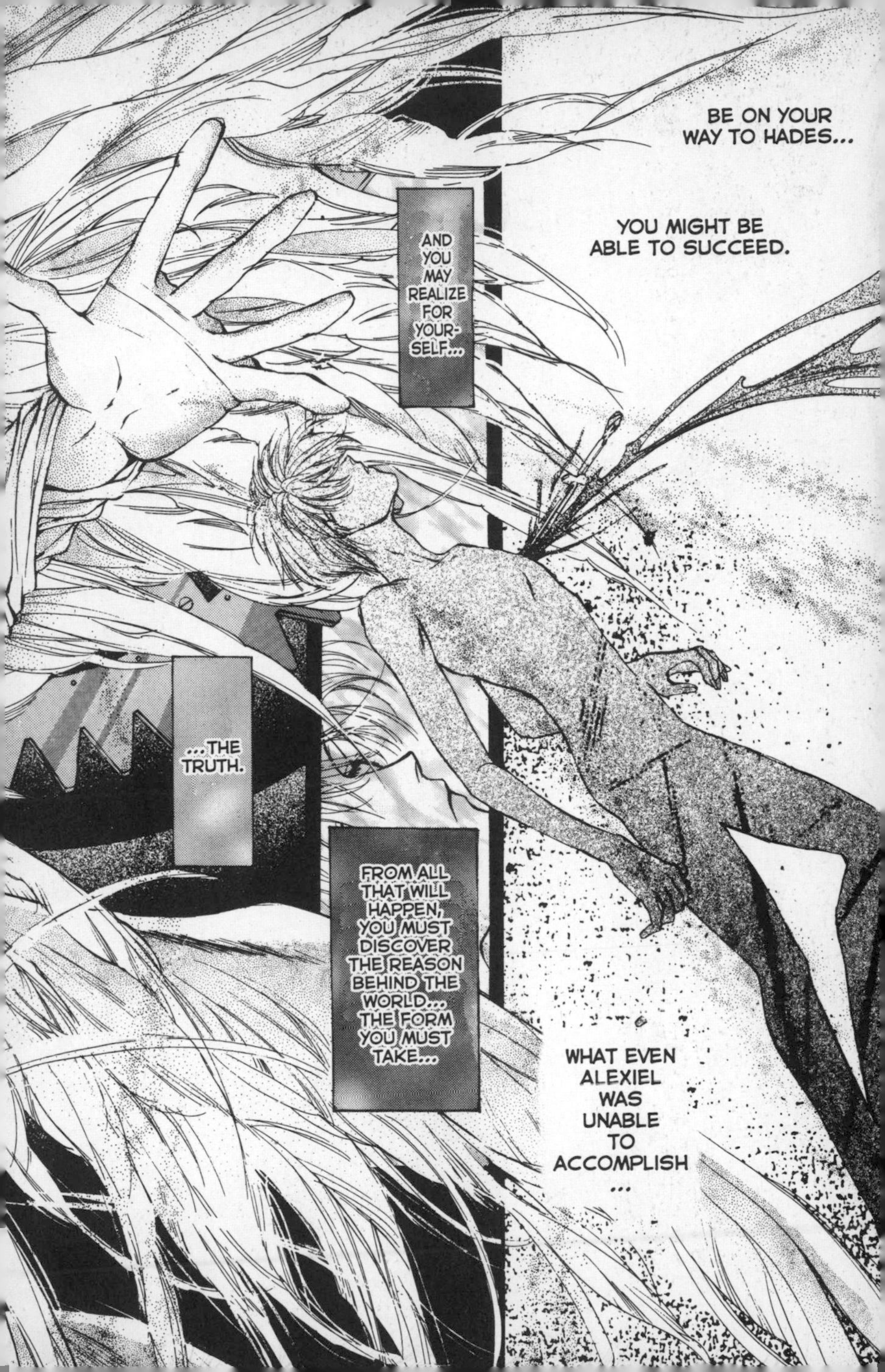
BE ON YOUR WAY TO HADES...
YOU MIGHT BE ABLE TO SUCCEED.
AND YOU MAY REALIZE FOR YOUR-SELF...
...THE TRUTH.
FROM ALL THAT WILL HAPPEN, YOU MUST DISCOVER THE REASON BEHIND THE WORLD... THE FORM YOU MUST TAKE...
WHAT EVEN ALEXIEL WAS UNABLE TO ACCOMPLISH ...

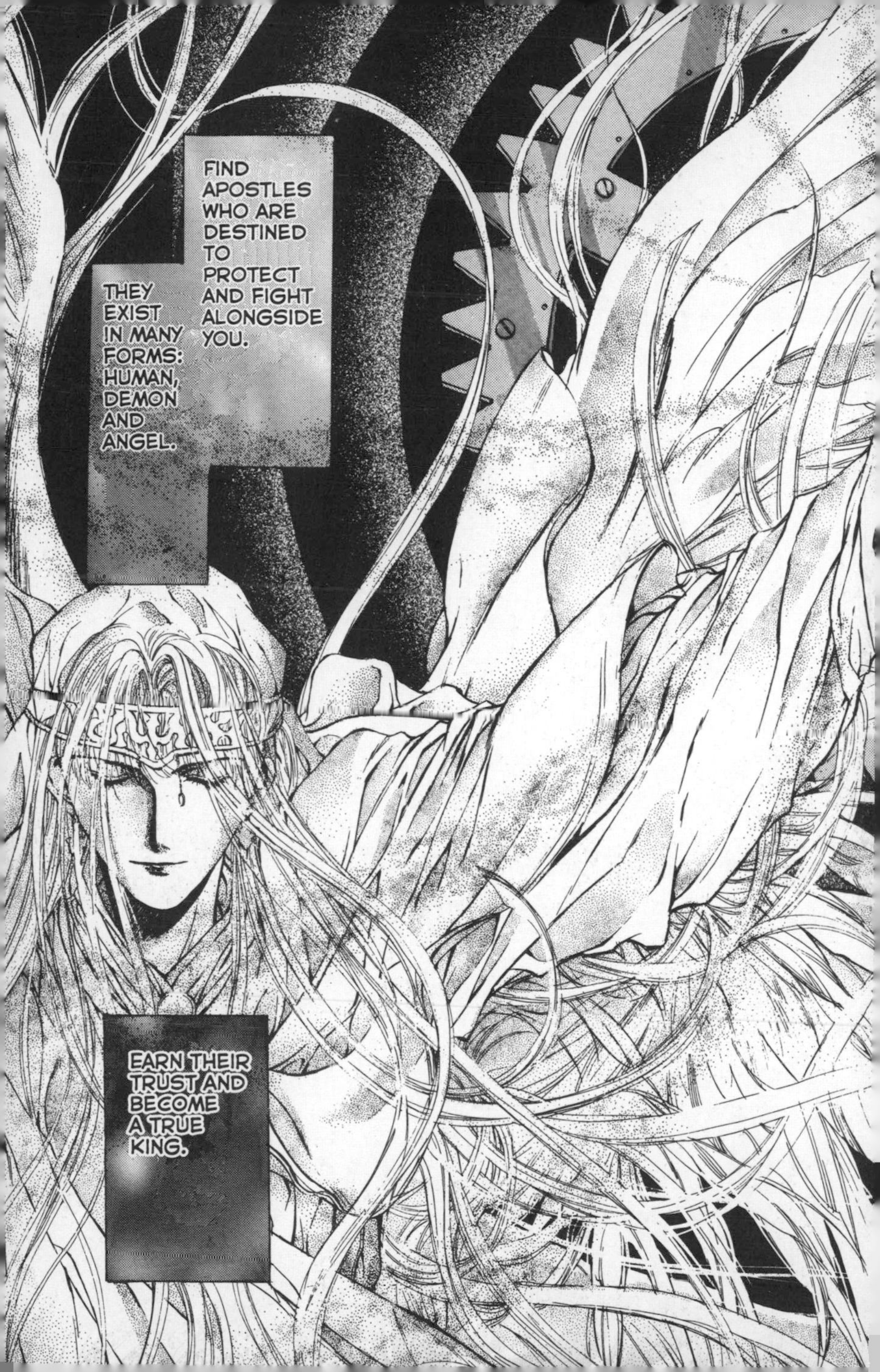
FIND APOSTLES WHO ARE DESTINED TO PROTECT AND FIGHT ALONGSIDE YOU.
THEY EXIST IN MANY FORMS: HUMAN, DEMON AND ANGEL.
EARN THEIR TRUST AND BECOME A TRUE KING.

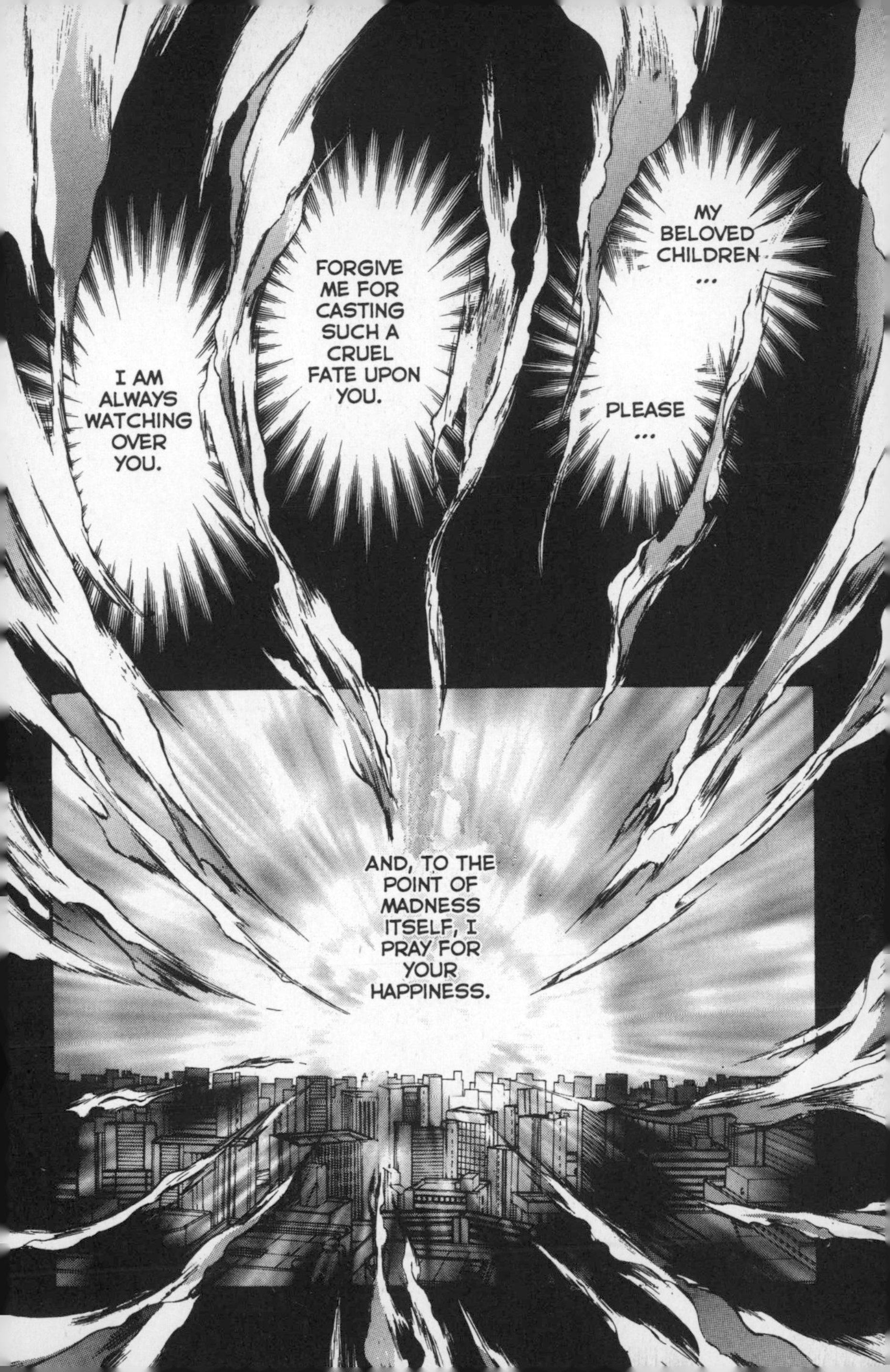
MY BELOVED CHILDREN ...
PLEASE ...
FORGIVE ME FOR CASTING SUCH A CRUEL FATE UPON YOU.
I AM ALWAYS WATCHING OVER YOU.
AND, TO THE POINT OF MADNESS ITSELF, I PRAY FOR YOUR HAPPINESS.

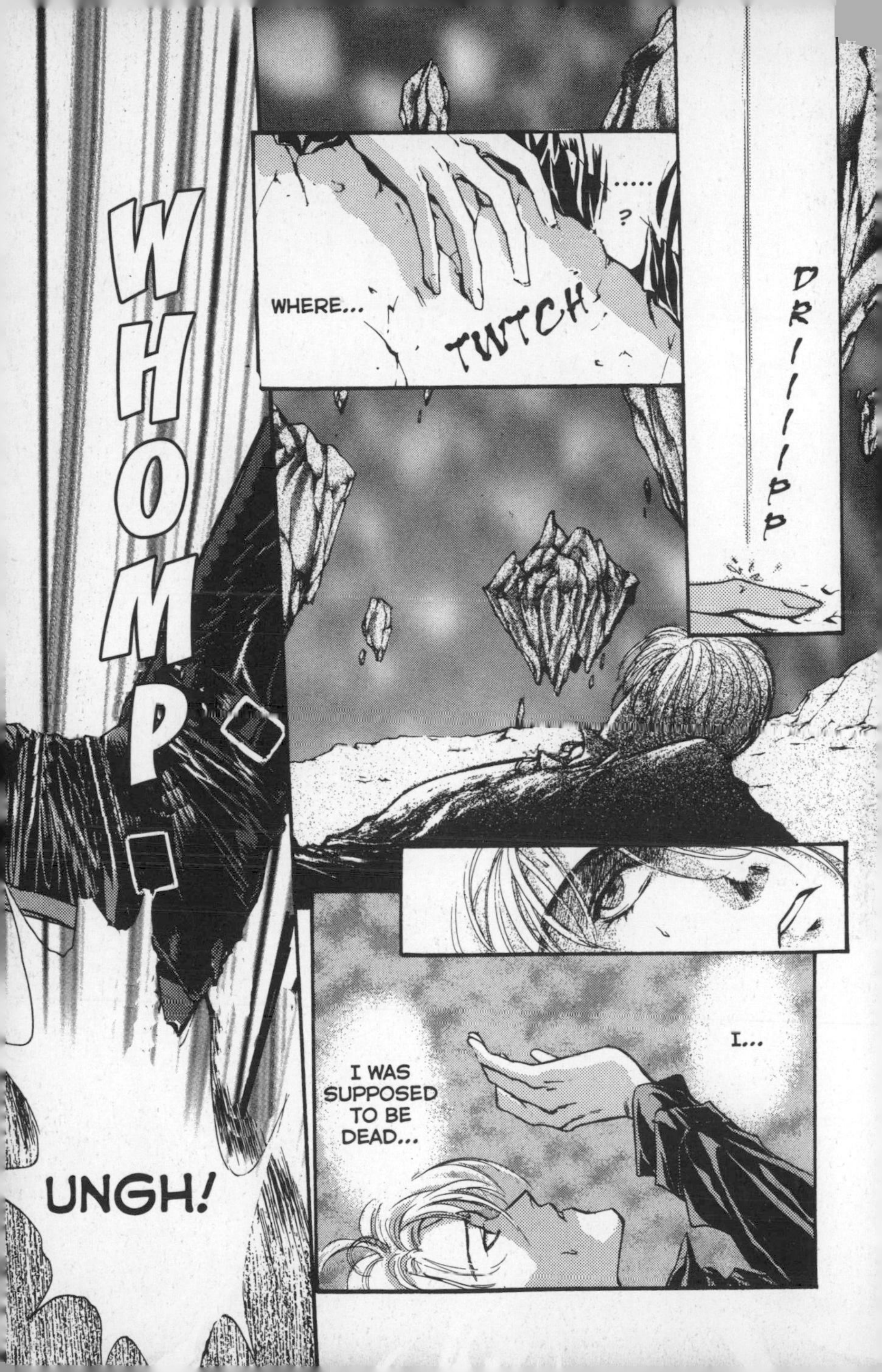
DRIIIIPP
.....
?
WHERE...
TWITCH
I...
I WAS SUPPOSED TO BE DEAD...
WHOMP
UNGH!

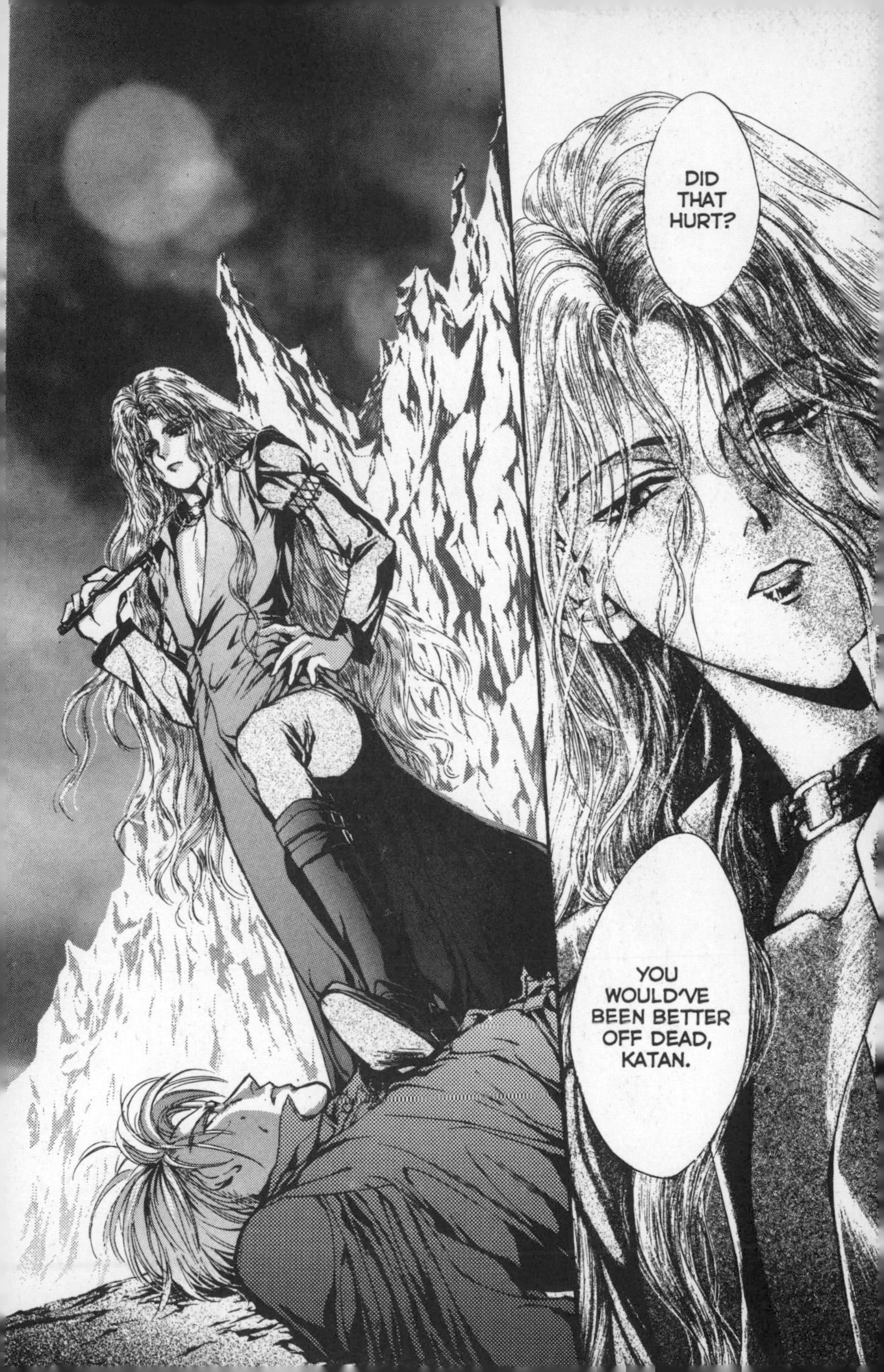
DID THAT HURT?
YOU WOULD'VE BEEN BETTER OFF DEAD, KATAN.

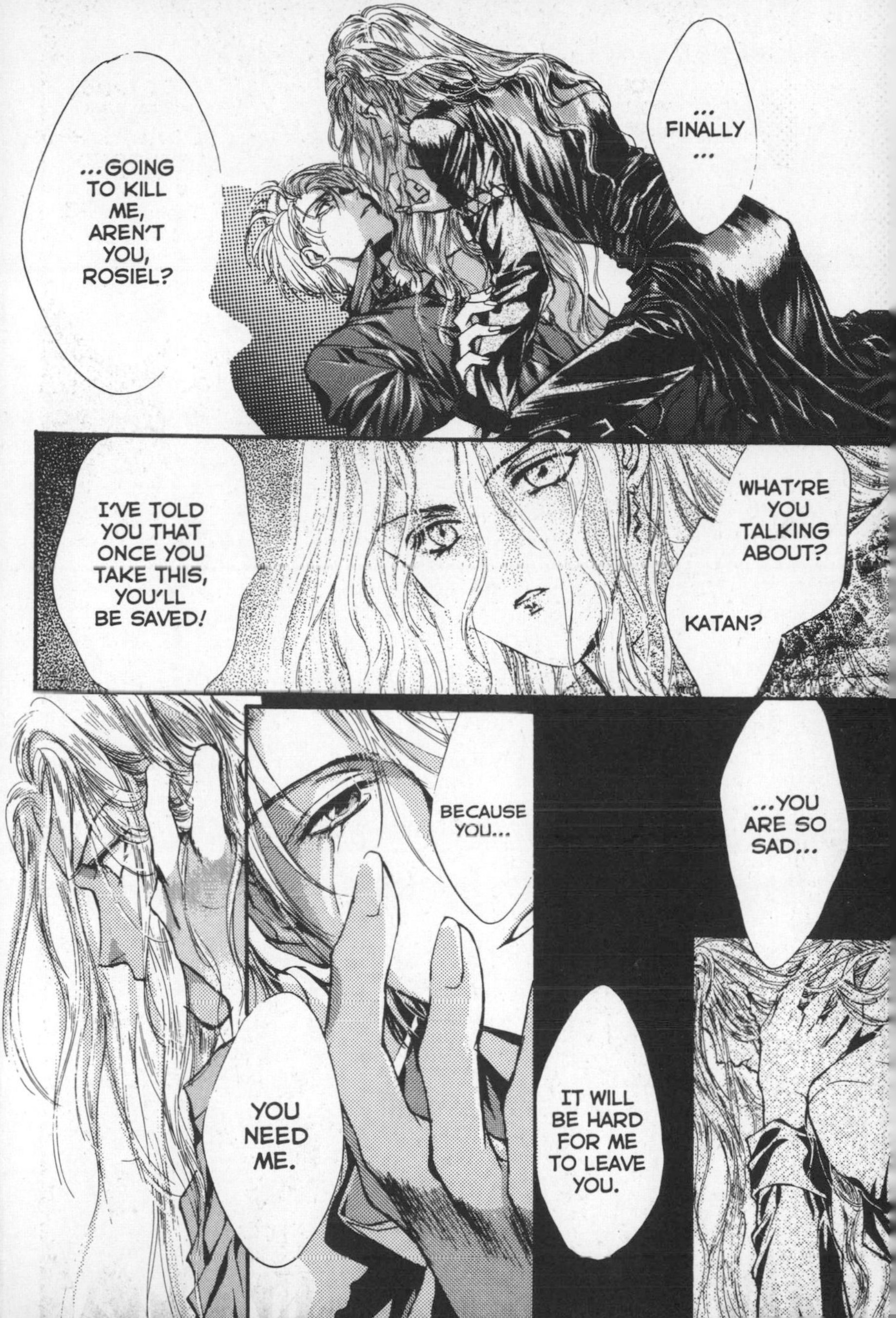
...FINALLY ...
...GOING TO KILL ME, AREN'T YOU, ROSIEL?
WHAT'RE YOU TALKING ABOUT?
KATAN?
I'VE TOLD YOU THAT ONCE YOU TAKE THIS, YOU'LL BE SAVED!
...YOU ARE SO SAD...
IT WILL BE HARD FOR ME TO LEAVE YOU.
BECAUSE YOU...
YOU NEED ME.

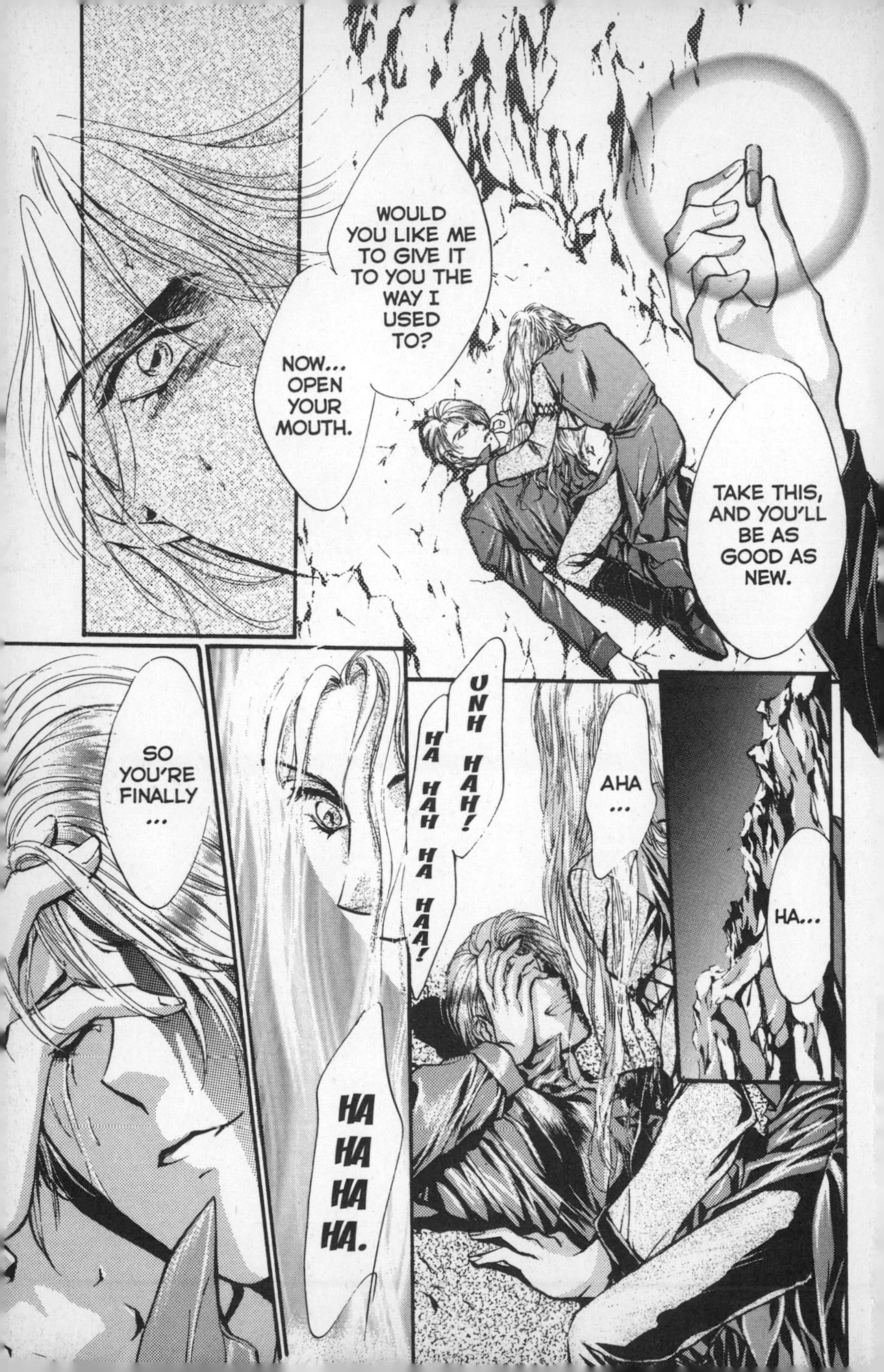
TAKE THIS, AND YOU'LL BE AS GOOD AS NEW.
WOULD YOU LIKE ME TO GIVE IT TO YOU THE WAY I USED TO?
NOW... OPEN YOUR MOUTH.
HA...
AHA ...
UNH HAH!
HA HAH HA HAA!
HA HA HA HA.
SO YOU'RE FINALLY ...

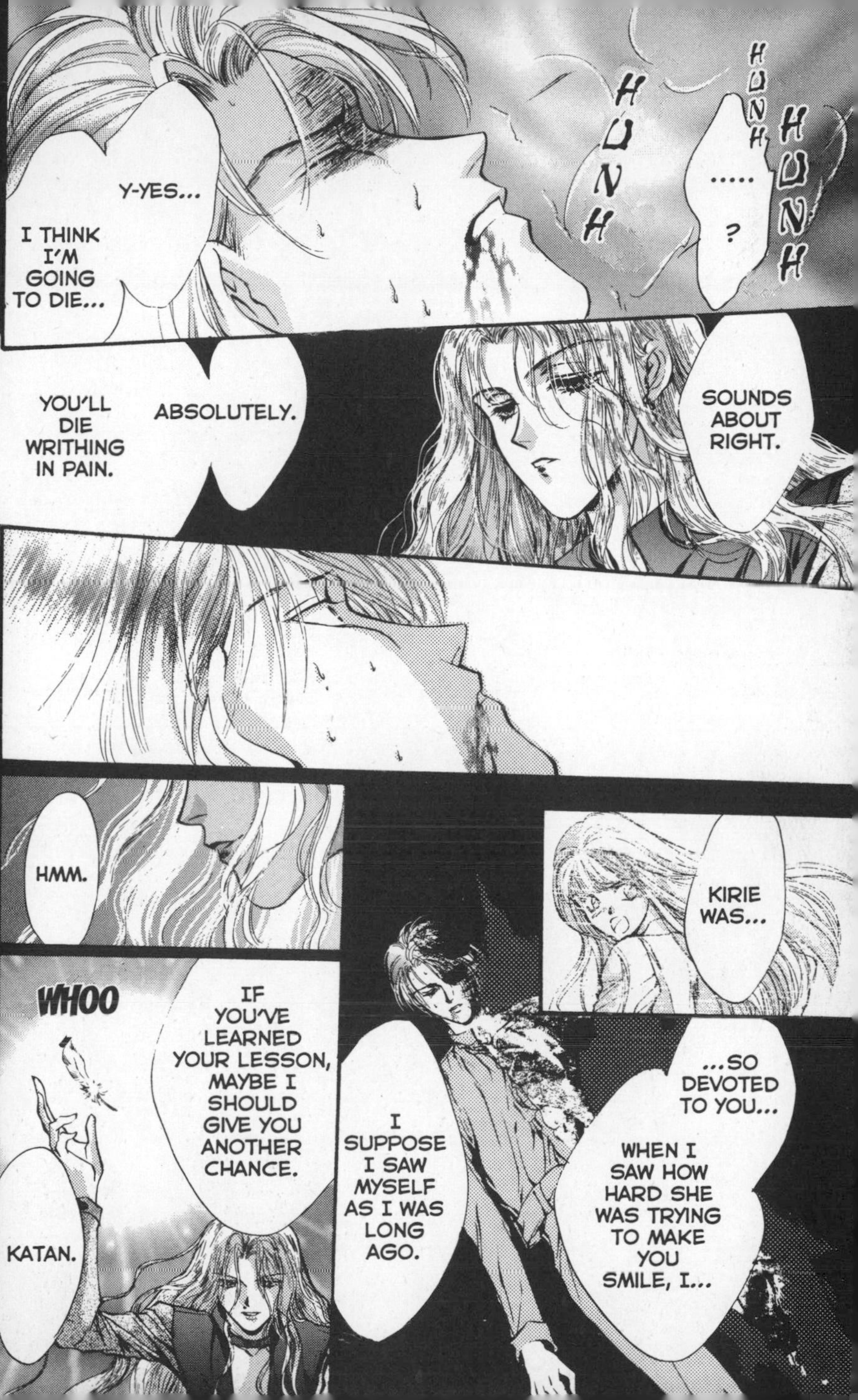
HUNH
HUNH
HUNH
.....
?
Y-YES...
I THINK I'M GOING TO DIE...
SOUNDS ABOUT RIGHT.
ABSOLUTELY.
YOU'LL DIE WRITHING IN PAIN.
KIRIE WAS...
HMM.
...SO DEVOTED TO YOU...
WHEN I SAW HOW HARD SHE WAS TRYING TO MAKE YOU SMILE, I...
I SUPPOSE I SAW MYSELF AS I WAS LONG AGO.
IF YOU'VE LEARNED YOUR LESSON, MAYBE I SHOULD GIVE YOU ANOTHER CHANCE.
WHOO
KATAN.

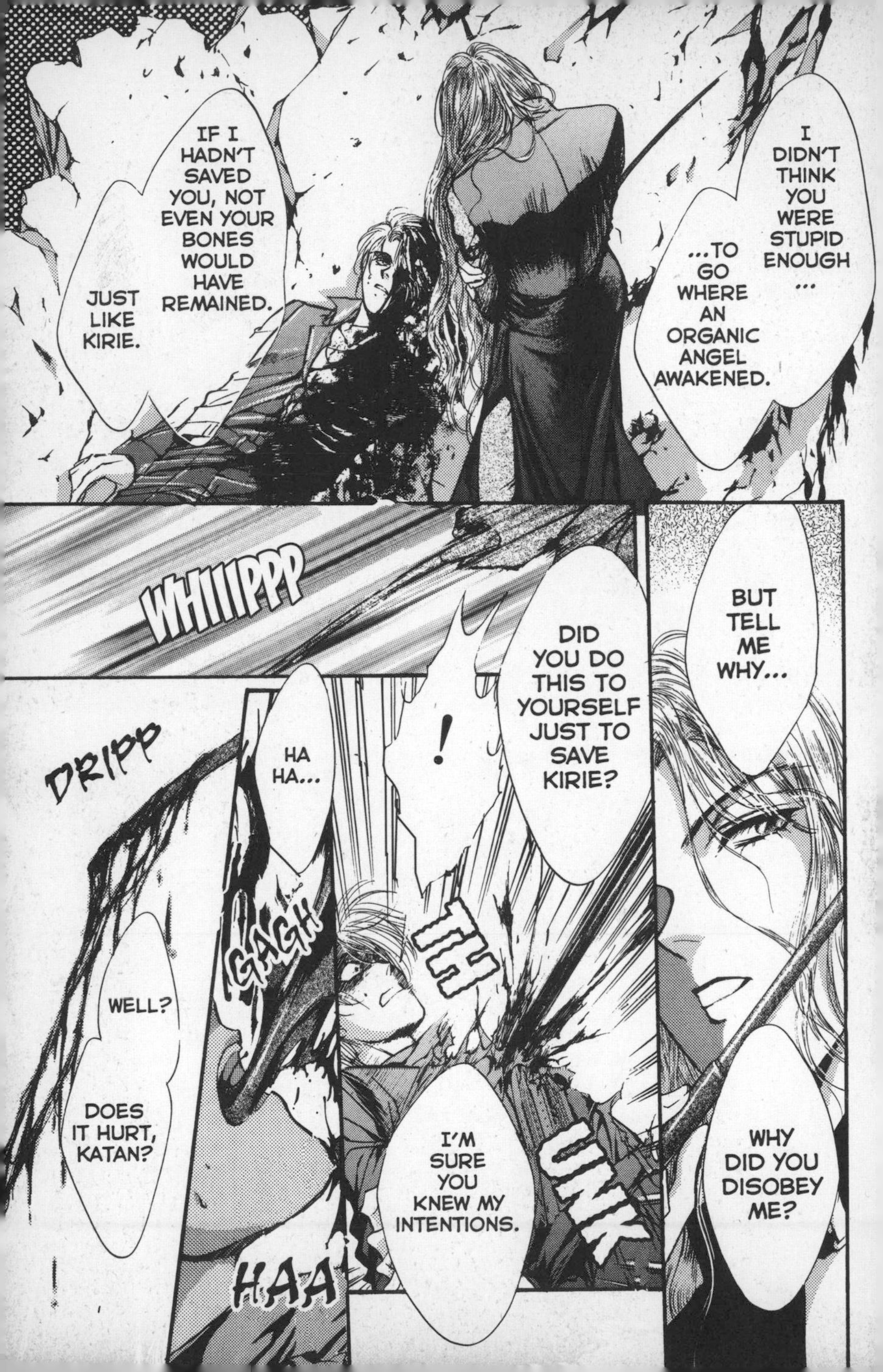
I DIDN'T THINK YOU WERE STUPID ENOUGH ...
...TO GO WHERE AN ORGANIC ANGEL AWAKENED.
IF I HADN'T SAVED YOU, NOT EVEN YOUR BONES WOULD HAVE REMAINED.
JUST LIKE KIRIE.
BUT TELL ME WHY...
WHY DID YOU DISOBEY ME?
WHIIIPPP
DID YOU DO THIS TO YOURSELF JUST TO SAVE KIRIE?
!
TH
UNK
I'M SURE YOU KNEW MY INTENTIONS.
HA HA...
GAGH
DRIPP
WELL?
DOES IT HURT, KATAN?
HAA

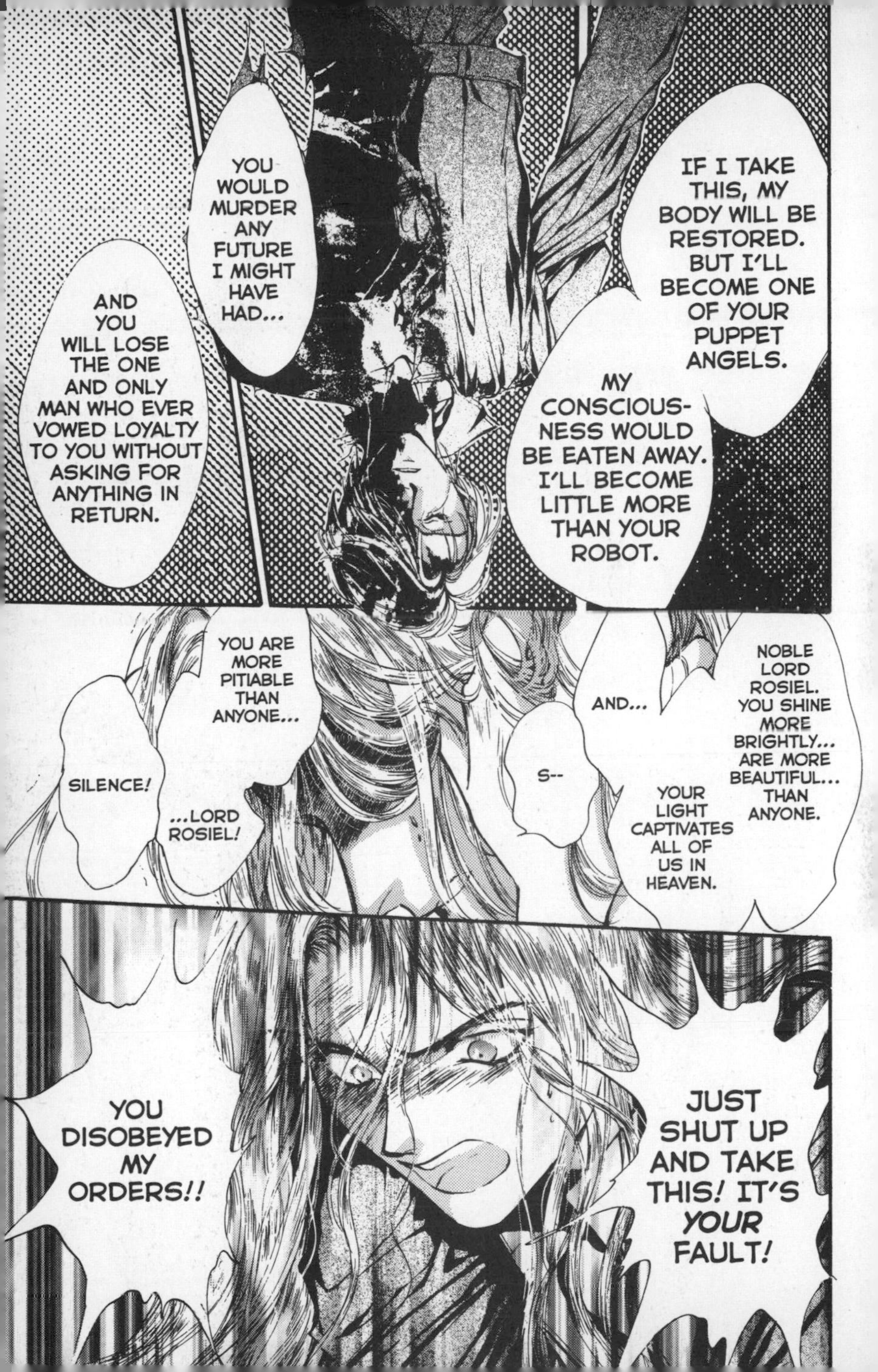
IF I TAKE THIS, MY BODY WILL BE RESTORED. BUT I'LL BECOME ONE OF YOUR PUPPET ANGELS.
MY CONSCIOUSNESS WOULD BE EATEN AWAY. I'LL BECOME LITTLE MORE THAN YOUR ROBOT.
YOU WOULD MURDER ANY FUTURE I MIGHT HAVE HAD...
AND YOU WILL LOSE THE ONE AND ONLY MAN WHO EVER VOWED LOYALTY TO YOU WITHOUT ASKING FOR ANYTHING IN RETURN.
NOBLE LORD ROSIEL. YOU SHINE MORE BRIGHTLY... ARE MORE BEAUTIFUL... THAN ANYONE.
YOUR LIGHT CAPTIVATES ALL OF US IN HEAVEN.
AND...
YOU ARE MORE PITIABLE THAN ANYONE...
...LORD ROSIEL!
S--
SILENCE!
JUST SHUT UP AND TAKE THIS! IT'S *YOUR* FAULT!
YOU DISOBEYED MY ORDERS!!

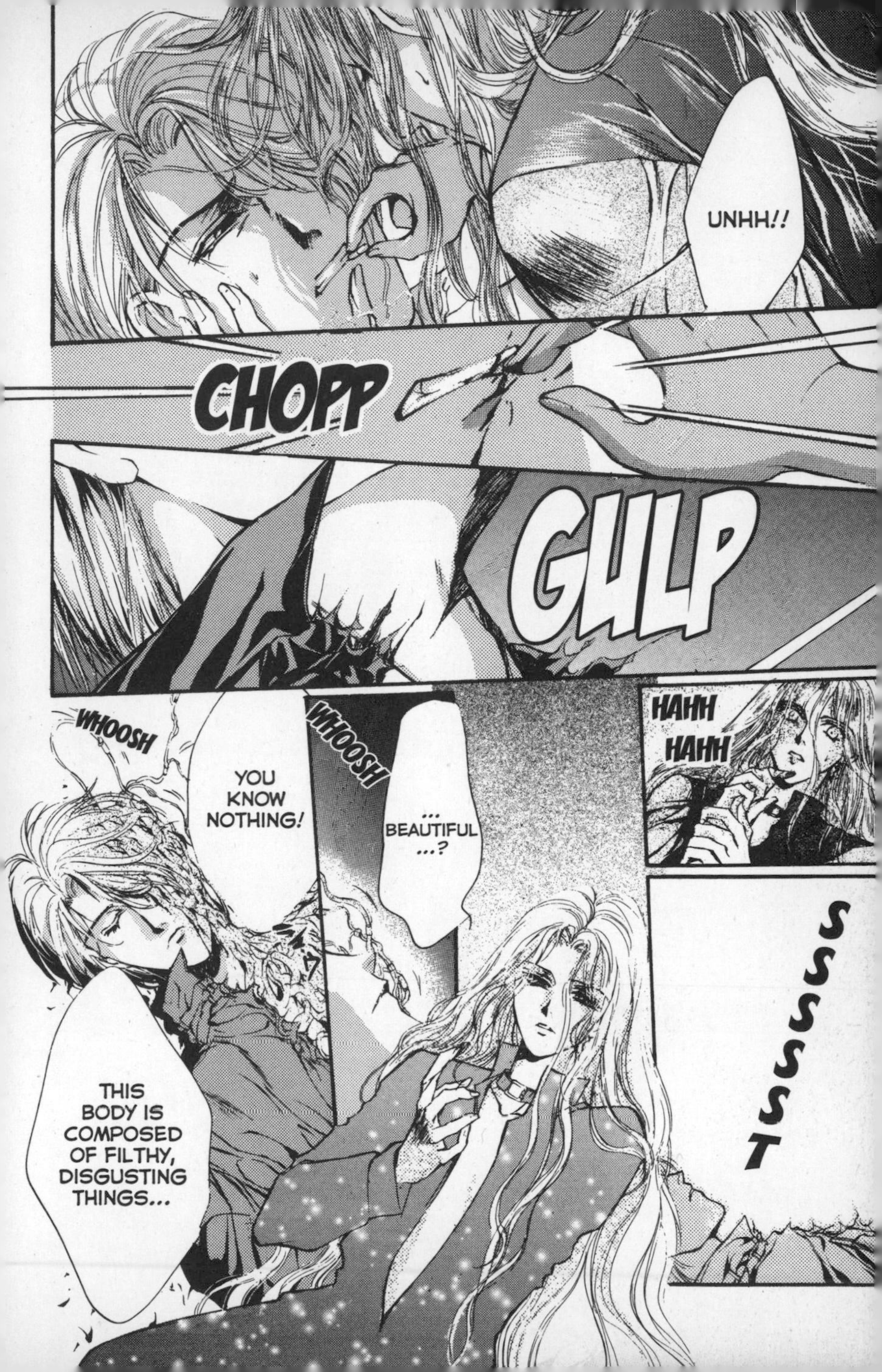
UNHH!!
CHOPP
GULP
HAHH HAHH
SSSSST
WHOOSH
... BEAUTIFUL ...?
WHOOSH
YOU KNOW NOTHING!
THIS BODY IS COMPOSED OF FILTHY, DISGUSTING THINGS...

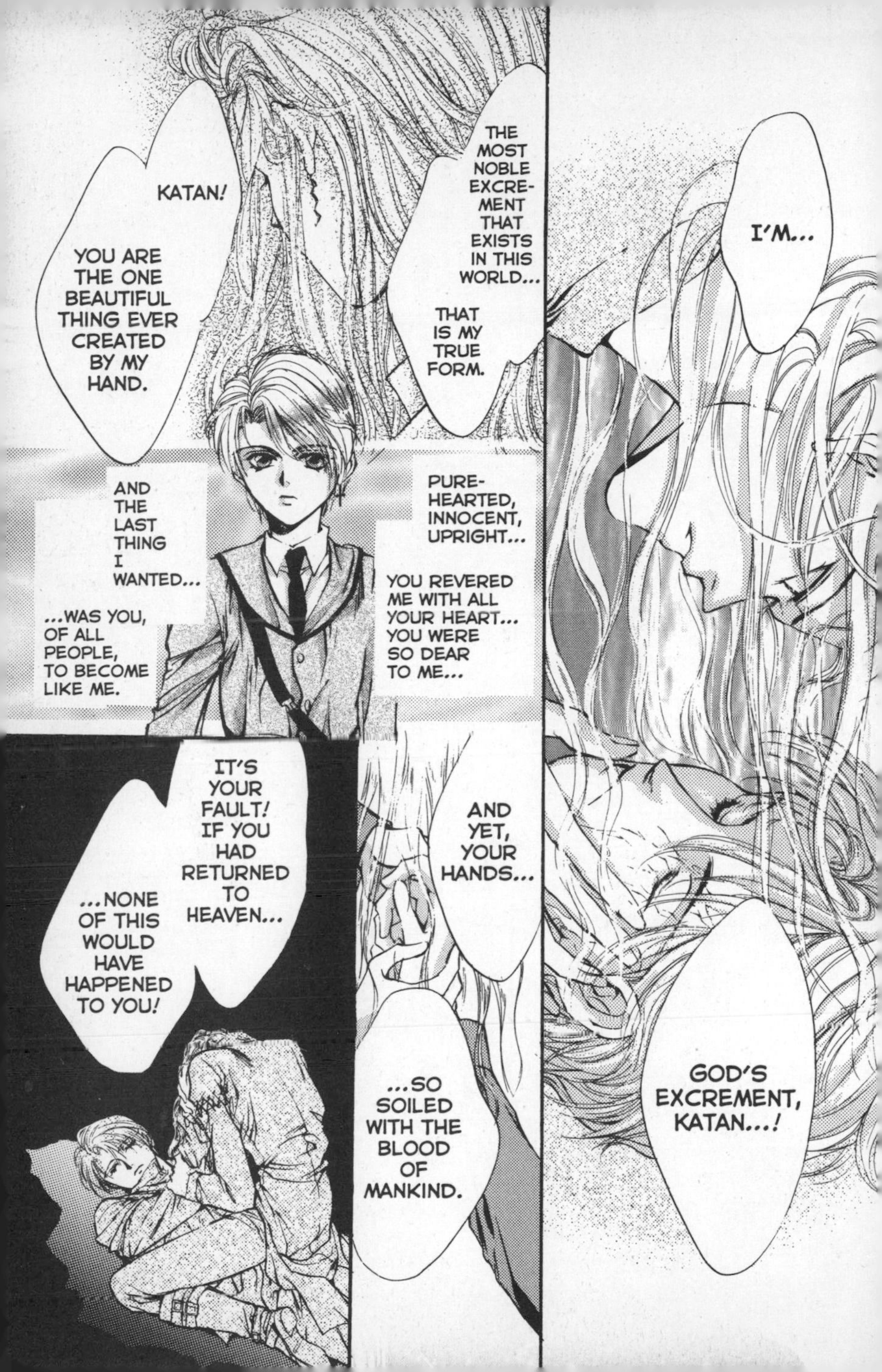
I'M...
GOD'S EXCREMENT, KATAN...!
THE MOST NOBLE EXCREMENT THAT EXISTS IN THIS WORLD...
THAT IS MY TRUE FORM.
KATAN!
YOU ARE THE ONE BEAUTIFUL THING EVER CREATED BY MY HAND.
PURE-HEARTED, INNOCENT, UPRIGHT...
YOU REVERED ME WITH ALL YOUR HEART... YOU WERE SO DEAR TO ME...
AND THE LAST THING I WANTED...
...WAS YOU, OF ALL PEOPLE, TO BECOME LIKE ME.
AND YET, YOUR HANDS...
...SO SOILED WITH THE BLOOD OF MANKIND.
IT'S YOUR FAULT! IF YOU HAD RETURNED TO HEAVEN...
...NONE OF THIS WOULD HAVE HAPPENED TO YOU!

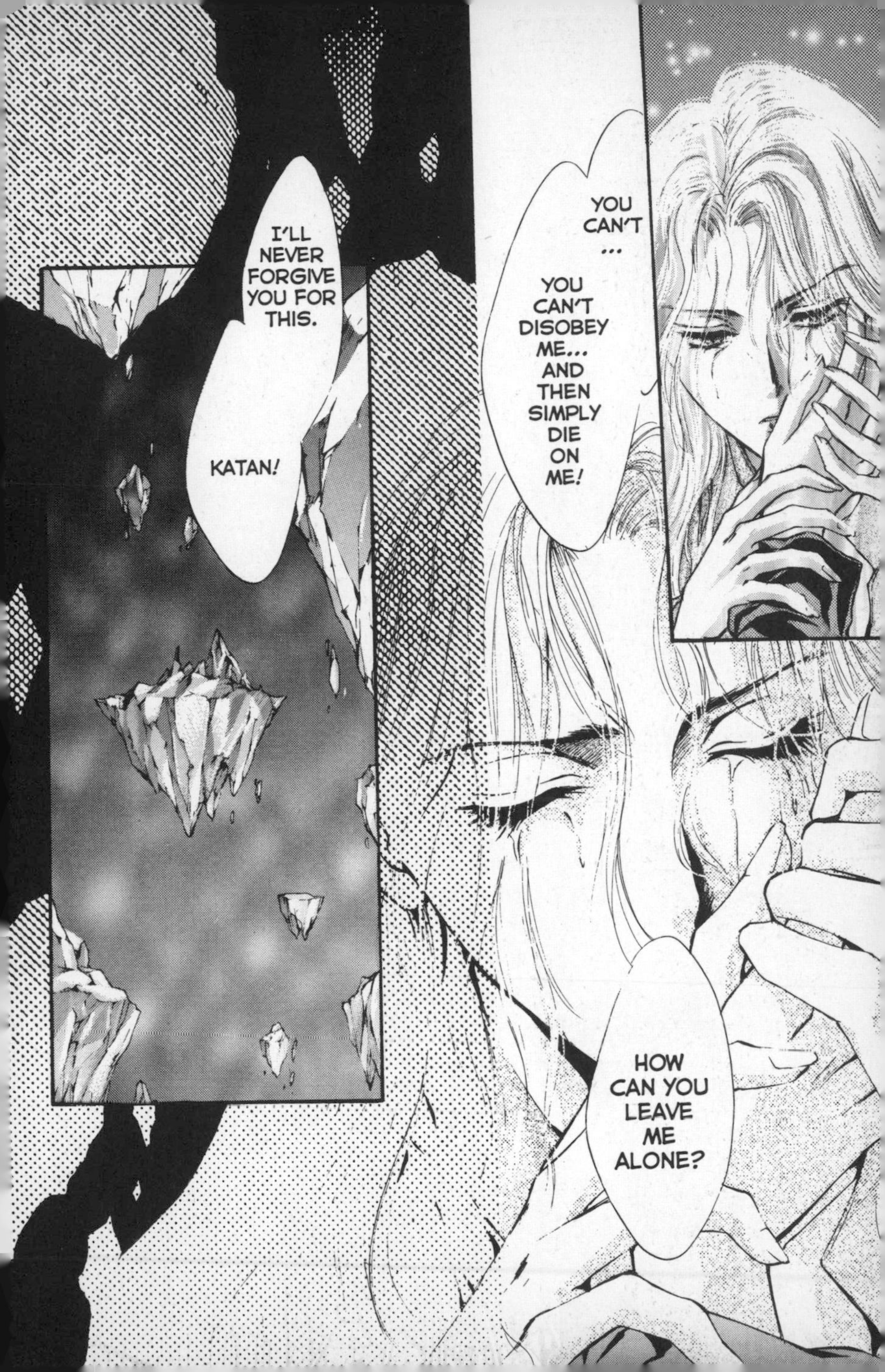
YOU CAN'T ...
YOU CAN'T DISOBEY ME... AND THEN SIMPLY DIE ON ME!
HOW CAN YOU LEAVE ME ALONE?
I'LL NEVER FORGIVE YOU FOR THIS.
KATAN!

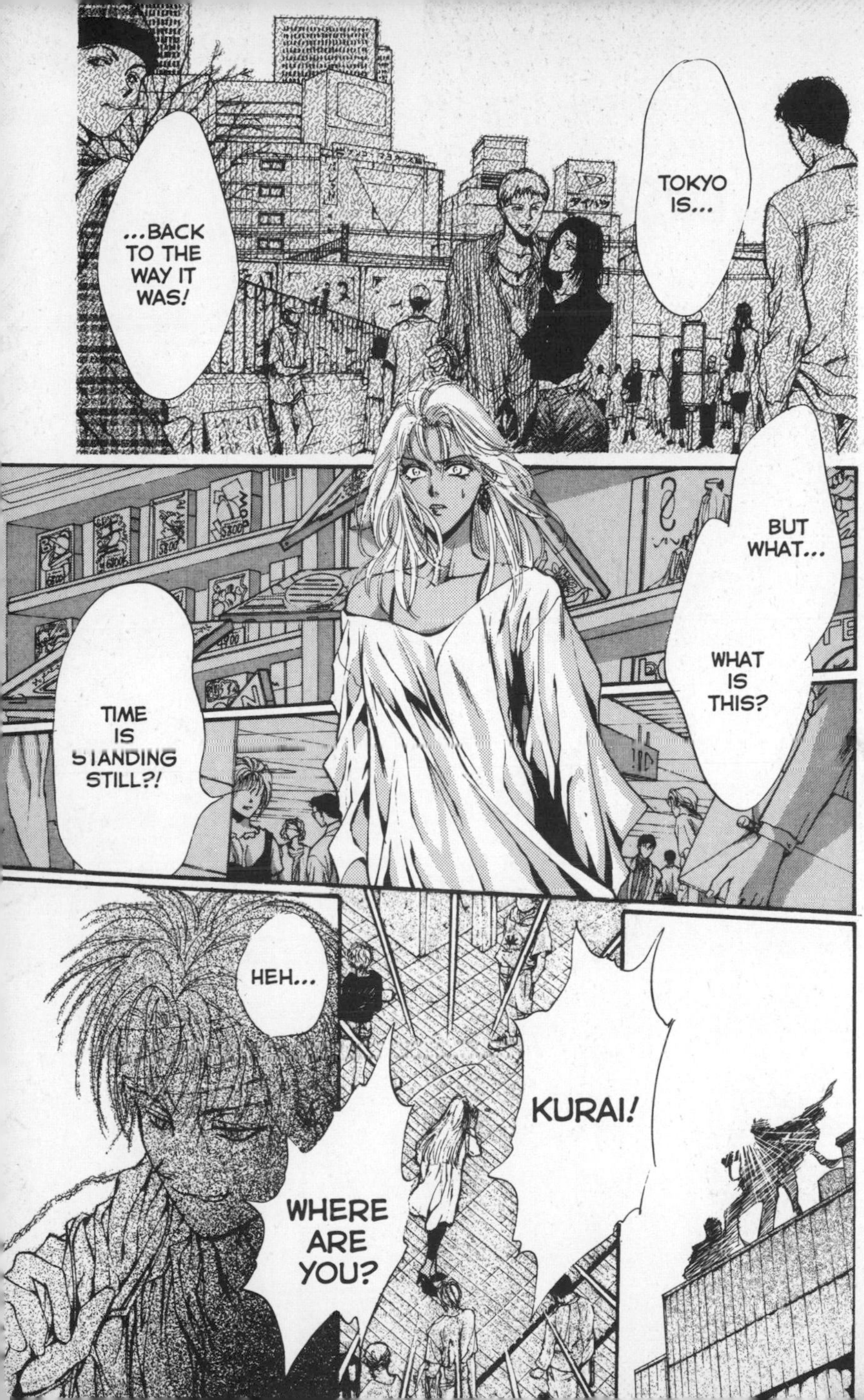
TOKYO IS...
...BACK TO THE WAY IT WAS!
BUT WHAT...
WHAT IS THIS?
TIME IS STANDING STILL?!
KURAI!
WHERE ARE YOU?
HEH...

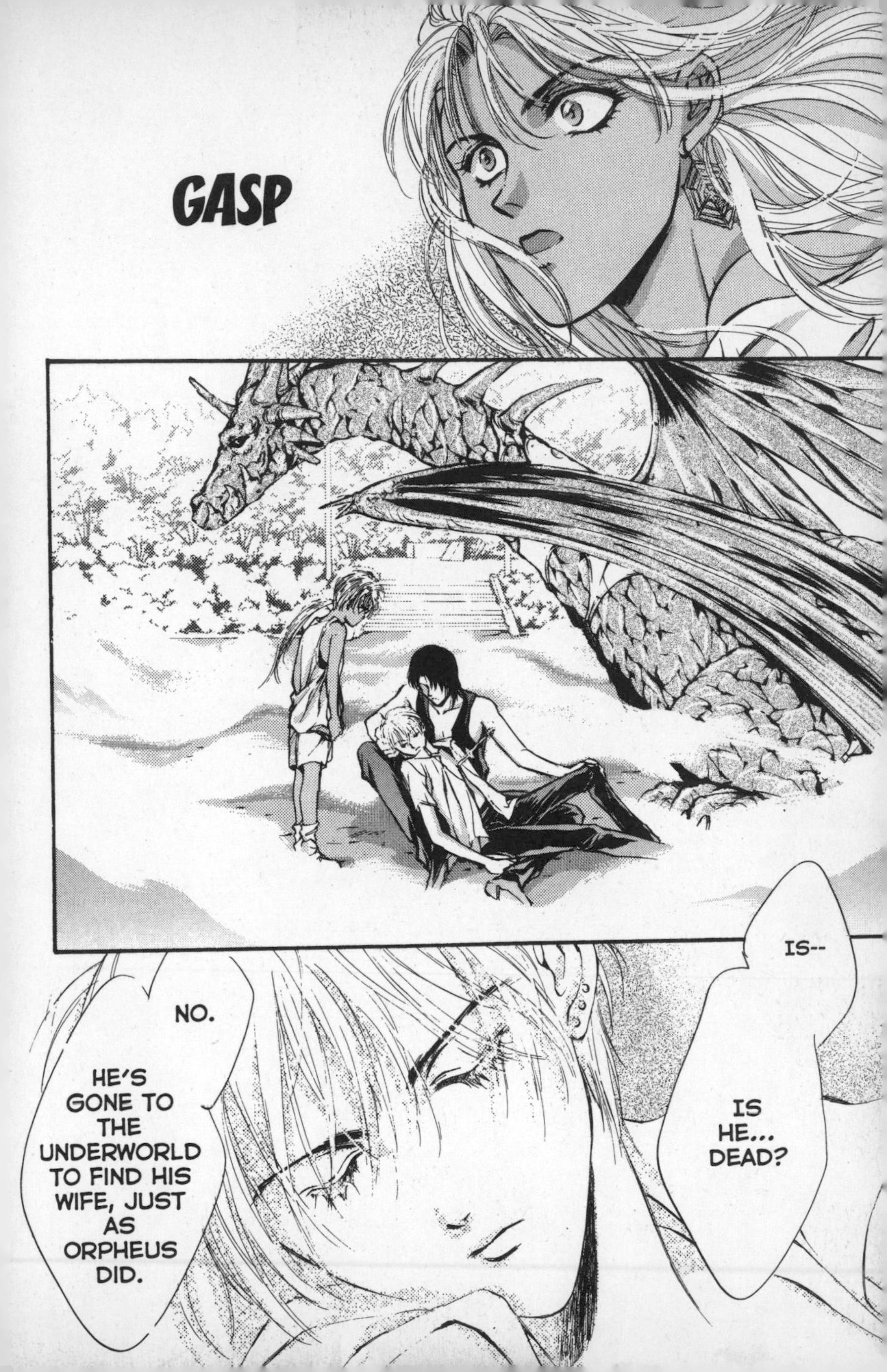
GASP
IS--
IS HE... DEAD?
NO.
HE'S GONE TO THE UNDERWORLD TO FIND HIS WIFE, JUST AS ORPHEUS DID.

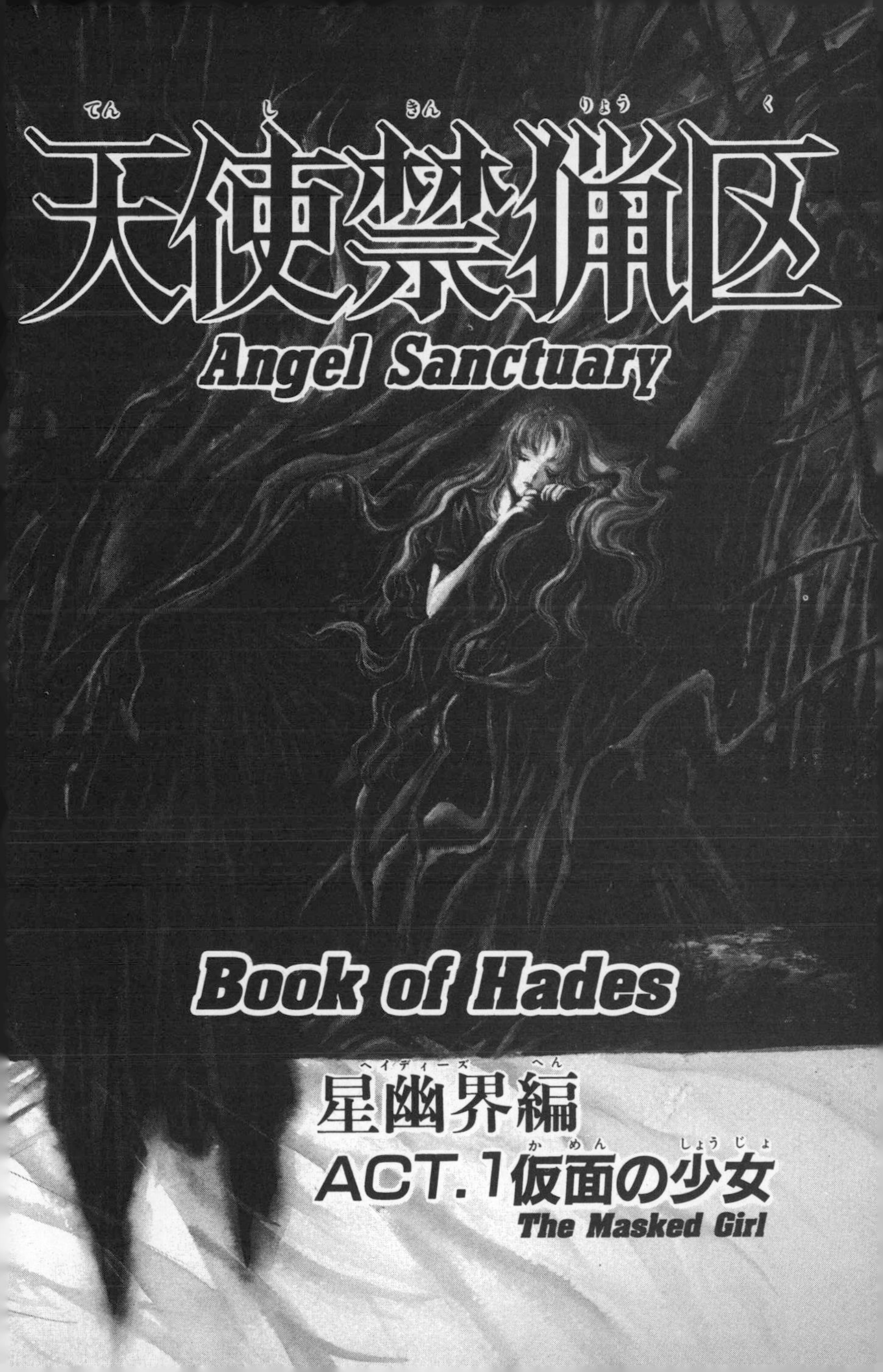
天使禁猟区
Angel Sanctuary
Book of Hades
星幽界編
ACT.1仮面の少女
The Masked Girl

天使禁猟区
ANGEL SANCTUARY

TRAITORS OF DESTRUCTION AND RESURRECTION BEHOLD! --YOUR TIME IS COMING--

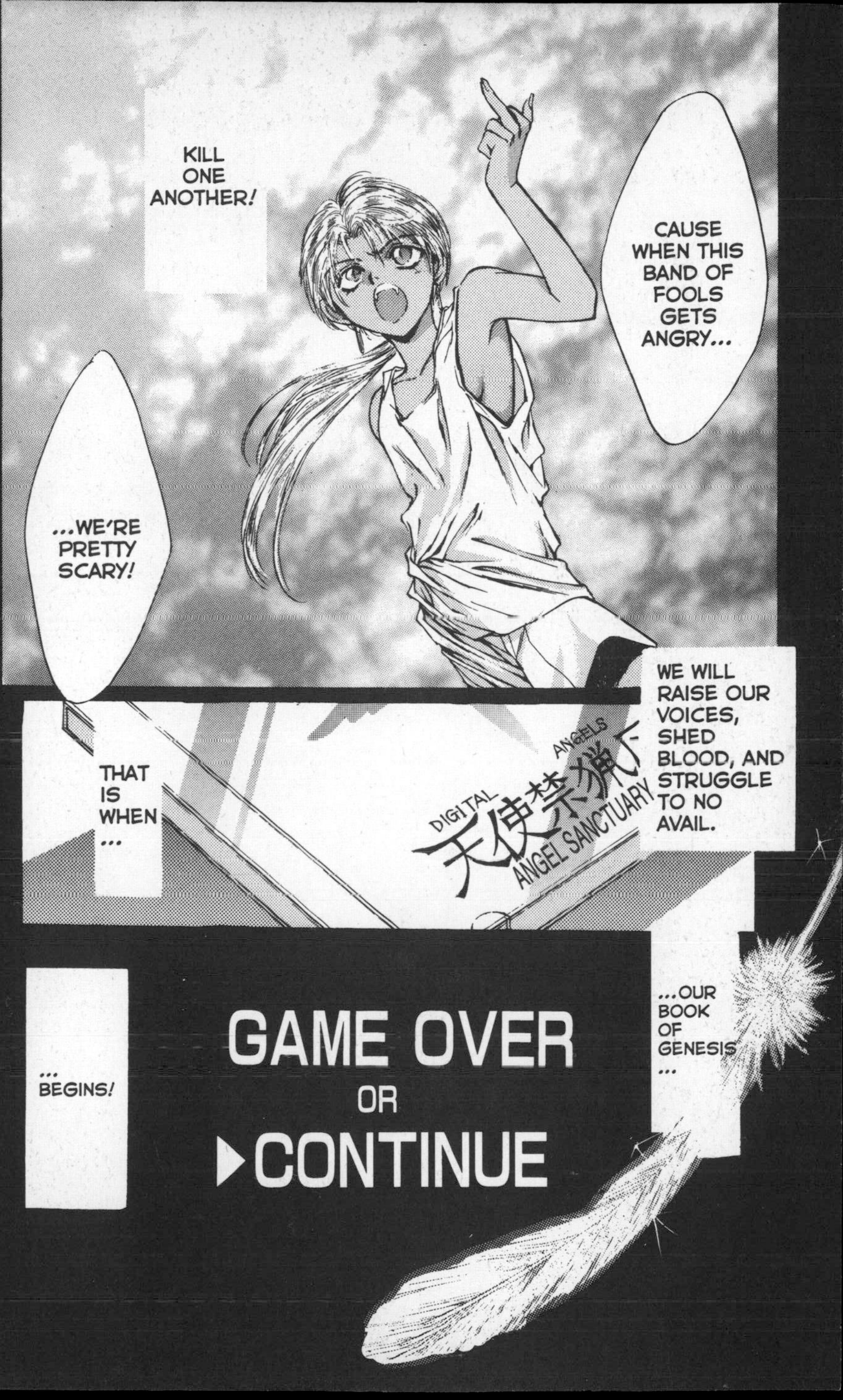
KILL ONE ANOTHER!
CAUSE WHEN THIS BAND OF FOOLS GETS ANGRY...
...WE'RE PRETTY SCARY!
WE WILL RAISE OUR VOICES, SHED BLOOD, AND STRUGGLE TO NO AVAIL.
DIGITAL ANGELS 天使禁猟区 ANGEL SANCTUARY
THAT IS WHEN ...
...OUR BOOK OF GENESIS ...
GAME OVER
OR
▶CONTINUE
... BEGINS!

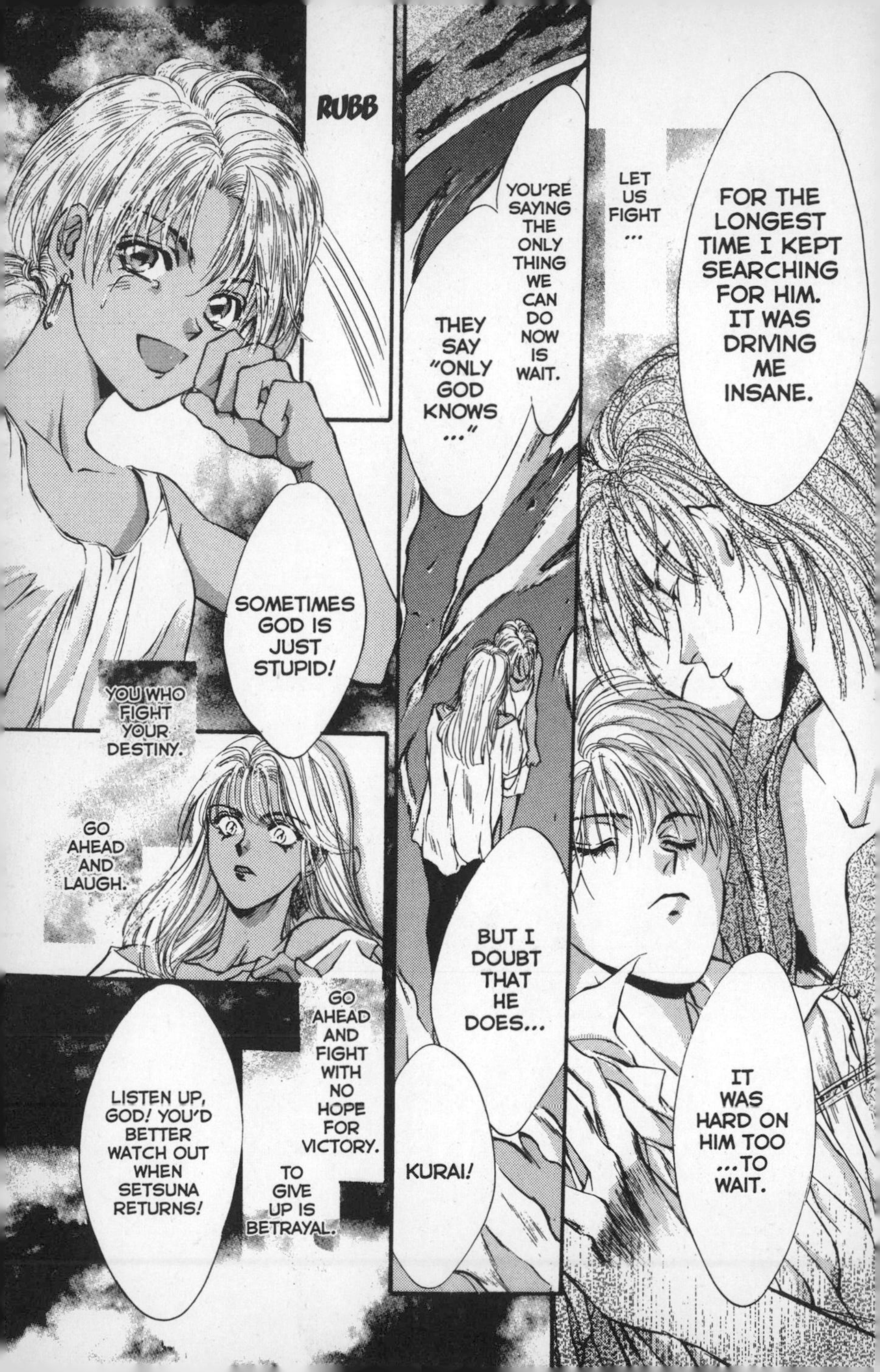
FOR THE LONGEST TIME I KEPT SEARCHING FOR HIM. IT WAS DRIVING ME INSANE.
LET US FIGHT ...
IT WAS HARD ON HIM TOO ...TO WAIT.
YOU'RE SAYING THE ONLY THING WE CAN DO NOW IS WAIT.
THEY SAY "ONLY GOD KNOWS ..."
BUT I DOUBT THAT HE DOES...
KURAI!
RUBB
SOMETIMES GOD IS JUST STUPID!
YOU WHO FIGHT YOUR DESTINY.
GO AHEAD AND LAUGH.
GO AHEAD AND FIGHT WITH NO HOPE FOR VICTORY.
TO GIVE UP IS BETRAYAL.
LISTEN UP, GOD! YOU'D BETTER WATCH OUT WHEN SETSUNA RETURNS!

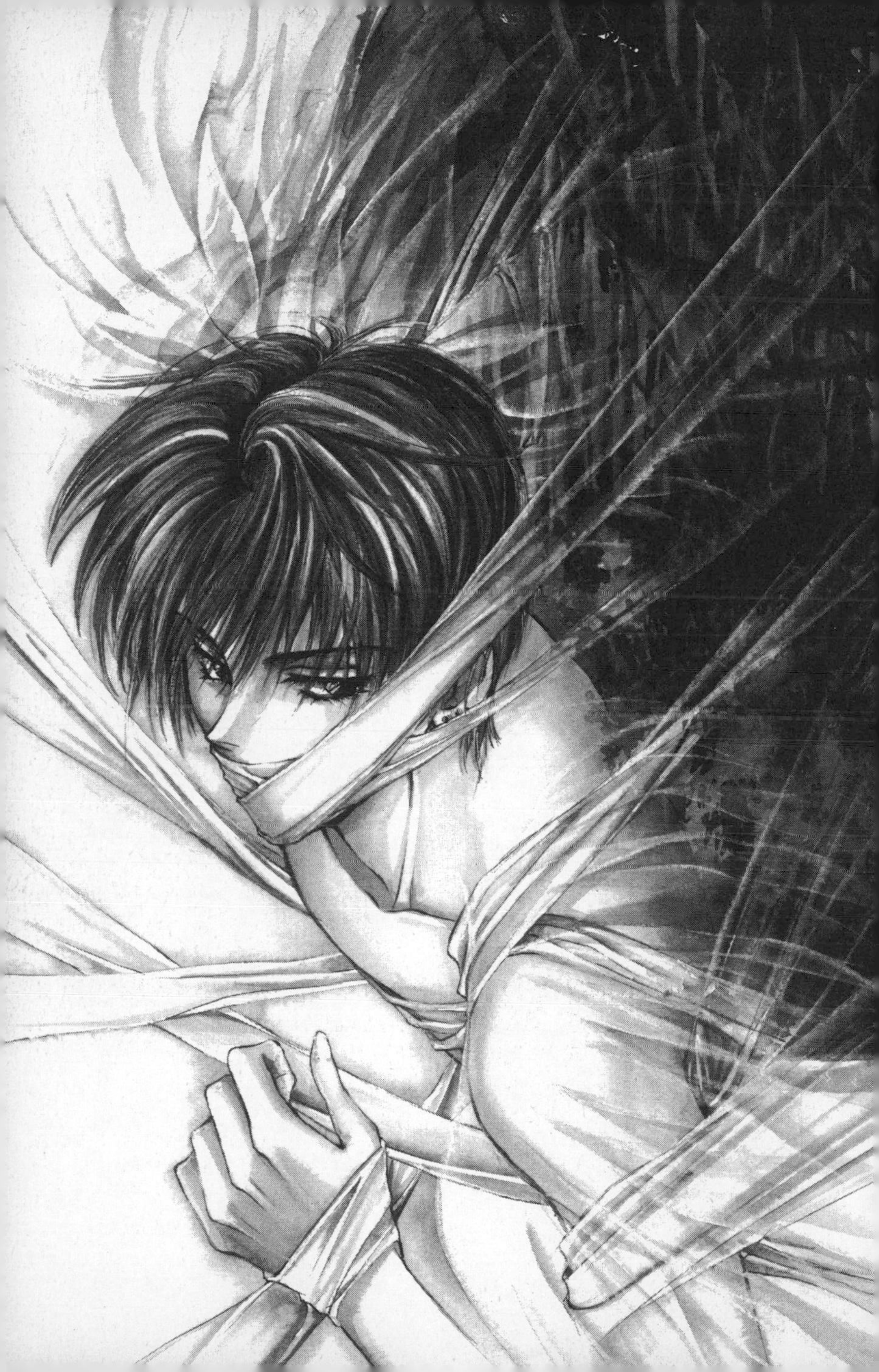

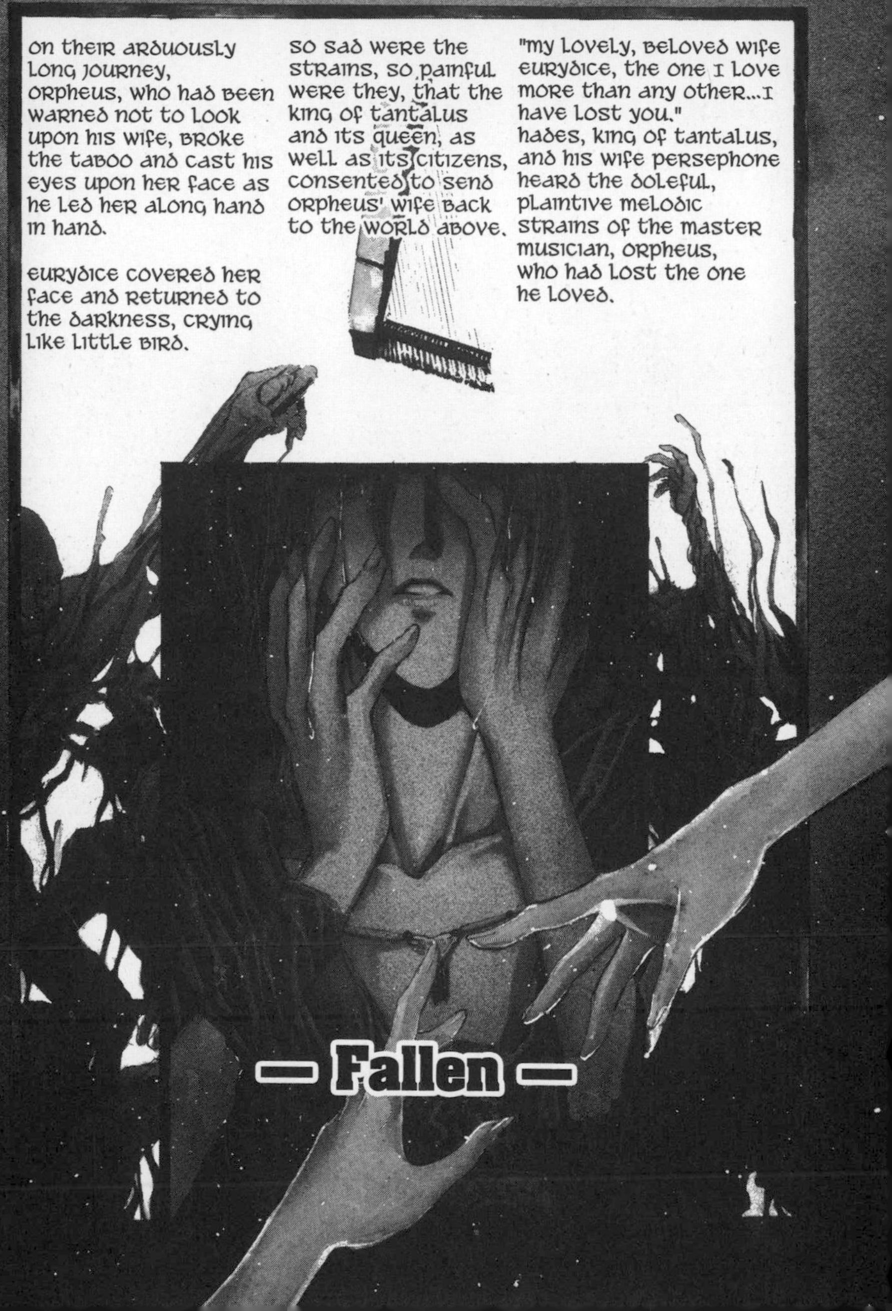
on their arduously long journey, orpheus, who had been warned not to look upon his wife, broke the taboo and cast his eyes upon her face as he led her along hand in hand.
eurydice covered her face and returned to the darkness, crying like little bird.
so sad were the strains, so painful were they, that the king of tantalus and its queen, as well as its citizens, consented to send orpheus' wife back to the world above.
"my lovely, beloved wife eurydice, the one I love more than any other...I have lost you."
hades, king of tantalus, and his wife persephone heard the doleful, plaintive melodic strains of the master musician, orpheus, who had lost the one he loved.
— Fallen —

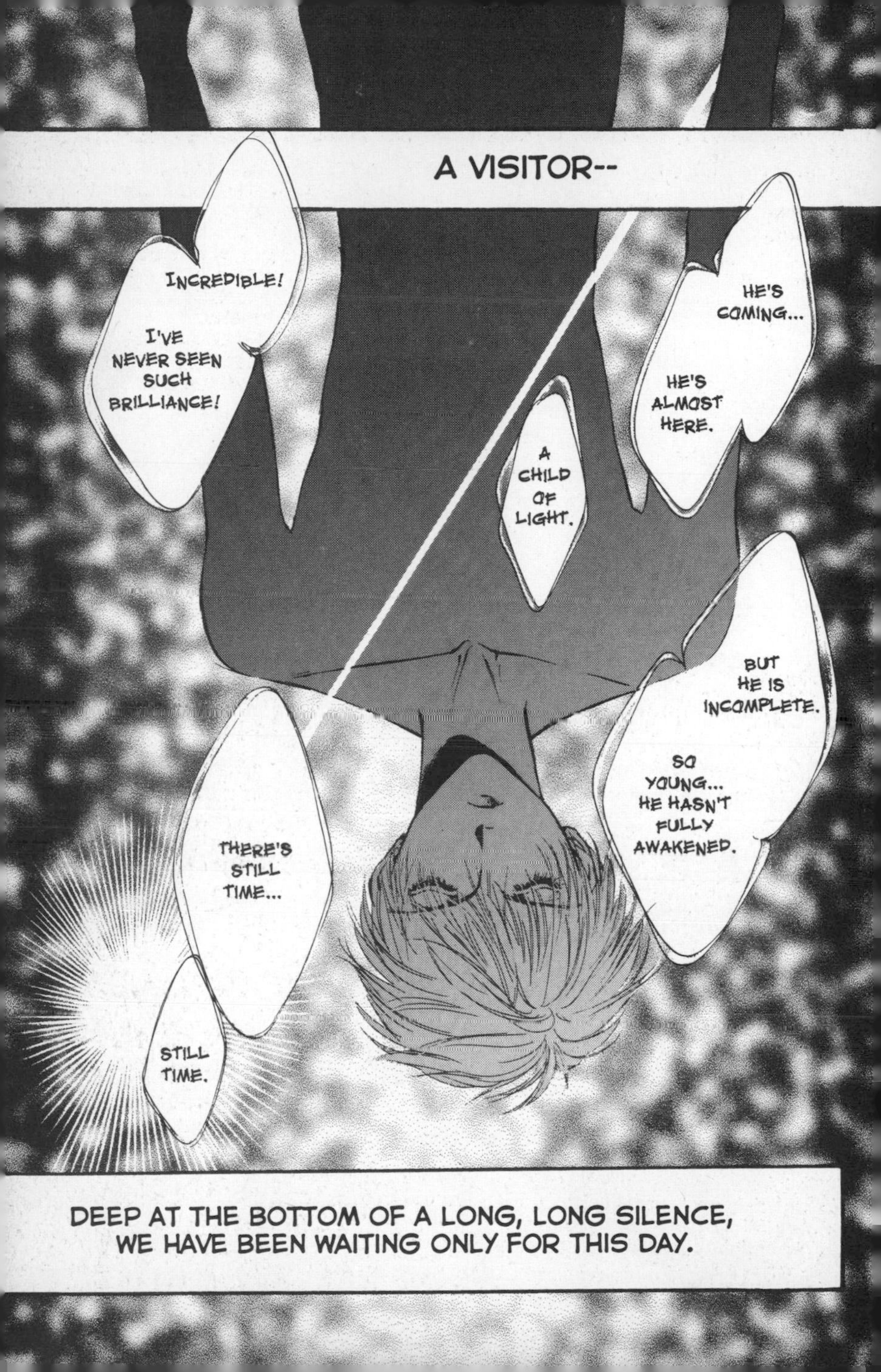
A VISITOR--
HE'S COMING... HE'S ALMOST HERE.
A CHILD OF LIGHT.
INCREDIBLE! I'VE NEVER SEEN SUCH BRILLIANCE!
BUT HE IS INCOMPLETE. SO YOUNG... HE HASN'T FULLY AWAKENED.
THERE'S STILL TIME...
STILL TIME.
DEEP AT THE BOTTOM OF A LONG, LONG SILENCE, WE HAVE BEEN WAITING ONLY FOR THIS DAY.

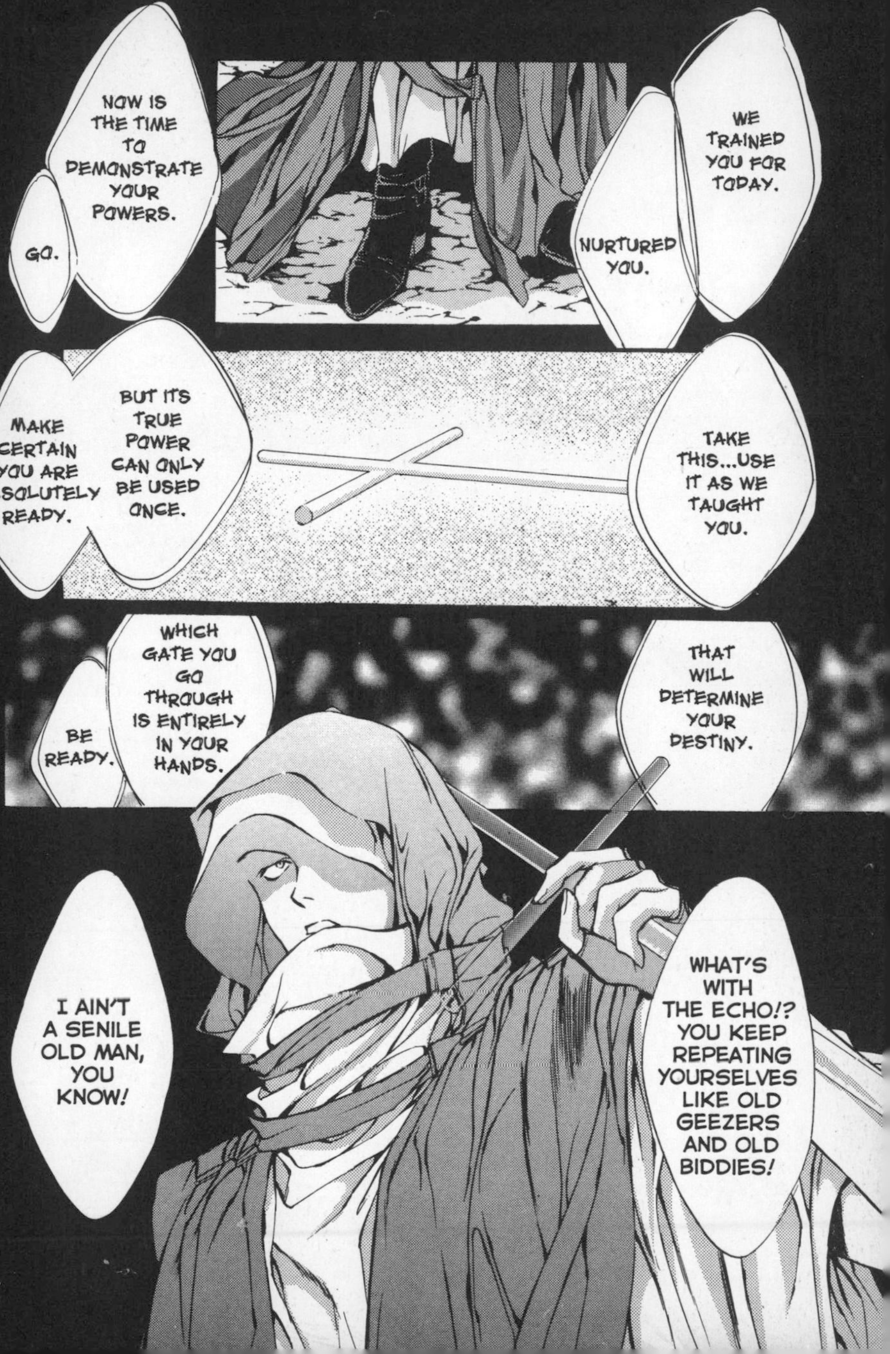
WE TRAINED YOU FOR TODAY.
NURTURED YOU.
NOW IS THE TIME TO DEMONSTRATE YOUR POWERS.
GO.
TAKE THIS...USE IT AS WE TAUGHT YOU.
BUT ITS TRUE POWER CAN ONLY BE USED ONCE.
MAKE CERTAIN YOU ARE ABSOLUTELY READY.
THAT WILL DETERMINE YOUR DESTINY.
WHICH GATE YOU GO THROUGH IS ENTIRELY IN YOUR HANDS.
BE READY.
WHAT'S WITH THE ECHO!? YOU KEEP REPEATING YOURSELVES LIKE OLD GEEZERS AND OLD BIDDIES!
I AIN'T A SENILE OLD MAN, YOU KNOW!

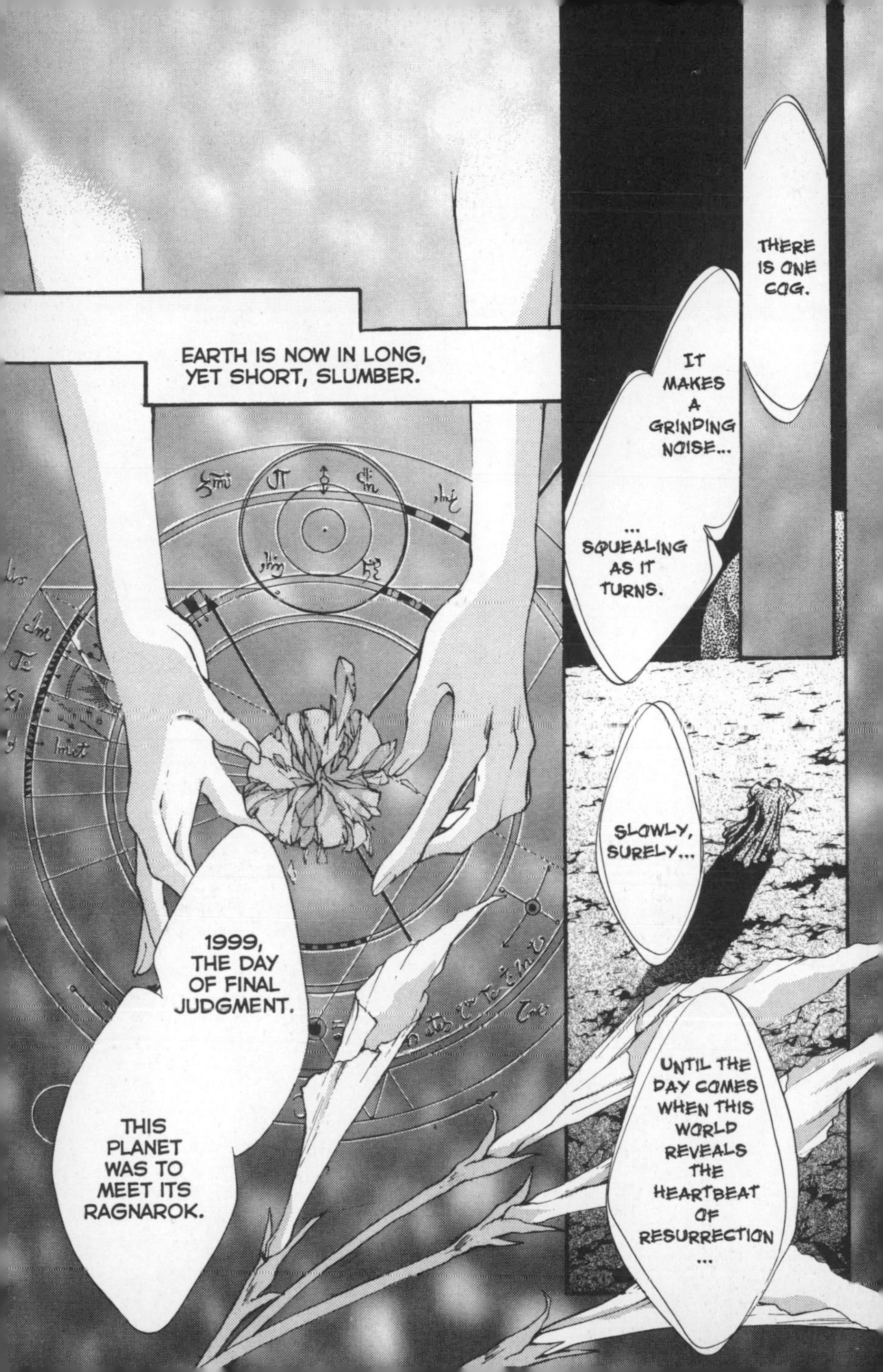
THERE IS ONE COG.
IT MAKES A GRINDING NOISE...
... SQUEALING AS IT TURNS.
SLOWLY, SURELY...
UNTIL THE DAY COMES WHEN THIS WORLD REVEALS THE HEARTBEAT OF RESURRECTION ...
EARTH IS NOW IN LONG, YET SHORT, SLUMBER.
1999, THE DAY OF FINAL JUDGMENT.
THIS PLANET WAS TO MEET ITS RAGNAROK.

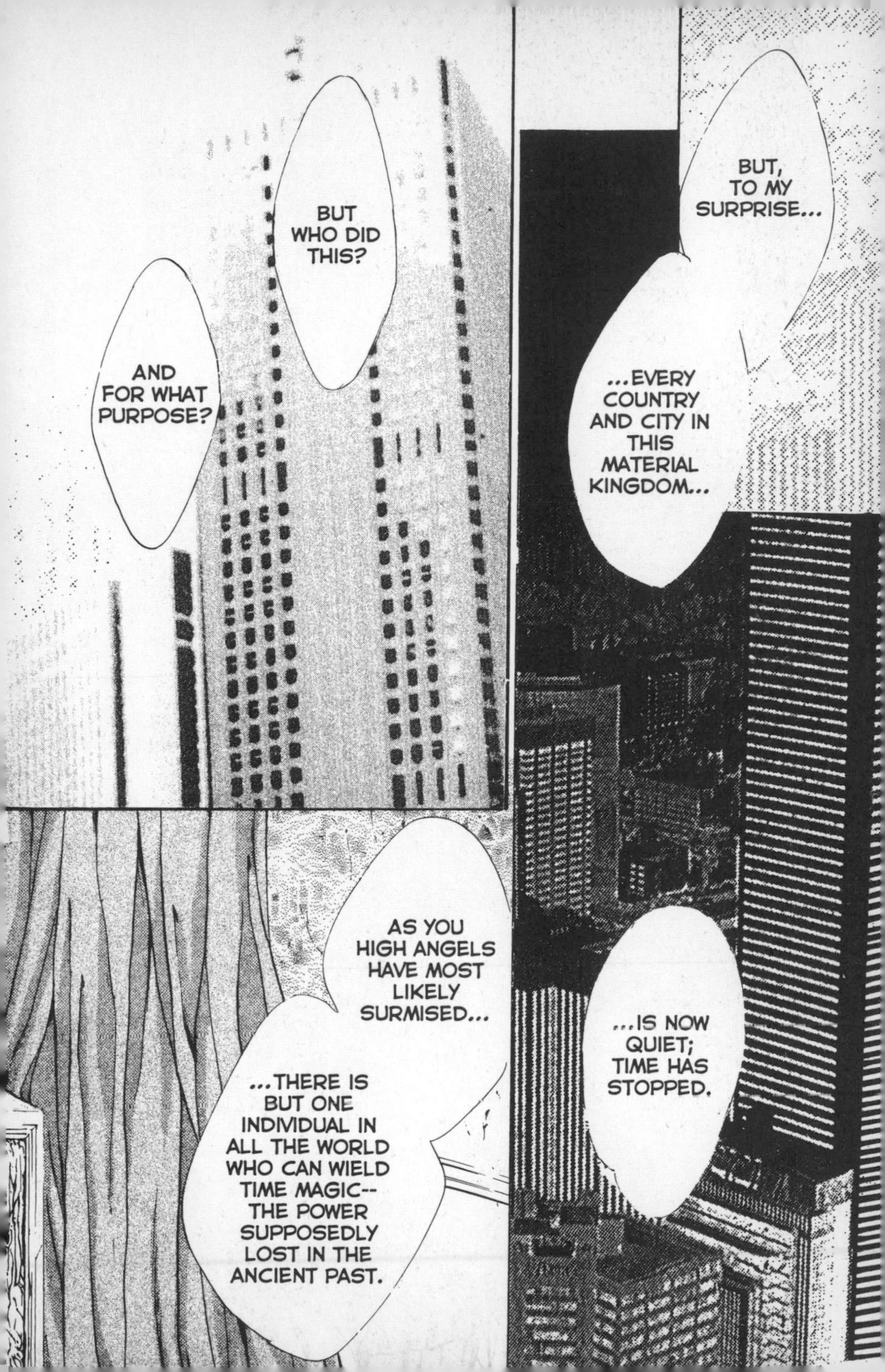
BUT, TO MY SURPRISE...
...EVERY COUNTRY AND CITY IN THIS MATERIAL KINGDOM...
...IS NOW QUIET; TIME HAS STOPPED.
BUT WHO DID THIS?
AND FOR WHAT PURPOSE?
AS YOU HIGH ANGELS HAVE MOST LIKELY SURMISED...
...THERE IS BUT ONE INDIVIDUAL IN ALL THE WORLD WHO CAN WIELD TIME MAGIC-- THE POWER SUPPOSEDLY LOST IN THE ANCIENT PAST.

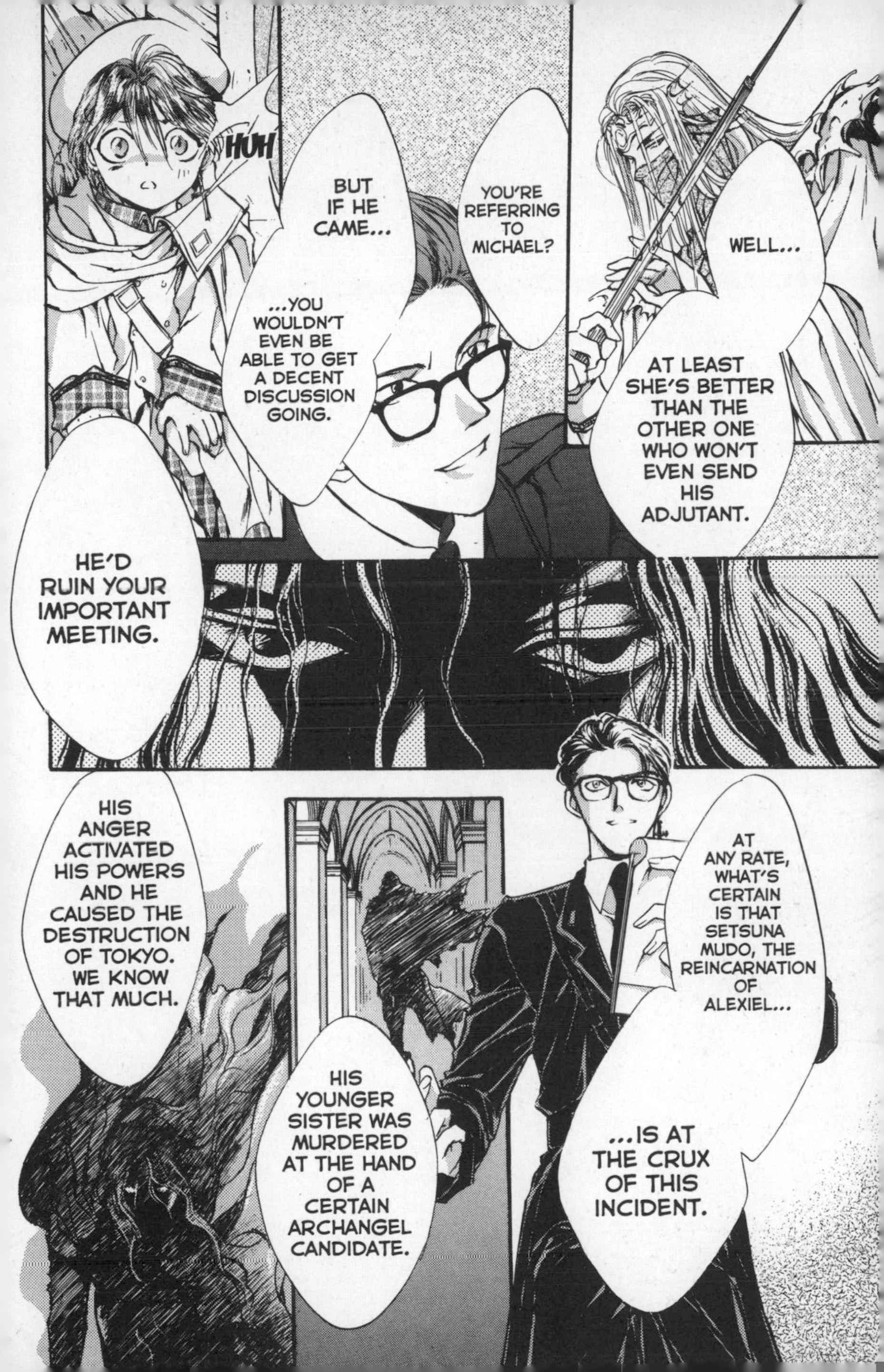
WELL...
AT LEAST SHE'S BETTER THAN THE OTHER ONE WHO WON'T EVEN SEND HIS ADJUTANT.
YOU'RE REFERRING TO MICHAEL?
BUT IF HE CAME...
...YOU WOULDN'T EVEN BE ABLE TO GET A DECENT DISCUSSION GOING.
HUH
HE'D RUIN YOUR IMPORTANT MEETING.
AT ANY RATE, WHAT'S CERTAIN IS THAT SETSUNA MUDO, THE REINCARNATION OF ALEXIEL...
...IS AT THE CRUX OF THIS INCIDENT.
HIS YOUNGER SISTER WAS MURDERED AT THE HAND OF A CERTAIN ARCHANGEL CANDIDATE.
HIS ANGER ACTIVATED HIS POWERS AND HE CAUSED THE DESTRUCTION OF TOKYO. WE KNOW THAT MUCH.

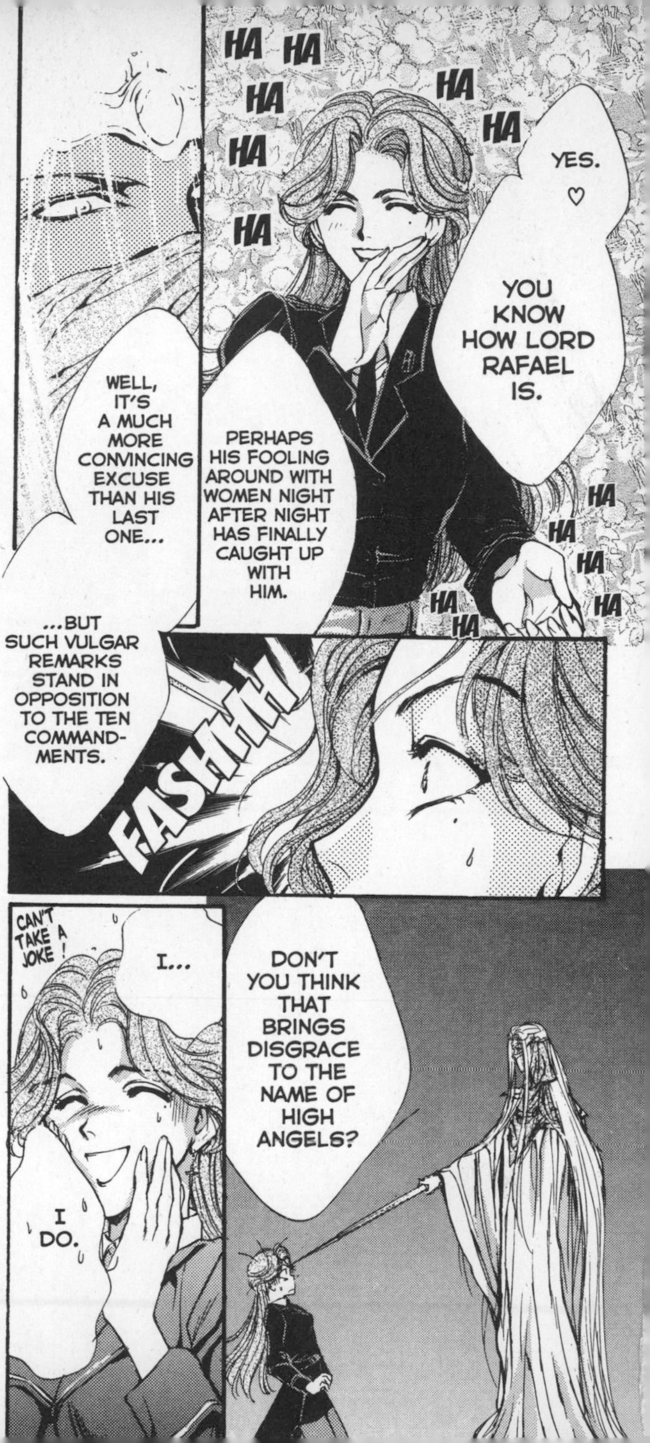
HA HA HA HA HA HA HA
YES. ♡
YOU KNOW HOW LORD RAFAEL IS.
PERHAPS HIS FOOLING AROUND WITH WOMEN NIGHT AFTER NIGHT HAS FINALLY CAUGHT UP WITH HIM.
HA HA HA HA HA HA
WELL, IT'S A MUCH MORE CONVINCING EXCUSE THAN HIS LAST ONE...
...BUT SUCH VULGAR REMARKS STAND IN OPPOSITION TO THE TEN COMMAND-MENTS.
FASHHH!
DON'T YOU THINK THAT BRINGS DISGRACE TO THE NAME OF HIGH ANGELS?
I...
CAN'T TAKE A JOKE!
I DO.

From here on, we're in a new chapter: Book of Hades. Yes, it was a long time getting here. There'll be less action than when the earth's surface was the stage, but it's going to be quite rough relaying information from three levels: Supreme Heaven, Hades, and Anagura. The human (well, not quite) relationships become quite messy, but please hang in and try to follow along. You'll need to have a firm understanding here in order to move on to the next chapter: Book of Gehenna. Although this has nothing to do with the story, a lot of people have been telling me I am obsessed with beauty. I don't care! I've recently come to realize that I love beauty.

Just recently? Yeah, right!

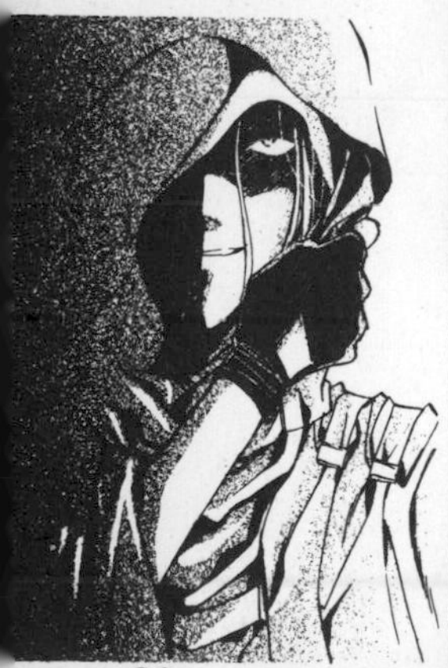

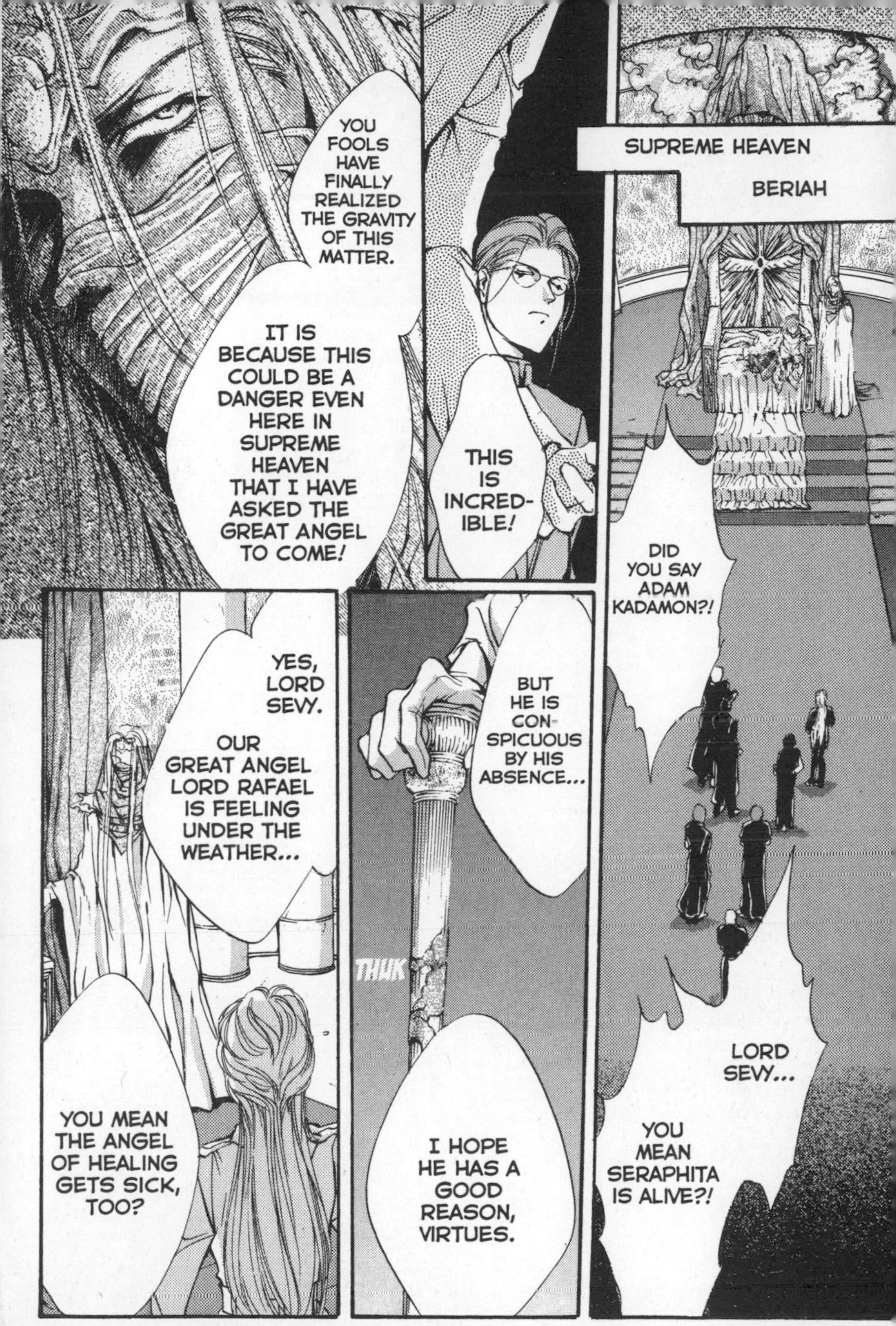
SUPREME HEAVEN
BERIAH
DID YOU SAY ADAM KADAMON?!
LORD SEVY...
YOU MEAN SERAPHITA IS ALIVE?!
THIS IS INCREDIBLE!
YOU FOOLS HAVE FINALLY REALIZED THE GRAVITY OF THIS MATTER.
IT IS BECAUSE THIS COULD BE A DANGER EVEN HERE IN SUPREME HEAVEN THAT I HAVE ASKED THE GREAT ANGEL TO COME!
BUT HE IS CONSPICUOUS BY HIS ABSENCE...
THUK
I HOPE HE HAS A GOOD REASON, VIRTUES.
YES, LORD SEVY.
OUR GREAT ANGEL LORD RAFAEL IS FEELING UNDER THE WEATHER...
YOU MEAN THE ANGEL OF HEALING GETS SICK, TOO?

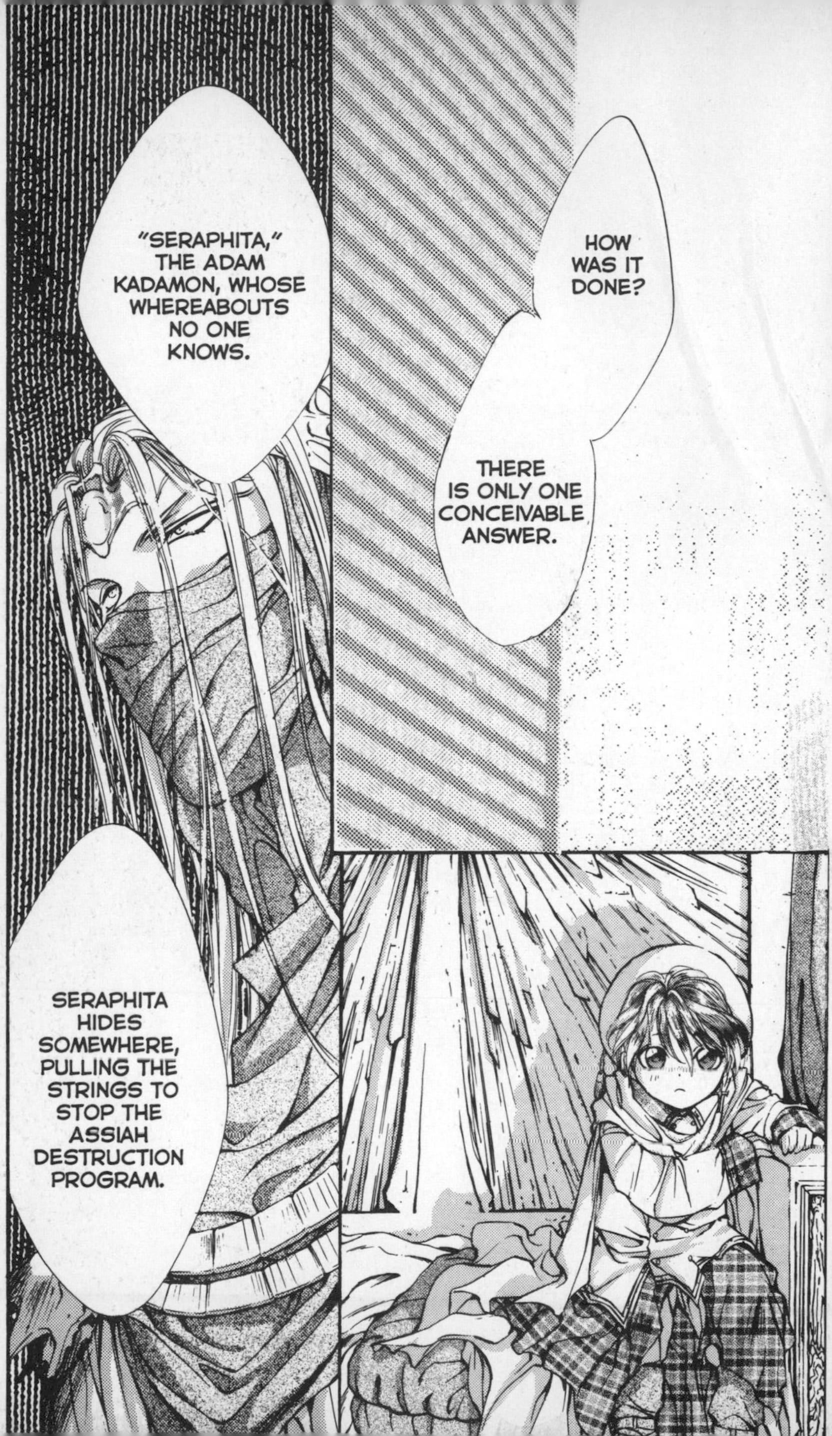
HOW WAS IT DONE?
THERE IS ONLY ONE CONCEIVABLE ANSWER.
"SERAPHITA," THE ADAM KADAMON, WHOSE WHEREABOUTS NO ONE KNOWS.
SERAPHITA HIDES SOMEWHERE, PULLING THE STRINGS TO STOP THE ASSIAH DESTRUCTION PROGRAM.

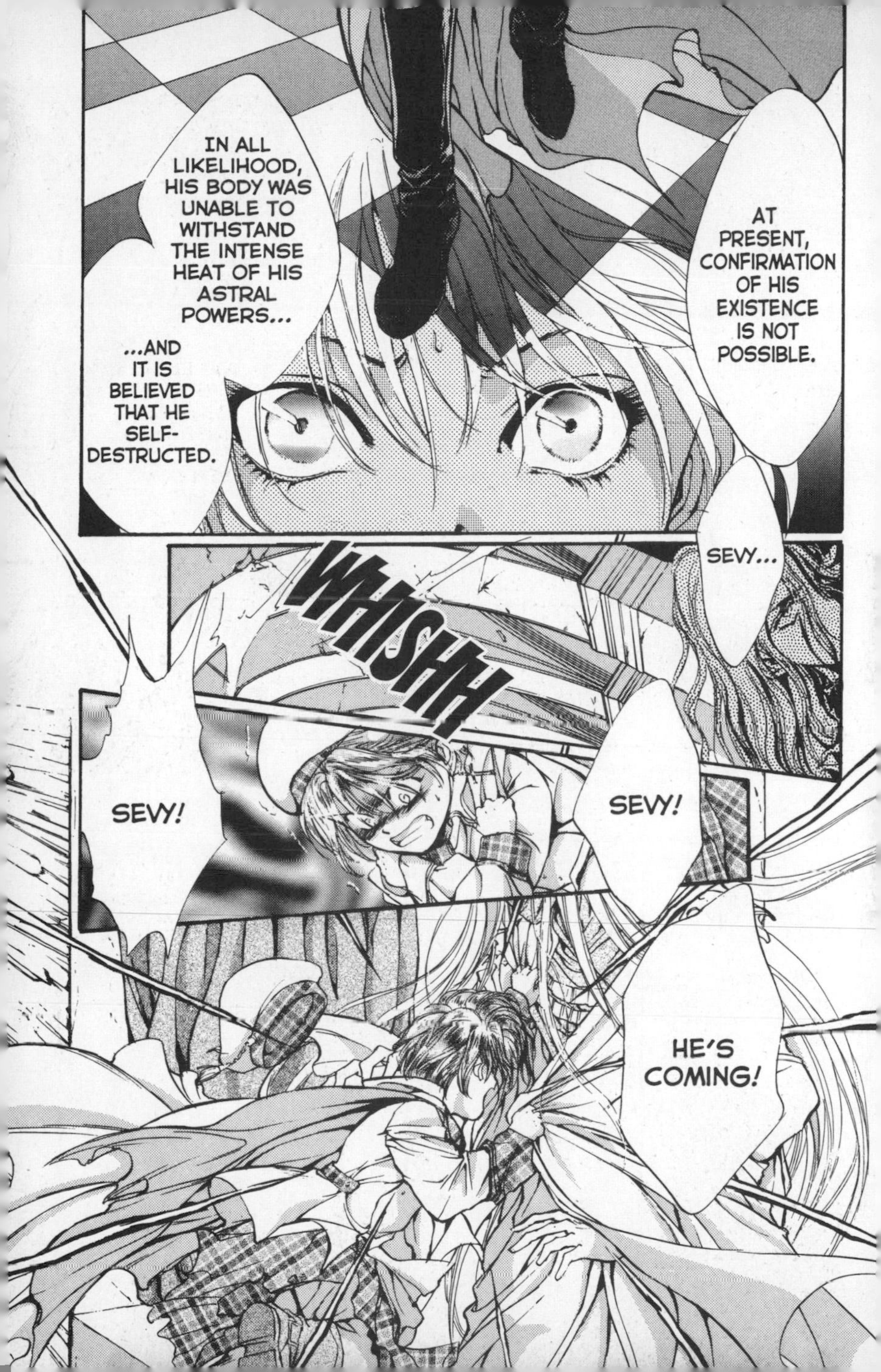
AT PRESENT, CONFIRMATION OF HIS EXISTENCE IS NOT POSSIBLE.
IN ALL LIKELIHOOD, HIS BODY WAS UNABLE TO WITHSTAND THE INTENSE HEAT OF HIS ASTRAL POWERS...
...AND IT IS BELIEVED THAT HE SELF-DESTRUCTED.
SEVY...
WHISH
SEVY!
SEVY!
HE'S COMING!

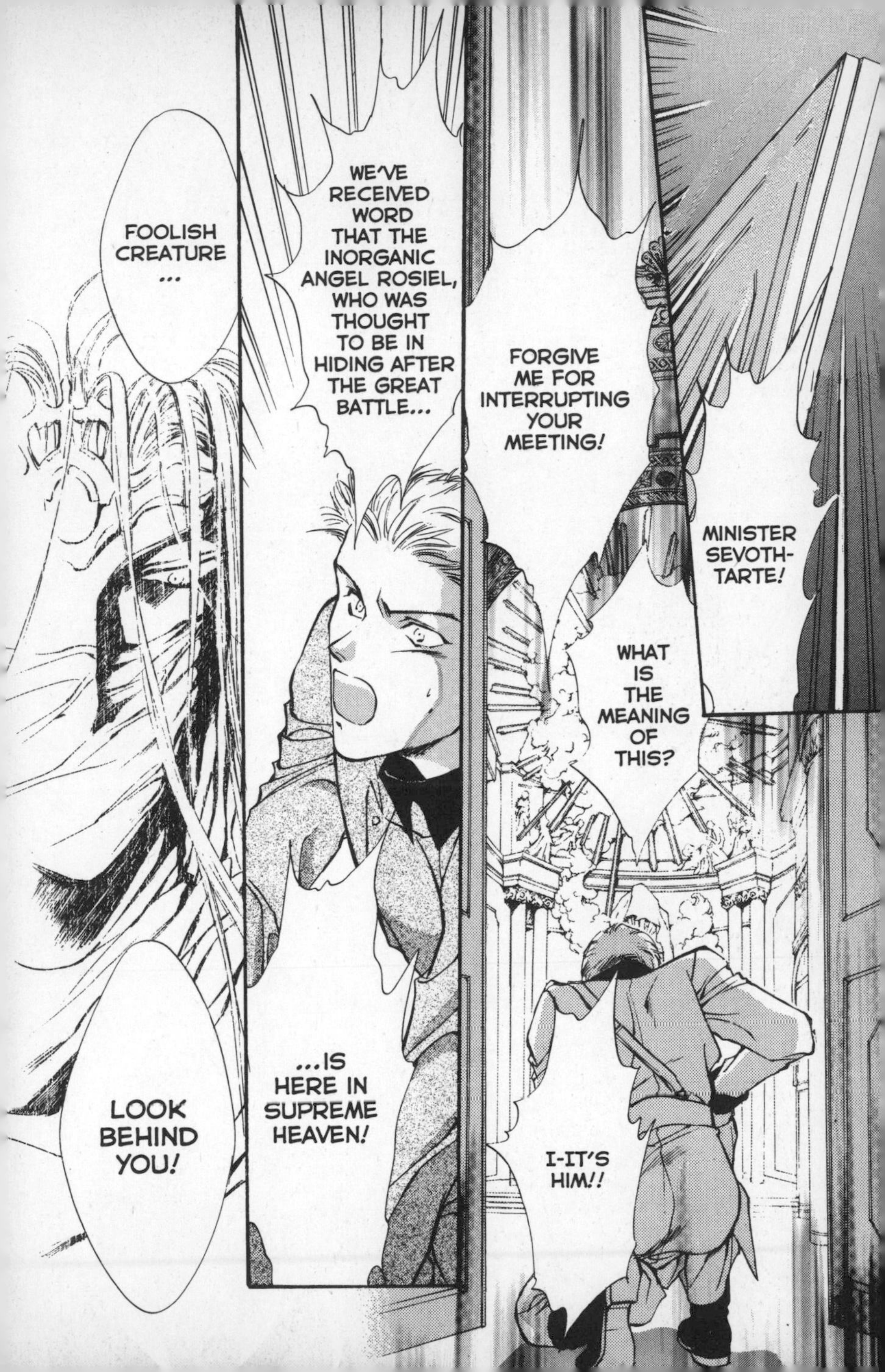
MINISTER SEVOTH-TARTE!
FORGIVE ME FOR INTERRUPTING YOUR MEETING!
WHAT IS THE MEANING OF THIS?
I-IT'S HIM!!
WE'VE RECEIVED WORD THAT THE INORGANIC ANGEL ROSIEL, WHO WAS THOUGHT TO BE IN HIDING AFTER THE GREAT BATTLE...
...IS HERE IN SUPREME HEAVEN!
FOOLISH CREATURE ...
LOOK BEHIND YOU!

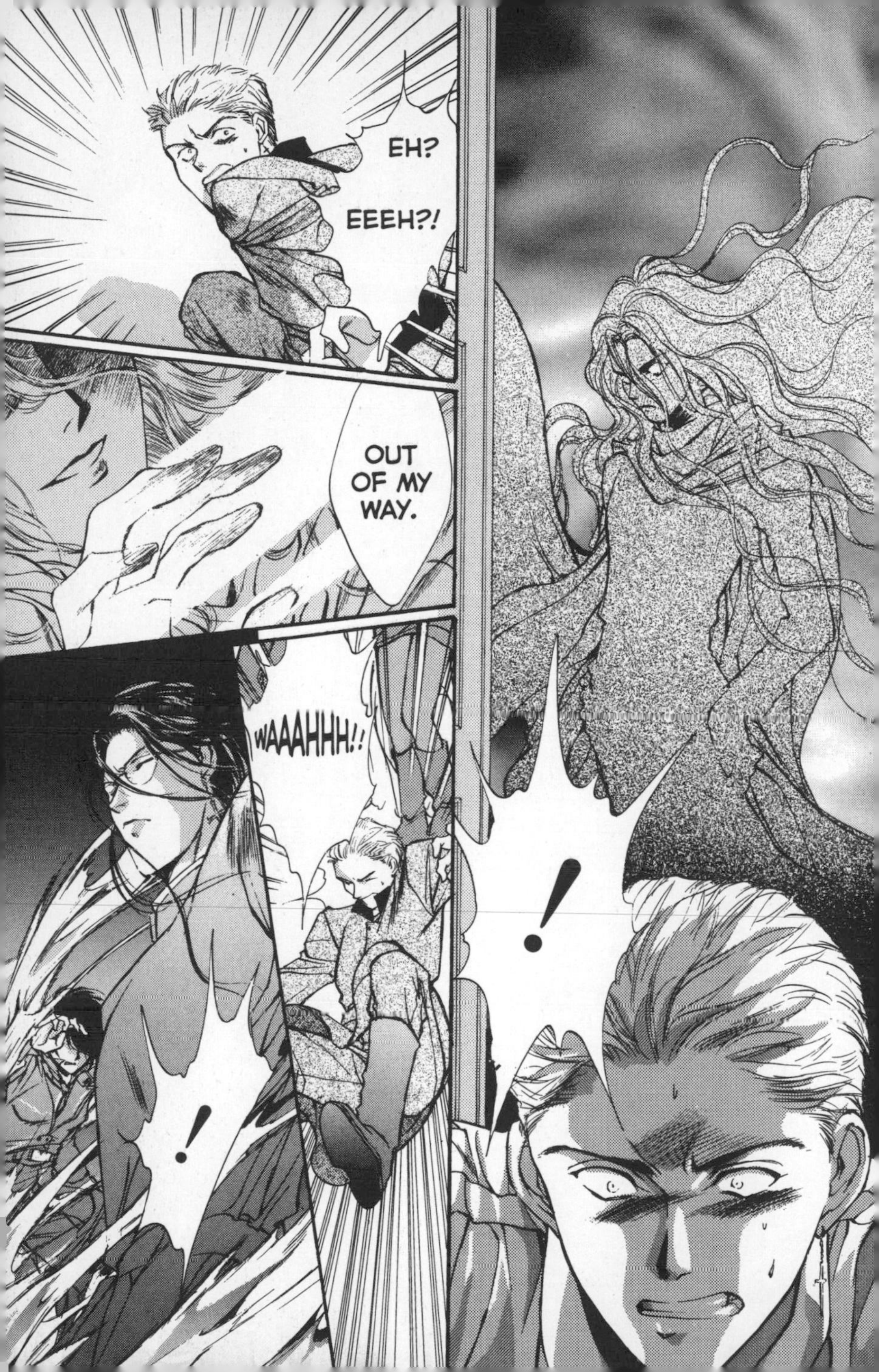
!
EH?
EEEH?!
OUT OF MY WAY.
WAAAHHH!!
!

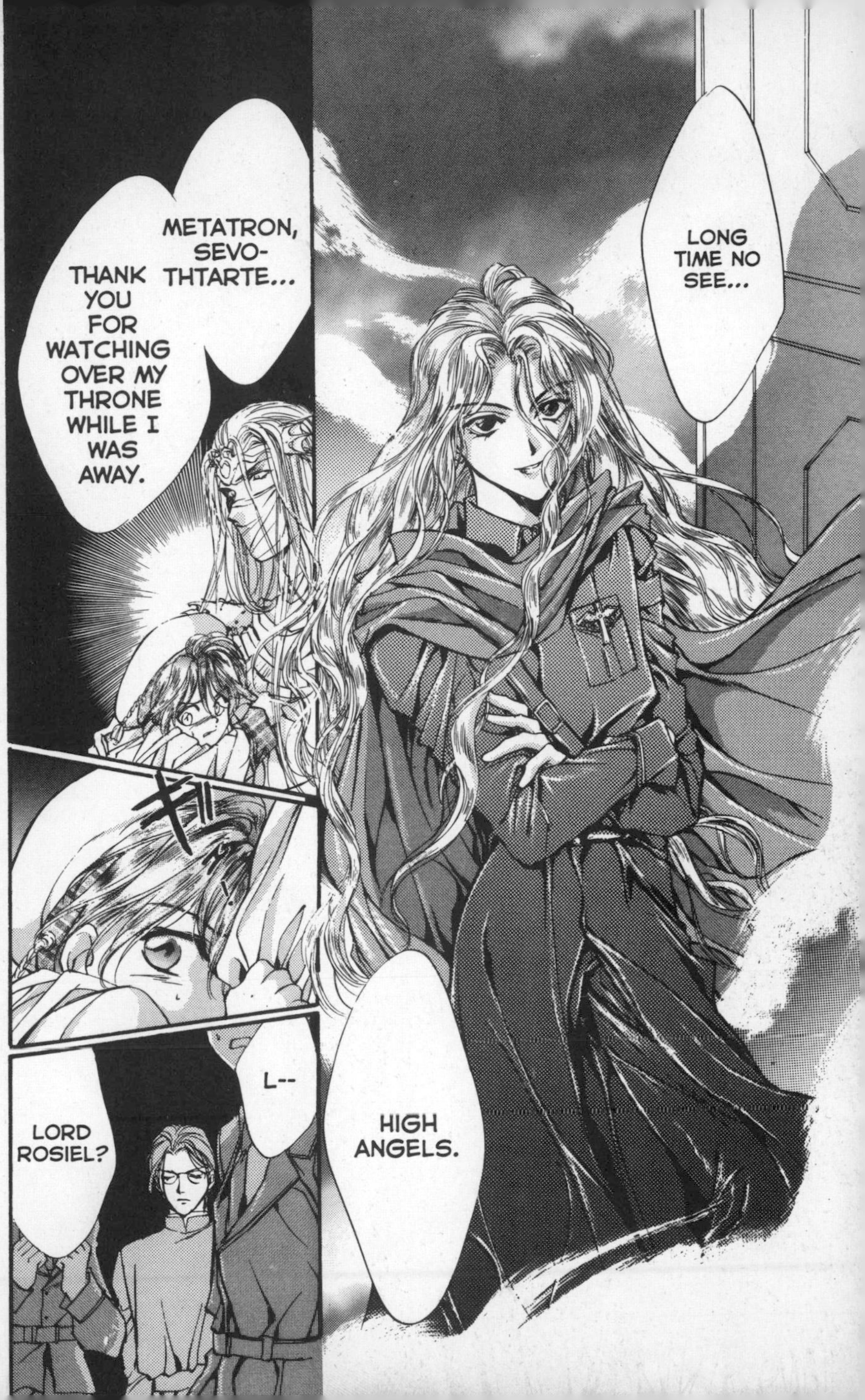
LONG TIME NO SEE...
HIGH ANGELS.
METATRON, SEVO-THTARTE...
THANK YOU FOR WATCHING OVER MY THRONE WHILE I WAS AWAY.
L--
LORD ROSIEL?

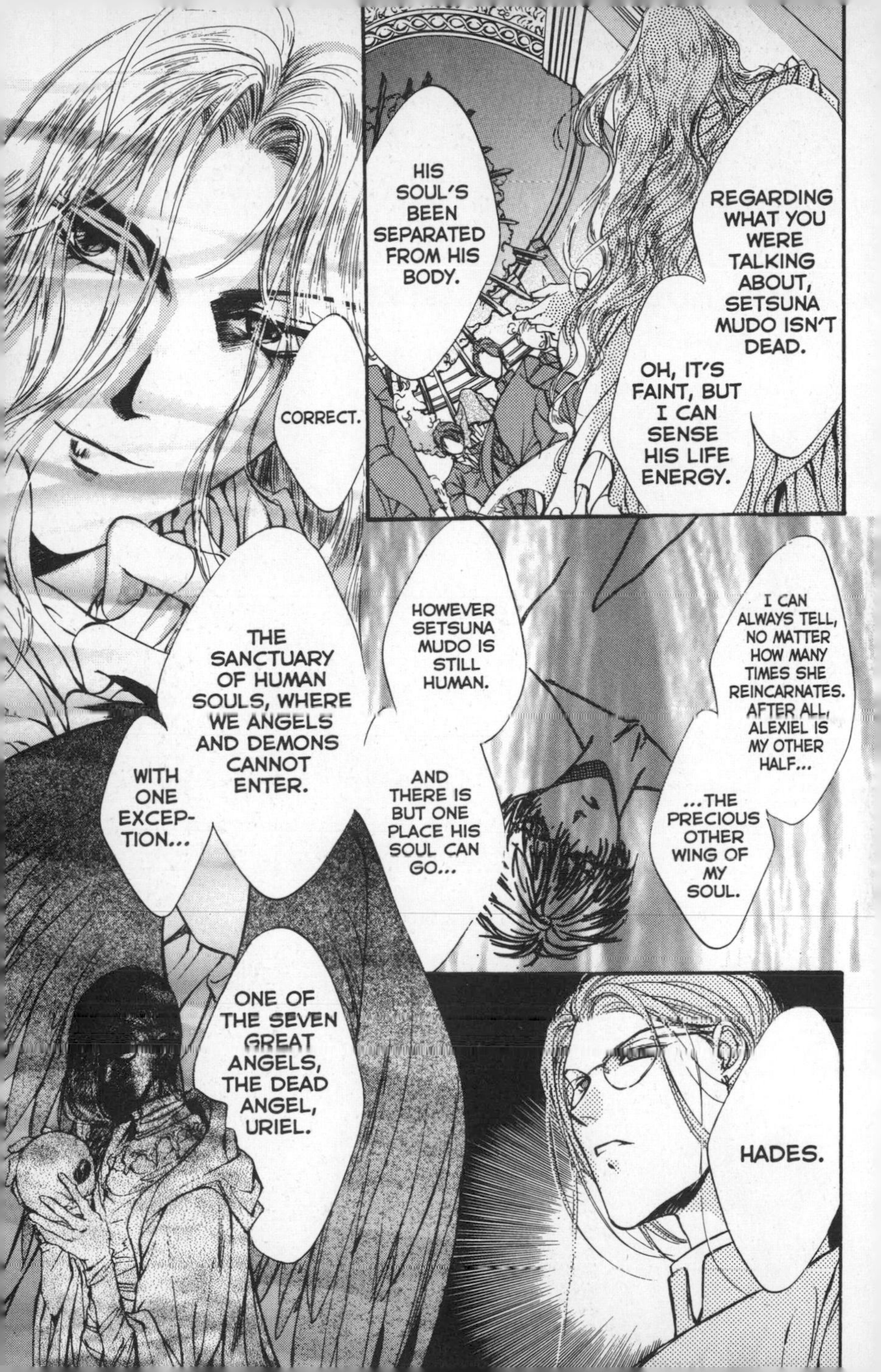
REGARDING WHAT YOU WERE TALKING ABOUT, SETSUNA MUDO ISN'T DEAD.
OH, IT'S FAINT, BUT I CAN SENSE HIS LIFE ENERGY.
HIS SOUL'S BEEN SEPARATED FROM HIS BODY.
CORRECT.
I CAN ALWAYS TELL, NO MATTER HOW MANY TIMES SHE REINCARNATES. AFTER ALL, ALEXIEL IS MY OTHER HALF...
...THE PRECIOUS OTHER WING OF MY SOUL.
HOWEVER SETSUNA MUDO IS STILL HUMAN.
AND THERE IS BUT ONE PLACE HIS SOUL CAN GO...
HADES.
THE SANCTUARY OF HUMAN SOULS, WHERE WE ANGELS AND DEMONS CANNOT ENTER.
WITH ONE EXCEPTION...
ONE OF THE SEVEN GREAT ANGELS, THE DEAD ANGEL, URIEL.

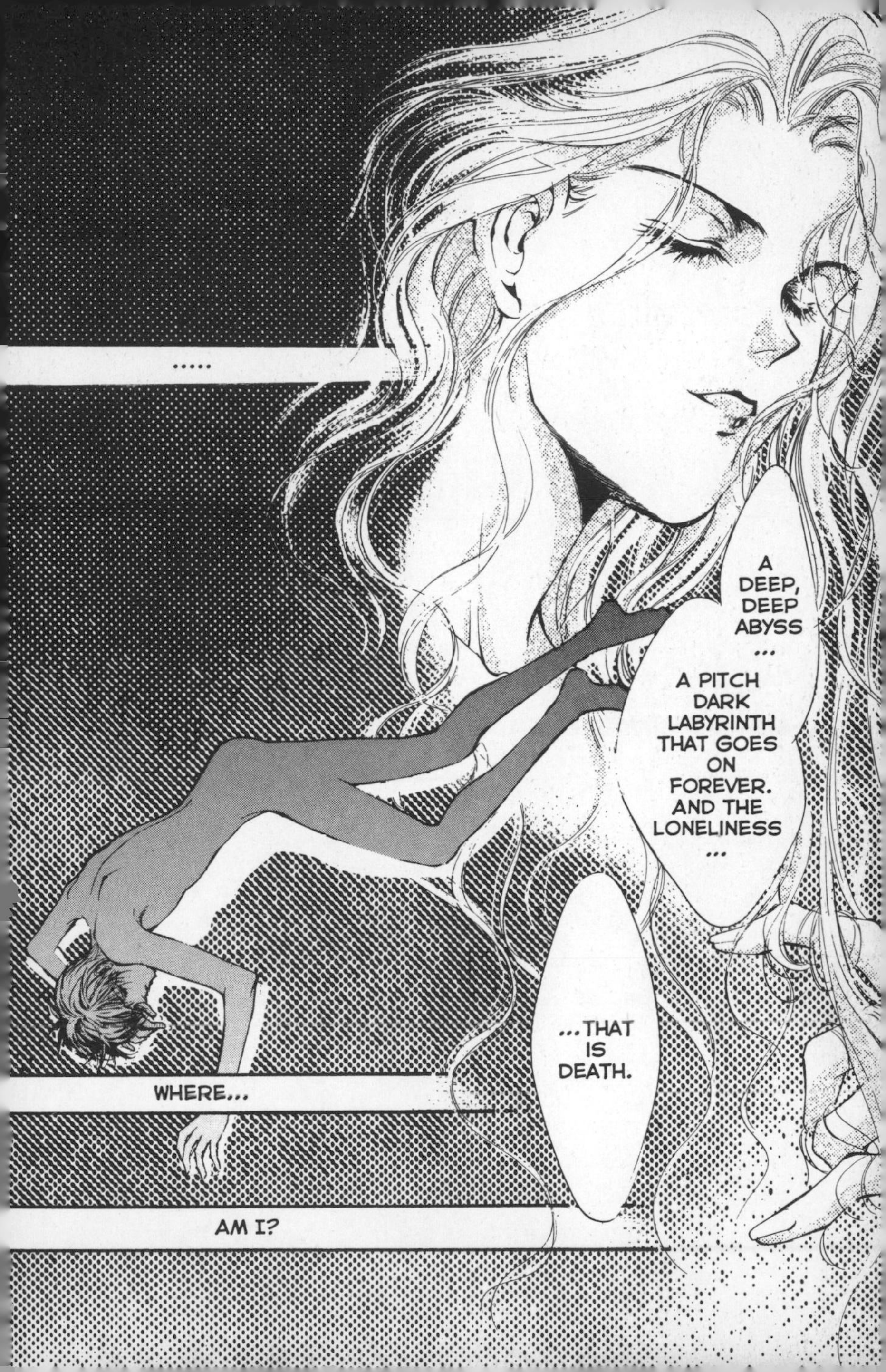
.....
A DEEP, DEEP ABYSS ... A PITCH DARK LABYRINTH THAT GOES ON FOREVER. AND THE LONELINESS ...
...THAT IS DEATH.
WHERE...
AM I?

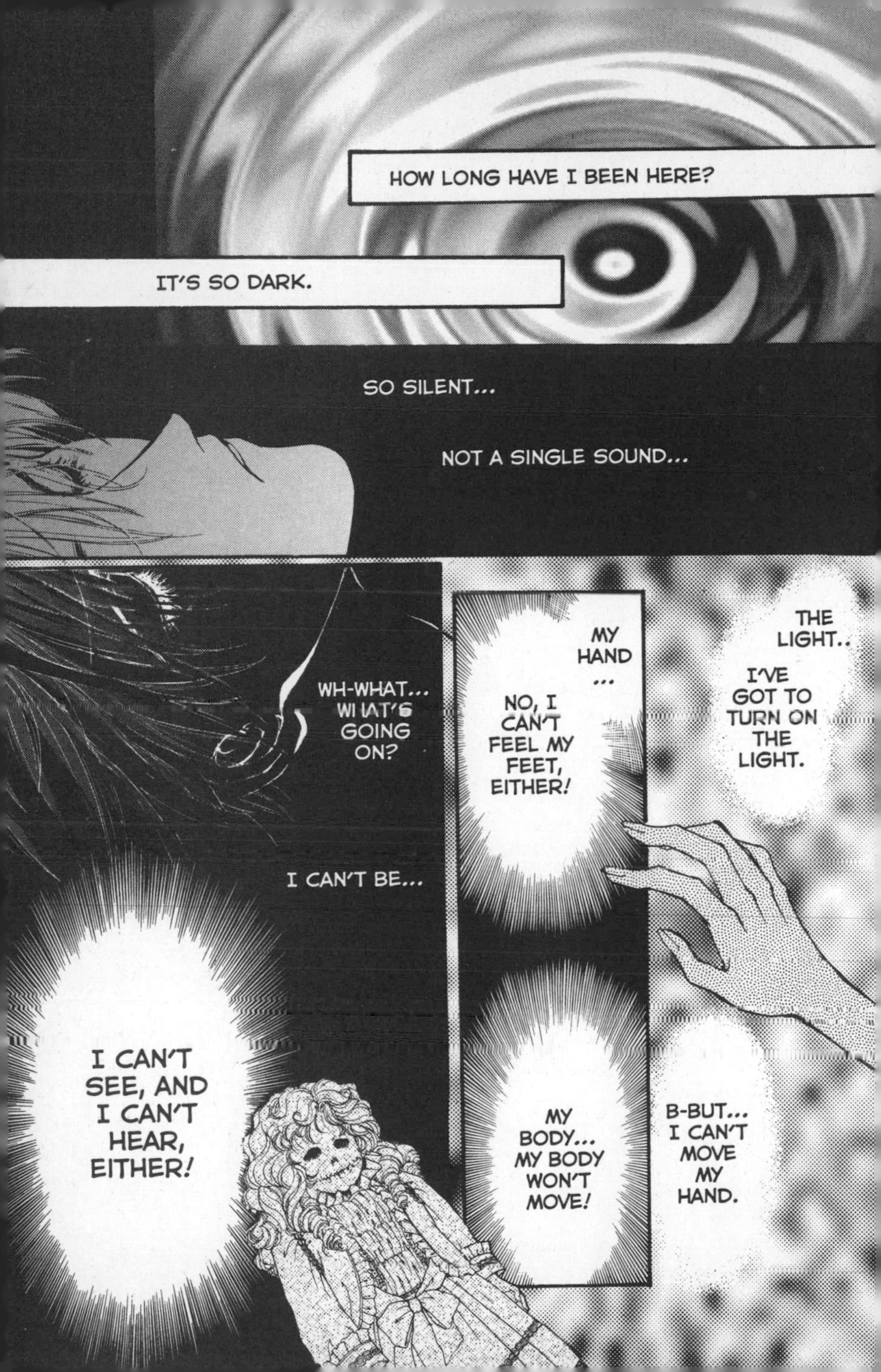
HOW LONG HAVE I BEEN HERE?
IT'S SO DARK.
SO SILENT...
NOT A SINGLE SOUND...
THE LIGHT..
I'VE GOT TO TURN ON THE LIGHT.
B-BUT... I CAN'T MOVE MY HAND.
MY HAND...
NO, I CAN'T FEEL MY FEET, EITHER!
MY BODY... MY BODY WON'T MOVE!
WH-WHAT... WHAT'S GOING ON?
I CAN'T BE...
I CAN'T SEE, AND I CAN'T HEAR, EITHER!

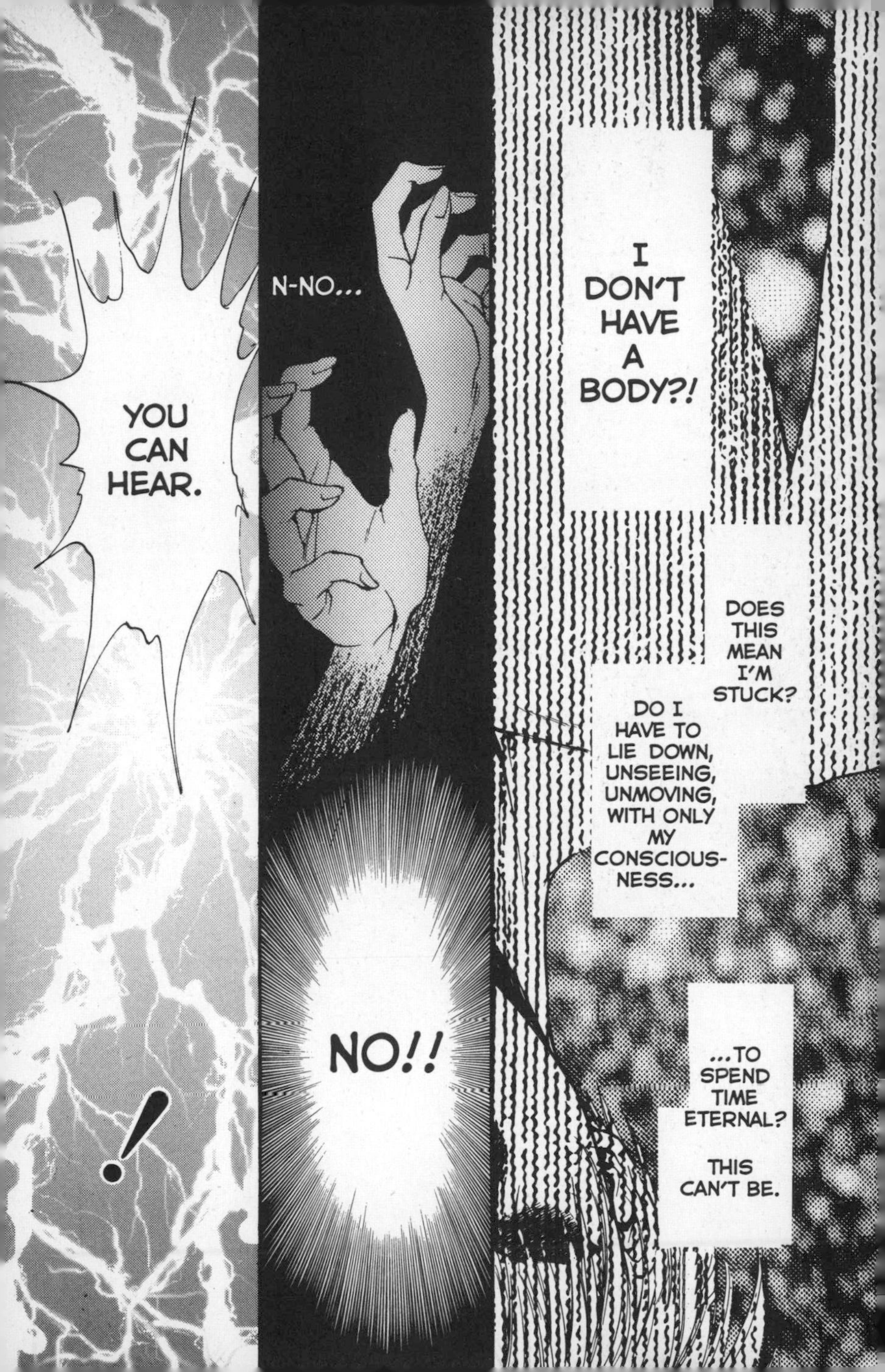

I DON'T HAVE A BODY?!
DOES THIS MEAN I'M STUCK?
DO I HAVE TO LIE DOWN, UNSEEING, UNMOVING, WITH ONLY MY CONSCIOUSNESS...
...TO SPEND TIME ETERNAL?
THIS CAN'T BE.
N-NO...
NO!!
YOU CAN HEAR.
!

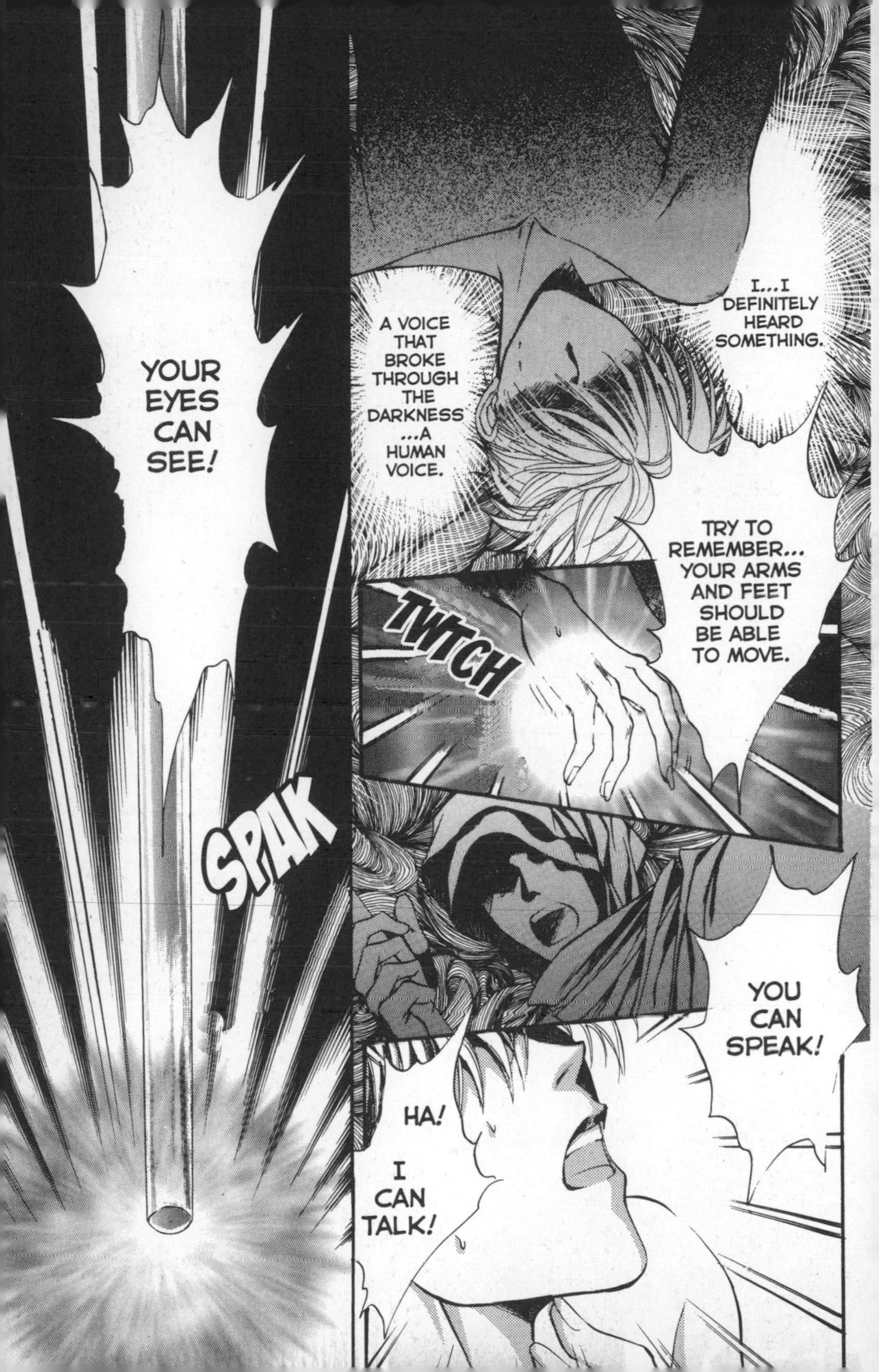
I...I DEFINITELY HEARD SOMETHING.
A VOICE THAT BROKE THROUGH THE DARKNESS ...A HUMAN VOICE.
TRY TO REMEMBER... YOUR ARMS AND FEET SHOULD BE ABLE TO MOVE.
TWITCH
YOU CAN SPEAK!
HA!
I CAN TALK!
YOUR EYES CAN SEE!
SPAK

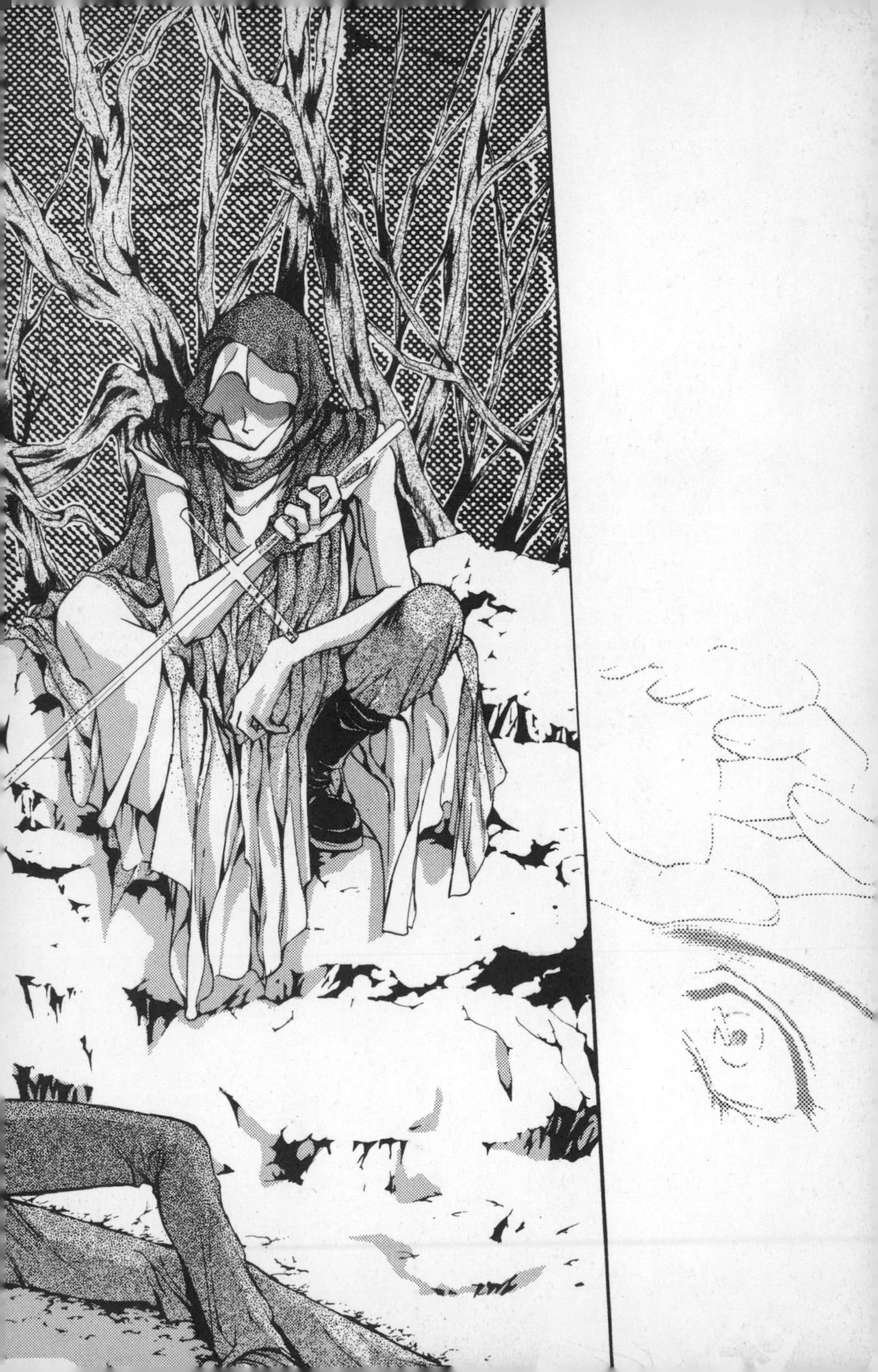

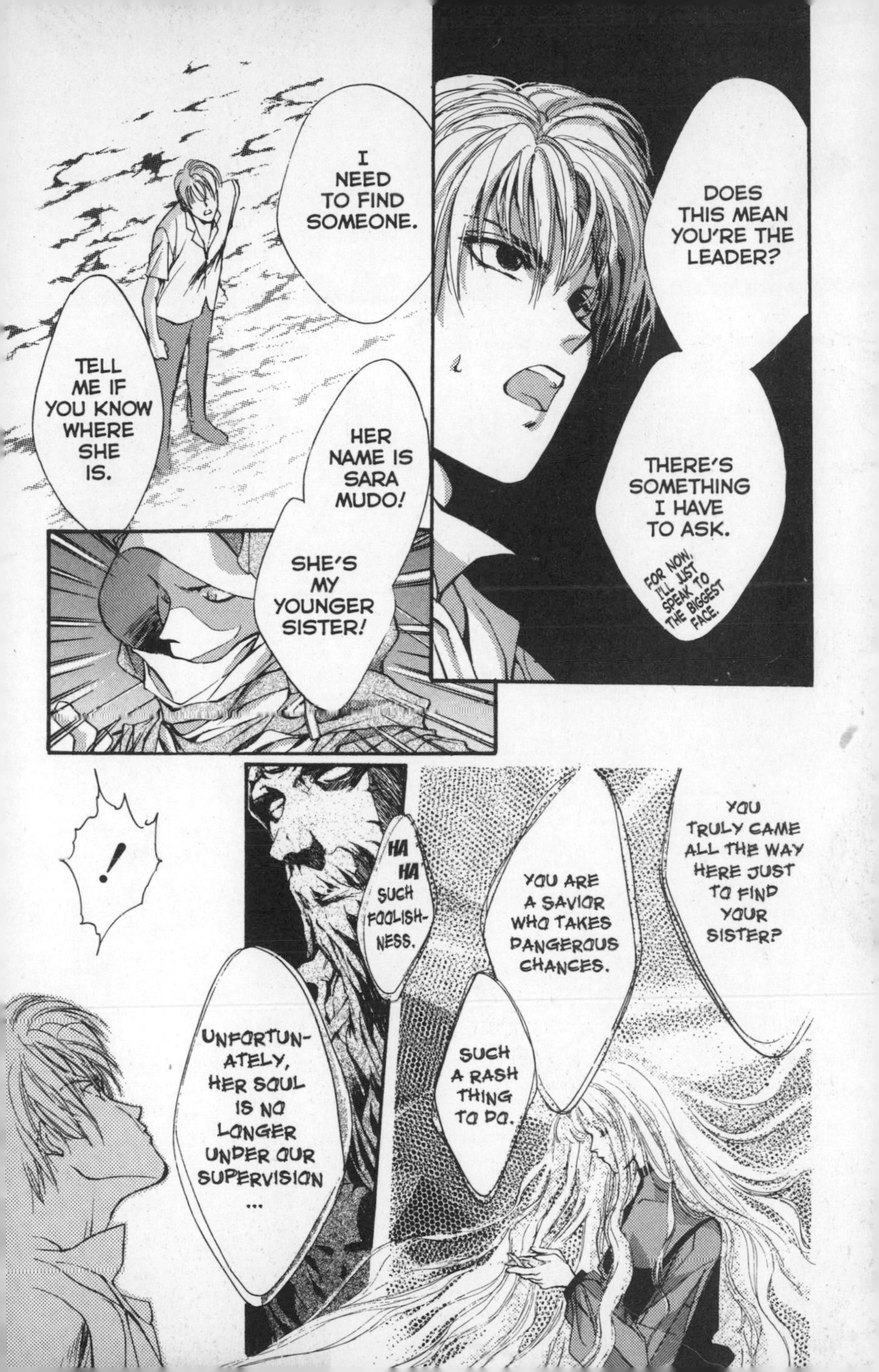
DOES THIS MEAN YOU'RE THE LEADER?
THERE'S SOMETHING I HAVE TO ASK.
FOR NOW, I'LL JUST SPEAK TO THE BIGGEST FACE.
I NEED TO FIND SOMEONE.
TELL ME IF YOU KNOW WHERE SHE IS.
HER NAME IS SARA MUDO!
SHE'S MY YOUNGER SISTER!
YOU TRULY CAME ALL THE WAY HERE JUST TO FIND YOUR SISTER?
YOU ARE A SAVIOR WHO TAKES DANGEROUS CHANCES.
SUCH A RASH THING TO DO.
HA HA
SUCH FOOLISH-NESS.
UNFORTUN-ATELY, HER SOUL IS NO LONGER UNDER OUR SUPERVISION ...
!

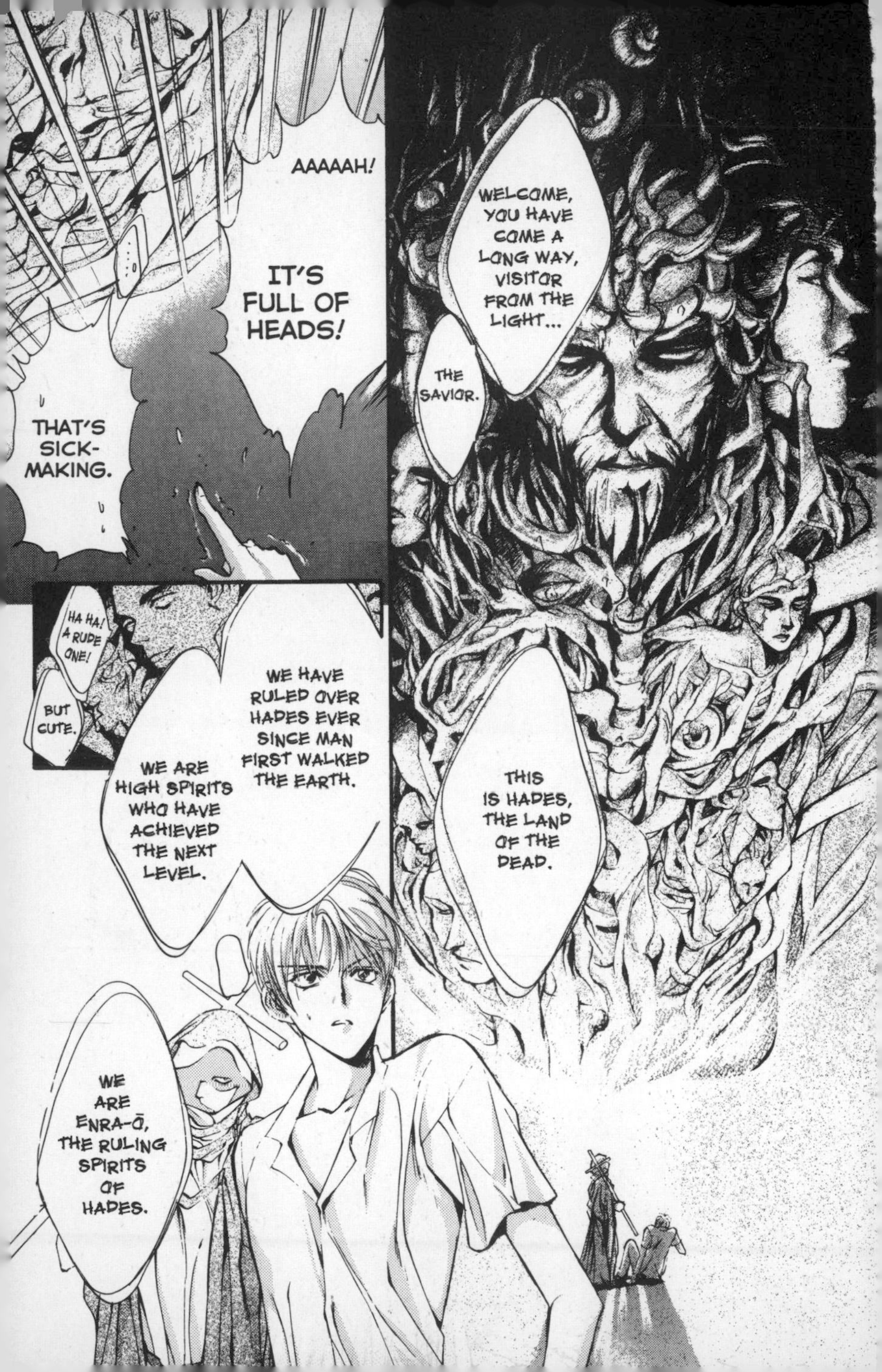
WELCOME, YOU HAVE COME A LONG WAY, VISITOR FROM THE LIGHT...
THE SAVIOR.
THIS IS HADES, THE LAND OF THE DEAD.
AAAAAH!
IT'S FULL OF HEADS!
THAT'S SICK-MAKING.
HA HA! A RUDE ONE!
BUT CUTE.
WE HAVE RULED OVER HADES EVER SINCE MAN FIRST WALKED THE EARTH.
WE ARE HIGH SPIRITS WHO HAVE ACHIEVED THE NEXT LEVEL.
WE ARE ENRA-Ō, THE RULING SPIRITS OF HADES.

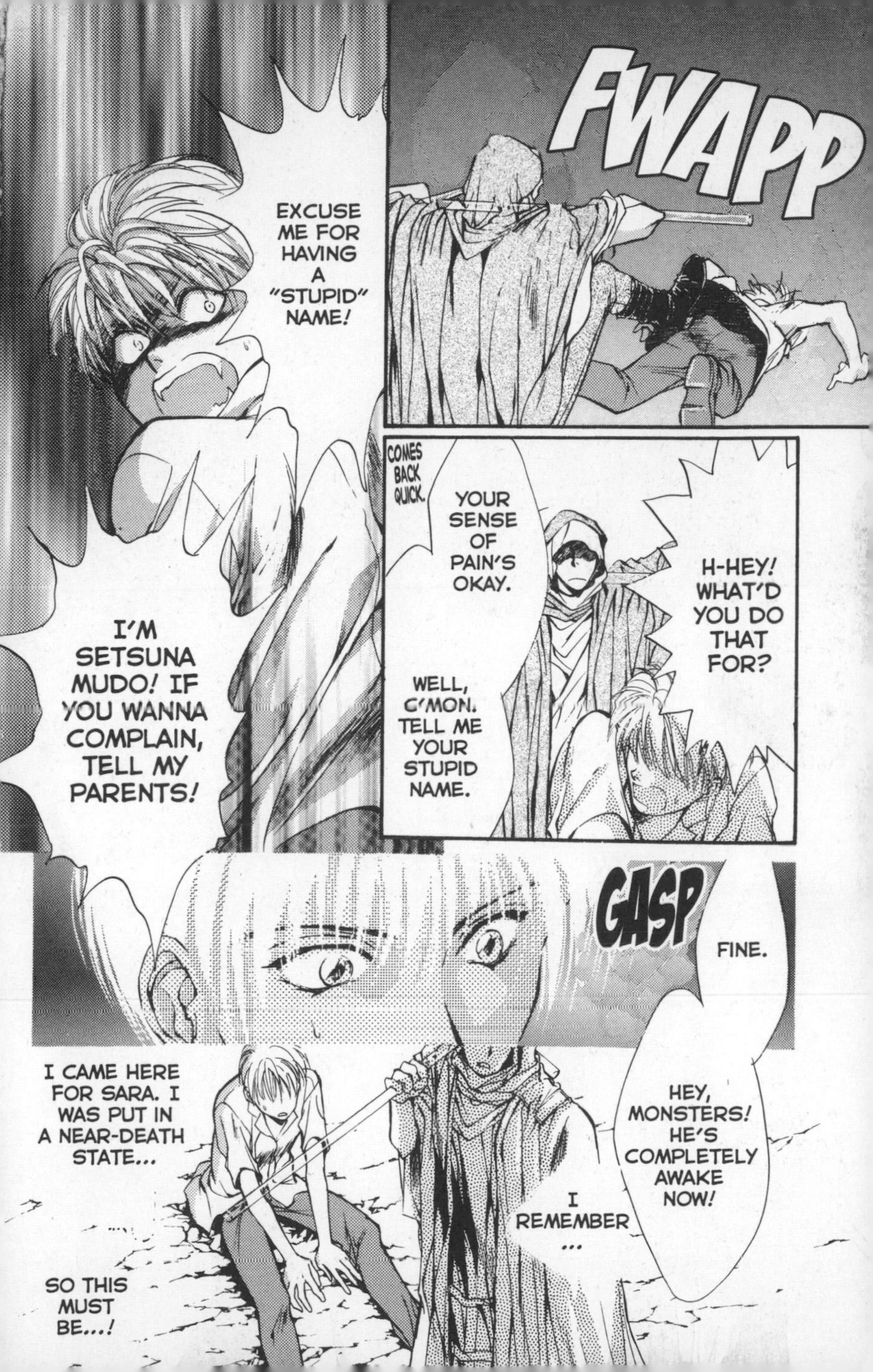
FWAPP
H-HEY! WHAT'D YOU DO THAT FOR?
YOUR SENSE OF PAIN'S OKAY.
COMES BACK QUICK.
WELL, C'MON. TELL ME YOUR STUPID NAME.
EXCUSE ME FOR HAVING A "STUPID" NAME!
I'M SETSUNA MUDO! IF YOU WANNA COMPLAIN, TELL MY PARENTS!
GASP
FINE.
HEY, MONSTERS! HE'S COMPLETELY AWAKE NOW!
I REMEMBER...
I CAME HERE FOR SARA. I WAS PUT IN A NEAR-DEATH STATE...
...
SO THIS MUST BE...!

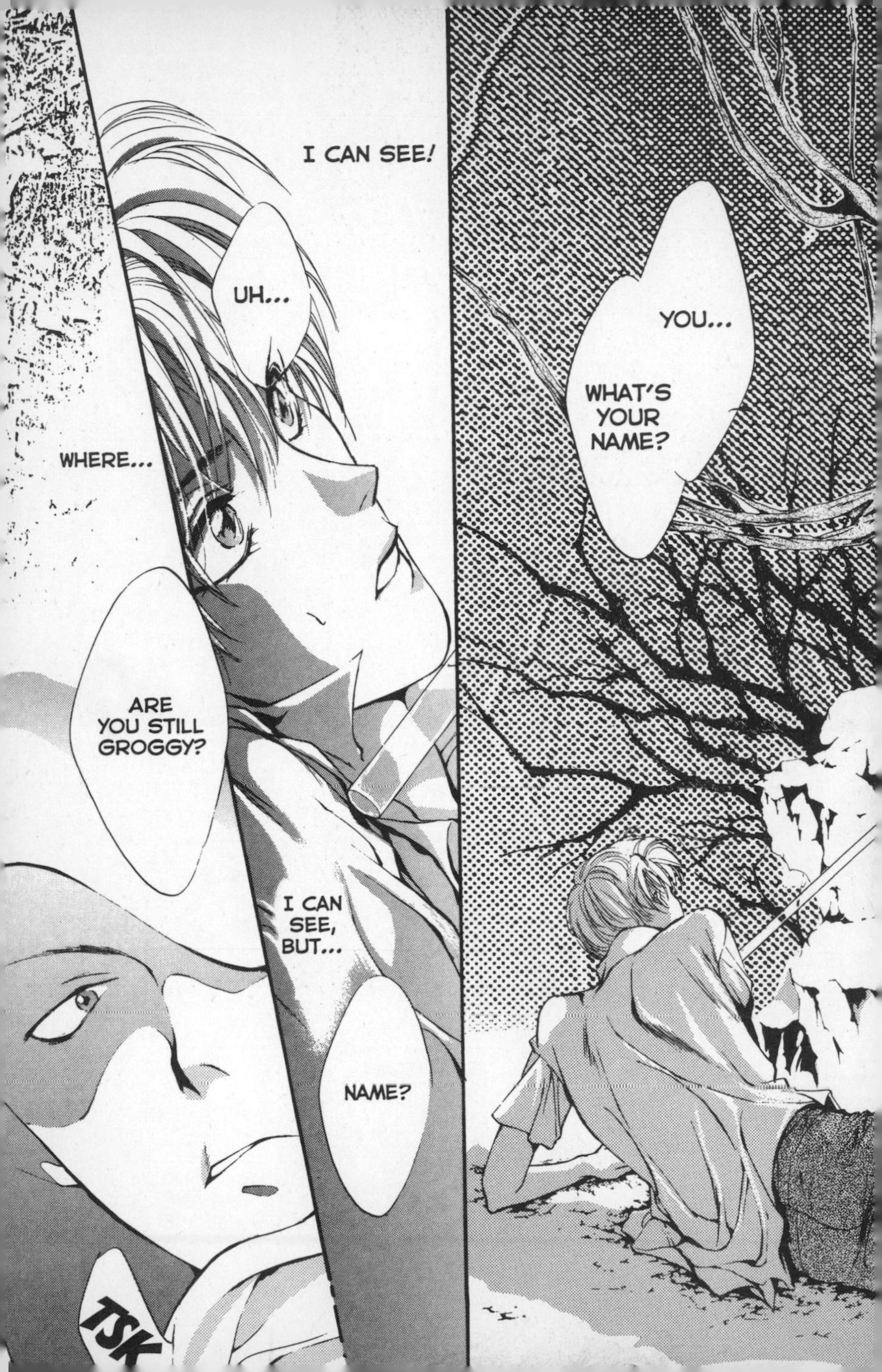
YOU...
WHAT'S YOUR NAME?
UH...
I CAN SEE!
WHERE...
ARE YOU STILL GROGGY?
I CAN SEE, BUT...
NAME?
TSK

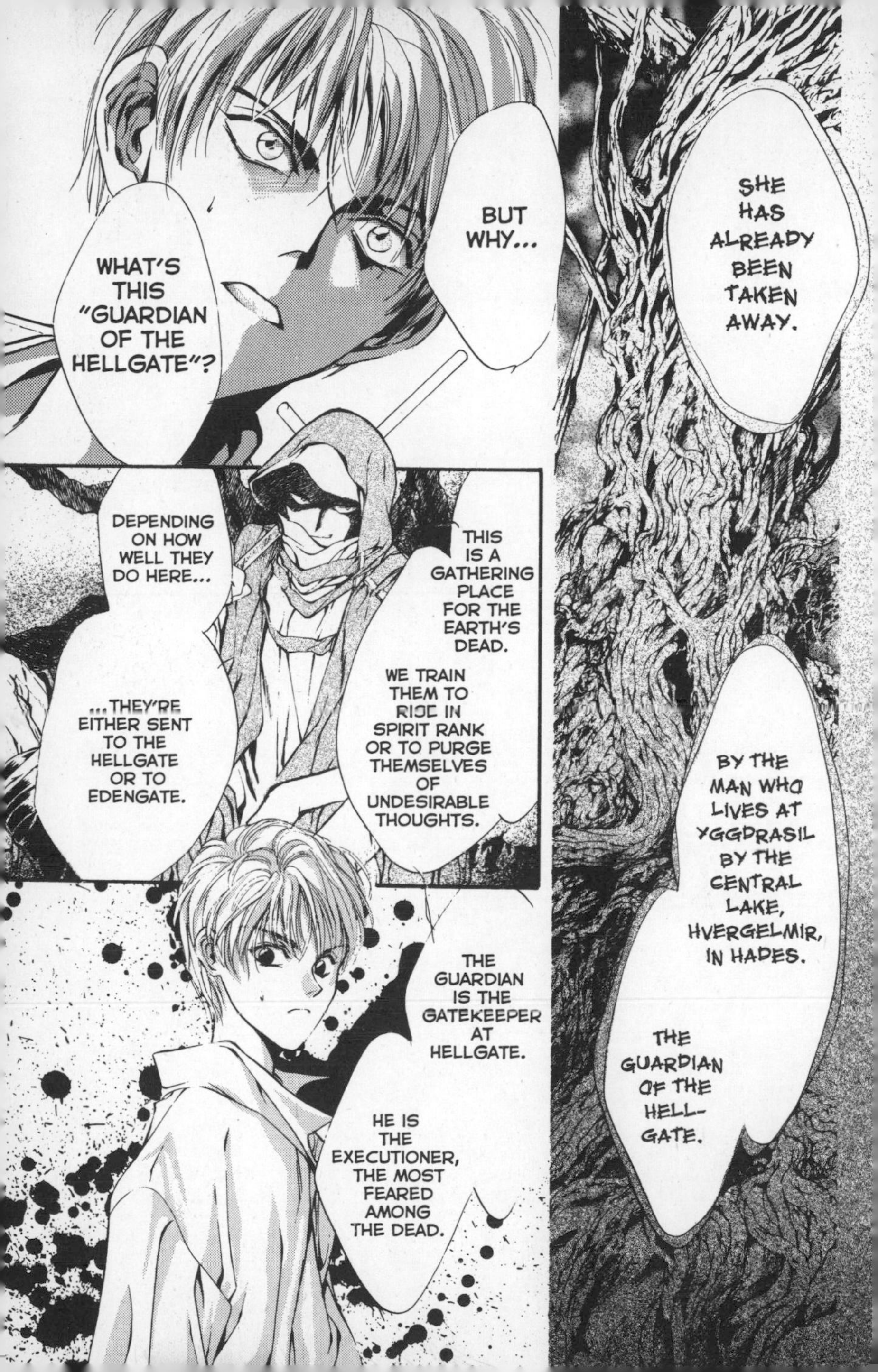
SHE HAS ALREADY BEEN TAKEN AWAY.
BY THE MAN WHO LIVES AT YGGDRASIL BY THE CENTRAL LAKE, HVERGELMIR, IN HADES.
THE GUARDIAN OF THE HELL-GATE.
BUT WHY...
WHAT'S THIS "GUARDIAN OF THE HELLGATE"?
THIS IS A GATHERING PLACE FOR THE EARTH'S DEAD.
WE TRAIN THEM TO RISE IN SPIRIT RANK OR TO PURGE THEMSELVES OF UNDESIRABLE THOUGHTS.
DEPENDING ON HOW WELL THEY DO HERE...
...THEY'RE EITHER SENT TO THE HELLGATE OR TO EDENGATE.
THE GUARDIAN IS THE GATEKEEPER AT HELLGATE.
HE IS THE EXECUTIONER, THE MOST FEARED AMONG THE DEAD.

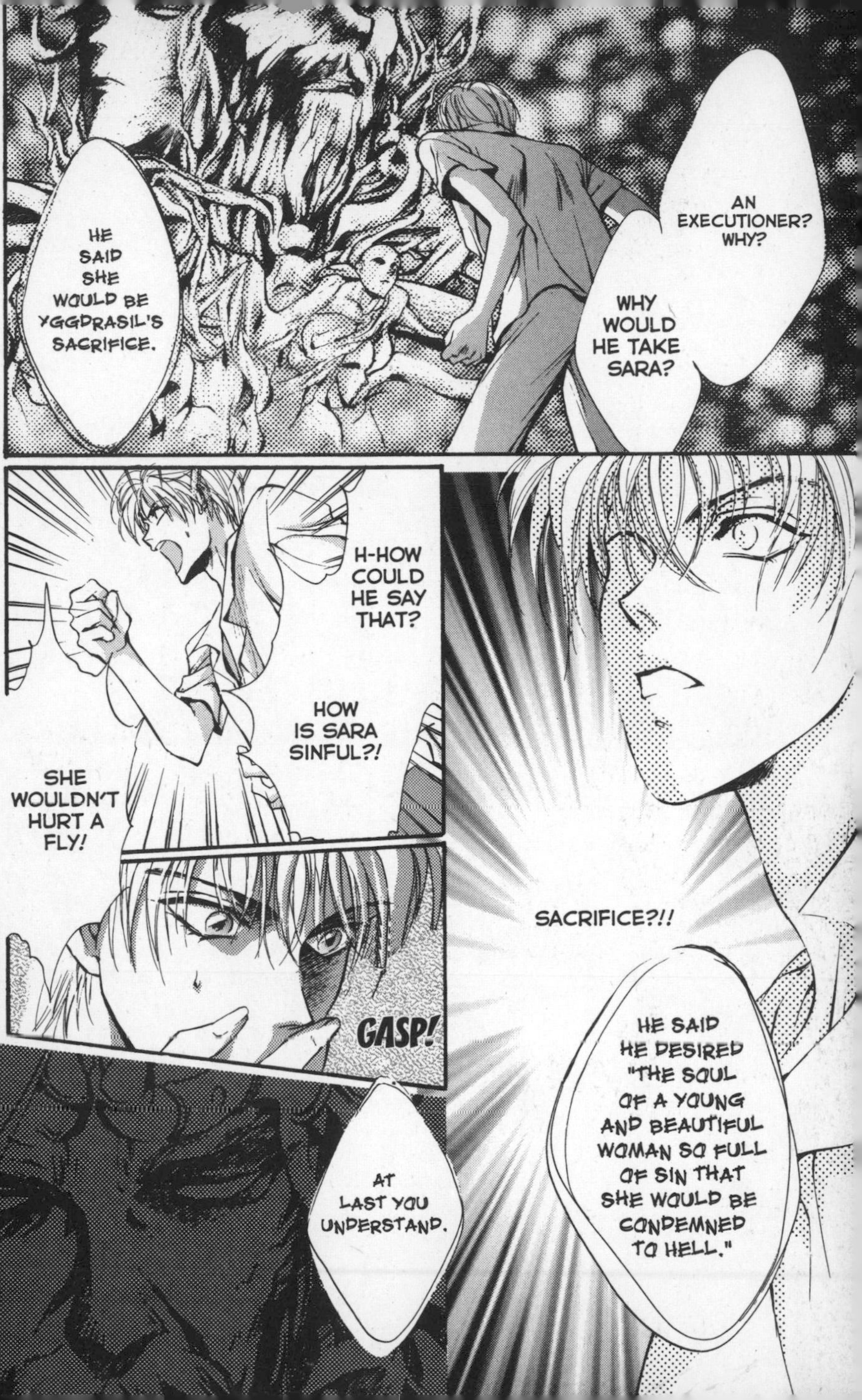
AN EXECUTIONER? WHY?
WHY WOULD HE TAKE SARA?
HE SAID SHE WOULD BE YGGDRASIL'S SACRIFICE.
SACRIFICE?!!
HE SAID HE DESIRED "THE SOUL OF A YOUNG AND BEAUTIFUL WOMAN SO FULL OF SIN THAT SHE WOULD BE CONDEMNED TO HELL."
H-HOW COULD HE SAY THAT?
HOW IS SARA SINFUL?!
SHE WOULDN'T HURT A FLY!
GASP!
AT LAST YOU UNDERSTAND.

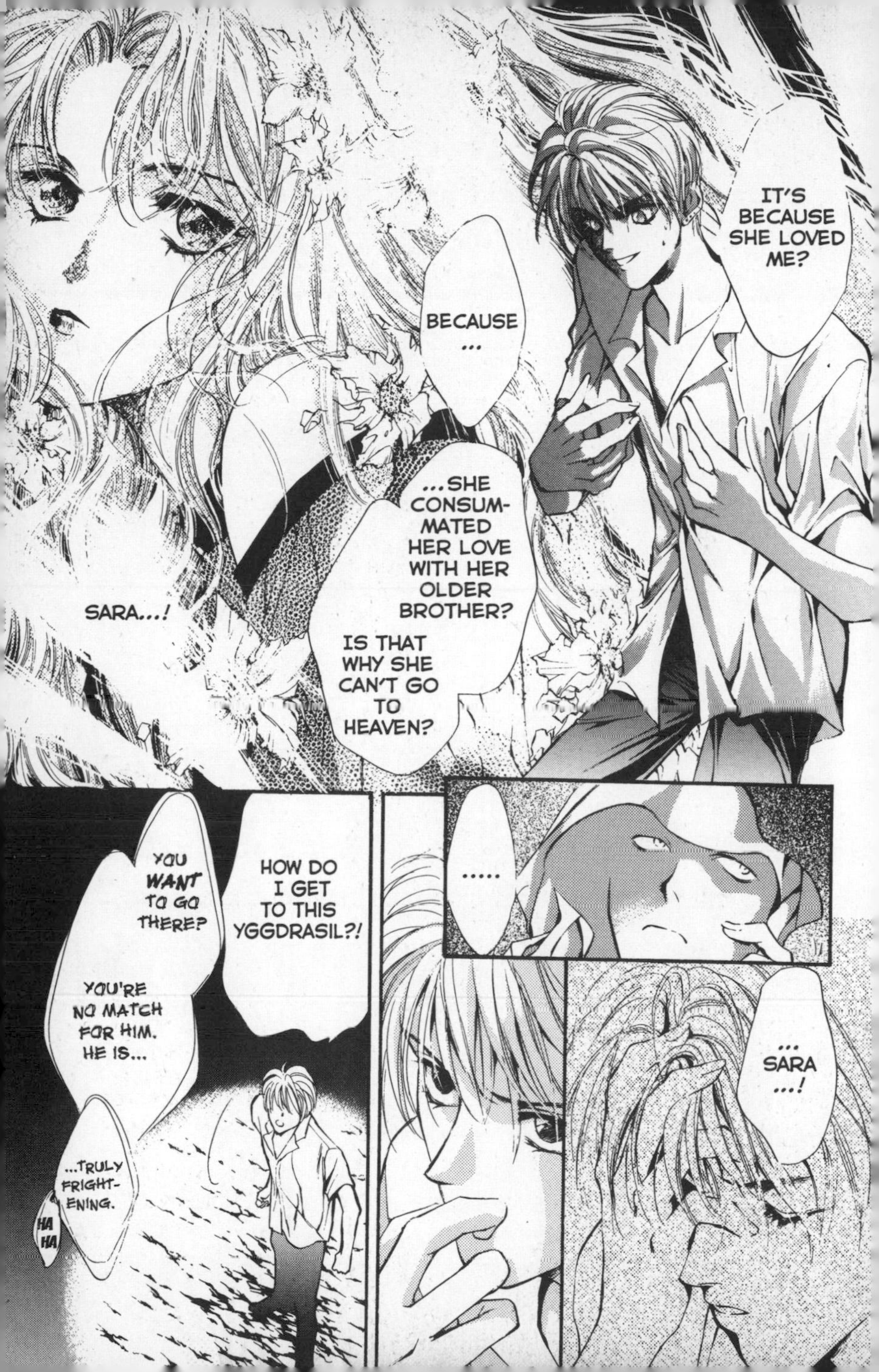
IT'S BECAUSE SHE LOVED ME?
BECAUSE ...
...SHE CONSUM-MATED HER LOVE WITH HER OLDER BROTHER?
IS THAT WHY SHE CAN'T GO TO HEAVEN?
SARA...!
.....
... SARA ...!
HOW DO I GET TO THIS YGGDRASIL?!
YOU WANT TO GO THERE?
YOU'RE NO MATCH FOR HIM. HE IS...
...TRULY FRIGHT-ENING.
HA HA

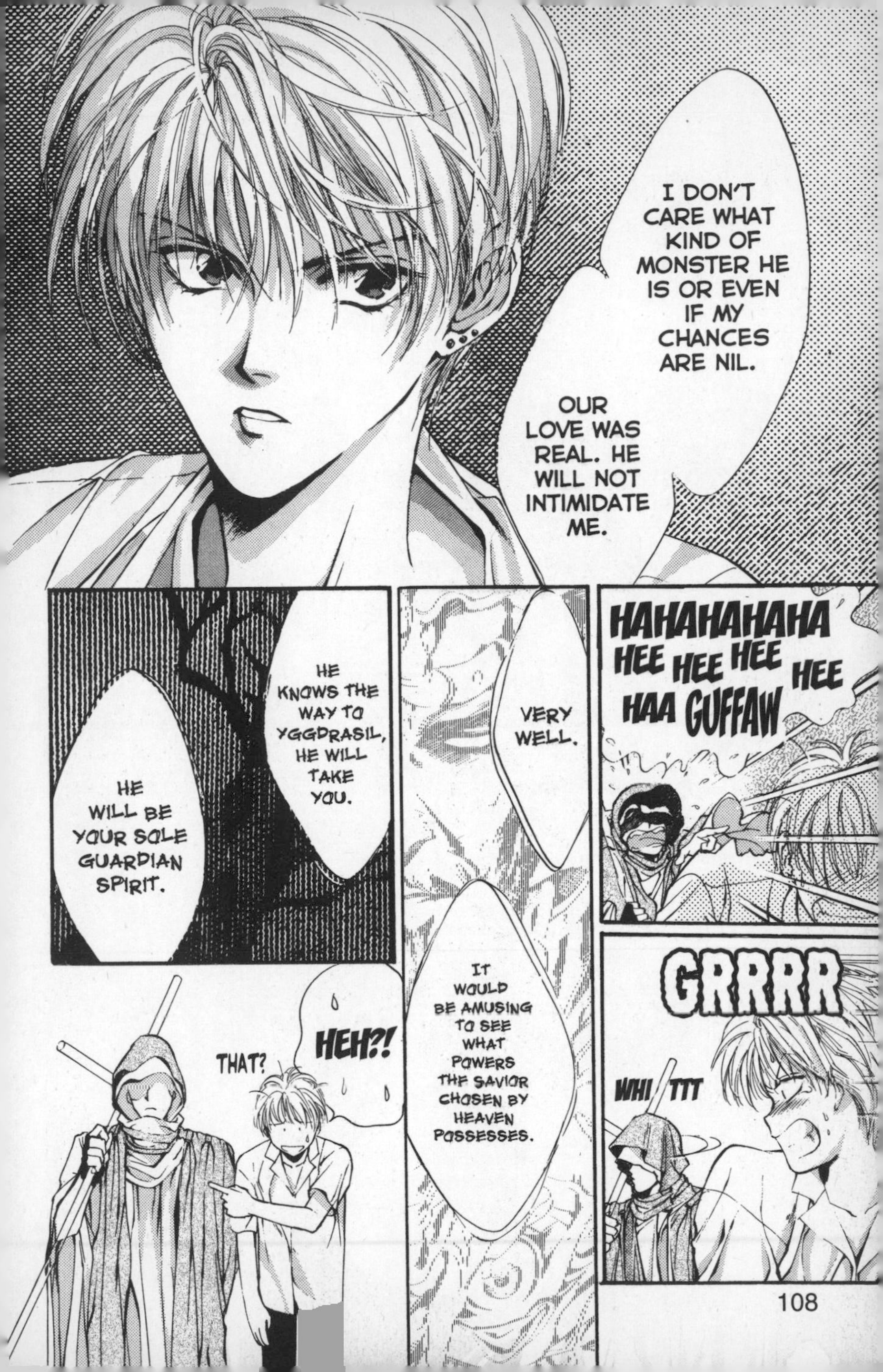
I DON'T CARE WHAT KIND OF MONSTER HE IS OR EVEN IF MY CHANCES ARE NIL.
OUR LOVE WAS REAL. HE WILL NOT INTIMIDATE ME.
HAHAHAHAHA HEE HEE HEE HEE HAA GUFFAW
GRRRR
WHI TTT
VERY WELL.
IT WOULD BE AMUSING TO SEE WHAT POWERS THE SAVIOR CHOSEN BY HEAVEN POSSESSES.
HE KNOWS THE WAY TO YGGDRASIL, HE WILL TAKE YOU.
HE WILL BE YOUR SOLE GUARDIAN SPIRIT.
HEH?!
THAT?

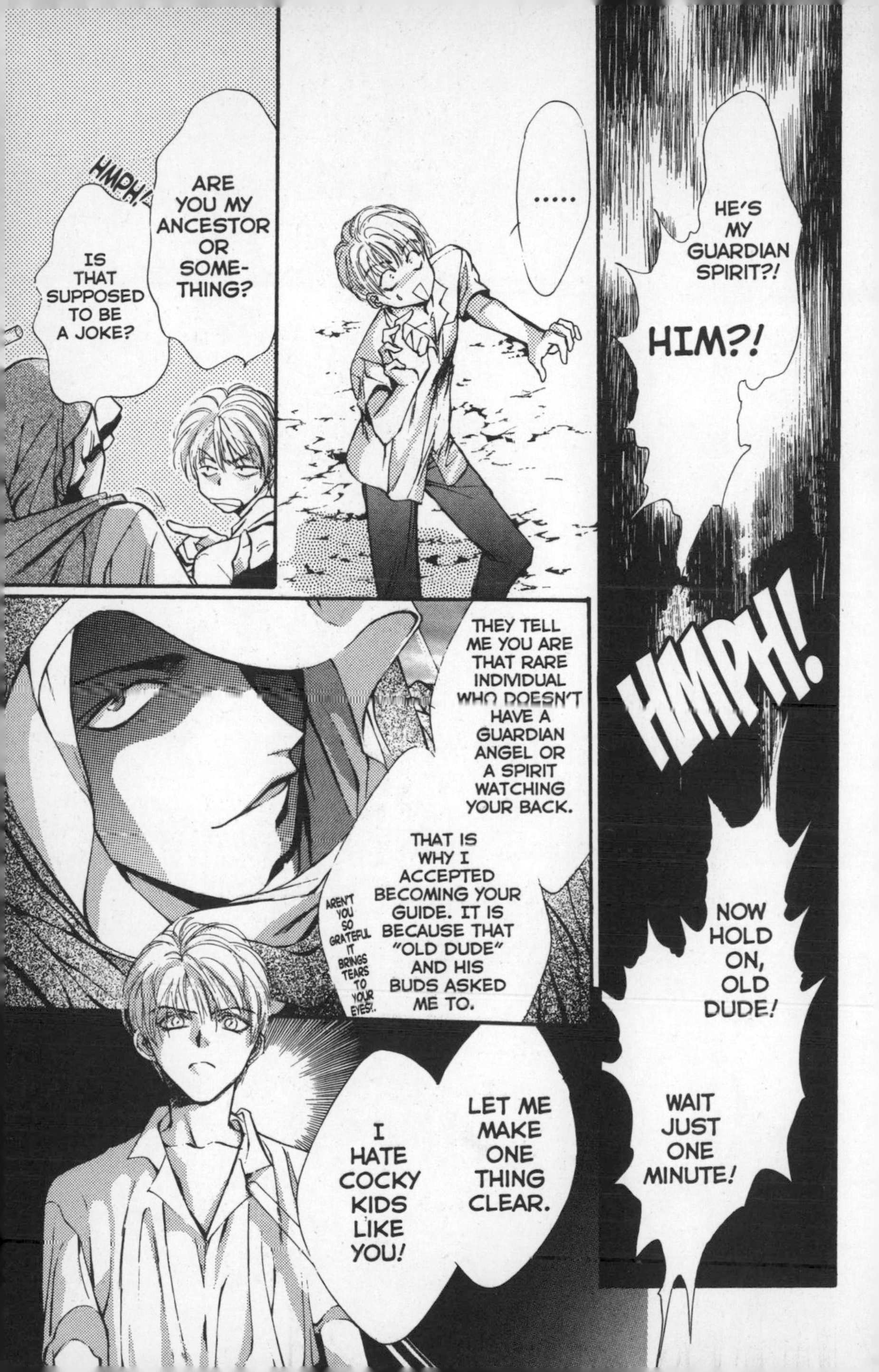
HE'S MY GUARDIAN SPIRIT?!
HIM?!
.....
ARE YOU MY ANCESTOR OR SOME-THING?
IS THAT SUPPOSED TO BE A JOKE?
HMPH!
THEY TELL ME YOU ARE THAT RARE INDIVIDUAL WHO DOESN'T HAVE A GUARDIAN ANGEL OR A SPIRIT WATCHING YOUR BACK.
THAT IS WHY I ACCEPTED BECOMING YOUR GUIDE. IT IS BECAUSE THAT "OLD DUDE" AND HIS BUDS ASKED ME TO.
AREN'T YOU SO GRATEFUL IT BRINGS TEARS TO YOUR EYES?!
HMPH!
NOW HOLD ON, OLD DUDE!
WAIT JUST ONE MINUTE!
LET ME MAKE ONE THING CLEAR.
I HATE COCKY KIDS LIKE YOU!

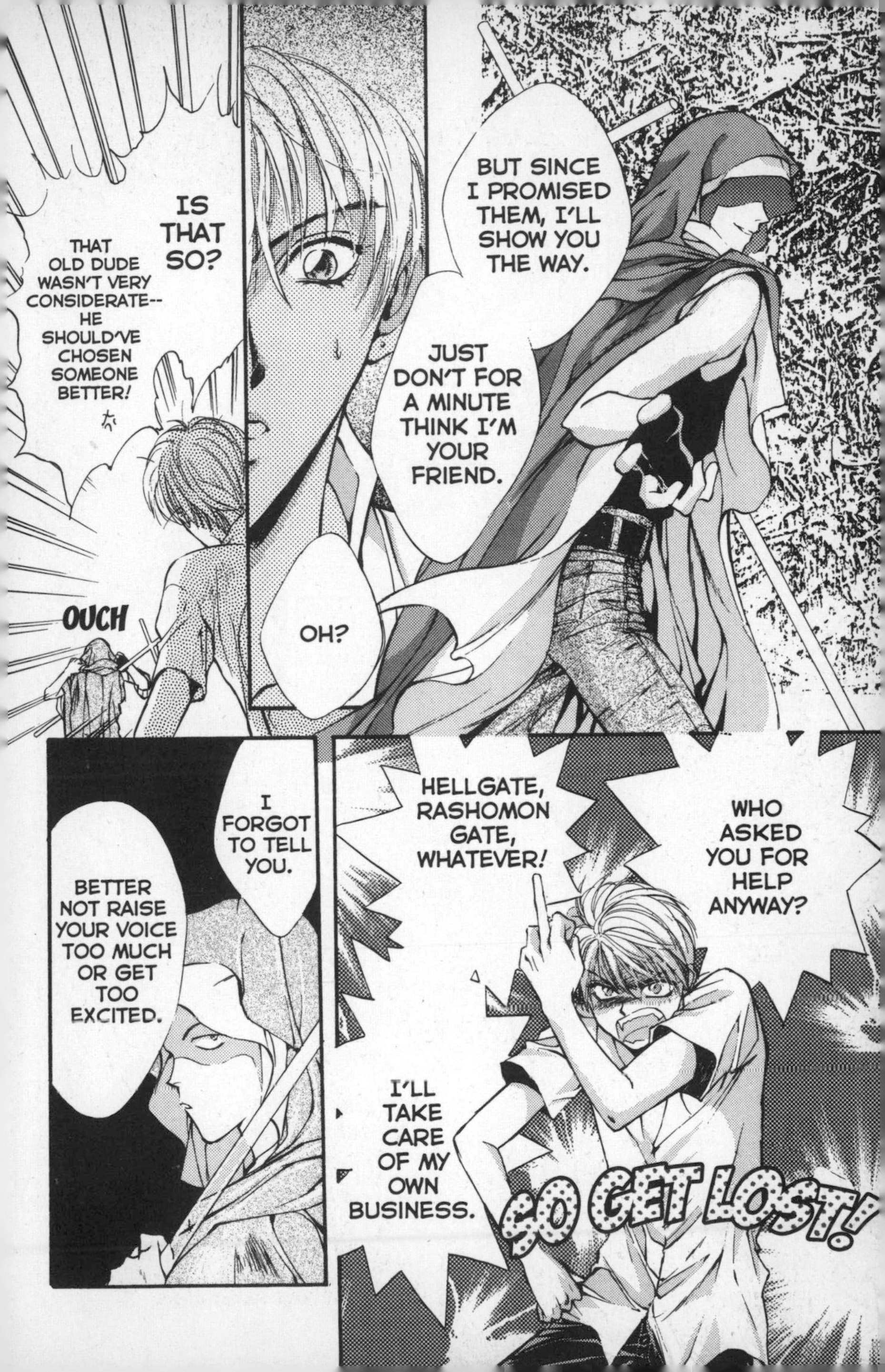
BUT SINCE I PROMISED THEM, I'LL SHOW YOU THE WAY.
JUST DON'T FOR A MINUTE THINK I'M YOUR FRIEND.
OH?
IS THAT SO?
THAT OLD DUDE WASN'T VERY CONSIDERATE-- HE SHOULD'VE CHOSEN SOMEONE BETTER!
OUCH
WHO ASKED YOU FOR HELP ANYWAY?
HELLGATE, RASHOMON GATE, WHATEVER!
I'LL TAKE CARE OF MY OWN BUSINESS.
GO GET LOST!
I FORGOT TO TELL YOU.
BETTER NOT RAISE YOUR VOICE TOO MUCH OR GET TOO EXCITED.

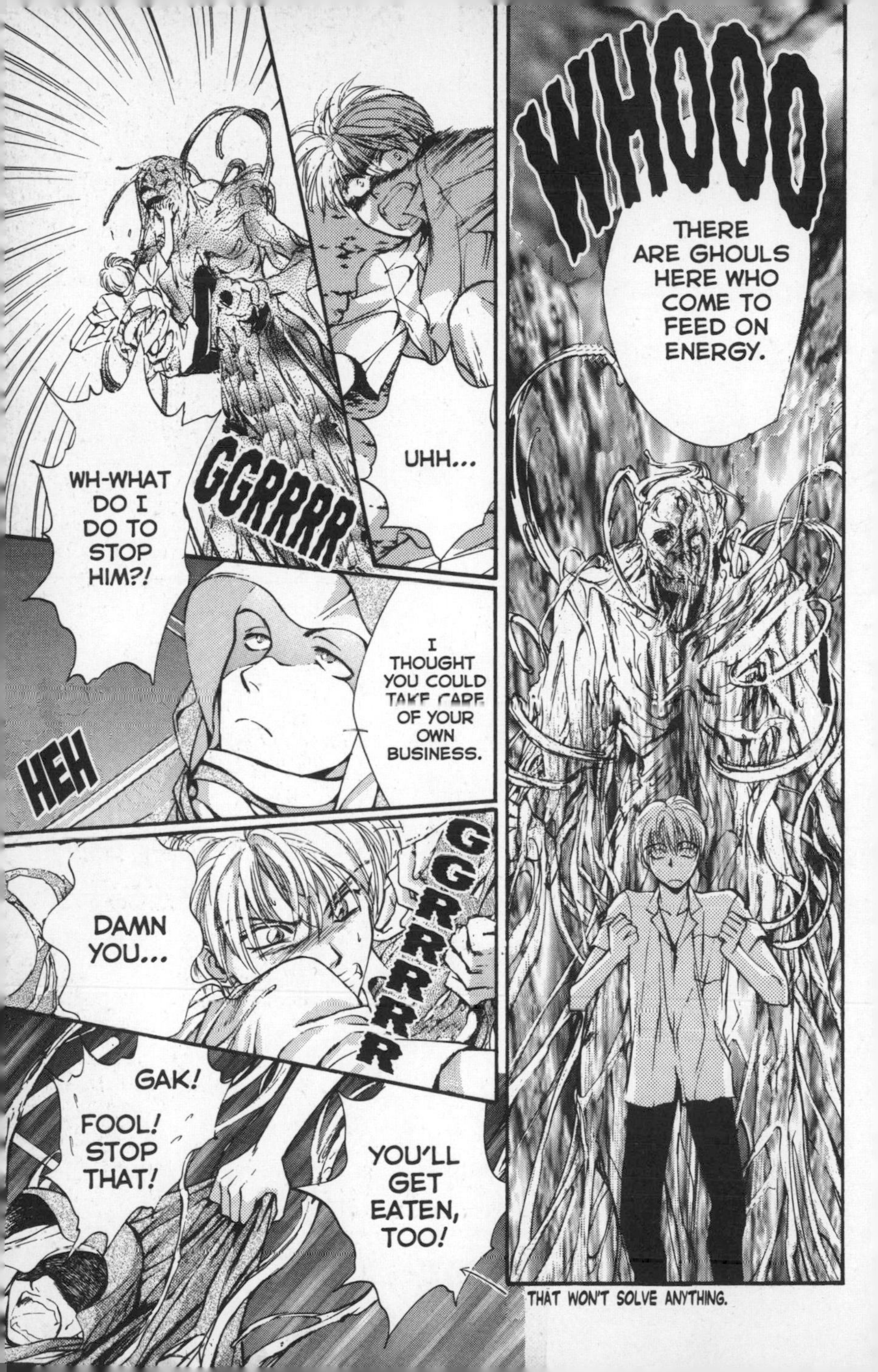
WHOOO
THERE ARE GHOULS HERE WHO COME TO FEED ON ENERGY.
THAT WON'T SOLVE ANYTHING.
UHH...
GGRRRRR
WH-WHAT DO I DO TO STOP HIM?!
I THOUGHT YOU COULD TAKE CARE OF YOUR OWN BUSINESS.
HEH
GGRRRRRR
DAMN YOU...
YOU'LL GET EATEN, TOO!
GAK!
FOOL! STOP THAT!

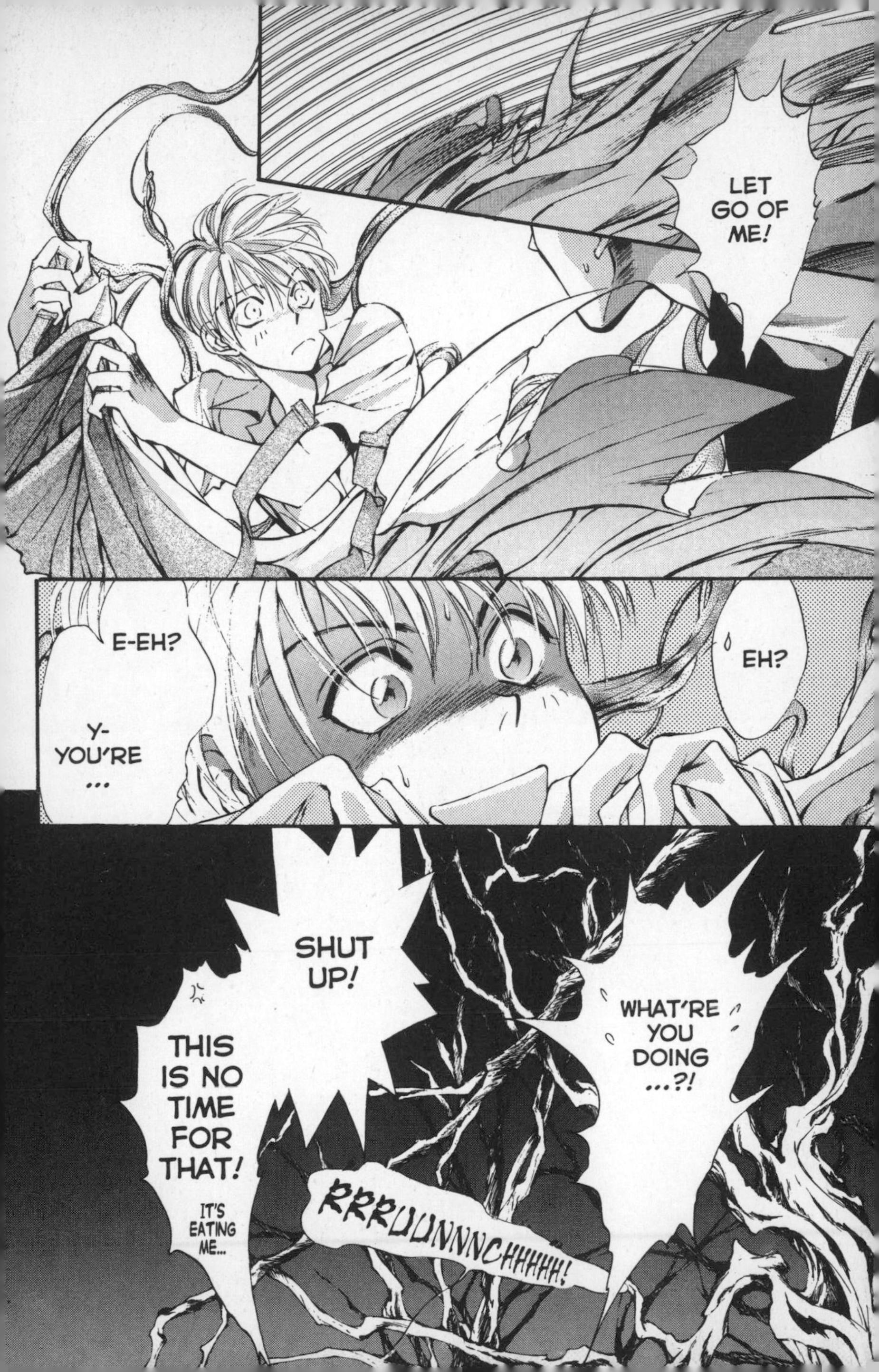
LET GO OF ME!
EH?
E-EH?
Y- YOU'RE ...
WHAT'RE YOU DOING ...?!
SHUT UP!
THIS IS NO TIME FOR THAT!
IT'S EATING ME...
RRRUUNNNCHHHHH!

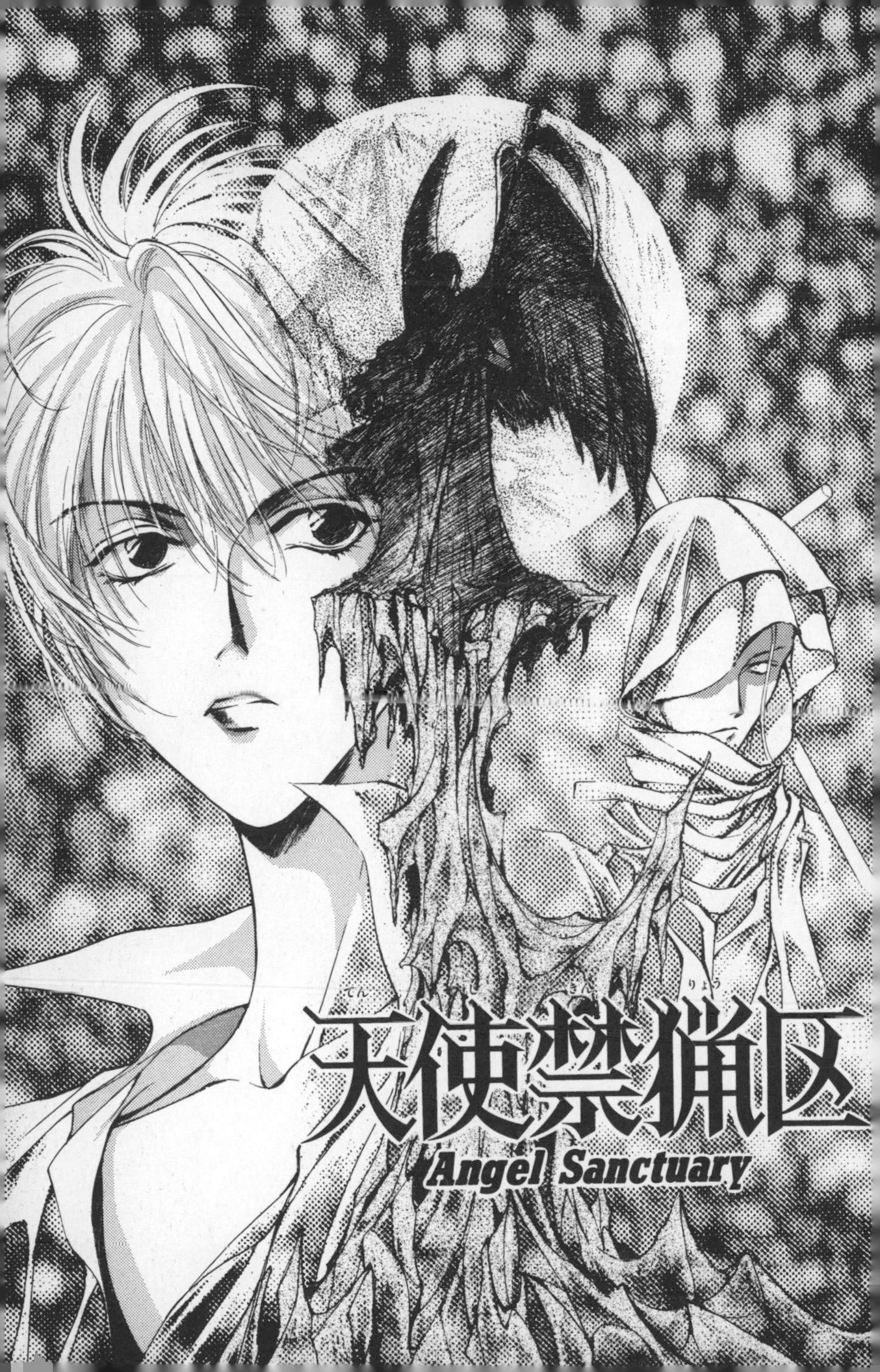
天使禁猟区
Angel Sanctuary

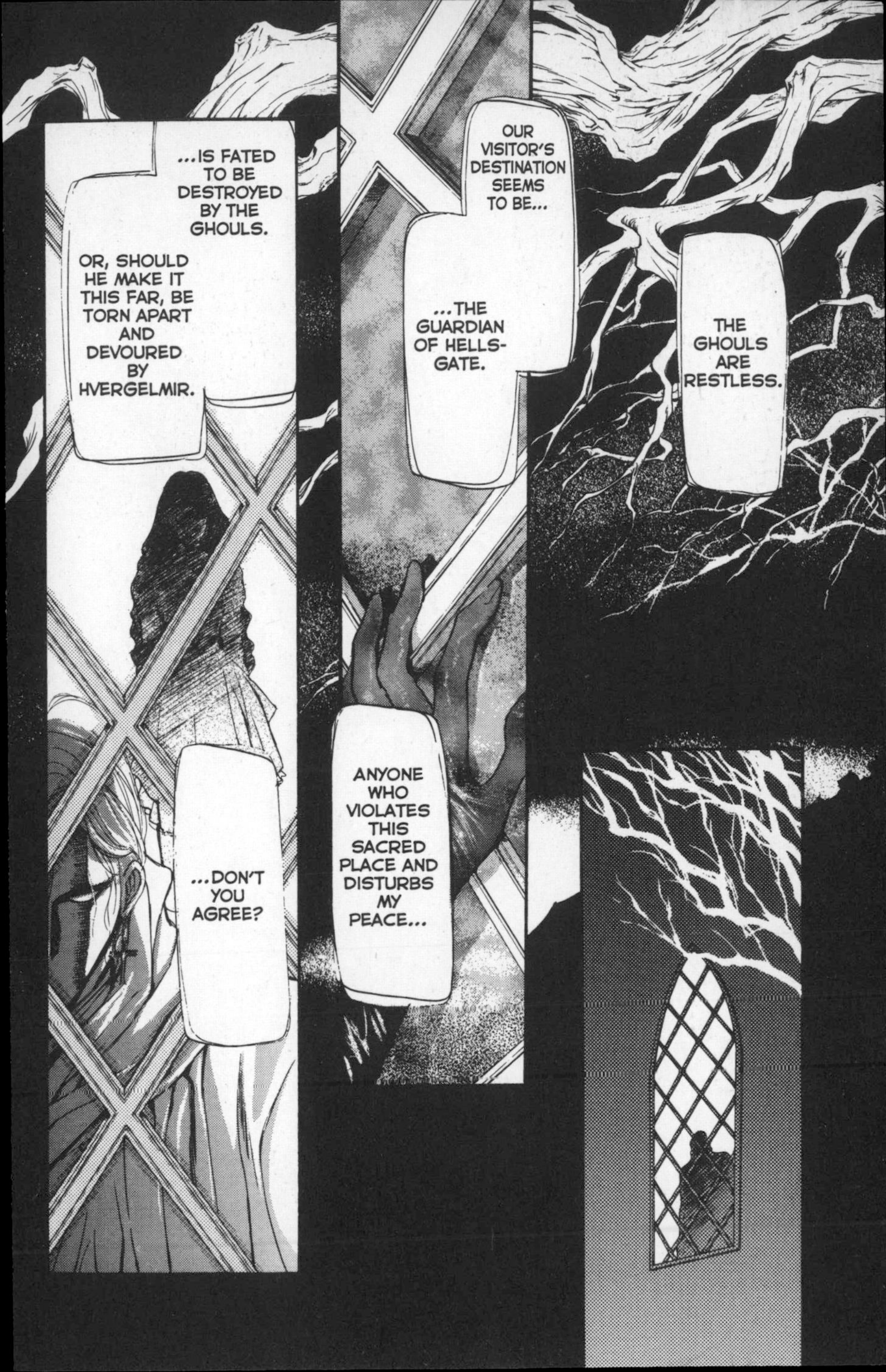
THE GHOULS ARE RESTLESS.
OUR VISITOR'S DESTINATION SEEMS TO BE...
...THE GUARDIAN OF HELLS-GATE.
ANYONE WHO VIOLATES THIS SACRED PLACE AND DISTURBS MY PEACE...
...IS FATED TO BE DESTROYED BY THE GHOULS.
OR, SHOULD HE MAKE IT THIS FAR, BE TORN APART AND DEVOURED BY HVERGELMIR.
...DON'T YOU AGREE?

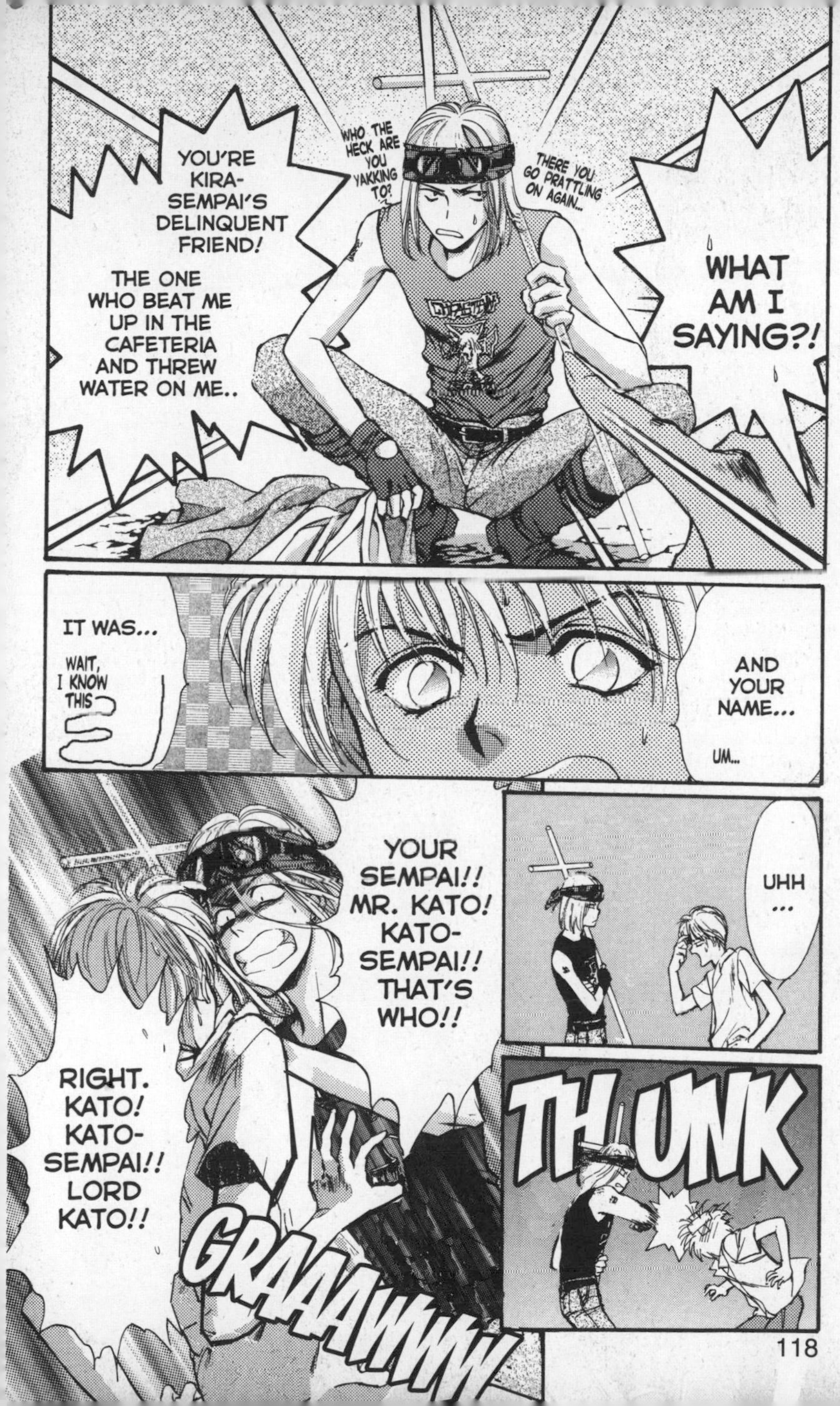
WHO THE HECK ARE YOU YAKKING TO?
THERE YOU GO PRATTLING ON AGAIN...
YOU'RE KIRA-SEMPAI'S DELINQUENT FRIEND!
THE ONE WHO BEAT ME UP IN THE CAFETERIA AND THREW WATER ON ME..
WHAT AM I SAYING?!
AND YOUR NAME...
UM...
IT WAS...
WAIT, I KNOW THIS
UHH ...
THUNK
YOUR SEMPAI!! MR. KATO! KATO-SEMPAI!! THAT'S WHO!!
RIGHT. KATO! KATO-SEMPAI!! LORD KATO!!
GRAAAWWWW

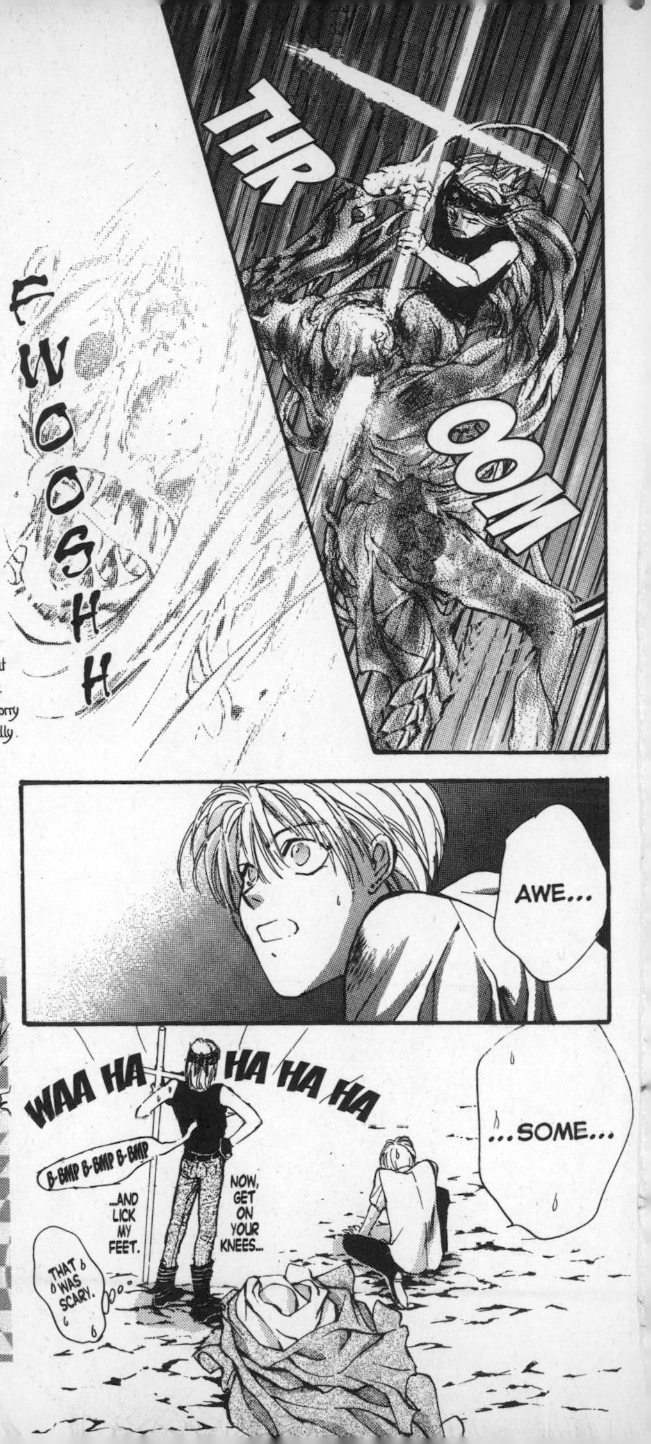
THR
OOM
FWOOSH
AWE...
...SOME...
WAA HA HA HA HA
NOW, GET ON YOUR KNEES...
...AND LICK MY FEET.
B-BMP B-BMP B-BMP
THAT WAS SCARY.

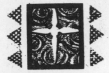

After all is said and done, you've probably guessed that it's Kato's spirit. Some of you wrote thinking it was "that delinquent" because you forgot his name, and some of you even thought it was Kira. Ahhh, I'm able to draw Kato at last. I have a thing for boys with hairstyles like his. And that's in real life, too. Just so you know, he's supposed to be a bleached blonde. The tattoo on his right shoulder is a rose and a rifle, but it really has nothing to do with guns. He seems like the type who might be in a band. What a lucky guy to be able to live his life as he does. Not a worry in the world. I envy him. Really. I think there are a lot of youngsters like him these days.

Don't you think so?

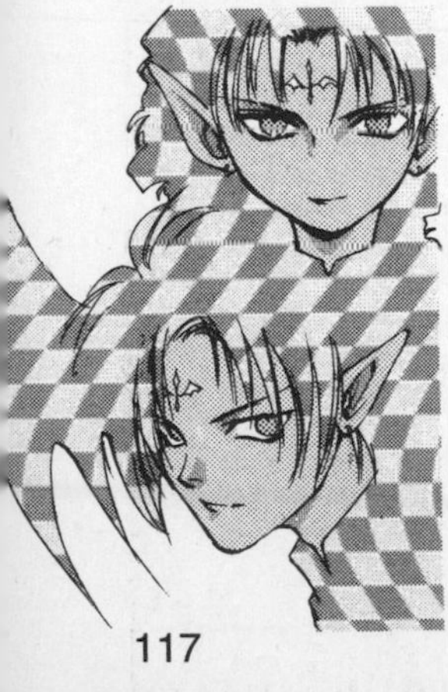

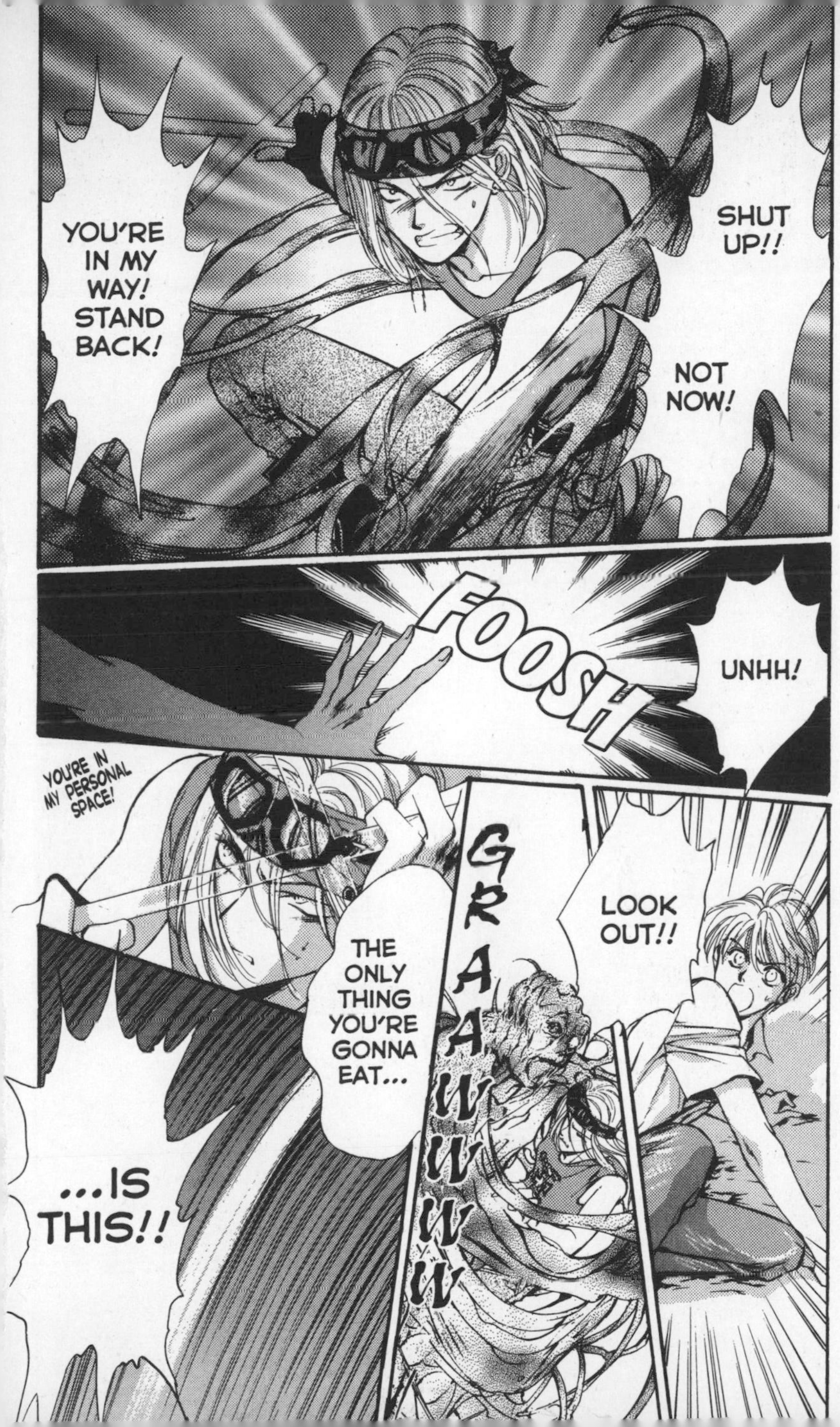
SHUT UP!!
NOT NOW!
YOU'RE IN MY WAY! STAND BACK!
FOOSH
UNHH!
LOOK OUT!!
GRAAWWWW
YOU'RE IN MY PERSONAL SPACE!
THE ONLY THING YOU'RE GONNA EAT...
...IS THIS!!

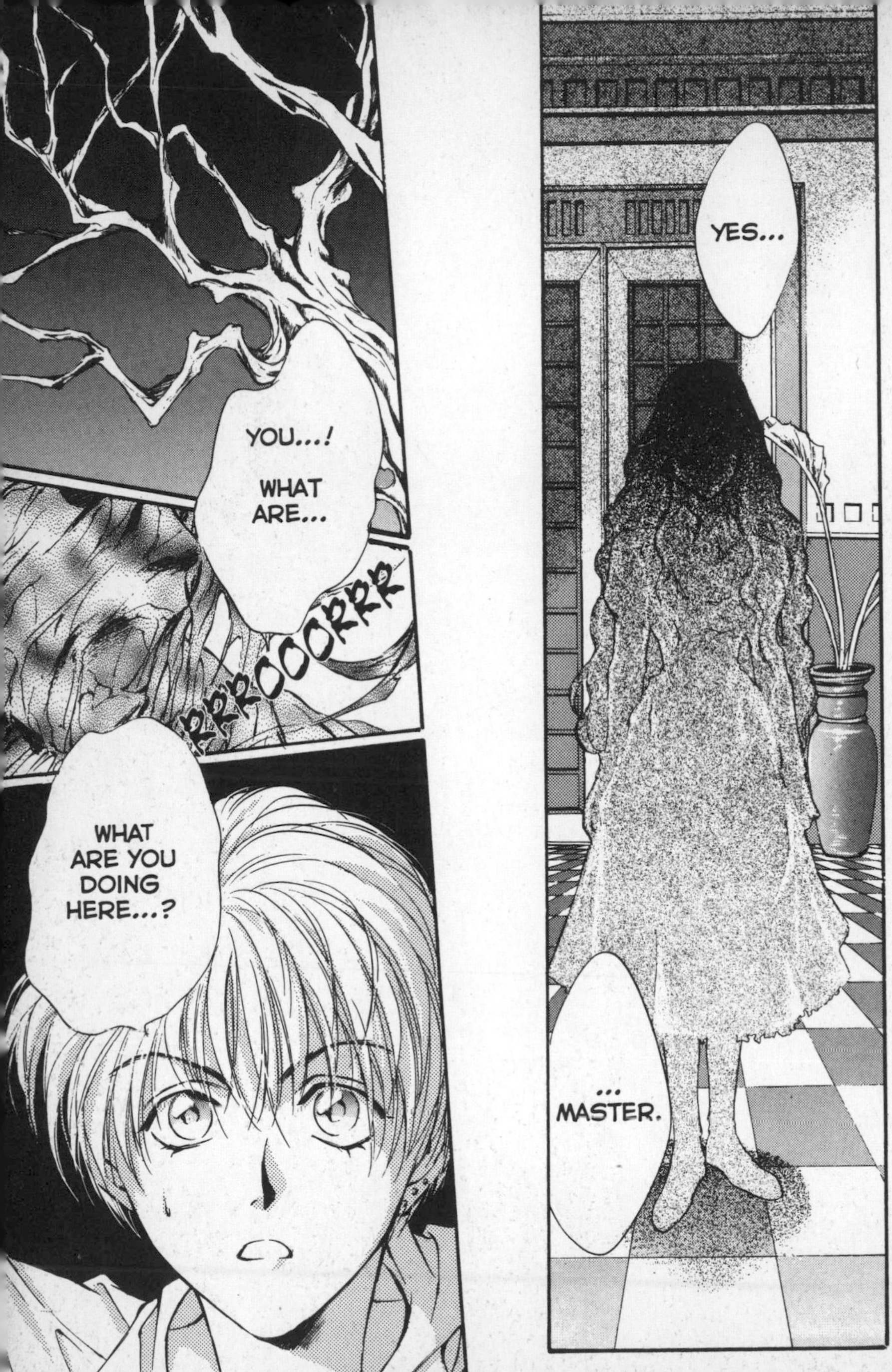
YES...
... MASTER.
YOU...! WHAT ARE...
RRROOORRR
WHAT ARE YOU DOING HERE...?

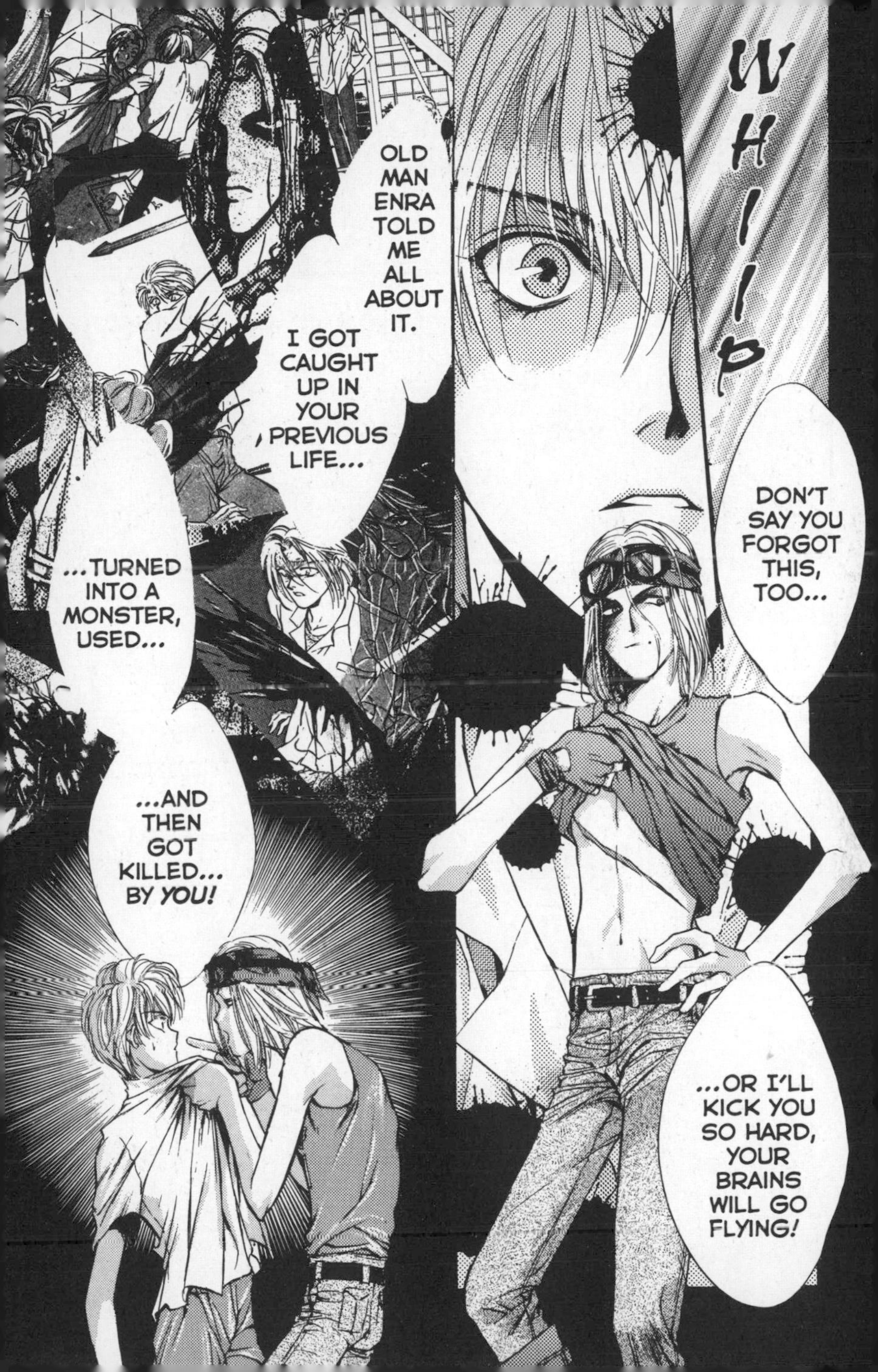
WHIIP
DON'T SAY YOU FORGOT THIS, TOO...
...OR I'LL KICK YOU SO HARD, YOUR BRAINS WILL GO FLYING!
OLD MAN ENRA TOLD ME ALL ABOUT IT.
I GOT CAUGHT UP IN YOUR PREVIOUS LIFE...
...TURNED INTO A MONSTER, USED...
...AND THEN GOT KILLED... BY *YOU!*

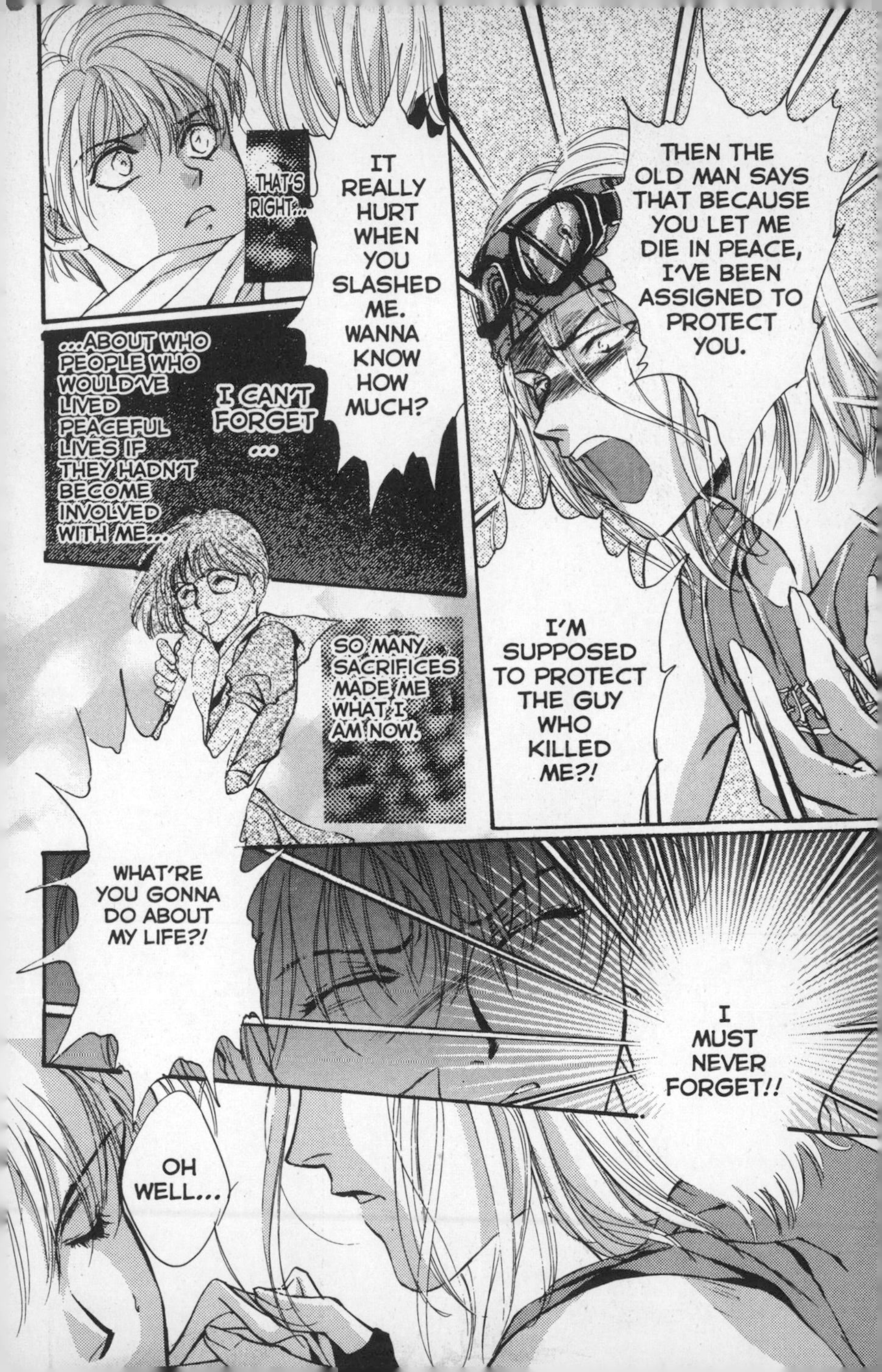

THEN THE OLD MAN SAYS THAT BECAUSE YOU LET ME DIE IN PEACE, I'VE BEEN ASSIGNED TO PROTECT YOU.
I'M SUPPOSED TO PROTECT THE GUY WHO KILLED ME?!
IT REALLY HURT WHEN YOU SLASHED ME. WANNA KNOW HOW MUCH?
THAT'S RIGHT...
I CAN'T FORGET ...
...ABOUT WHO PEOPLE WHO WOULD'VE LIVED PEACEFUL LIVES IF THEY HADN'T BECOME INVOLVED WITH ME...
SO MANY SACRIFICES MADE ME WHAT I AM NOW.
I MUST NEVER FORGET!!
WHAT'RE YOU GONNA DO ABOUT MY LIFE?!
OH WELL...

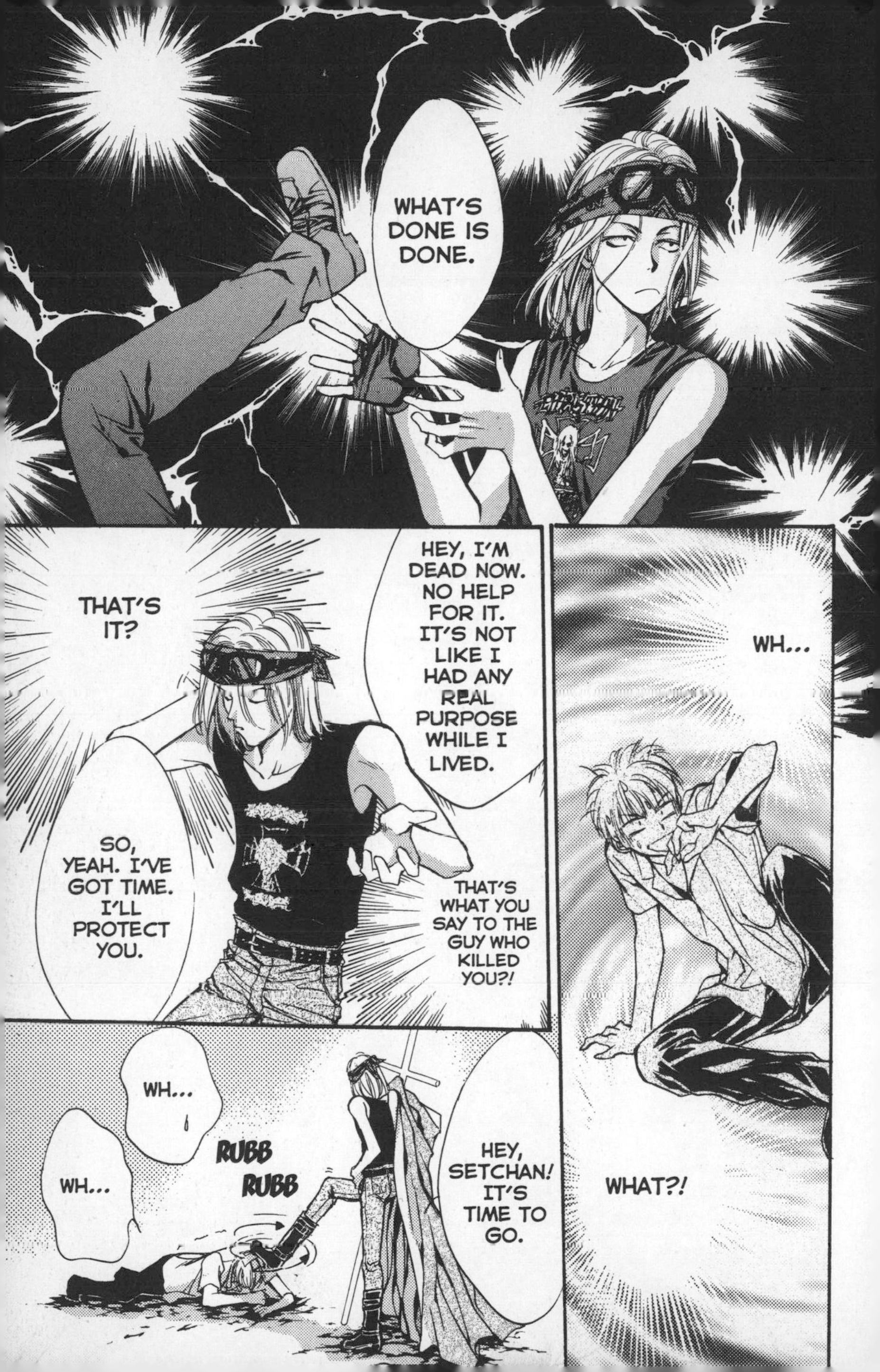
WHAT'S DONE IS DONE.
WH...
WHAT?!
THAT'S IT?
HEY, I'M DEAD NOW. NO HELP FOR IT. IT'S NOT LIKE I HAD ANY REAL PURPOSE WHILE I LIVED.
SO, YEAH. I'VE GOT TIME. I'LL PROTECT YOU.
THAT'S WHAT YOU SAY TO THE GUY WHO KILLED YOU?!
HEY, SETCHAN! IT'S TIME TO GO.
WH...
RUBB
RUBB
WH...

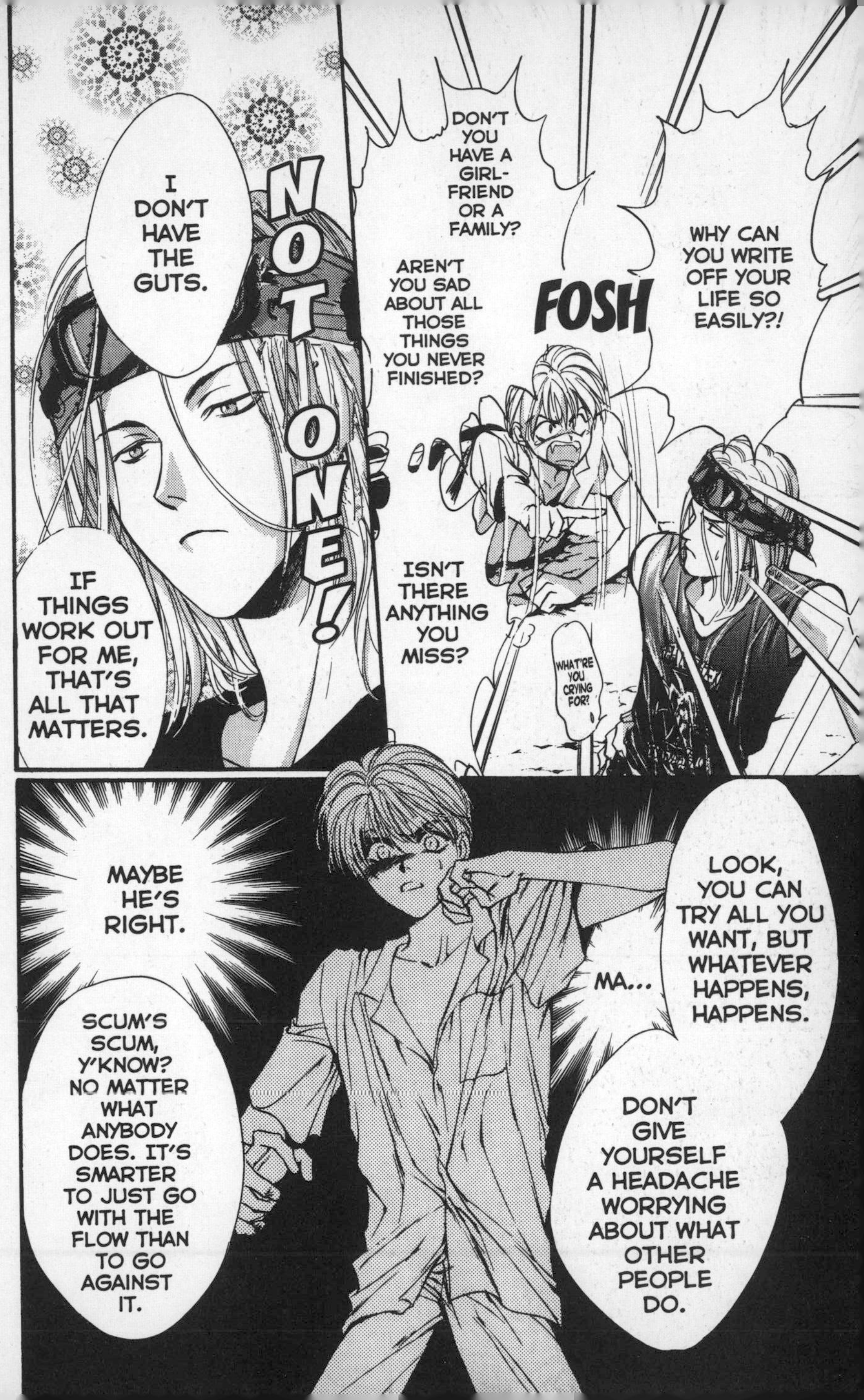
WHY CAN YOU WRITE OFF YOUR LIFE SO EASILY?!
DON'T YOU HAVE A GIRL-FRIEND OR A FAMILY?
FOSH
AREN'T YOU SAD ABOUT ALL THOSE THINGS YOU NEVER FINISHED?
WHAT'RE YOU CRYING FOR?
ISN'T THERE ANYTHING YOU MISS?
NOT ONE!
I DON'T HAVE THE GUTS.
IF THINGS WORK OUT FOR ME, THAT'S ALL THAT MATTERS.
LOOK, YOU CAN TRY ALL YOU WANT, BUT WHATEVER HAPPENS, HAPPENS.
MA...
MAYBE HE'S RIGHT.
DON'T GIVE YOURSELF A HEADACHE WORRYING ABOUT WHAT OTHER PEOPLE DO.
SCUM'S SCUM, Y'KNOW? NO MATTER WHAT ANYBODY DOES. IT'S SMARTER TO JUST GO WITH THE FLOW THAN TO GO AGAINST IT.

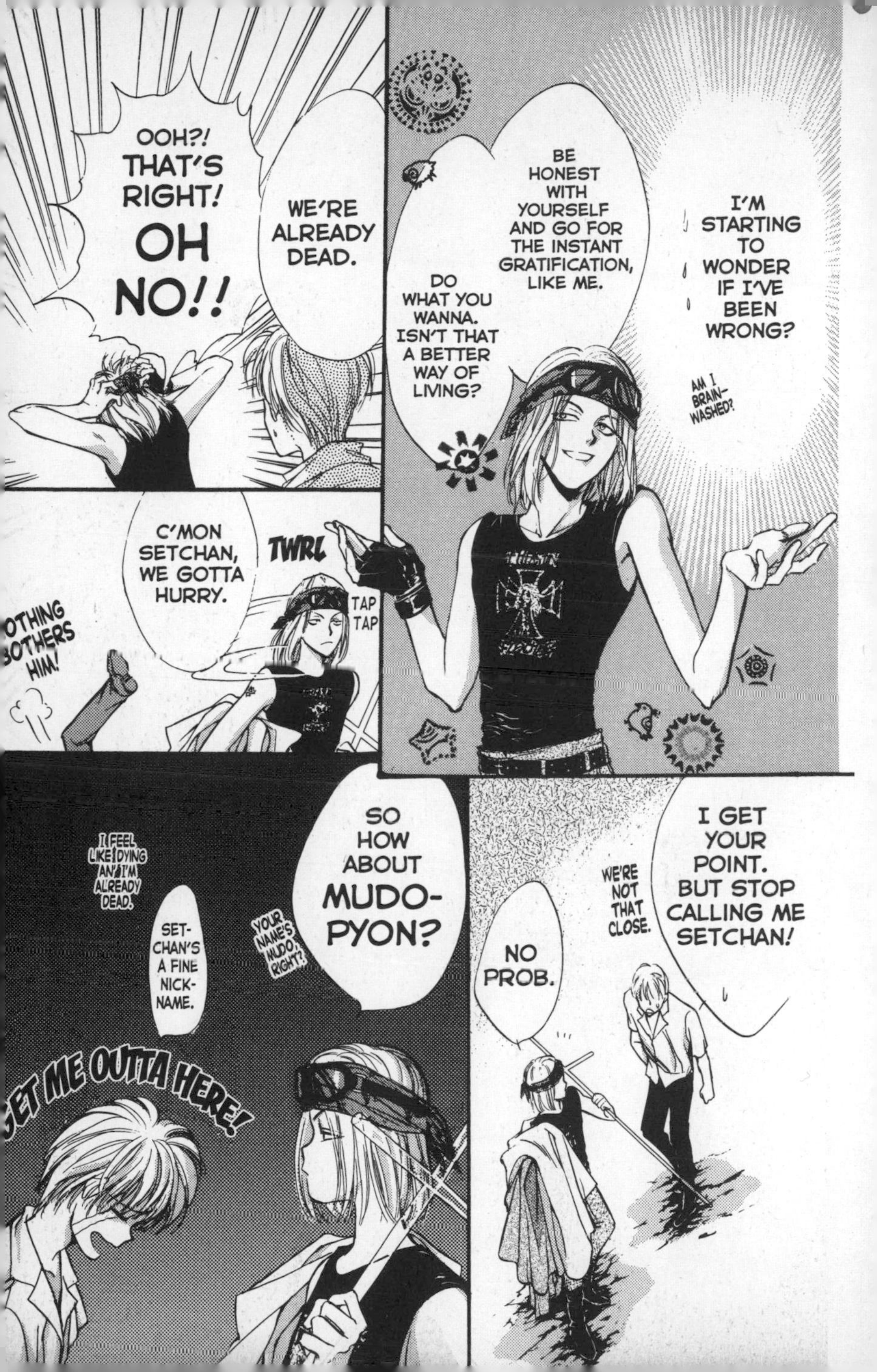
I'M STARTING TO WONDER IF I'VE BEEN WRONG?
AM I BRAIN-WASHED?
BE HONEST WITH YOURSELF AND GO FOR THE INSTANT GRATIFICATION, LIKE ME.
DO WHAT YOU WANNA. ISN'T THAT A BETTER WAY OF LIVING?
WE'RE ALREADY DEAD.
OOH?! THAT'S RIGHT! OH NO!!
TAP TAP
TWRL
C'MON SETCHAN, WE GOTTA HURRY.
OTHING BOTHERS HIM!
I GET YOUR POINT. BUT STOP CALLING ME SETCHAN!
WE'RE NOT THAT CLOSE.
NO PROB.
SO HOW ABOUT MUDO-PYON?
YOUR NAME'S MUDO, RIGHT?
SET-CHAN'S A FINE NICK-NAME.
I FEEL LIKE DYING AN' I'M ALREADY DEAD.
GET ME OUTTA HERE!

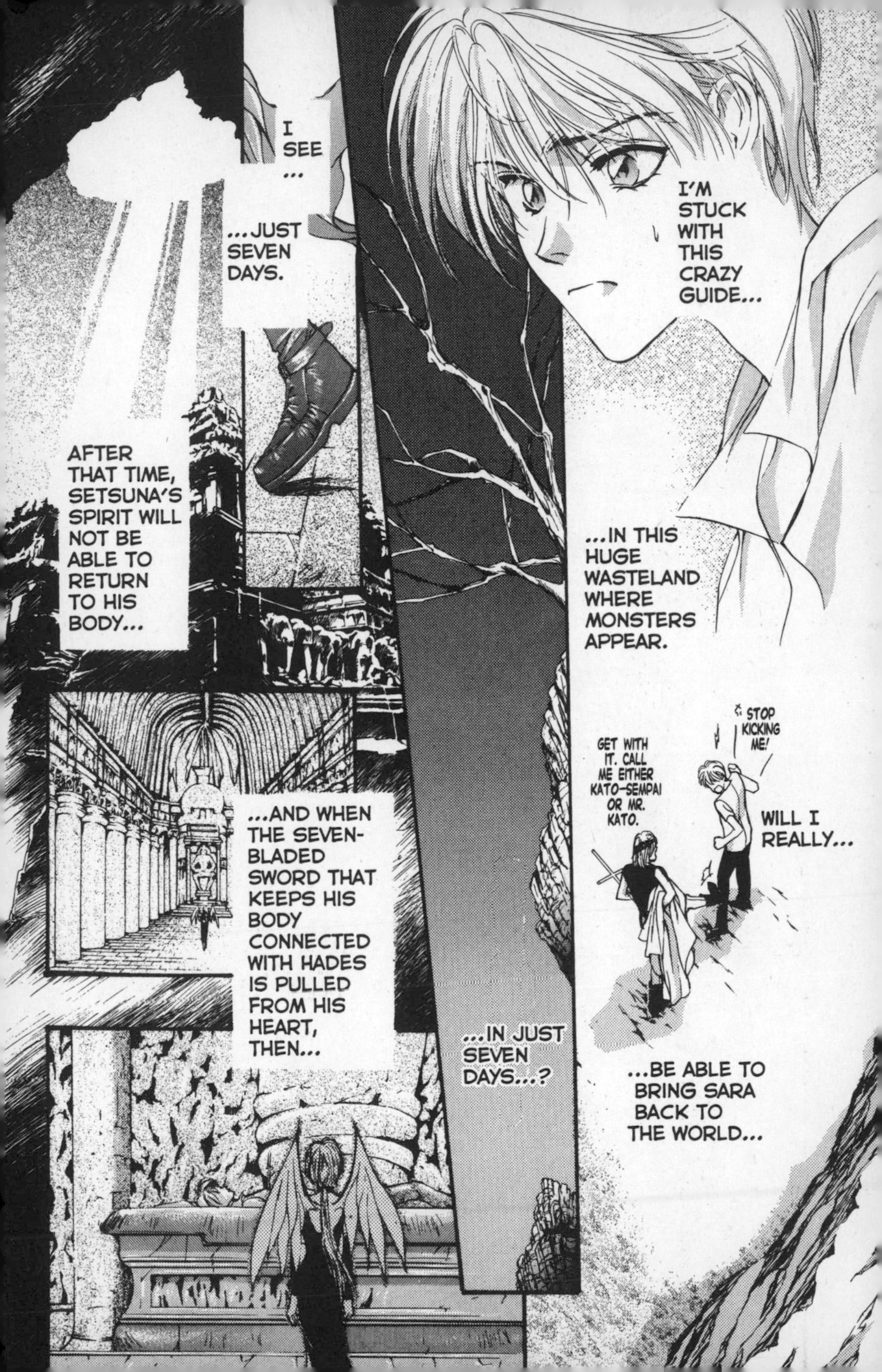
I'M STUCK WITH THIS CRAZY GUIDE...
...IN THIS HUGE WASTELAND WHERE MONSTERS APPEAR.
STOP KICKING ME!
GET WITH IT. CALL ME EITHER KATO-SEMPAI OR MR. KATO.
WILL I REALLY...
...BE ABLE TO BRING SARA BACK TO THE WORLD...
...IN JUST SEVEN DAYS...?
I SEE ...
...JUST SEVEN DAYS.
AFTER THAT TIME, SETSUNA'S SPIRIT WILL NOT BE ABLE TO RETURN TO HIS BODY...
...AND WHEN THE SEVEN-BLADED SWORD THAT KEEPS HIS BODY CONNECTED WITH HADES IS PULLED FROM HIS HEART, THEN...

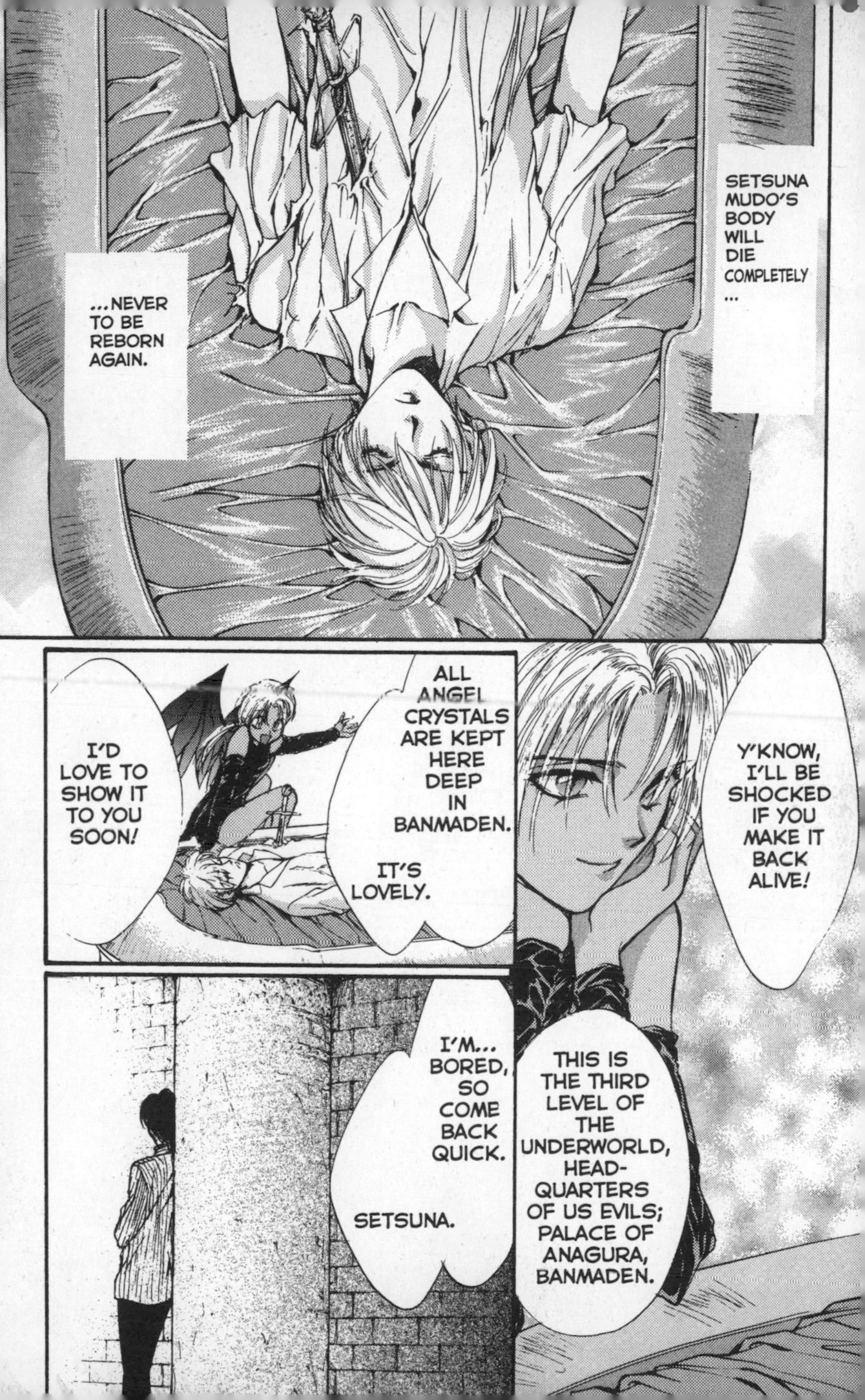
SETSUNA MUDO'S BODY WILL DIE COMPLETELY...
...NEVER TO BE REBORN AGAIN.
Y'KNOW, I'LL BE SHOCKED IF YOU MAKE IT BACK ALIVE!
THIS IS THE THIRD LEVEL OF THE UNDERWORLD, HEAD-QUARTERS OF US EVILS; PALACE OF ANAGURA, BANMADEN.
ALL ANGEL CRYSTALS ARE KEPT HERE DEEP IN BANMADEN.
IT'S LOVELY.
I'D LOVE TO SHOW IT TO YOU SOON!
I'M... BORED, SO COME BACK QUICK.
SETSUNA.

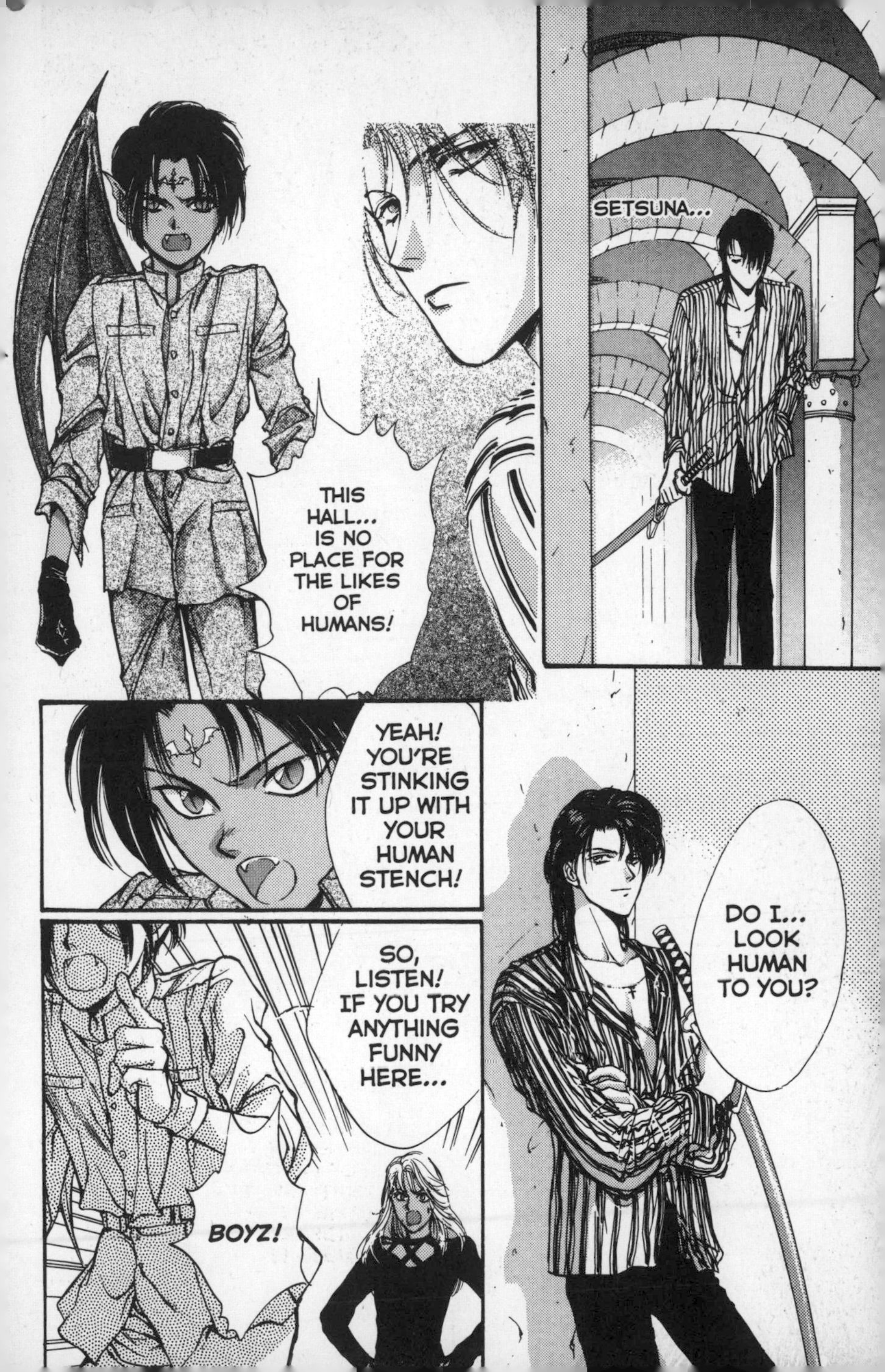
SETSUNA...
THIS HALL... IS NO PLACE FOR THE LIKES OF HUMANS!
DO I... LOOK HUMAN TO YOU?
YEAH! YOU'RE STINKING IT UP WITH YOUR HUMAN STENCH!
SO, LISTEN! IF YOU TRY ANYTHING FUNNY HERE...
BOYZ!

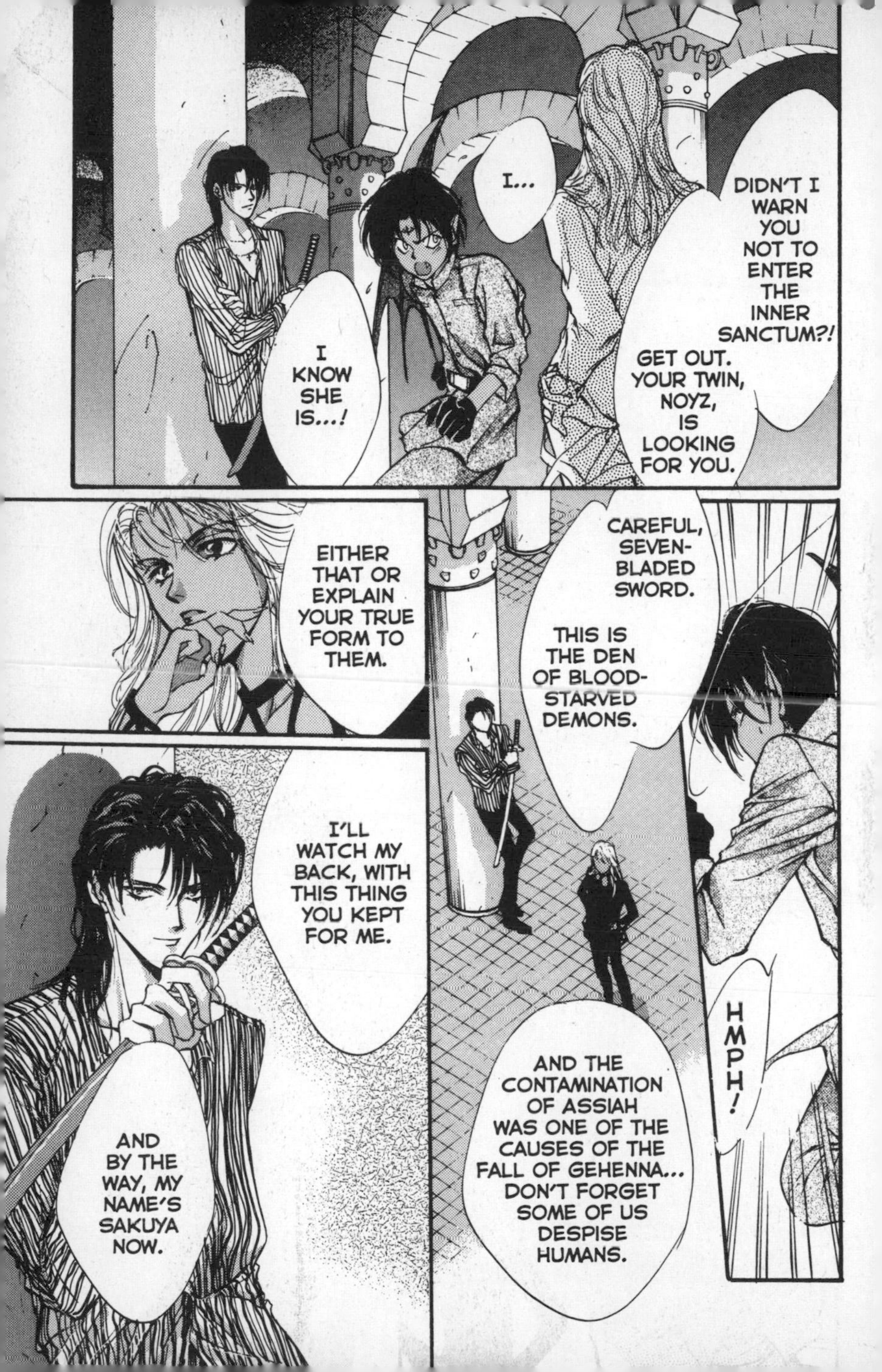
DIDN'T I WARN YOU NOT TO ENTER THE INNER SANCTUM?!
GET OUT. YOUR TWIN, NOYZ, IS LOOKING FOR YOU.
I...
I KNOW SHE IS...!
HMPH!
CAREFUL, SEVEN-BLADED SWORD.
THIS IS THE DEN OF BLOOD-STARVED DEMONS.
AND THE CONTAMINATION OF ASSIAH WAS ONE OF THE CAUSES OF THE FALL OF GEHENNA... DON'T FORGET SOME OF US DESPISE HUMANS.
EITHER THAT OR EXPLAIN YOUR TRUE FORM TO THEM.
I'LL WATCH MY BACK, WITH THIS THING YOU KEPT FOR ME.
AND BY THE WAY, MY NAME'S SAKUYA NOW.

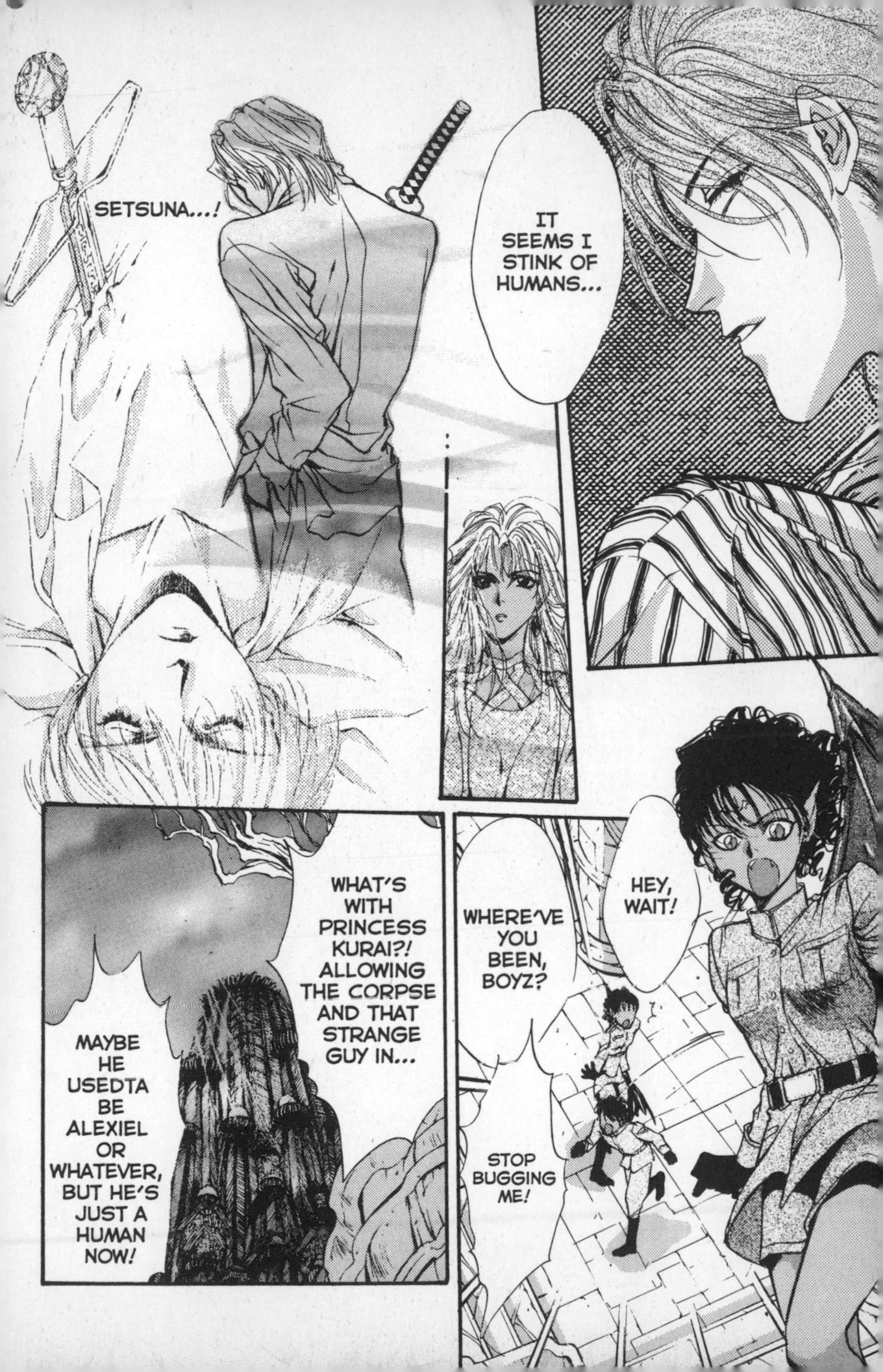
IT SEEMS I STINK OF HUMANS...
SETSUNA...!
HEY, WAIT!
WHERE'VE YOU BEEN, BOYZ?
STOP BUGGING ME!
WHAT'S WITH PRINCESS KURAI?! ALLOWING THE CORPSE AND THAT STRANGE GUY IN...
MAYBE HE USEDTA BE ALEXIEL OR WHATEVER, BUT HE'S JUST A HUMAN NOW!

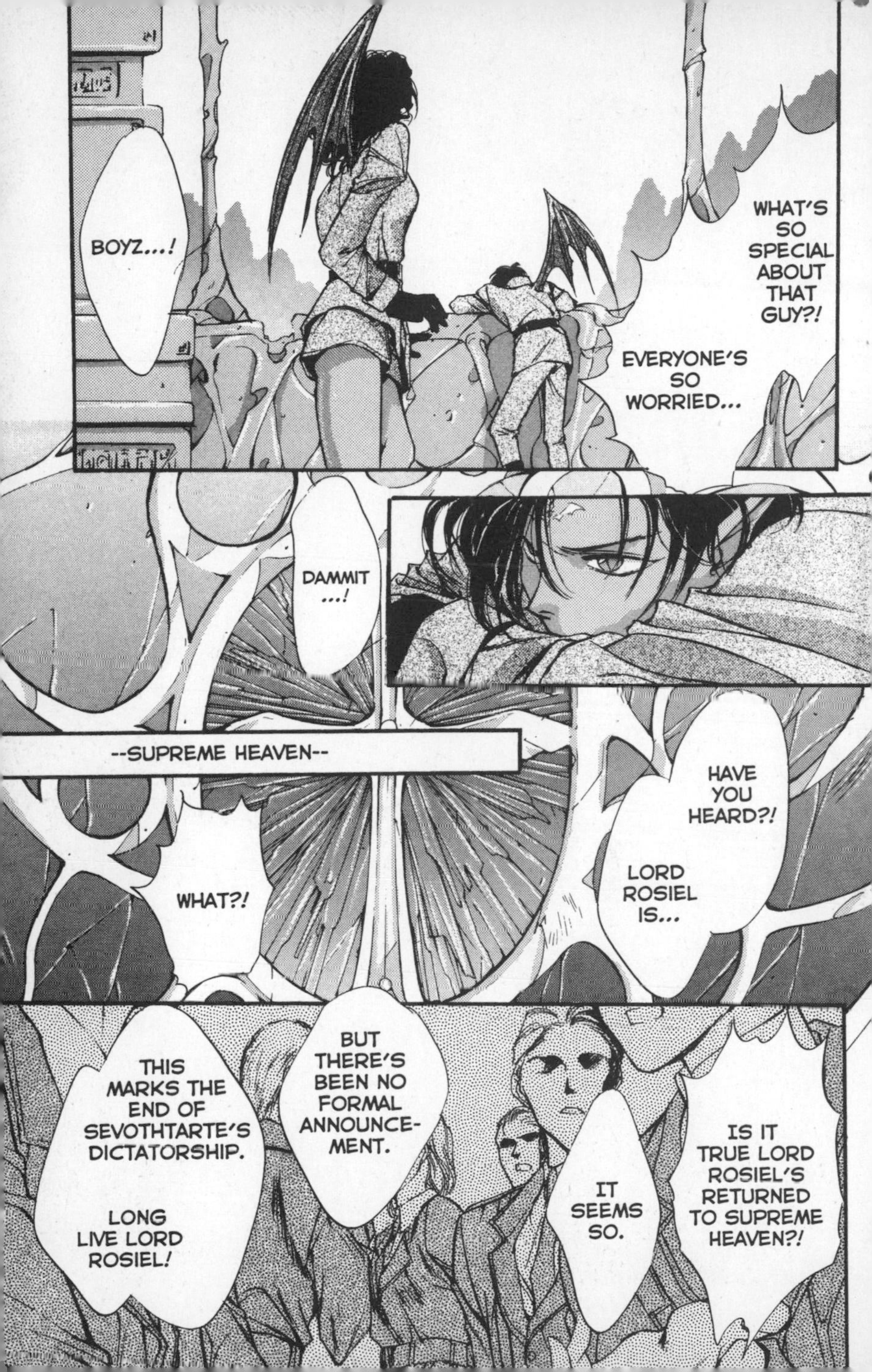
WHAT'S SO SPECIAL ABOUT THAT GUY?!
EVERYONE'S SO WORRIED...
BOYZ...!
DAMMIT...!
--SUPREME HEAVEN--
HAVE YOU HEARD?!
LORD ROSIEL IS...
WHAT?!
IS IT TRUE LORD ROSIEL'S RETURNED TO SUPREME HEAVEN?!
IT SEEMS SO.
BUT THERE'S BEEN NO FORMAL ANNOUNCE-MENT.
THIS MARKS THE END OF SEVOTHTARTE'S DICTATORSHIP.
LONG LIVE LORD ROSIEL!

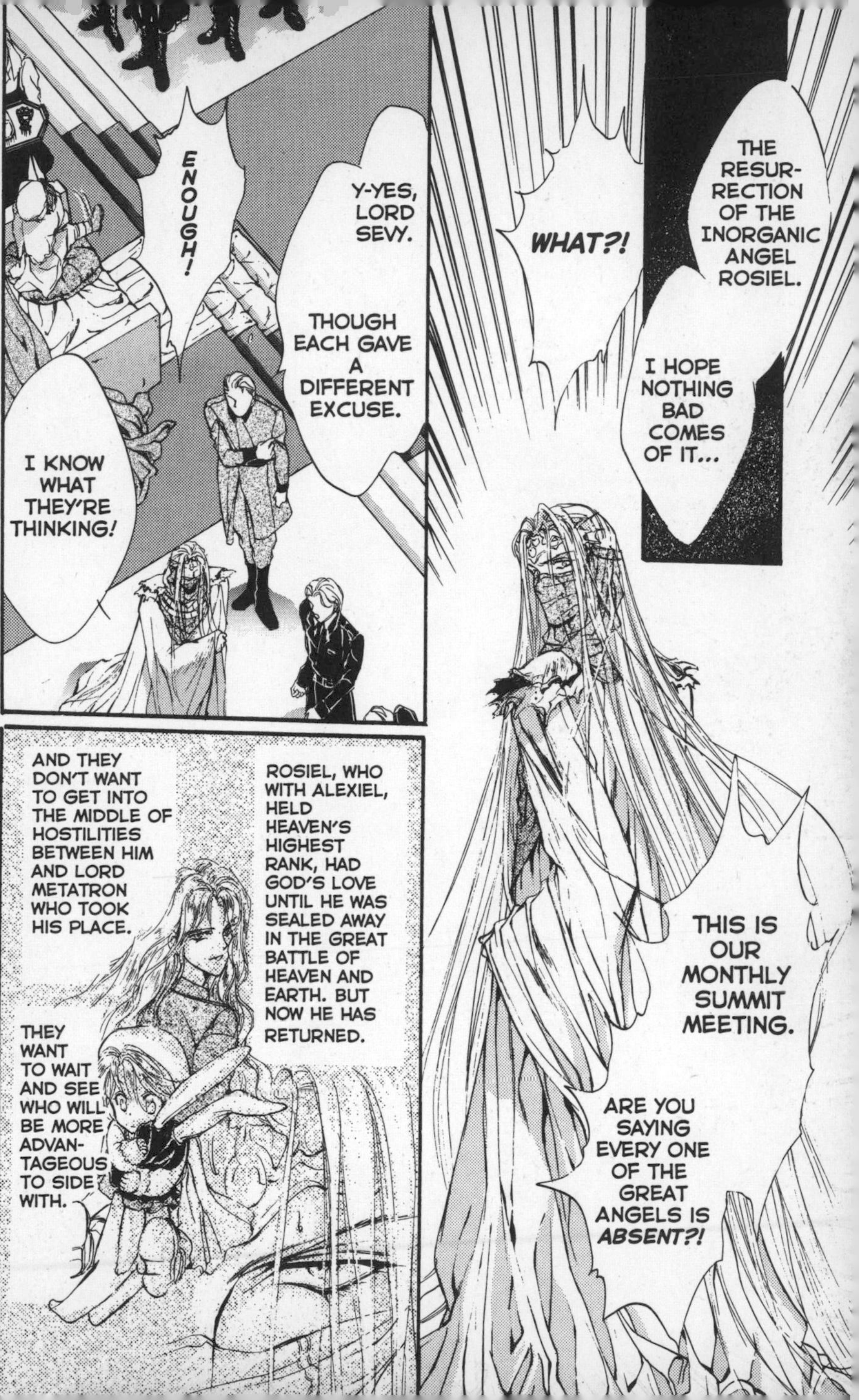
THE RESURRECTION OF THE INORGANIC ANGEL ROSIEL.
I HOPE NOTHING BAD COMES OF IT...
WHAT?!
THIS IS OUR MONTHLY SUMMIT MEETING.
ARE YOU SAYING EVERY ONE OF THE GREAT ANGELS IS ABSENT?!
Y-YES, LORD SEVY.
THOUGH EACH GAVE A DIFFERENT EXCUSE.
ENOUGH!
I KNOW WHAT THEY'RE THINKING!
ROSIEL, WHO WITH ALEXIEL, HELD HEAVEN'S HIGHEST RANK, HAD GOD'S LOVE UNTIL HE WAS SEALED AWAY IN THE GREAT BATTLE OF HEAVEN AND EARTH. BUT NOW HE HAS RETURNED.
AND THEY DON'T WANT TO GET INTO THE MIDDLE OF HOSTILITIES BETWEEN HIM AND LORD METATRON WHO TOOK HIS PLACE.
THEY WANT TO WAIT AND SEE WHO WILL BE MORE ADVANTAGEOUS TO SIDE WITH.

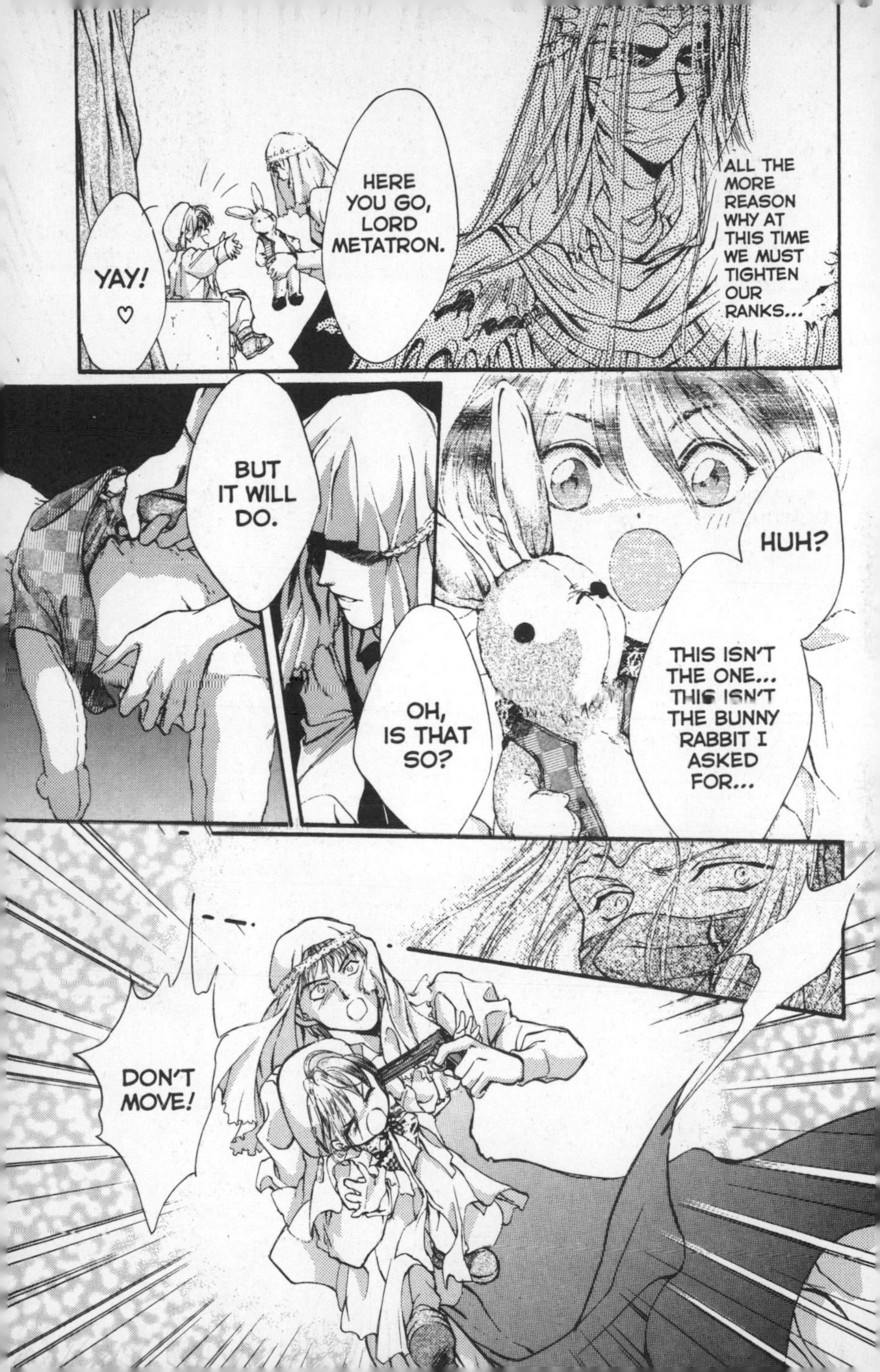
ALL THE MORE REASON WHY AT THIS TIME WE MUST TIGHTEN OUR RANKS...
HERE YOU GO, LORD METATRON.
YAY! ♡
HUH?
THIS ISN'T THE ONE... THIS ISN'T THE BUNNY RABBIT I ASKED FOR...
OH, IS THAT SO?
BUT IT WILL DO.
--!
DON'T MOVE!

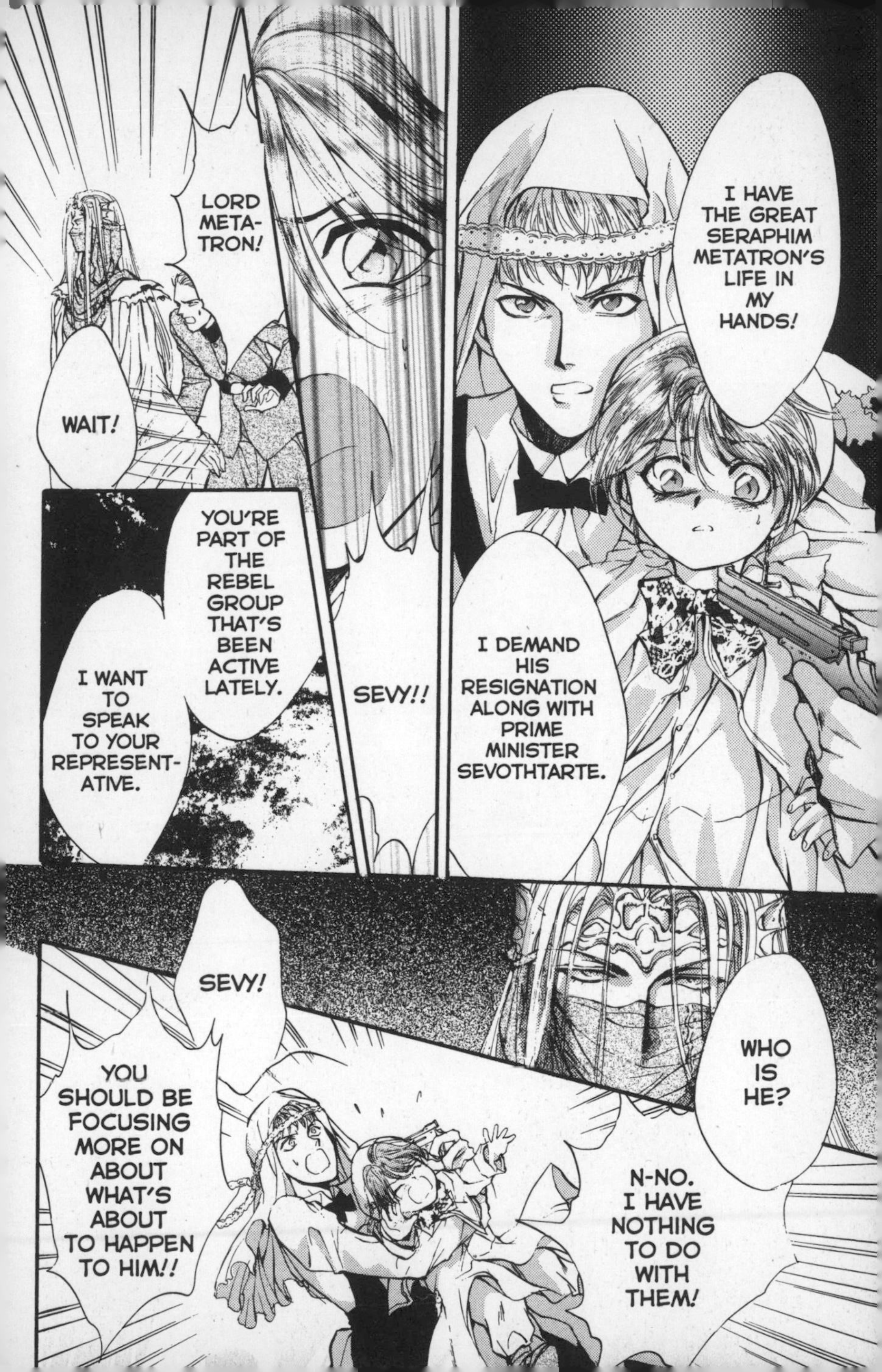
I HAVE THE GREAT SERAPHIM METATRON'S LIFE IN MY HANDS!
I DEMAND HIS RESIGNATION ALONG WITH PRIME MINISTER SEVOTHTARTE.
SEVY!!
LORD META-TRON!
WAIT!
YOU'RE PART OF THE REBEL GROUP THAT'S BEEN ACTIVE LATELY.
I WANT TO SPEAK TO YOUR REPRESENT-ATIVE.
WHO IS HE?
N-NO. I HAVE NOTHING TO DO WITH THEM!
SEVY!
YOU SHOULD BE FOCUSING MORE ON ABOUT WHAT'S ABOUT TO HAPPEN TO HIM!!

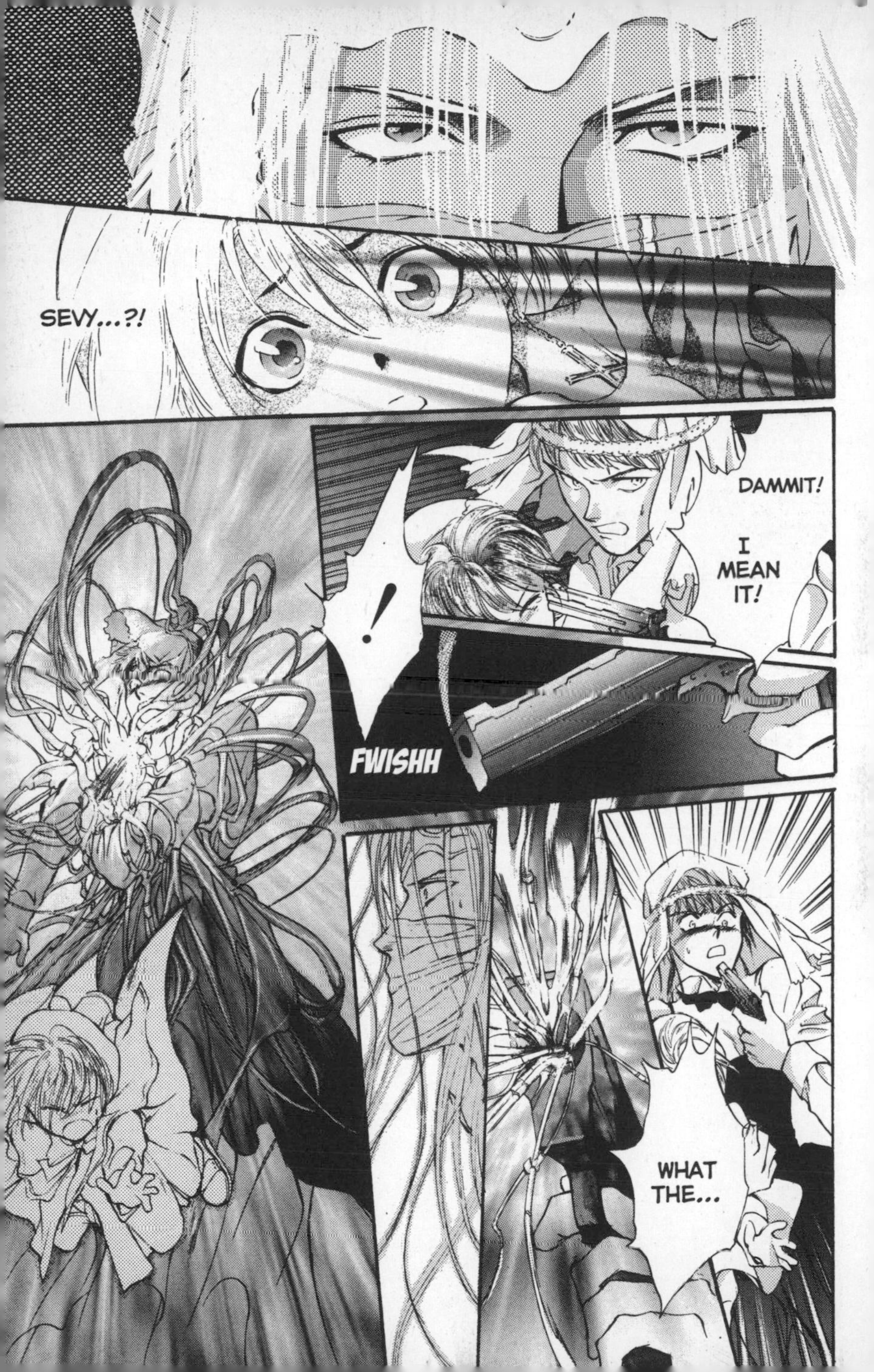
SEVY...?!
DAMMIT!
I MEAN IT!
!
FWISHH
WHAT THE...

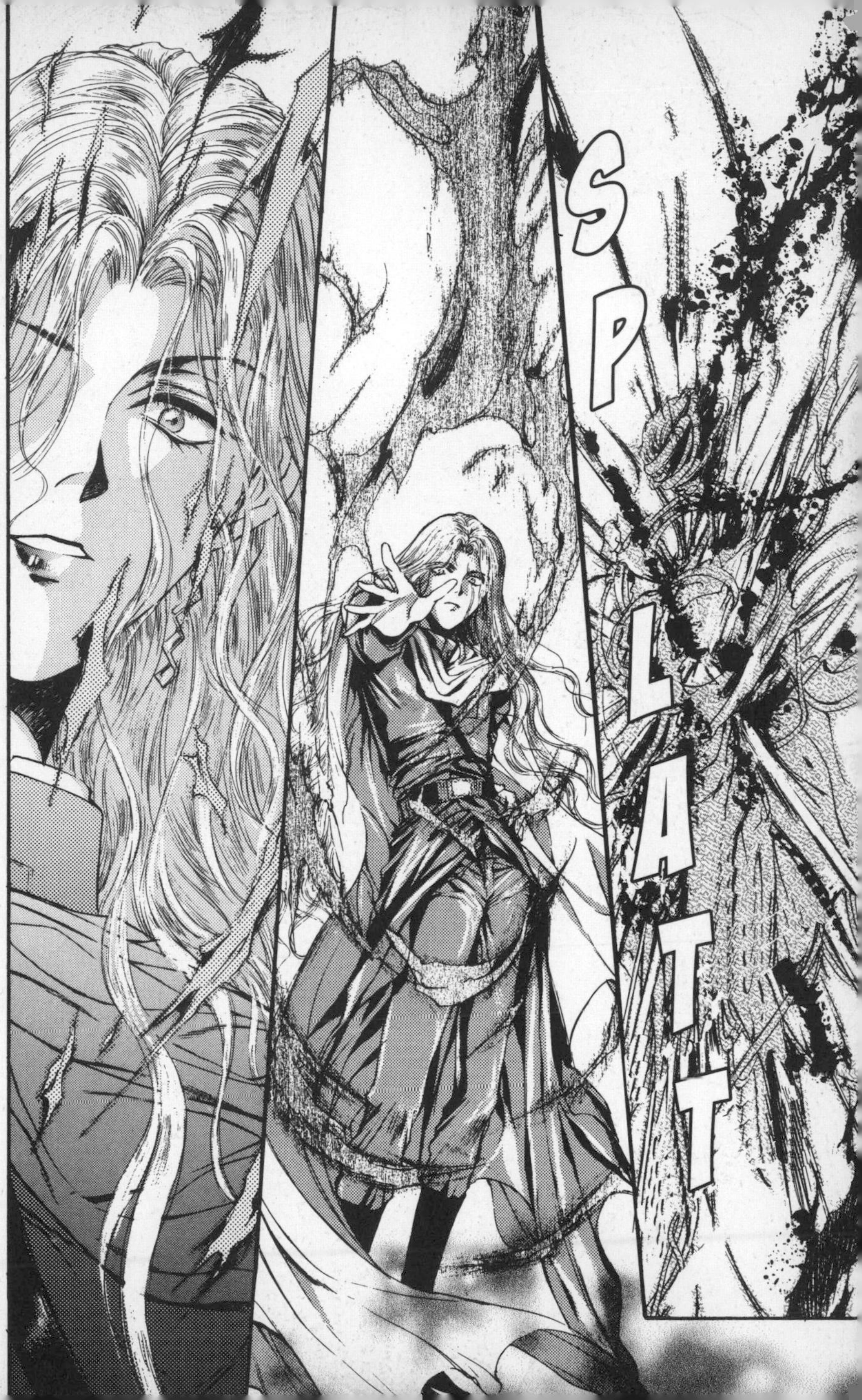
SPLATT

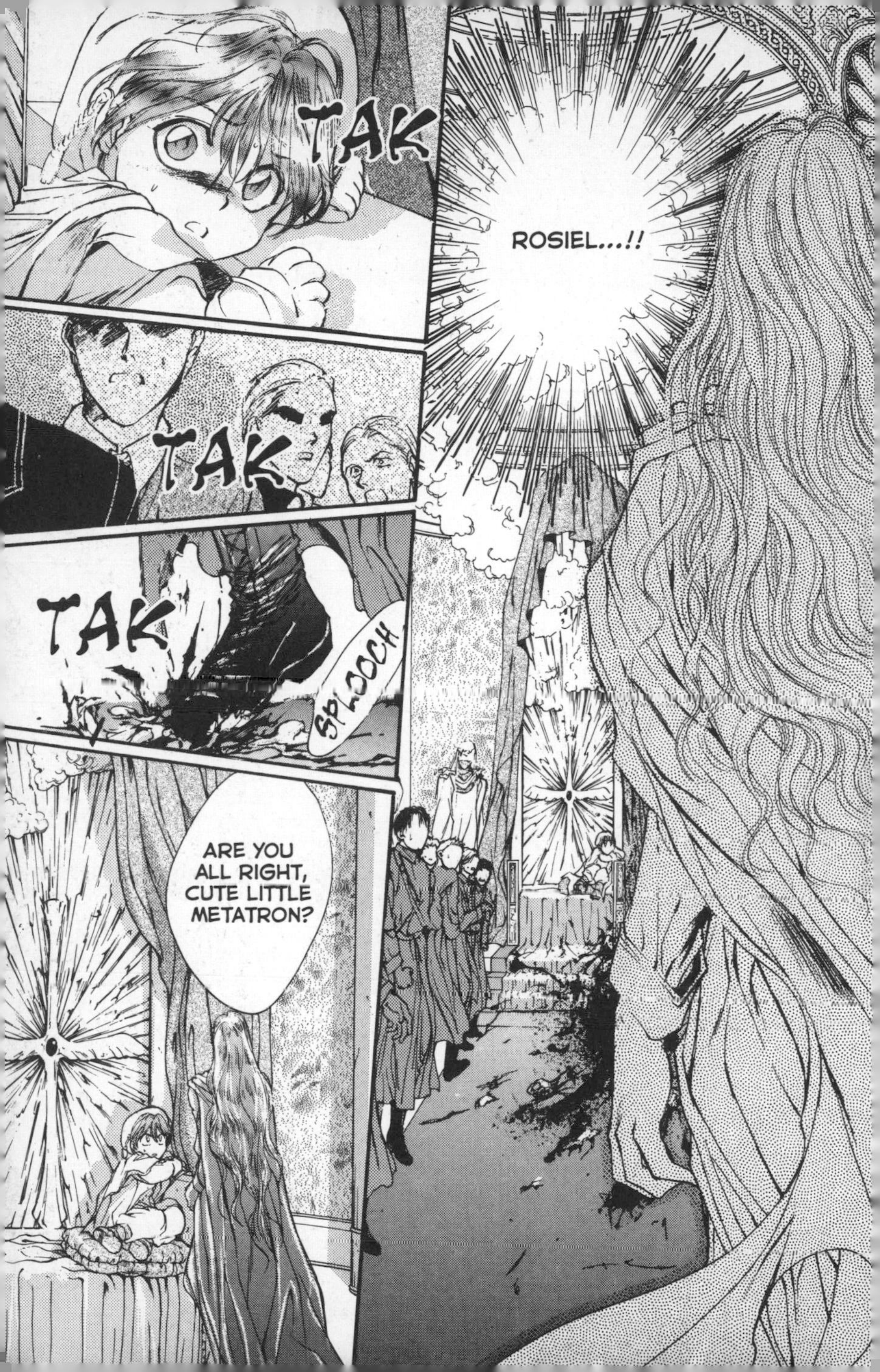
ROSIEL...!!
TAK
TAK
TAK
SPLOOCH
ARE YOU ALL RIGHT, CUTE LITTLE METATRON?

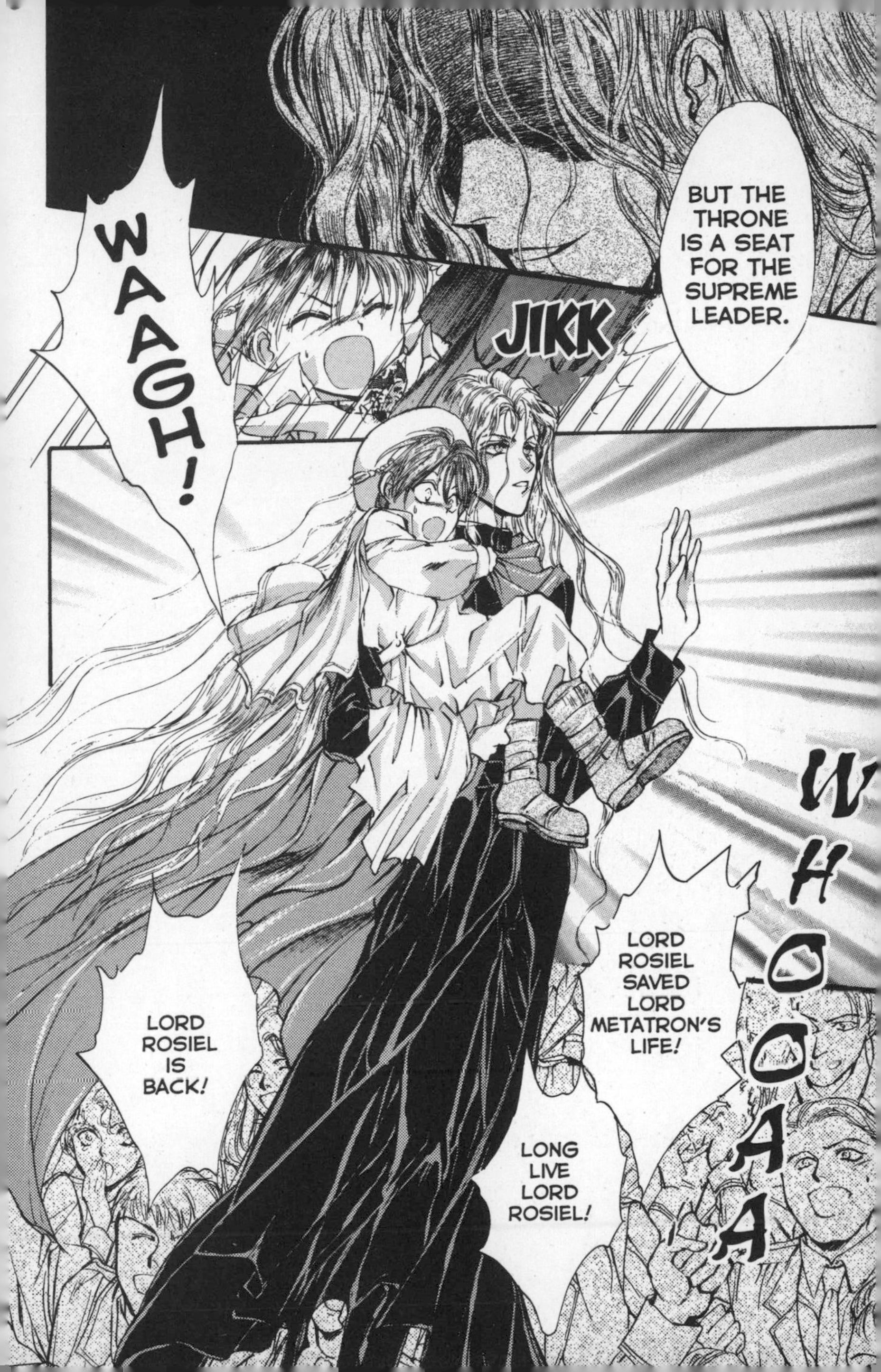
BUT THE THRONE IS A SEAT FOR THE SUPREME LEADER.
JIKK
WAAGH!
WHOOOAAA
LORD ROSIEL SAVED LORD METATRON'S LIFE!
LONG LIVE LORD ROSIEL!
LORD ROSIEL IS BACK!

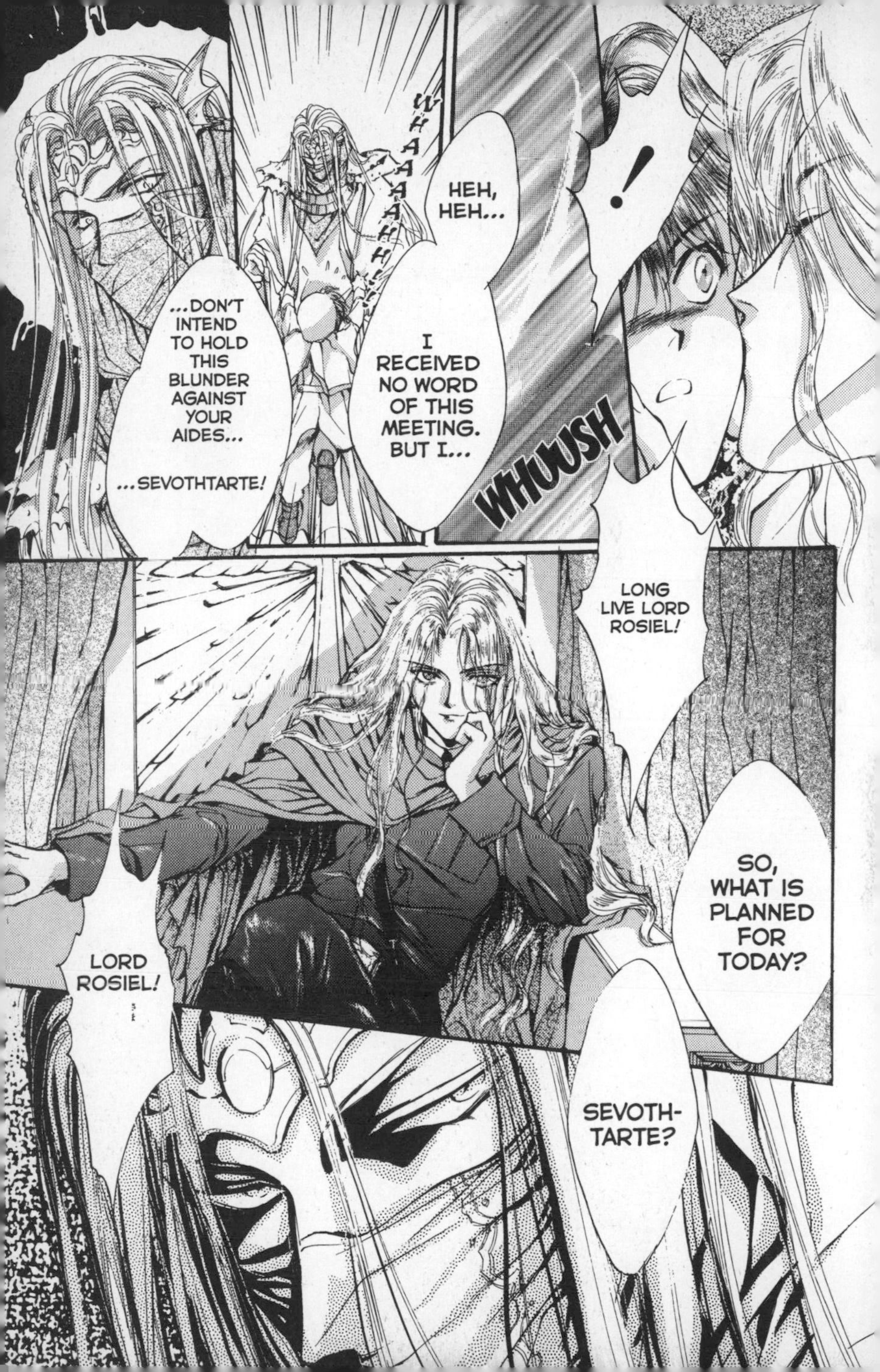
!
WHAAAAAHH!!
HEH, HEH...
I RECEIVED NO WORD OF THIS MEETING. BUT I...
WHUUSH
...DON'T INTEND TO HOLD THIS BLUNDER AGAINST YOUR AIDES...
...SEVOTHTARTE!
LONG LIVE LORD ROSIEL!
SO, WHAT IS PLANNED FOR TODAY?
SEVOTH-TARTE?
LORD ROSIEL!

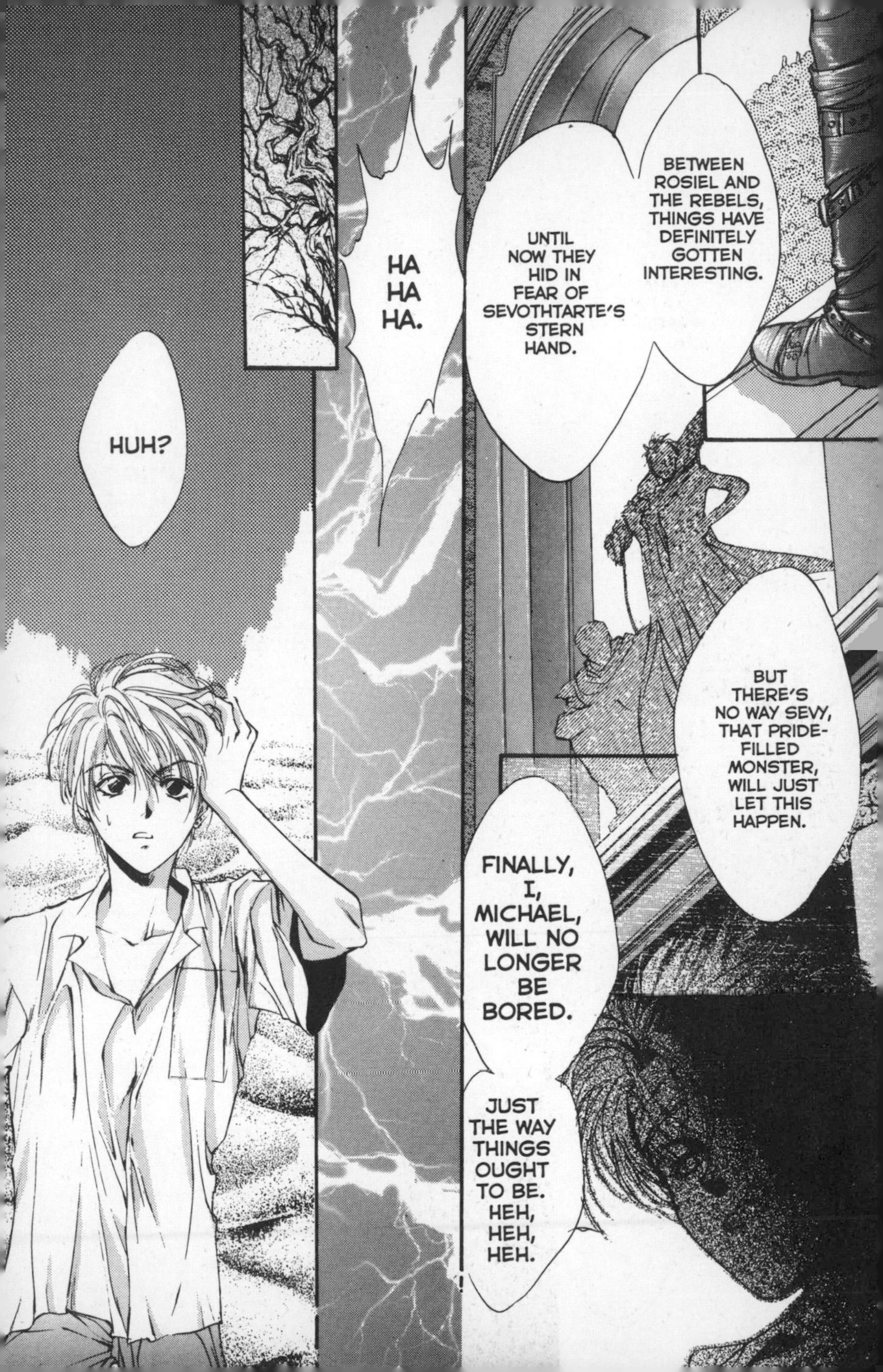
BETWEEN ROSIEL AND THE REBELS, THINGS HAVE DEFINITELY GOTTEN INTERESTING.
UNTIL NOW THEY HID IN FEAR OF SEVOTHTARTE'S STERN HAND.
BUT THERE'S NO WAY SEVY, THAT PRIDE-FILLED MONSTER, WILL JUST LET THIS HAPPEN.
FINALLY, I, MICHAEL, WILL NO LONGER BE BORED.
JUST THE WAY THINGS OUGHT TO BE. HEH, HEH, HEH.
HA HA HA.
HUH?

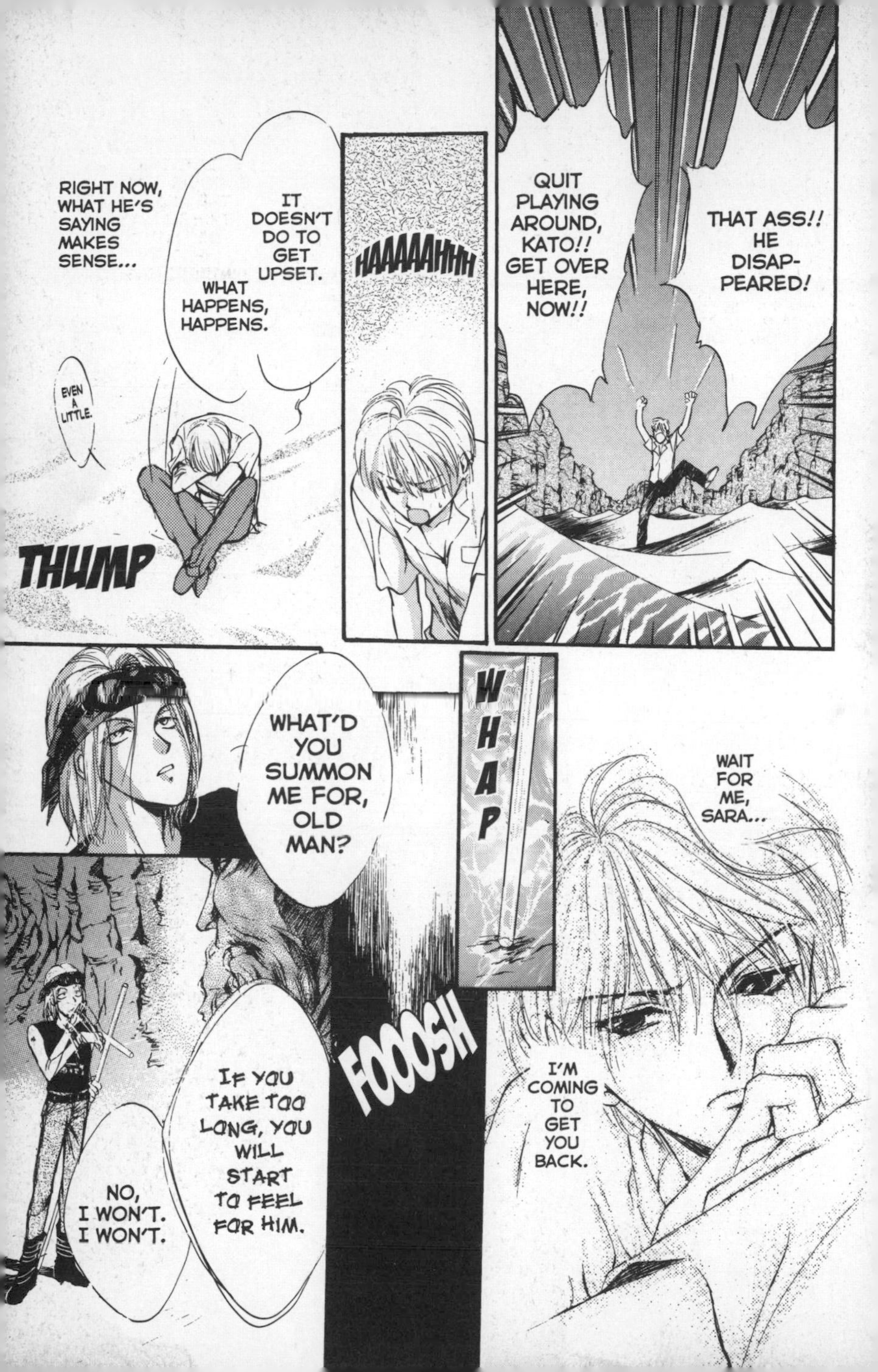
THAT ASS!! HE DISAP-PEARED!
QUIT PLAYING AROUND, KATO!! GET OVER HERE, NOW!!
HAAAAAHHH
IT DOESN'T DO TO GET UPSET.
WHAT HAPPENS, HAPPENS.
RIGHT NOW, WHAT HE'S SAYING MAKES SENSE...
EVEN A LITTLE.
THUMP
WAIT FOR ME, SARA...
I'M COMING TO GET YOU BACK.
WHAP
WHAT'D YOU SUMMON ME FOR, OLD MAN?
FOOOSH
IF YOU TAKE TOO LONG, YOU WILL START TO FEEL FOR HIM.
NO, I WON'T. I WON'T.

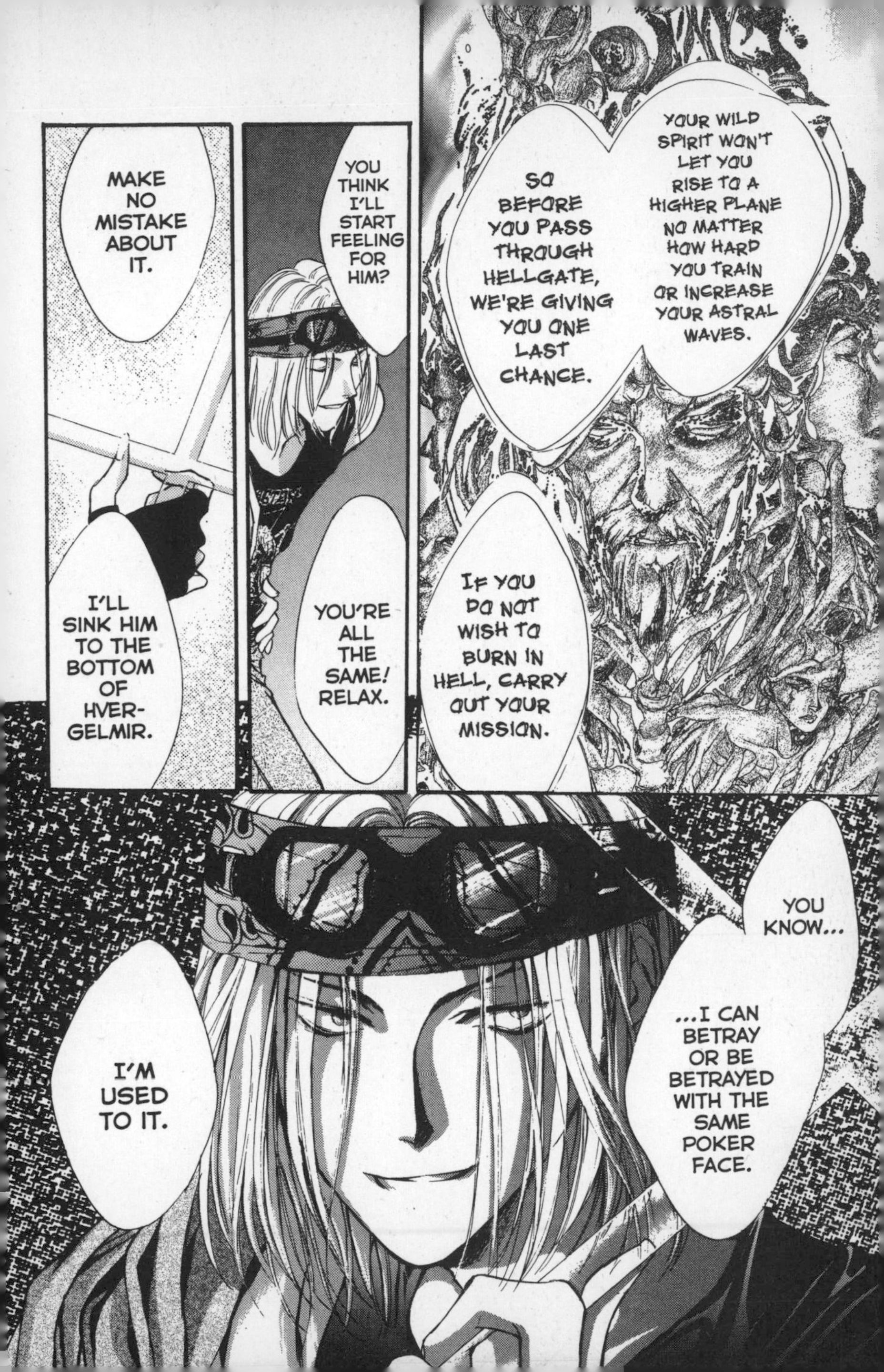
YOUR WILD SPIRIT WON'T LET YOU RISE TO A HIGHER PLANE NO MATTER HOW HARD YOU TRAIN OR INCREASE YOUR ASTRAL WAVES.
SO BEFORE YOU PASS THROUGH HELLGATE, WE'RE GIVING YOU ONE LAST CHANCE.
IF YOU DO NOT WISH TO BURN IN HELL, CARRY OUT YOUR MISSION.
YOU THINK I'LL START FEELING FOR HIM?
YOU'RE ALL THE SAME! RELAX.
MAKE NO MISTAKE ABOUT IT.
I'LL SINK HIM TO THE BOTTOM OF HVER-GELMIR.
YOU KNOW...
...I CAN BETRAY OR BE BETRAYED WITH THE SAME POKER FACE.
I'M USED TO IT.

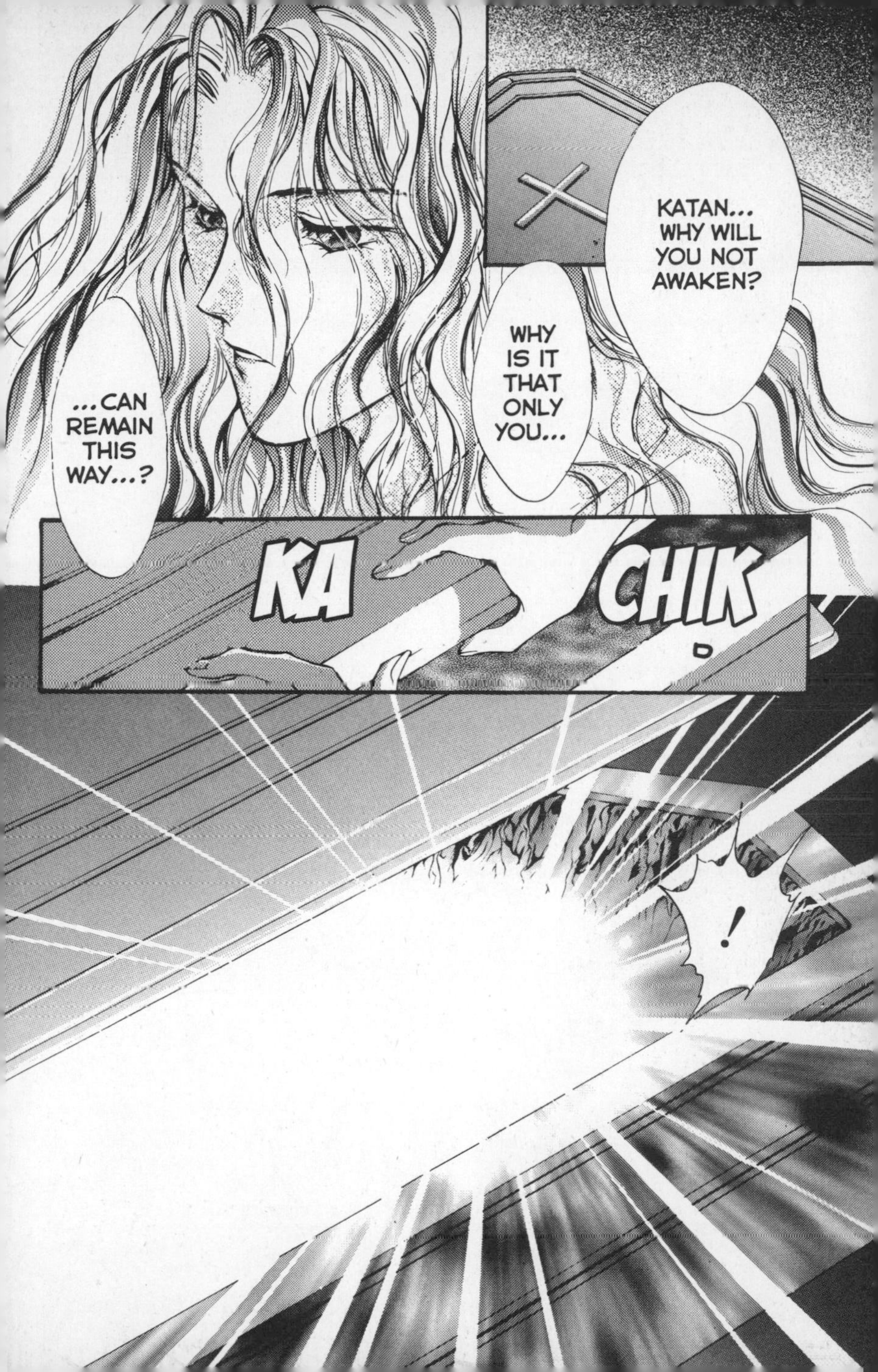
KATAN... WHY WILL YOU NOT AWAKEN?
WHY IS IT THAT ONLY YOU...
...CAN REMAIN THIS WAY...?
KA CHIK
!

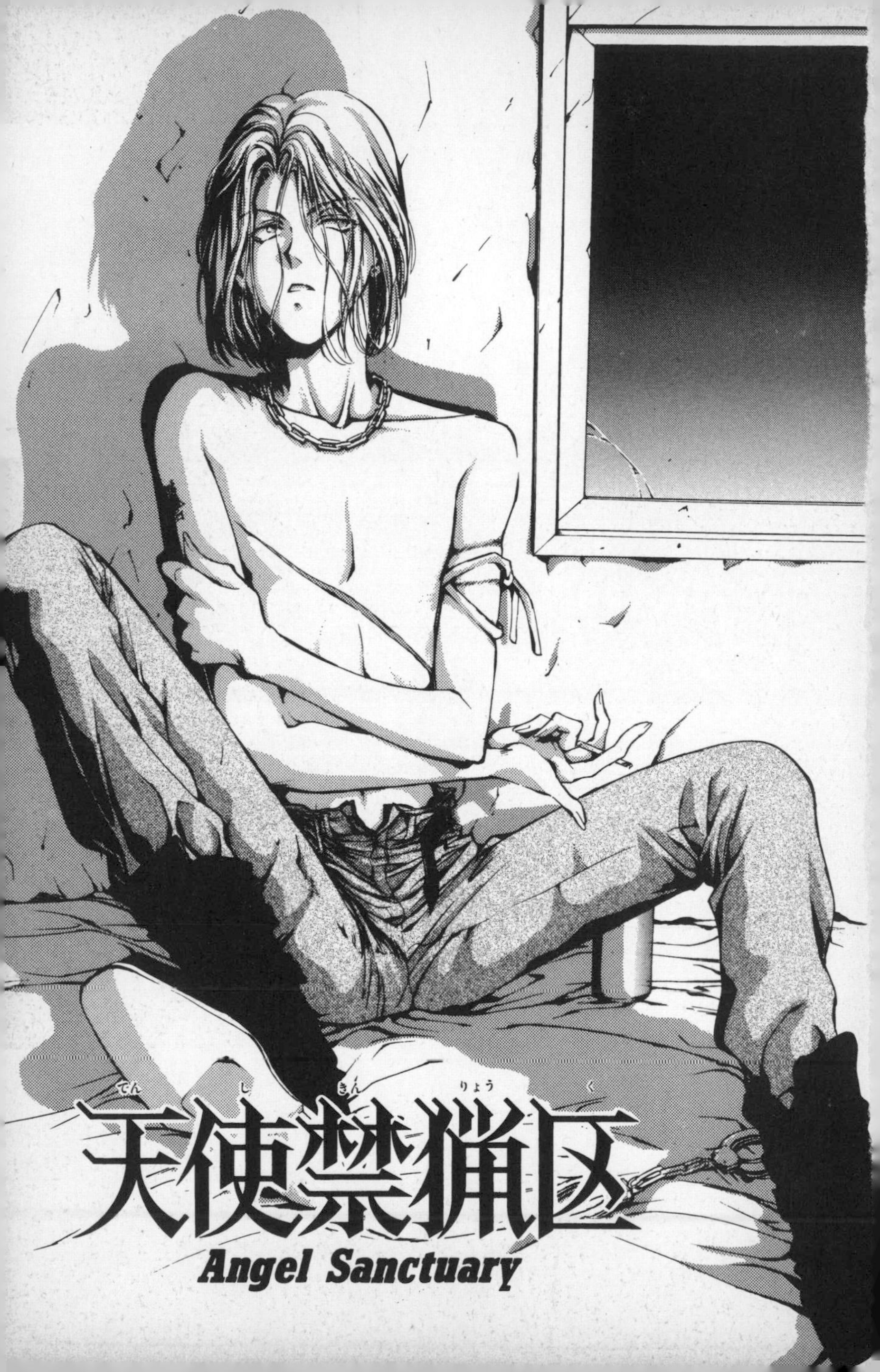
てんしきんりょうく
天使禁猟区
Angel Sanctuary

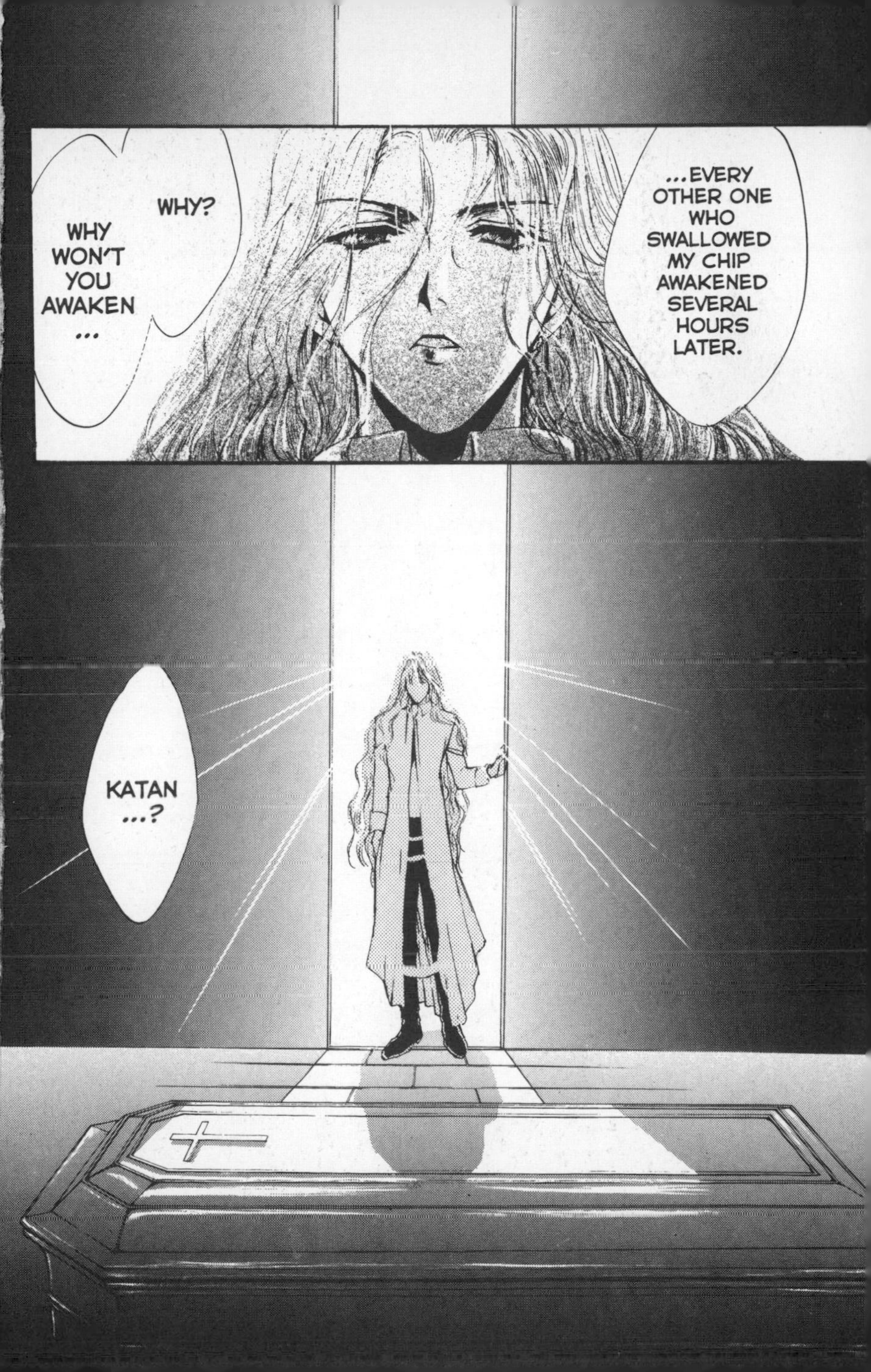
...EVERY OTHER ONE WHO SWALLOWED MY CHIP AWAKENED SEVERAL HOURS LATER.
WHY?
WHY WON'T YOU AWAKEN ...
KATAN ...?

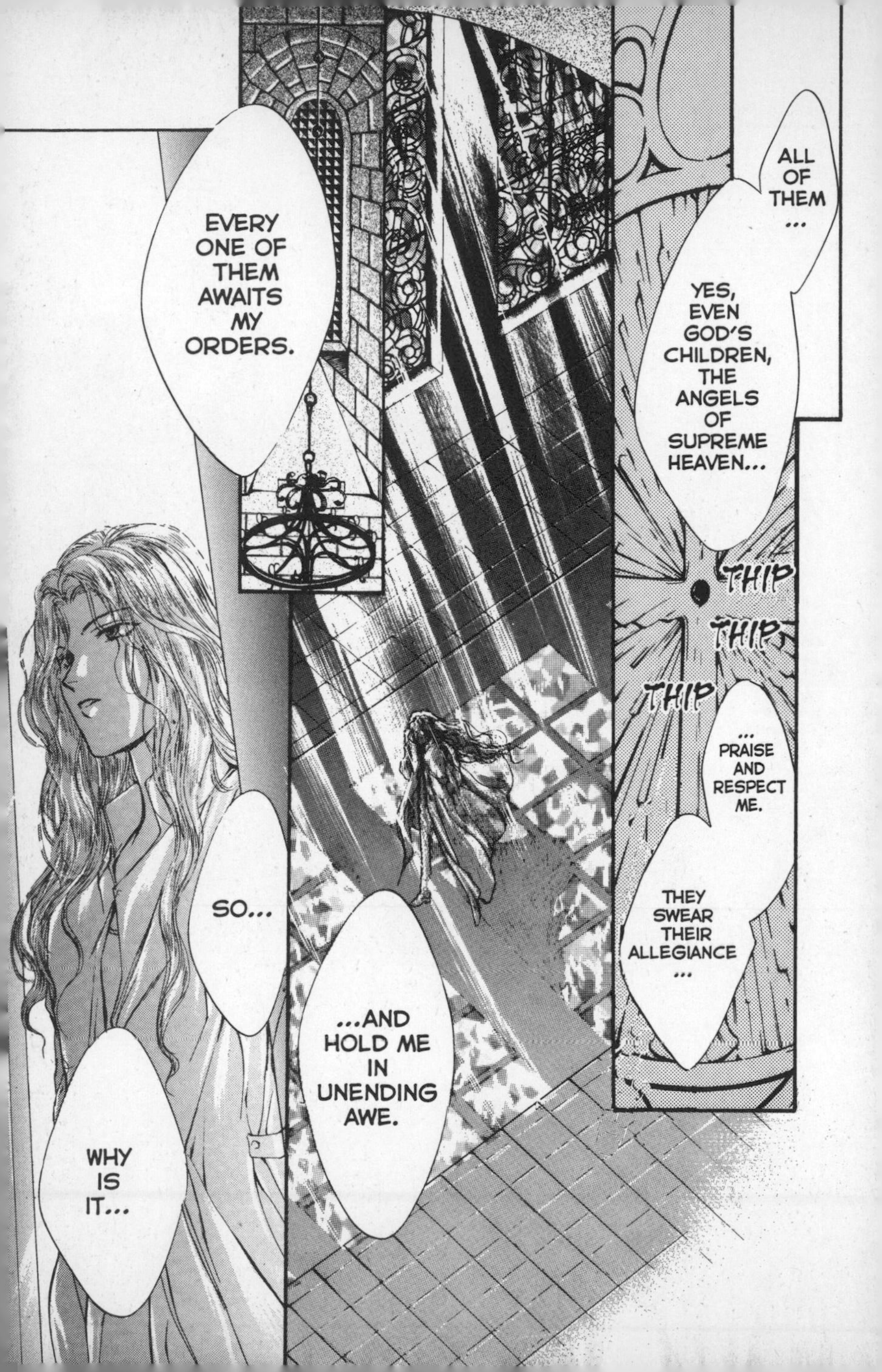
ALL OF THEM ...
YES, EVEN GOD'S CHILDREN, THE ANGELS OF SUPREME HEAVEN...
THIP
THIP
THIP
... PRAISE AND RESPECT ME.
THEY SWEAR THEIR ALLEGIANCE ...
...AND HOLD ME IN UNENDING AWE.
EVERY ONE OF THEM AWAITS MY ORDERS.
SO...
WHY IS IT...

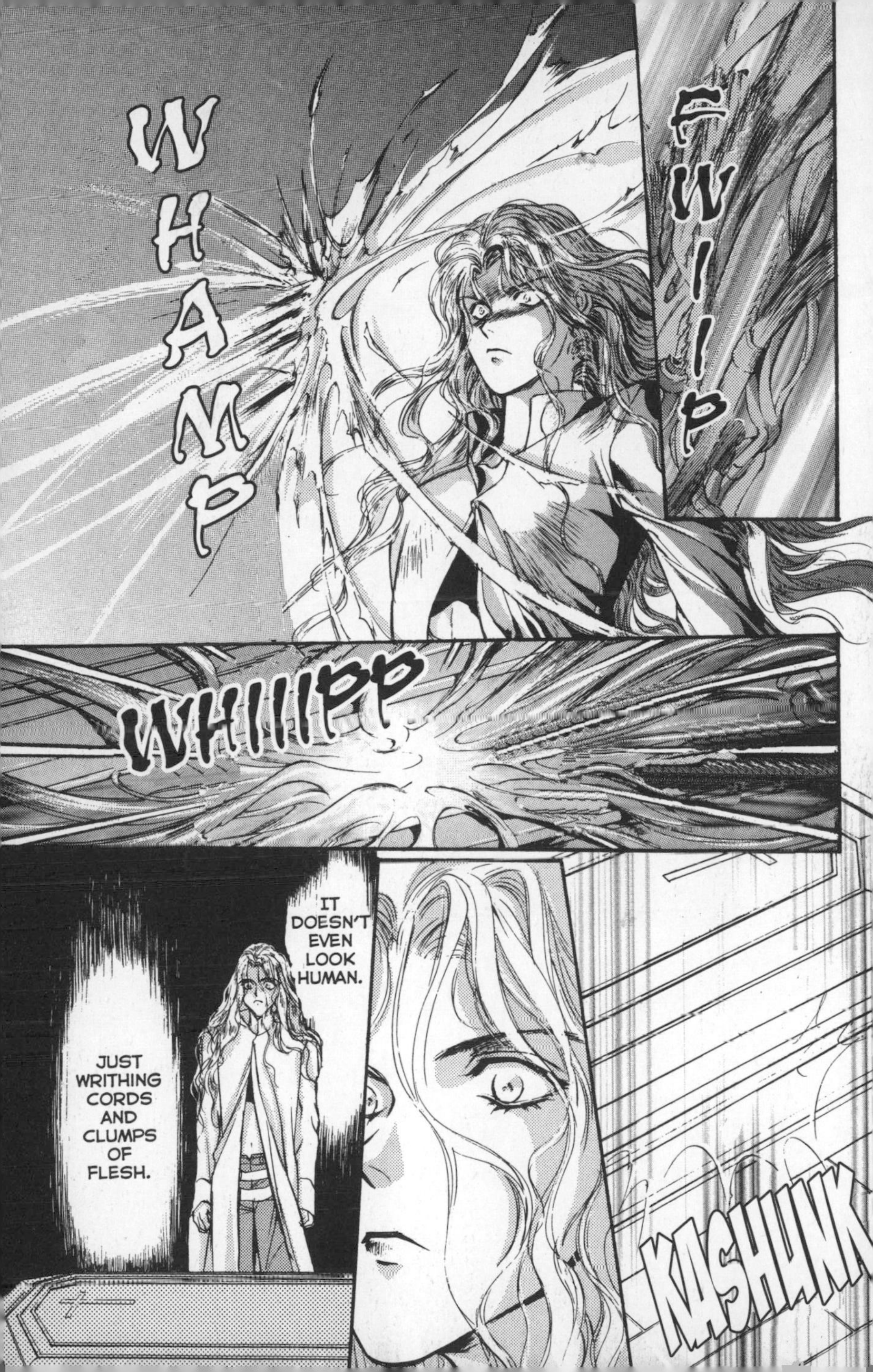
FWIIIP
WHAMP
WHIIIPP
KASHUNK
IT DOESN'T EVEN LOOK HUMAN.
JUST WRITHING CORDS AND CLUMPS OF FLESH.

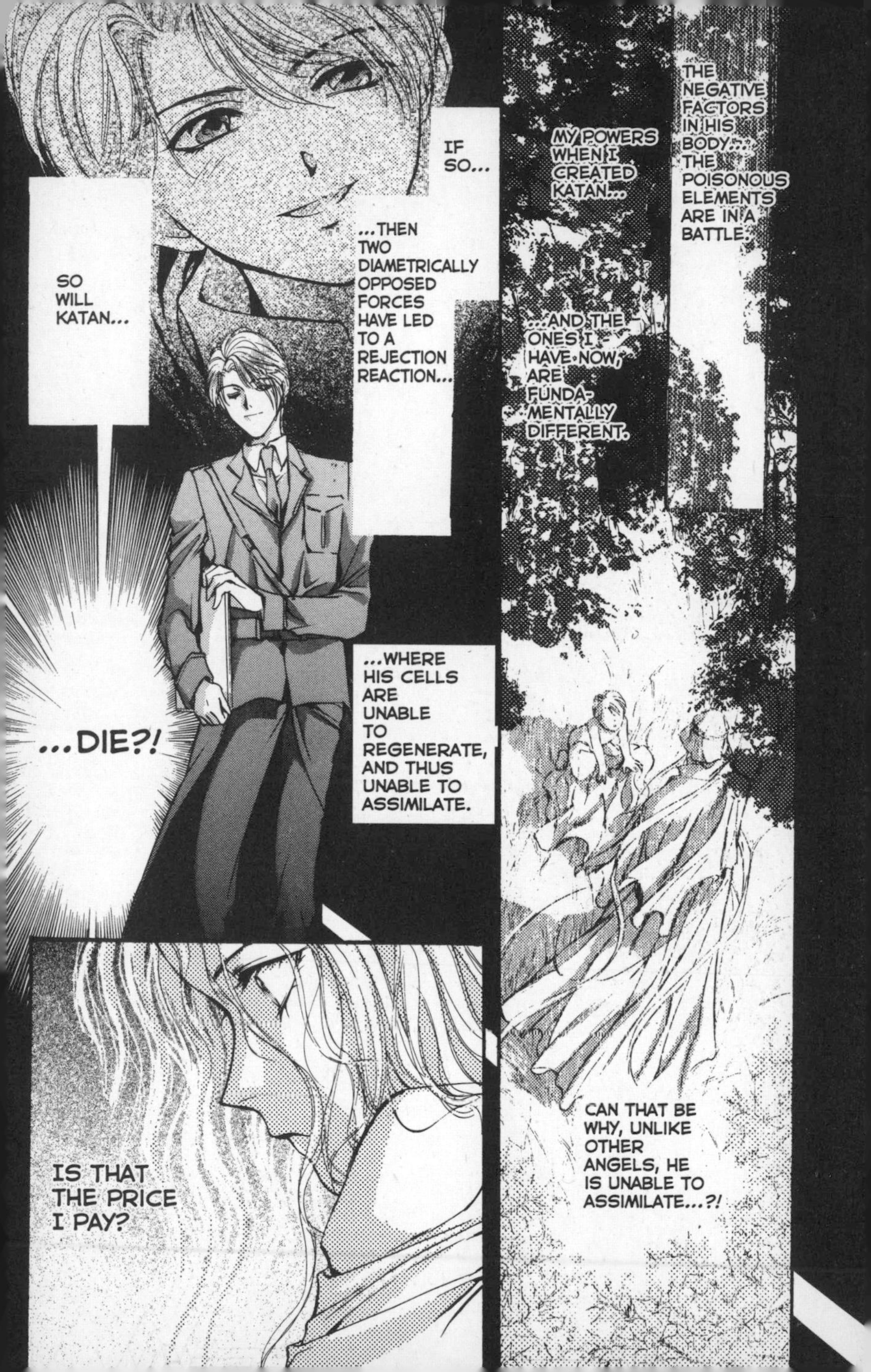
THE NEGATIVE FACTORS IN HIS BODY... THE POISONOUS ELEMENTS ARE IN A BATTLE.
MY POWERS WHEN I CREATED KATAN...
...AND THE ONES I HAVE NOW, ARE FUNDAMENTALLY DIFFERENT.
CAN THAT BE WHY, UNLIKE OTHER ANGELS, HE IS UNABLE TO ASSIMILATE...?!
IF SO...
...THEN TWO DIAMETRICALLY OPPOSED FORCES HAVE LED TO A REJECTION REACTION...
...WHERE HIS CELLS ARE UNABLE TO REGENERATE, AND THUS UNABLE TO ASSIMILATE.
SO WILL KATAN...
...DIE?!
IS THAT THE PRICE I PAY?

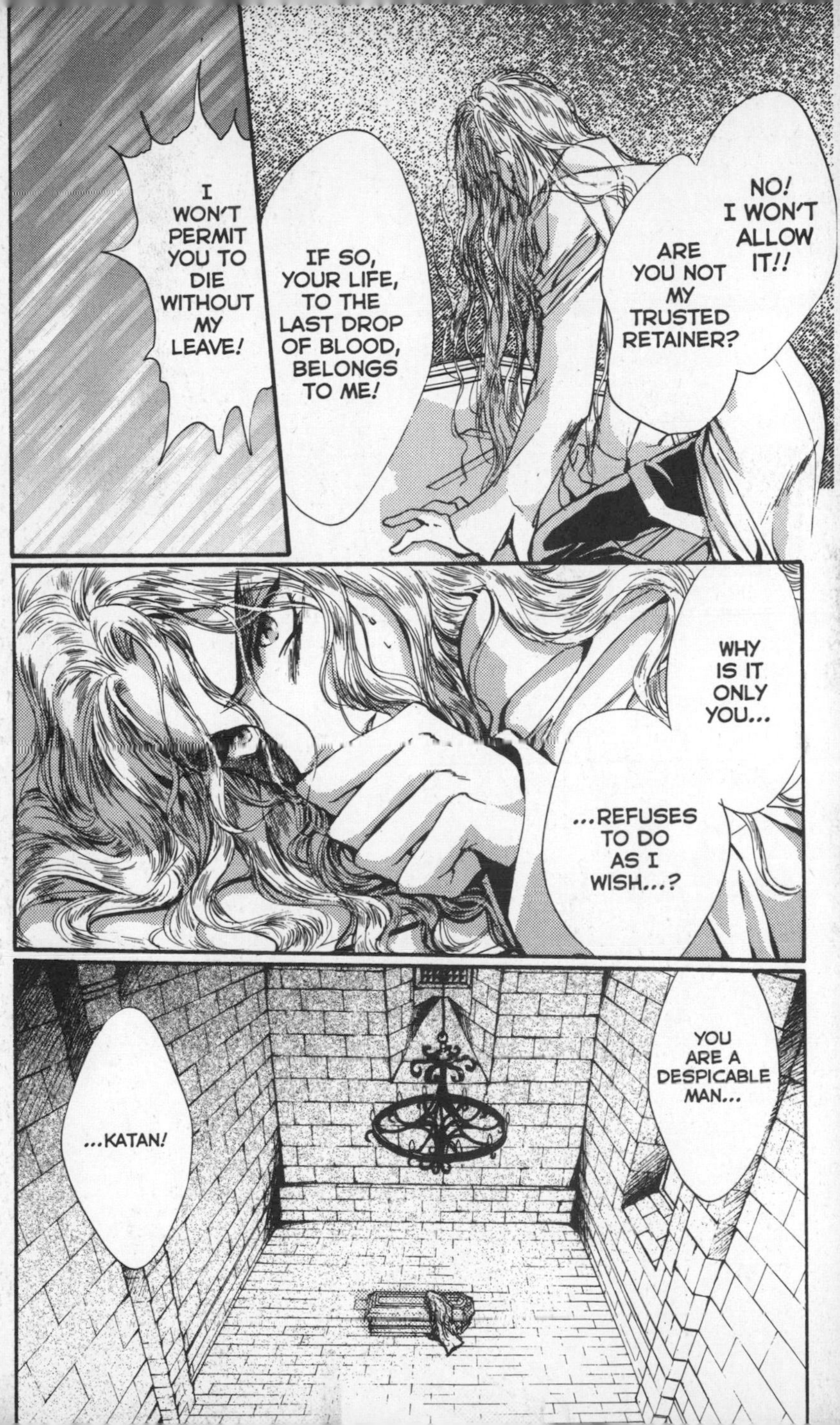
NO! I WON'T ALLOW IT!!
ARE YOU NOT MY TRUSTED RETAINER?
IF SO, YOUR LIFE, TO THE LAST DROP OF BLOOD, BELONGS TO ME!
I WON'T PERMIT YOU TO DIE WITHOUT MY LEAVE!
WHY IS IT ONLY YOU...
...REFUSES TO DO AS I WISH...?
YOU ARE A DESPICABLE MAN...
...KATAN!

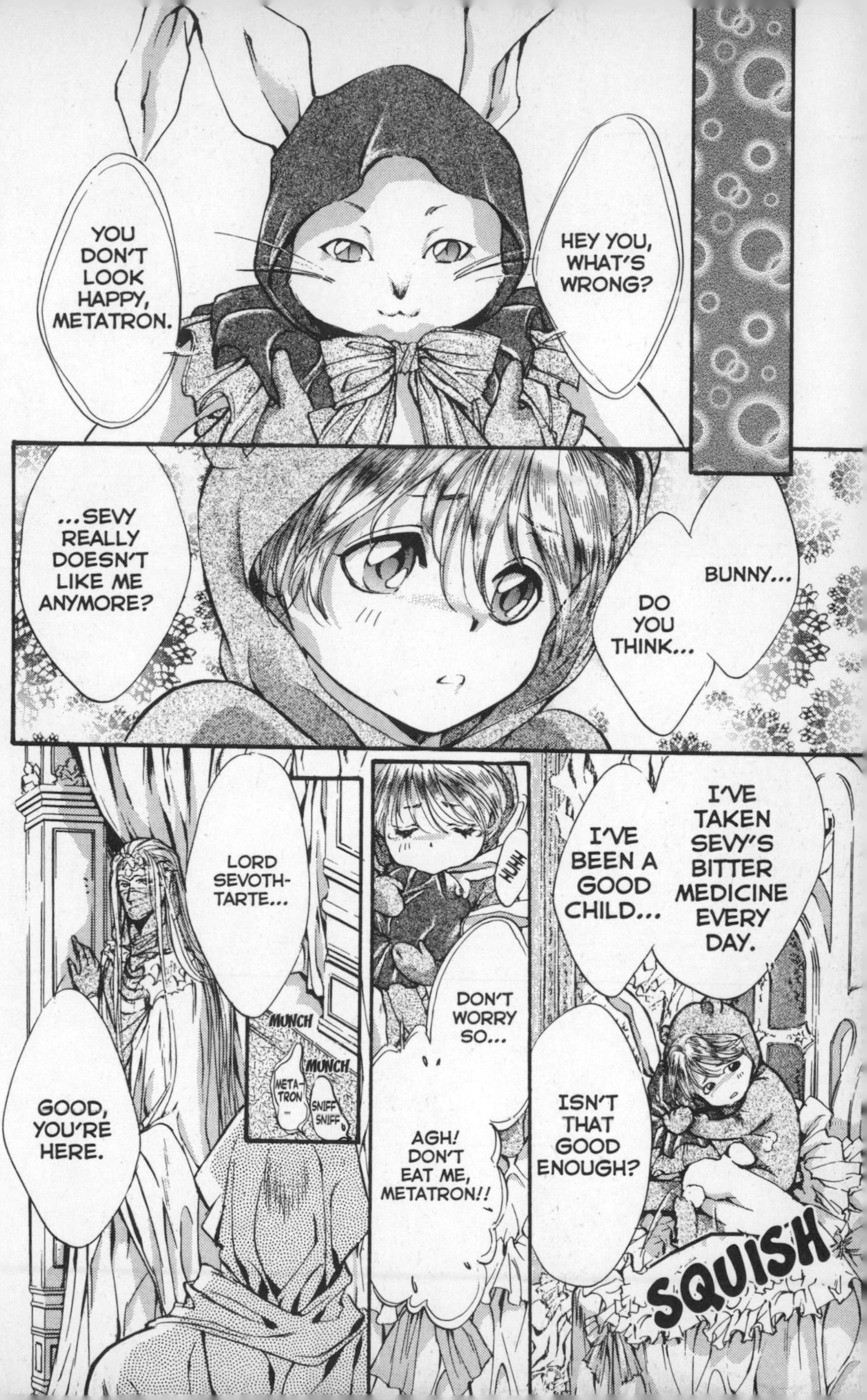
HEY YOU, WHAT'S WRONG?
YOU DON'T LOOK HAPPY, METATRON.
BUNNY...
DO YOU THINK...
...SEVY REALLY DOESN'T LIKE ME ANYMORE?
I'VE TAKEN SEVY'S BITTER MEDICINE EVERY DAY.
I'VE BEEN A GOOD CHILD...
ISN'T THAT GOOD ENOUGH?
SQUISH
HUHH
DON'T WORRY SO...
AGH! DON'T EAT ME, METATRON!!
LORD SEVOTH-TARTE...
MUNCH
MUNCH
METATRON...
SNIFF SNIFF
GOOD, YOU'RE HERE.

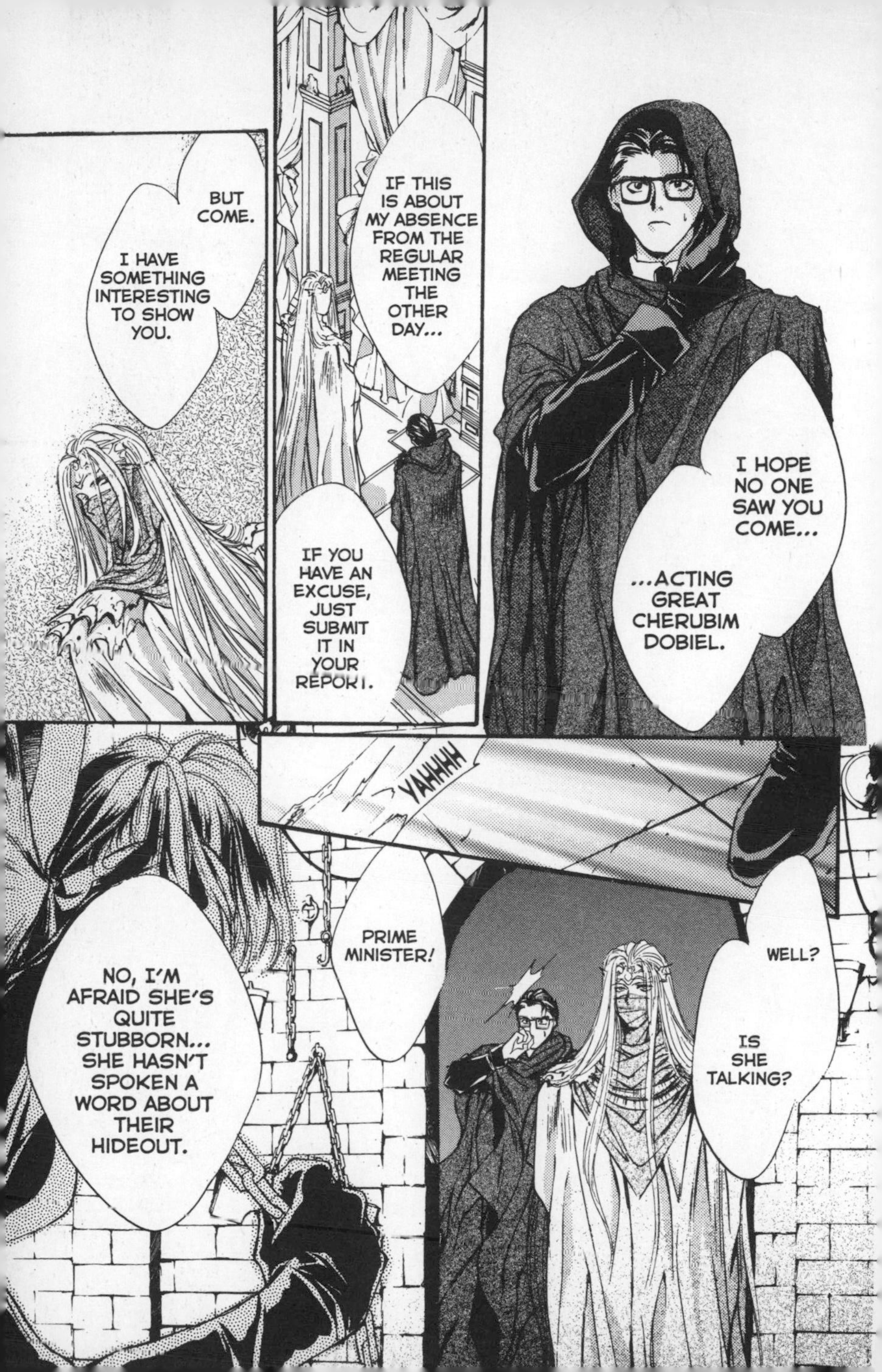
I HOPE NO ONE SAW YOU COME...
...ACTING GREAT CHERUBIM DOBIEL.
IF THIS IS ABOUT MY ABSENCE FROM THE REGULAR MEETING THE OTHER DAY...
IF YOU HAVE AN EXCUSE, JUST SUBMIT IT IN YOUR REPORT.
BUT COME.
I HAVE SOMETHING INTERESTING TO SHOW YOU.
YAHHHH
WELL?
IS SHE TALKING?
PRIME MINISTER!
NO, I'M AFRAID SHE'S QUITE STUBBORN... SHE HASN'T SPOKEN A WORD ABOUT THEIR HIDEOUT.

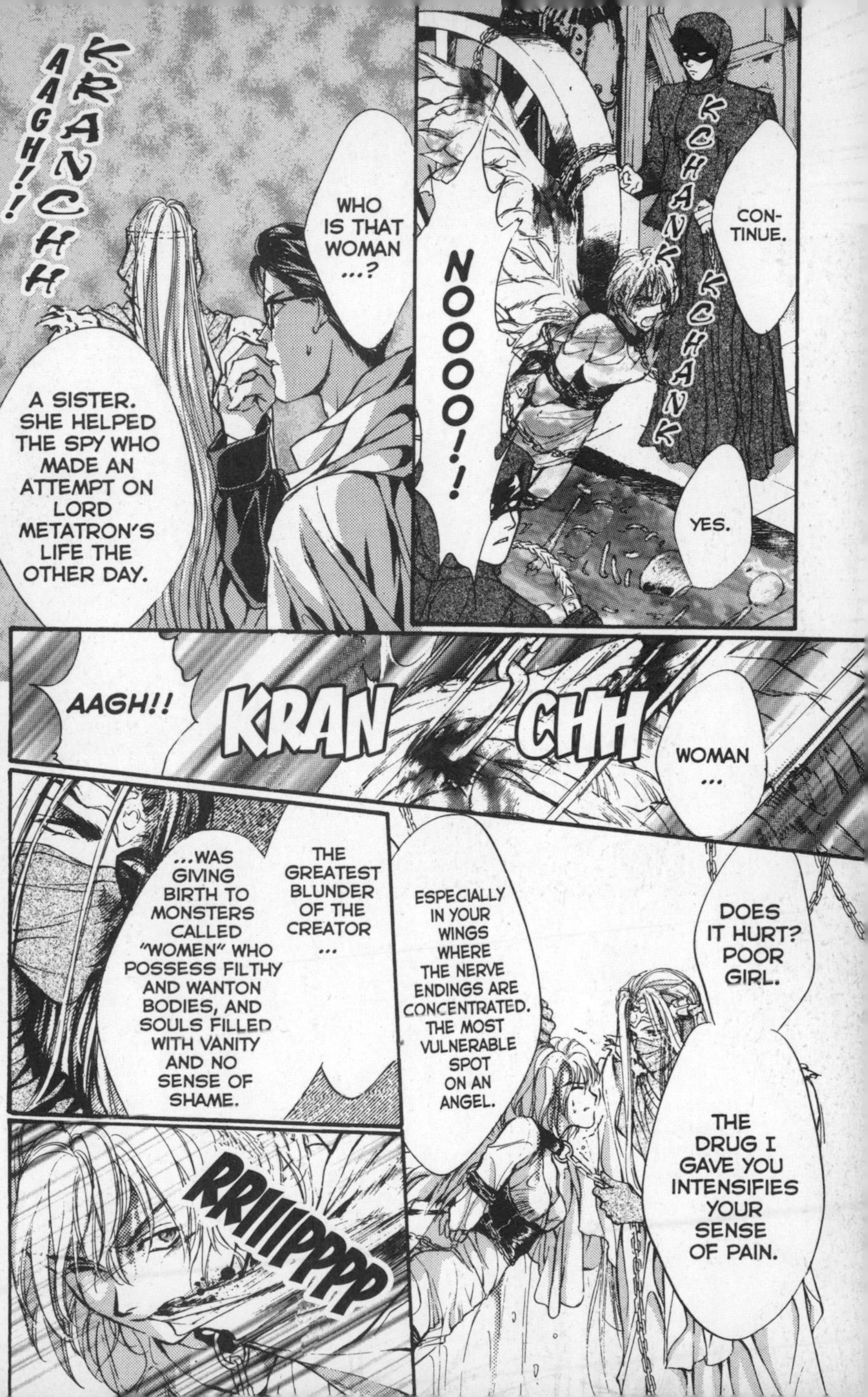
CON-TINUE.
KCHANK KCHANK
NOOOOO!!
YES.
KRANCHH
AAGH!!
WHO IS THAT WOMAN ...?
A SISTER. SHE HELPED THE SPY WHO MADE AN ATTEMPT ON LORD METATRON'S LIFE THE OTHER DAY.
WOMAN ...
KRAN CHH
AAGH!!
DOES IT HURT? POOR GIRL.
THE DRUG I GAVE YOU INTENSIFIES YOUR SENSE OF PAIN.
ESPECIALLY IN YOUR WINGS WHERE THE NERVE ENDINGS ARE CONCENTRATED. THE MOST VULNERABLE SPOT ON AN ANGEL.
THE GREATEST BLUNDER OF THE CREATOR ...
...WAS GIVING BIRTH TO MONSTERS CALLED "WOMEN" WHO POSSESS FILTHY AND WANTON BODIES, AND SOULS FILLED WITH VANITY AND NO SENSE OF SHAME.
RRIIIPPPPP

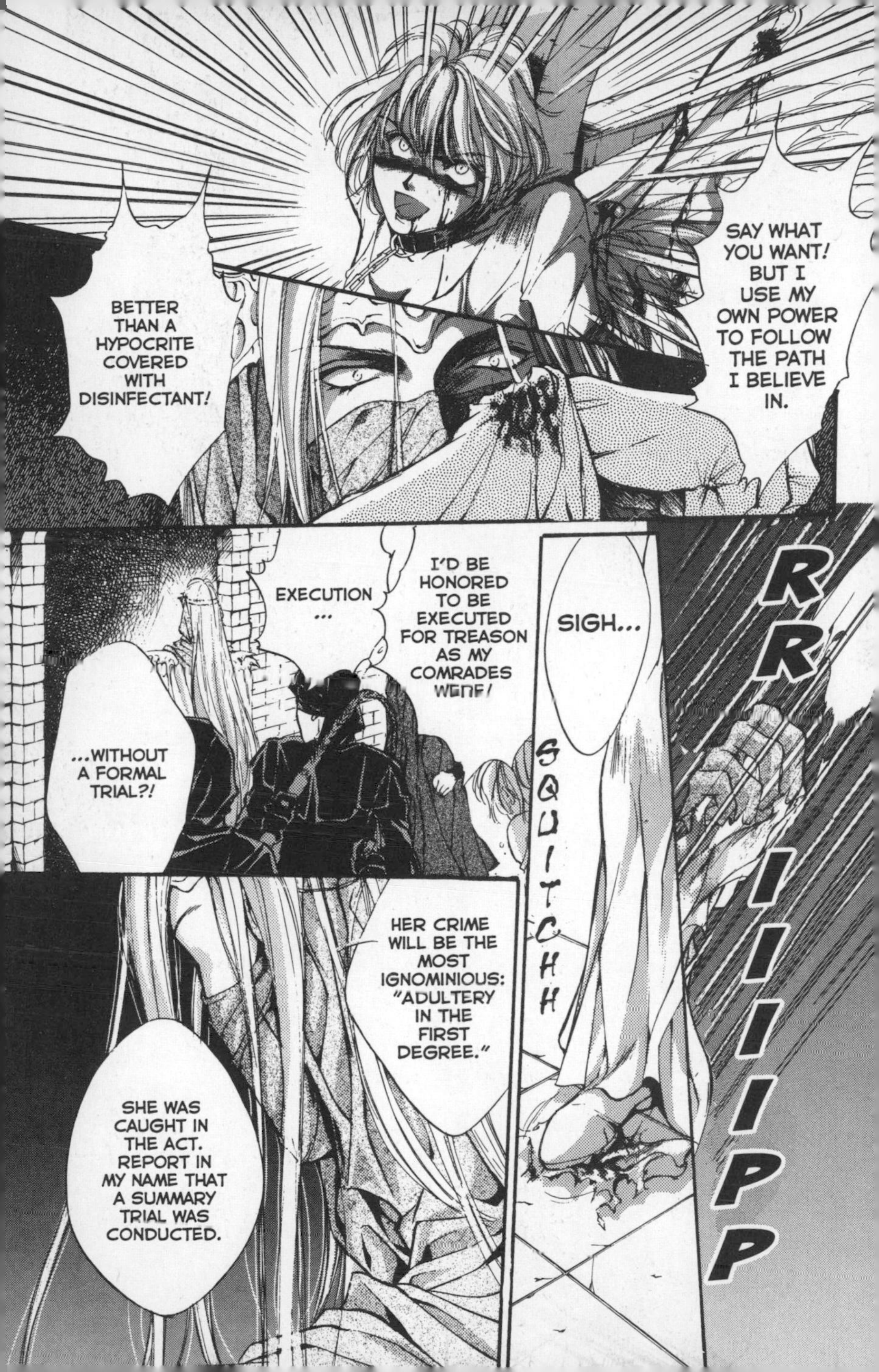
SAY WHAT YOU WANT! BUT I USE MY OWN POWER TO FOLLOW THE PATH I BELIEVE IN.
BETTER THAN A HYPOCRITE COVERED WITH DISINFECTANT!
RRIIIPP
SIGH...
SQUITCHH
I'D BE HONORED TO BE EXECUTED FOR TREASON AS MY COMRADES WERE!
EXECUTION ...
...WITHOUT A FORMAL TRIAL?!
HER CRIME WILL BE THE MOST IGNOMINIOUS: "ADULTERY IN THE FIRST DEGREE."
SHE WAS CAUGHT IN THE ACT. REPORT IN MY NAME THAT A SUMMARY TRIAL WAS CONDUCTED.

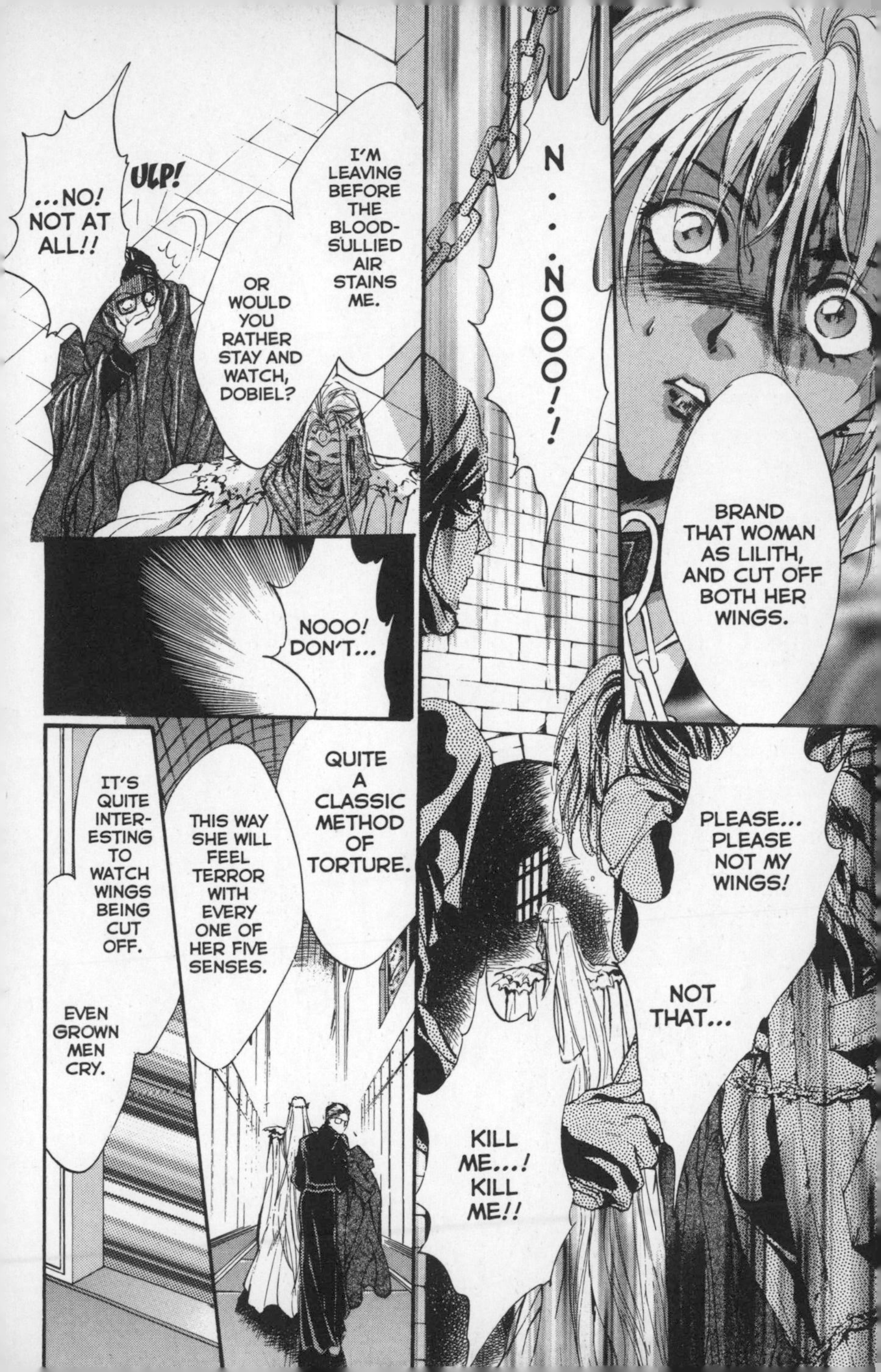
BRAND THAT WOMAN AS LILITH, AND CUT OFF BOTH HER WINGS.
N... NOOO!!
I'M LEAVING BEFORE THE BLOOD-SULLIED AIR STAINS ME.
OR WOULD YOU RATHER STAY AND WATCH, DOBIEL?
ULP!
...NO! NOT AT ALL!!
NOOO! DON'T...
PLEASE... PLEASE NOT MY WINGS!
NOT THAT...
KILL ME...! KILL ME!!
QUITE A CLASSIC METHOD OF TORTURE.
THIS WAY SHE WILL FEEL TERROR WITH EVERY ONE OF HER FIVE SENSES.
IT'S QUITE INTER-ESTING TO WATCH WINGS BEING CUT OFF.
EVEN GROWN MEN CRY.

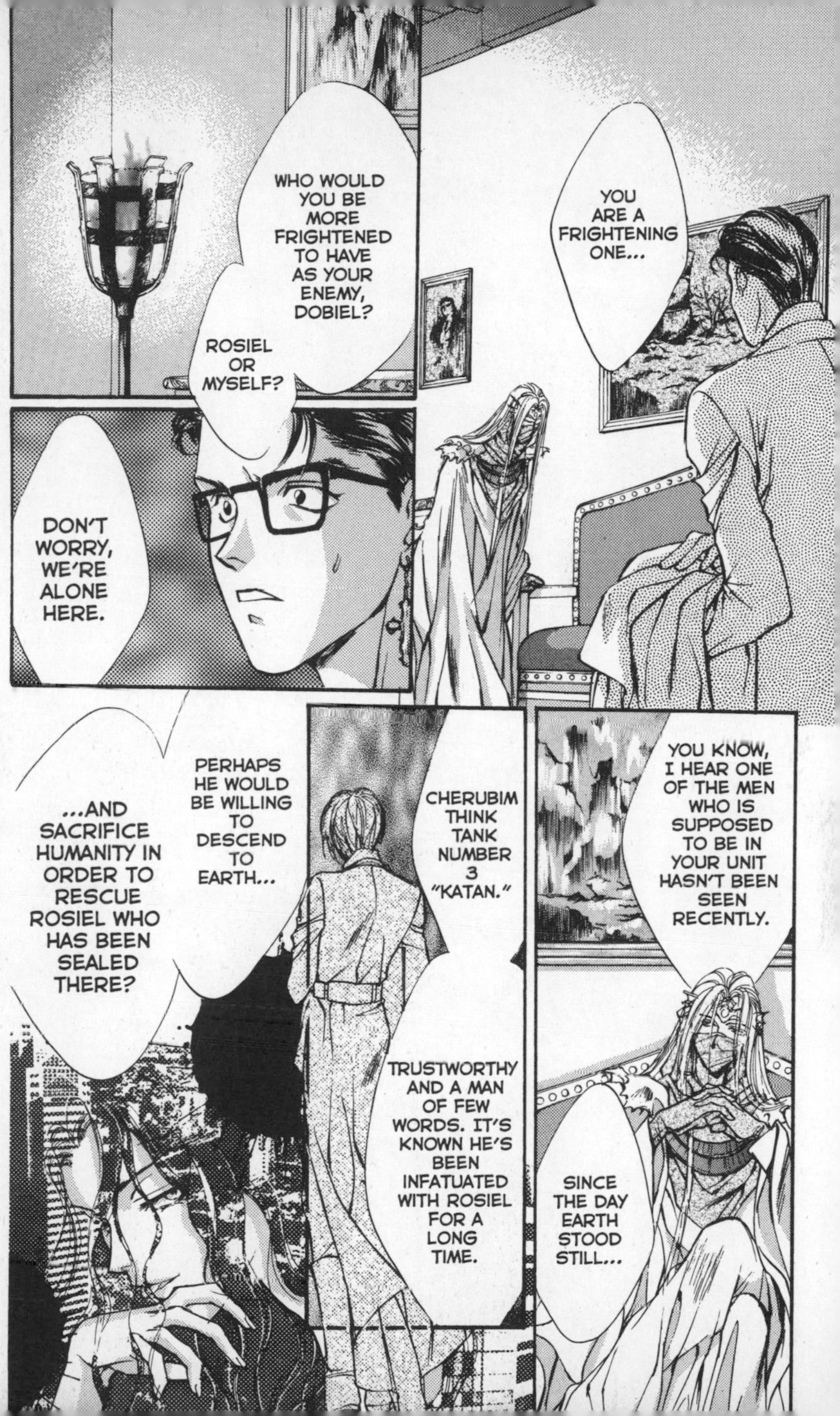
YOU ARE A FRIGHTENING ONE...
WHO WOULD YOU BE MORE FRIGHTENED TO HAVE AS YOUR ENEMY, DOBIEL?
ROSIEL OR MYSELF?
DON'T WORRY, WE'RE ALONE HERE.
YOU KNOW, I HEAR ONE OF THE MEN WHO IS SUPPOSED TO BE IN YOUR UNIT HASN'T BEEN SEEN RECENTLY.
SINCE THE DAY EARTH STOOD STILL...
CHERUBIM THINK TANK NUMBER 3 "KATAN."
TRUSTWORTHY AND A MAN OF FEW WORDS. IT'S KNOWN HE'S BEEN INFATUATED WITH ROSIEL FOR A LONG TIME.
PERHAPS HE WOULD BE WILLING TO DESCEND TO EARTH...
...AND SACRIFICE HUMANITY IN ORDER TO RESCUE ROSIEL WHO HAS BEEN SEALED THERE?

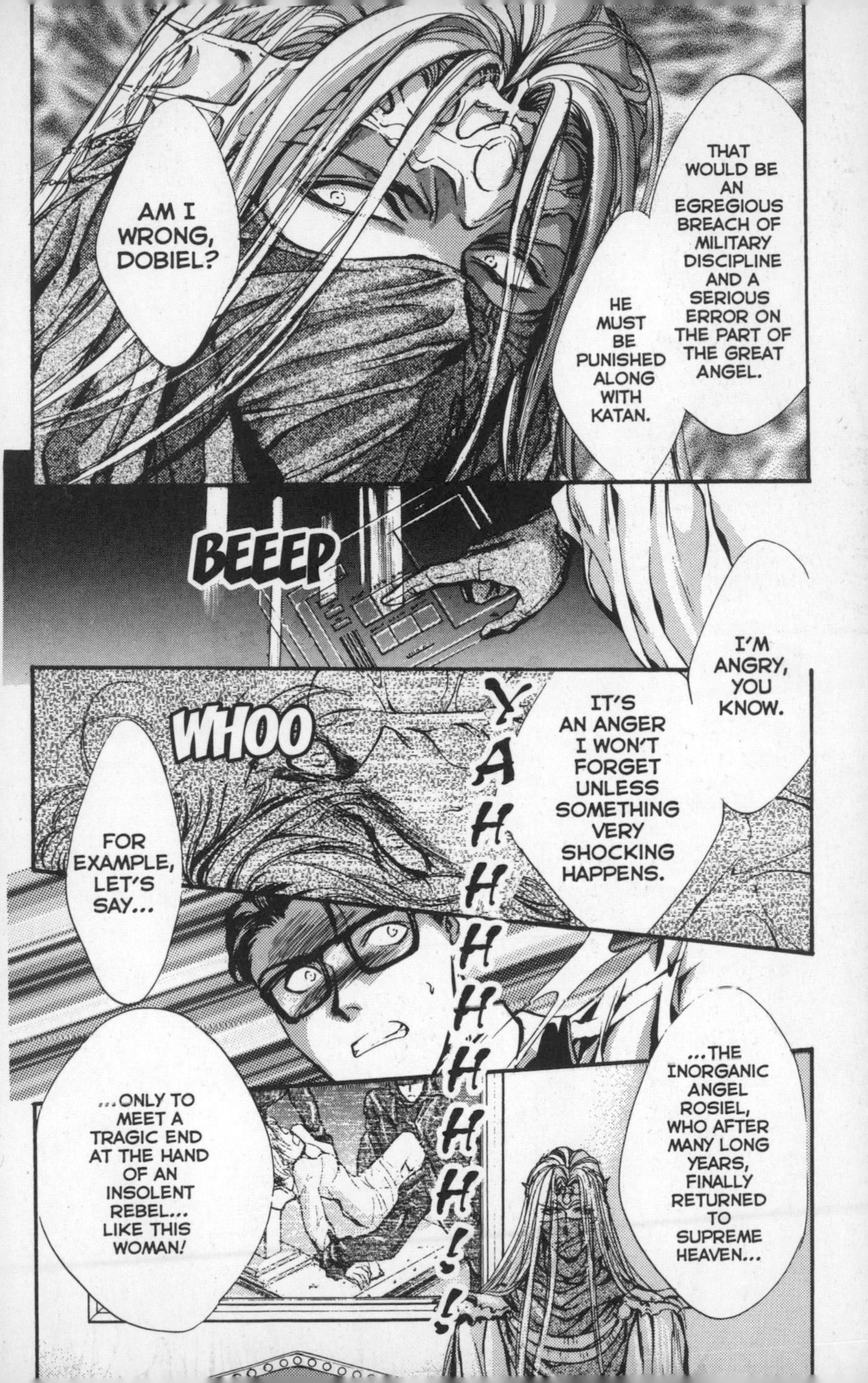
THAT WOULD BE AN EGREGIOUS BREACH OF MILITARY DISCIPLINE AND A SERIOUS ERROR ON THE PART OF THE GREAT ANGEL.
HE MUST BE PUNISHED ALONG WITH KATAN.
AM I WRONG, DOBIEL?
BEEEP
I'M ANGRY, YOU KNOW.
IT'S AN ANGER I WON'T FORGET UNLESS SOMETHING VERY SHOCKING HAPPENS.
WHOO
FOR EXAMPLE, LET'S SAY...
YAHHHHHHHHH!!
...THE INORGANIC ANGEL ROSIEL, WHO AFTER MANY LONG YEARS, FINALLY RETURNED TO SUPREME HEAVEN...
...ONLY TO MEET A TRAGIC END AT THE HAND OF AN INSOLENT REBEL... LIKE THIS WOMAN!

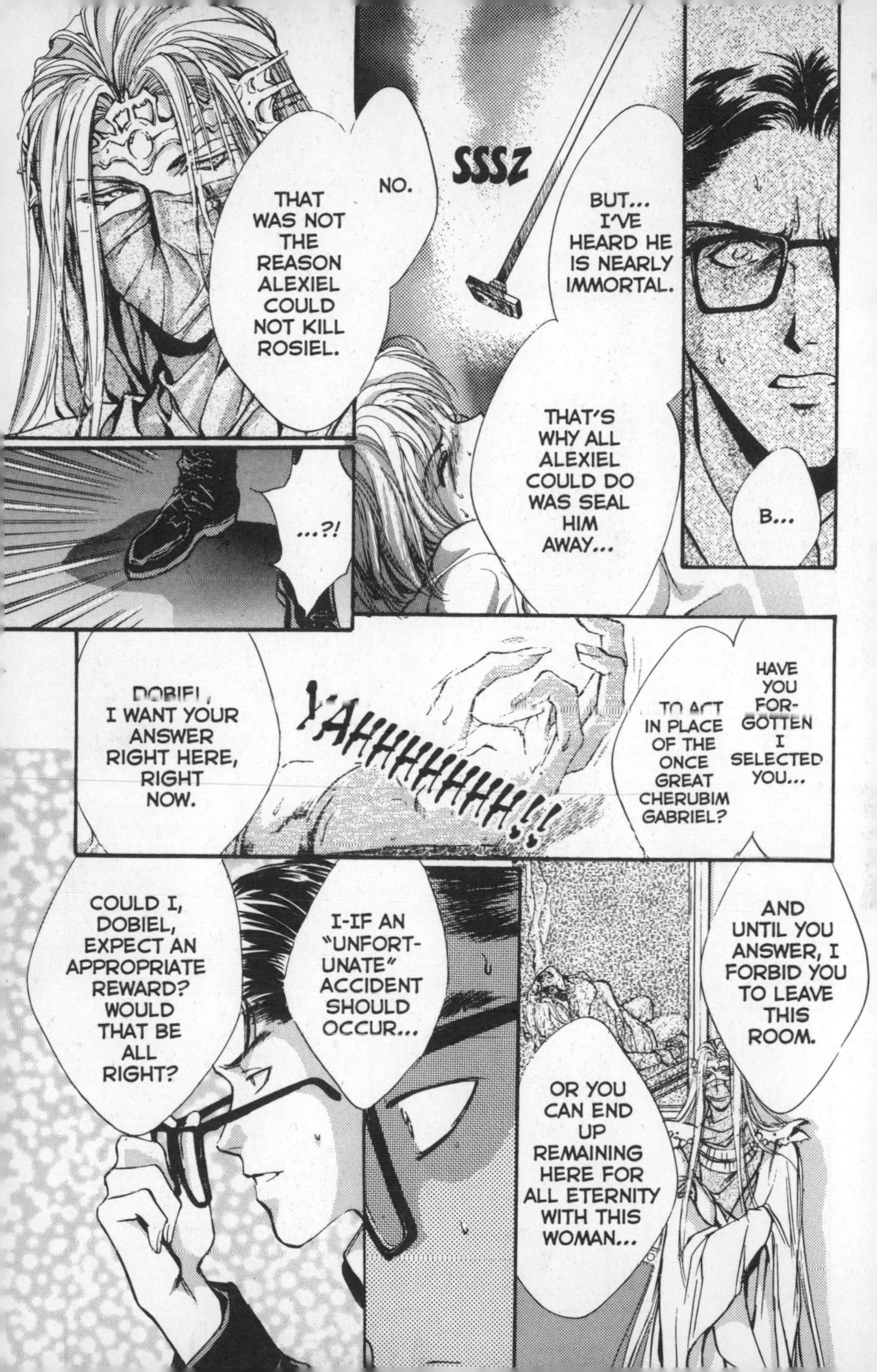
BUT... I'VE HEARD HE IS NEARLY IMMORTAL.
THAT'S WHY ALL ALEXIEL COULD DO WAS SEAL HIM AWAY...
B...
SSSZ
NO.
THAT WAS NOT THE REASON ALEXIEL COULD NOT KILL ROSIEL.
...?!
HAVE YOU FOR-GOTTEN I SELECTED YOU...
TO ACT IN PLACE OF THE ONCE GREAT CHERUBIM GABRIEL?
YAHHHHHHHH!!
DOBIEL, I WANT YOUR ANSWER RIGHT HERE, RIGHT NOW.
AND UNTIL YOU ANSWER, I FORBID YOU TO LEAVE THIS ROOM.
OR YOU CAN END UP REMAINING HERE FOR ALL ETERNITY WITH THIS WOMAN...
I-IF AN "UNFORT-UNATE" ACCIDENT SHOULD OCCUR...
COULD I, DOBIEL, EXPECT AN APPROPRIATE REWARD? WOULD THAT BE ALL RIGHT?

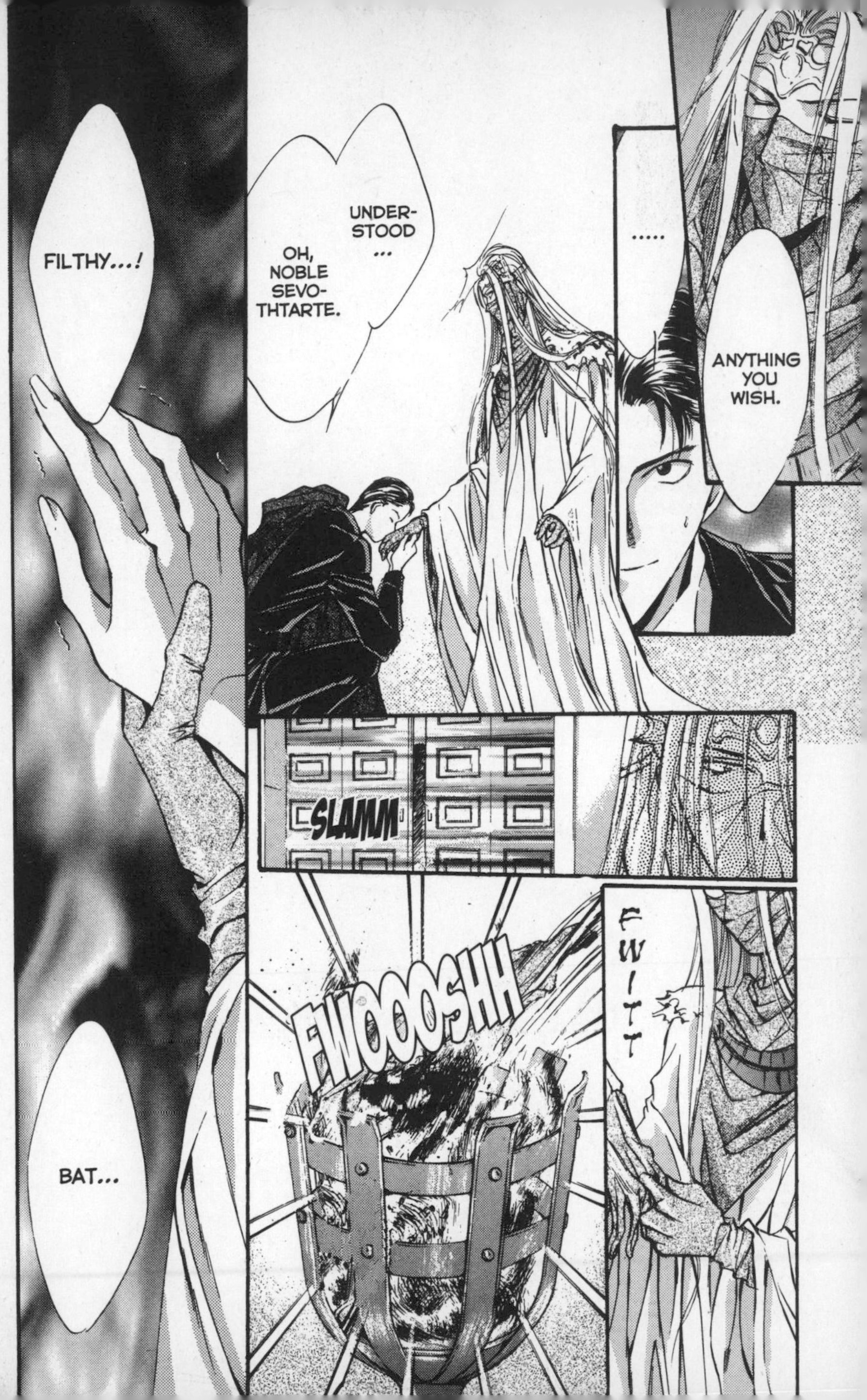
.....
ANYTHING YOU WISH.
UNDER-STOOD ...
OH, NOBLE SEVO-THTARTE.
SLAMM
FWITT
FWOOOSHH
FILTHY...!
BAT...

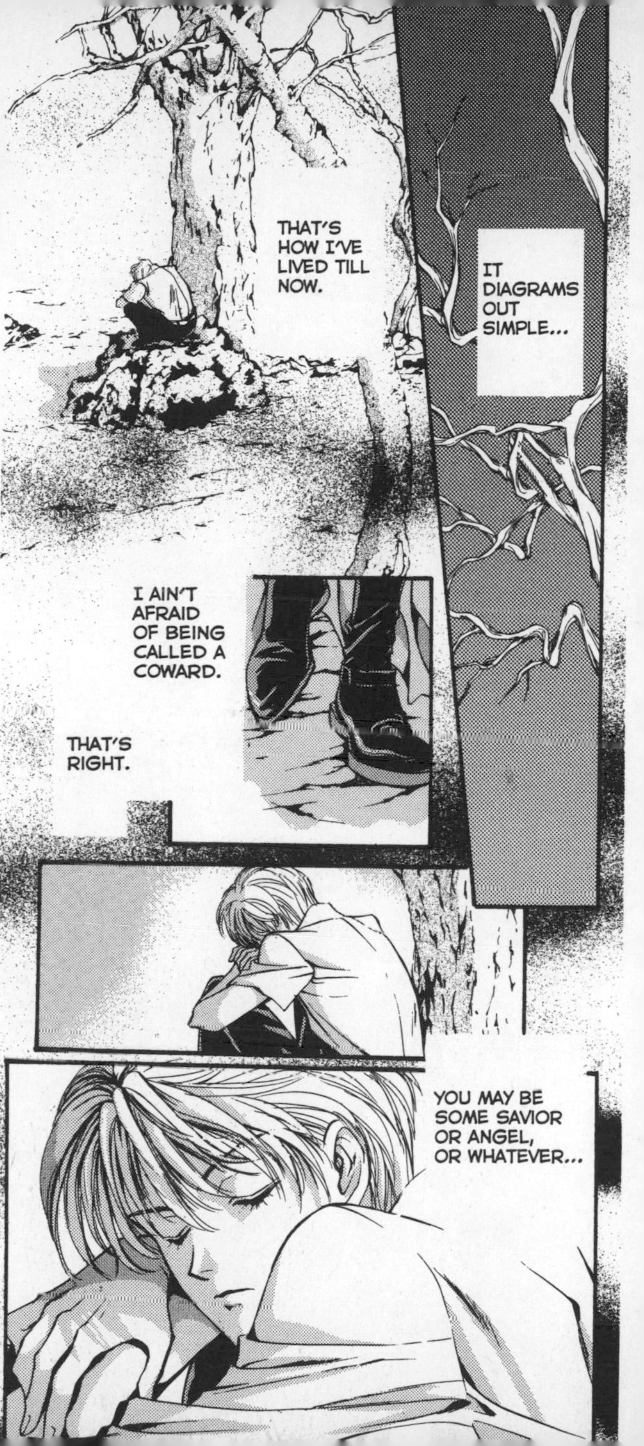
IT DIAGRAMS OUT SIMPLE...
THAT'S HOW I'VE LIVED TILL NOW.
I AIN'T AFRAID OF BEING CALLED A COWARD.
THAT'S RIGHT.
YOU MAY BE SOME SAVIOR OR ANGEL, OR WHATEVER...

I may be repeating myself, but Kato is not a minor character. Ever since this serial began, I have been anxiously waiting for the Hades chapter, where his character begins to play a role. I hinted at it by doing a lot of close-ups of him in the first volume--things like that. Even back then I was itching to draw the interaction between Setchan and Kato-chan. But I held back all this time.

It was so long!!

I'm glad to say he's quite popular, even though he isn't handsome or anything of the sort. Strangely, there are people who even think he's cool.♪ Actually, his actions, dialog, etc., are filled with many of my own troubles, and things I cry out for in my heart. He seems almost too close to be someone else.

You never can tell...!

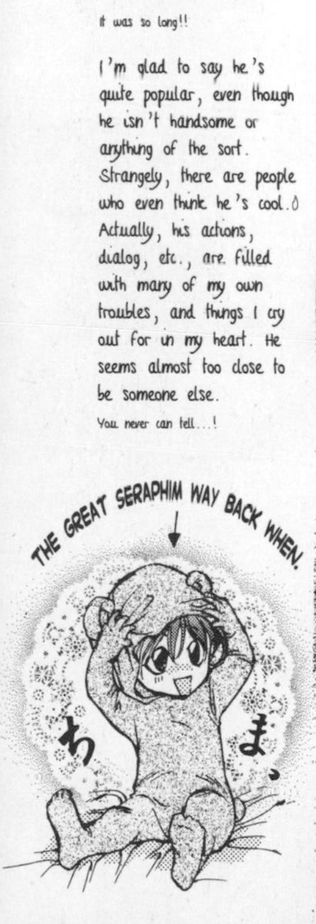
THE GREAT SERAPHIM WAY BACK WHEN.
ち
ま。

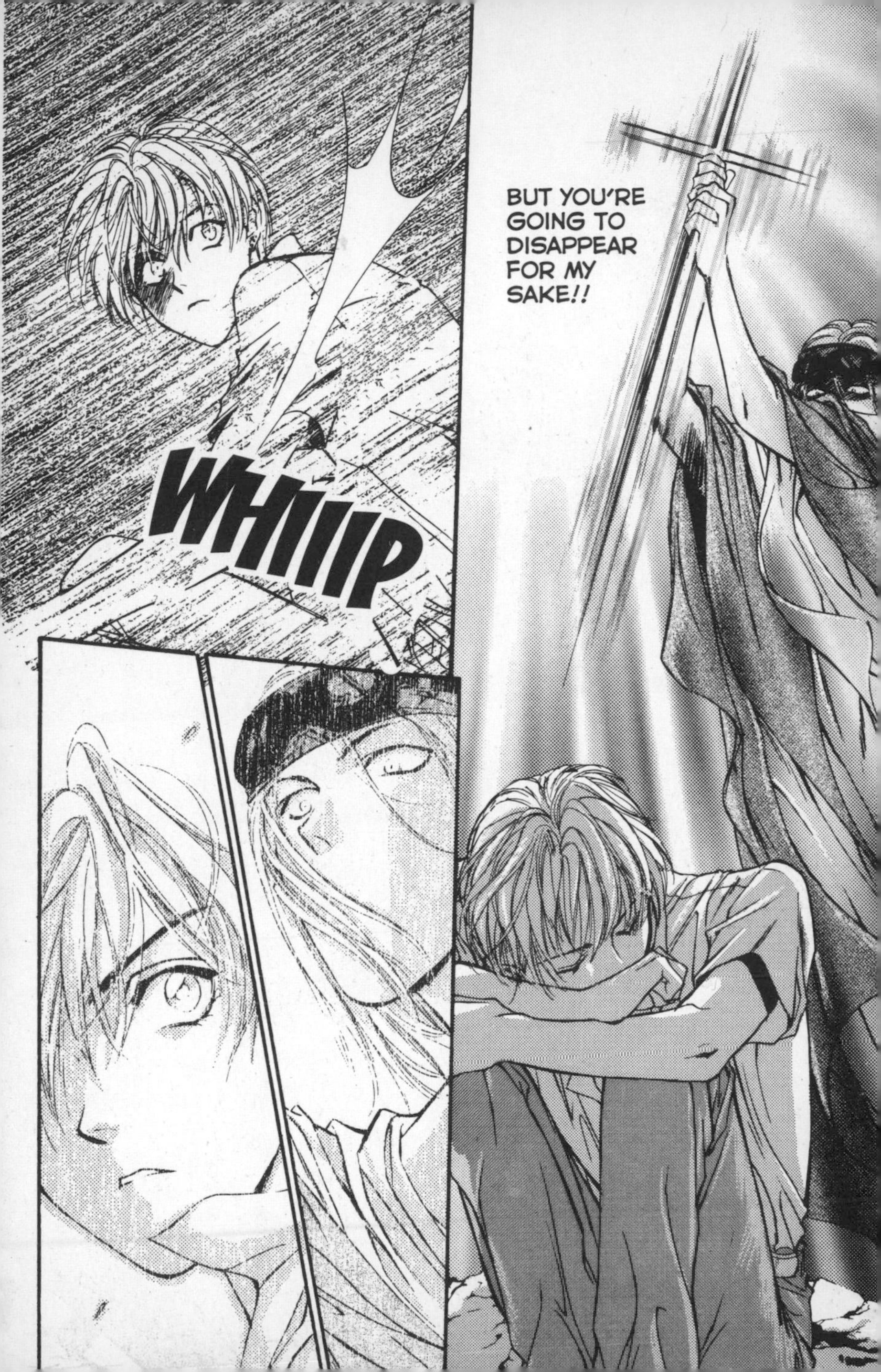
BUT YOU'RE GOING TO DISAPPEAR FOR MY SAKE!!
WHIIP

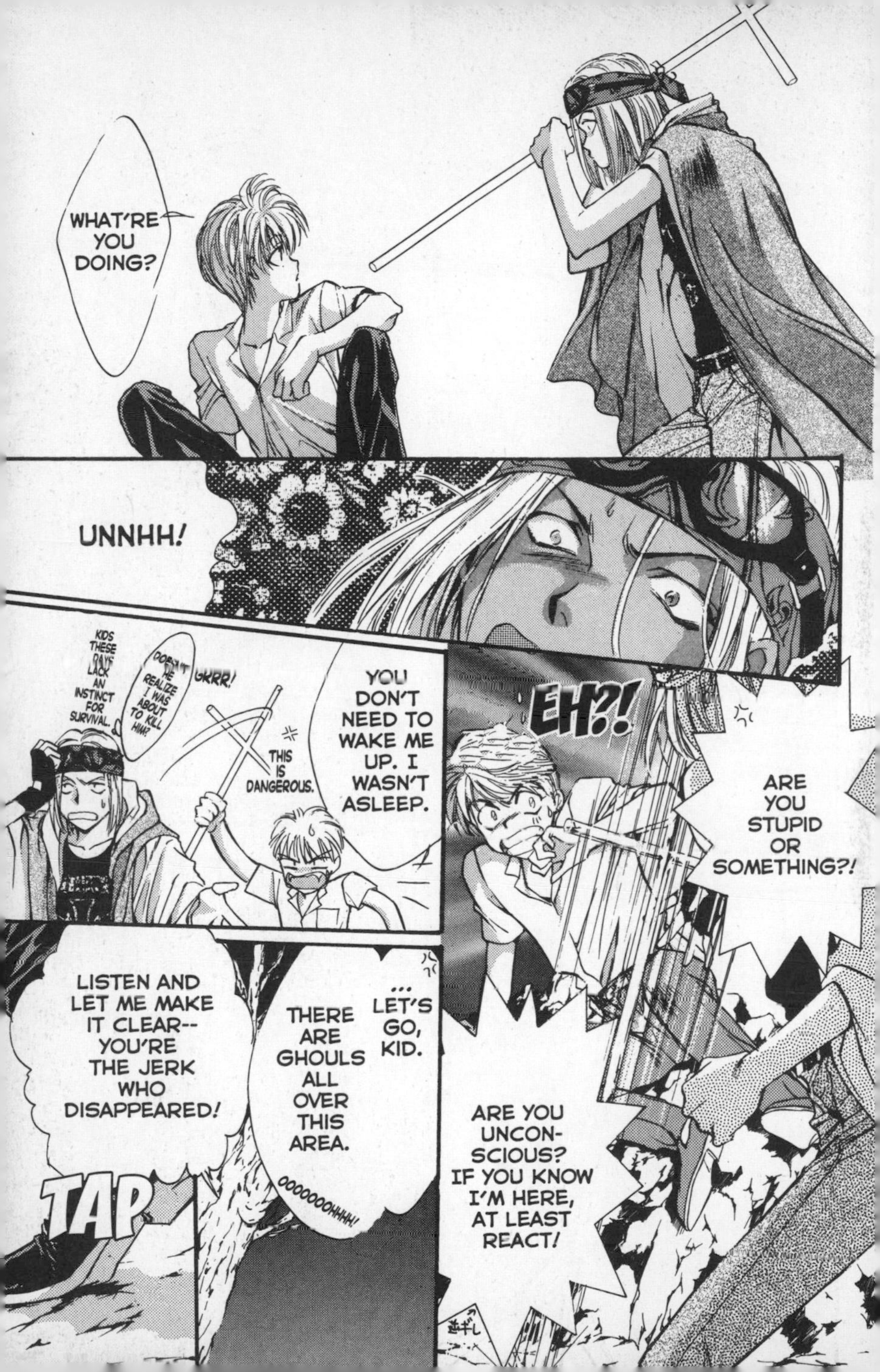
WHAT'RE YOU DOING?
UNNHH!
EH?!
ARE YOU STUPID OR SOMETHING?!
ARE YOU UNCONSCIOUS? IF YOU KNOW I'M HERE, AT LEAST REACT!
YOU DON'T NEED TO WAKE ME UP. I WASN'T ASLEEP.
THIS IS DANGEROUS.
GRRR!
DOESN'T HE REALIZE I WAS ABOUT TO KILL HIM?
KIDS THESE DAYS LACK AN INSTINCT FOR SURVIVAL.
... LET'S GO, KID.
THERE ARE GHOULS ALL OVER THIS AREA.
OOOOOOOHHHH!
LISTEN AND LET ME MAKE IT CLEAR-- YOU'RE THE JERK WHO DISAPPEARED!
TAP

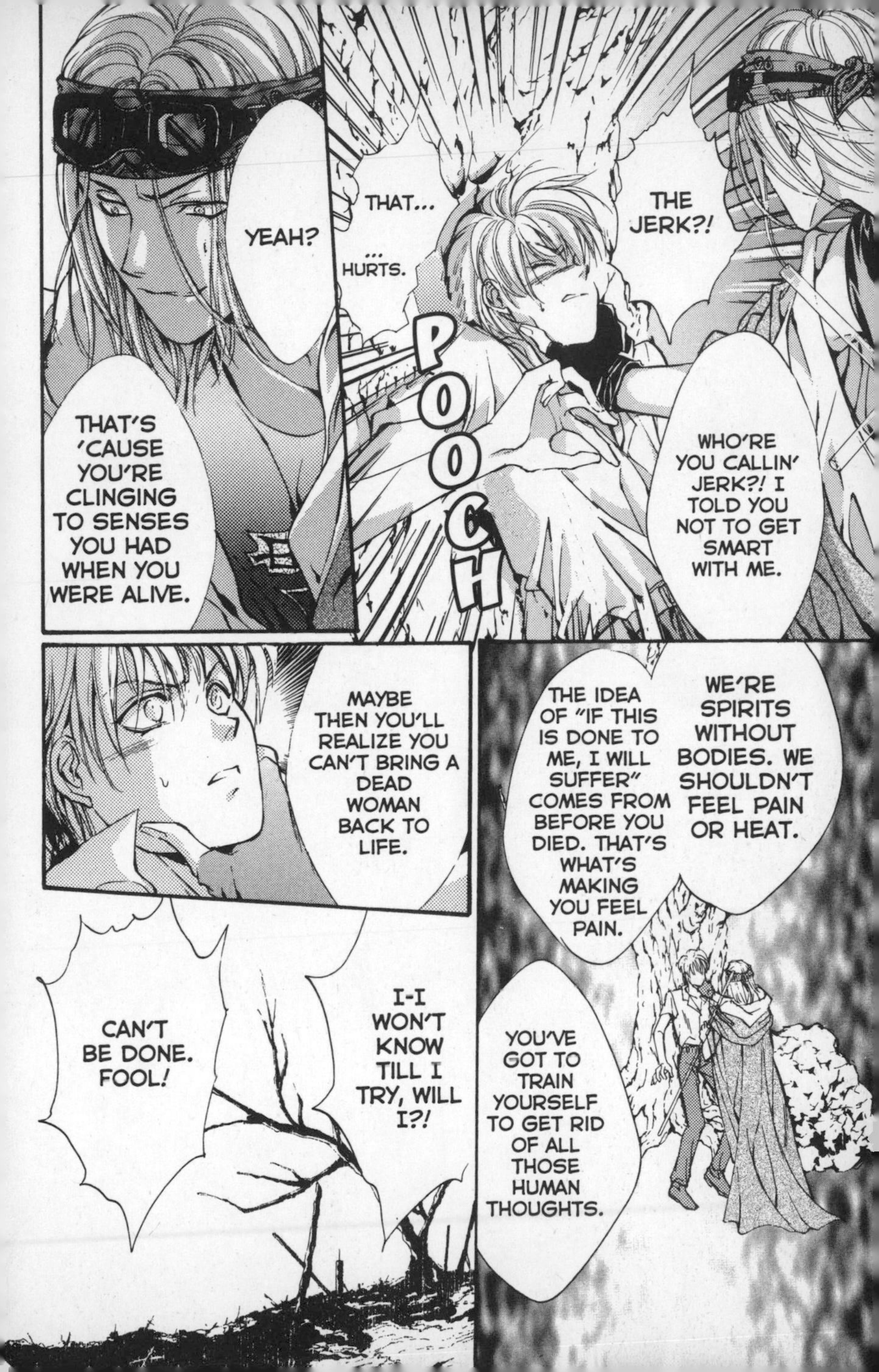
THE JERK?!
THAT...
... HURTS.
POOCH
WHO'RE YOU CALLIN' JERK?! I TOLD YOU NOT TO GET SMART WITH ME.
YEAH?
THAT'S 'CAUSE YOU'RE CLINGING TO SENSES YOU HAD WHEN YOU WERE ALIVE.
WE'RE SPIRITS WITHOUT BODIES. WE SHOULDN'T FEEL PAIN OR HEAT.
THE IDEA OF "IF THIS IS DONE TO ME, I WILL SUFFER" COMES FROM BEFORE YOU DIED. THAT'S WHAT'S MAKING YOU FEEL PAIN.
YOU'VE GOT TO TRAIN YOURSELF TO GET RID OF ALL THOSE HUMAN THOUGHTS.
MAYBE THEN YOU'LL REALIZE YOU CAN'T BRING A DEAD WOMAN BACK TO LIFE.
I-I WON'T KNOW TILL I TRY, WILL I?!
CAN'T BE DONE. FOOL!

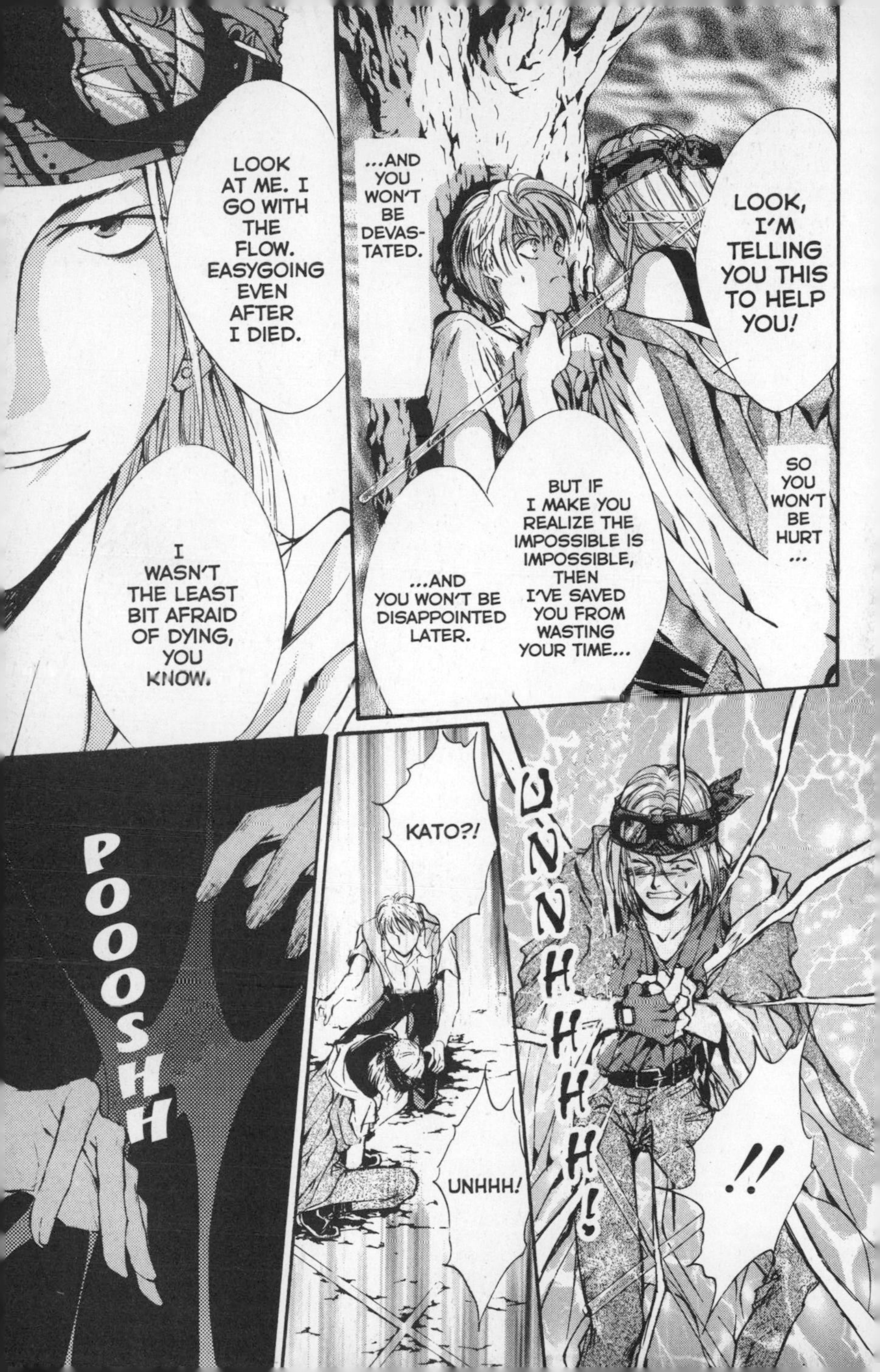
LOOK, I'M TELLING YOU THIS TO HELP YOU!
SO YOU WON'T BE HURT...
...AND YOU WON'T BE DEVASTATED.
BUT IF I MAKE YOU REALIZE THE IMPOSSIBLE IS IMPOSSIBLE, THEN I'VE SAVED YOU FROM WASTING YOUR TIME...
...AND YOU WON'T BE DISAPPOINTED LATER.
LOOK AT ME. I GO WITH THE FLOW. EASYGOING EVEN AFTER I DIED.
I WASN'T THE LEAST BIT AFRAID OF DYING, YOU KNOW.
UNNHHHH!
!!
KATO?!
UNHHH!
POOOSHH

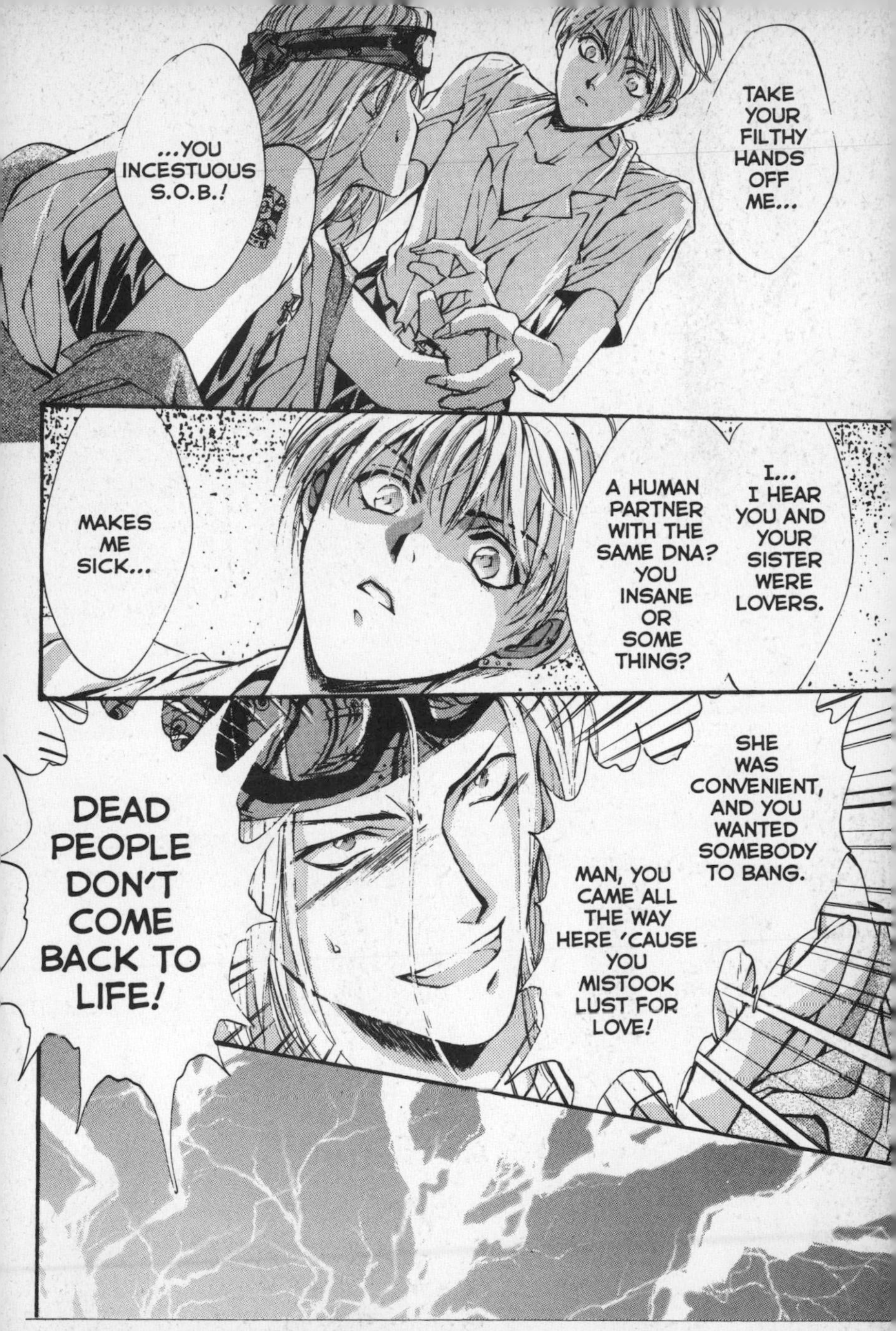
TAKE YOUR FILTHY HANDS OFF ME...
...YOU INCESTUOUS S.O.B.!
I... I HEAR YOU AND YOUR SISTER WERE LOVERS.
A HUMAN PARTNER WITH THE SAME DNA? YOU INSANE OR SOME THING?
MAKES ME SICK...
SHE WAS CONVENIENT, AND YOU WANTED SOMEBODY TO BANG.
MAN, YOU CAME ALL THE WAY HERE 'CAUSE YOU MISTOOK LUST FOR LOVE!
DEAD PEOPLE DON'T COME BACK TO LIFE!

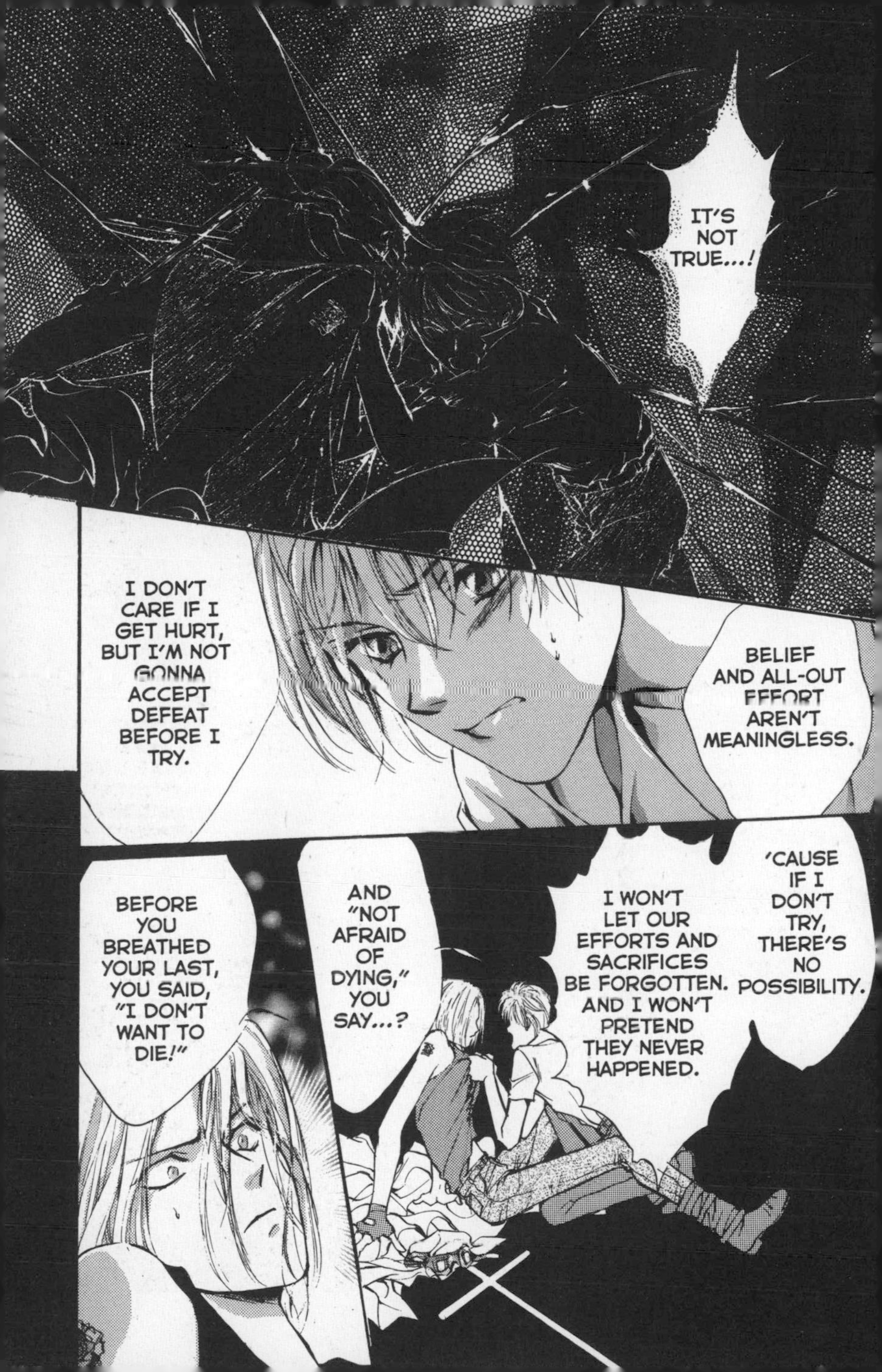
IT'S NOT TRUE...!
BELIEF AND ALL-OUT EFFORT AREN'T MEANINGLESS.
I DON'T CARE IF I GET HURT, BUT I'M NOT GONNA ACCEPT DEFEAT BEFORE I TRY.
'CAUSE IF I DON'T TRY, THERE'S NO POSSIBILITY.
I WON'T LET OUR EFFORTS AND SACRIFICES BE FORGOTTEN. AND I WON'T PRETEND THEY NEVER HAPPENED.
AND "NOT AFRAID OF DYING," YOU SAY...?
BEFORE YOU BREATHED YOUR LAST, YOU SAID, "I DON'T WANT TO DIE!"

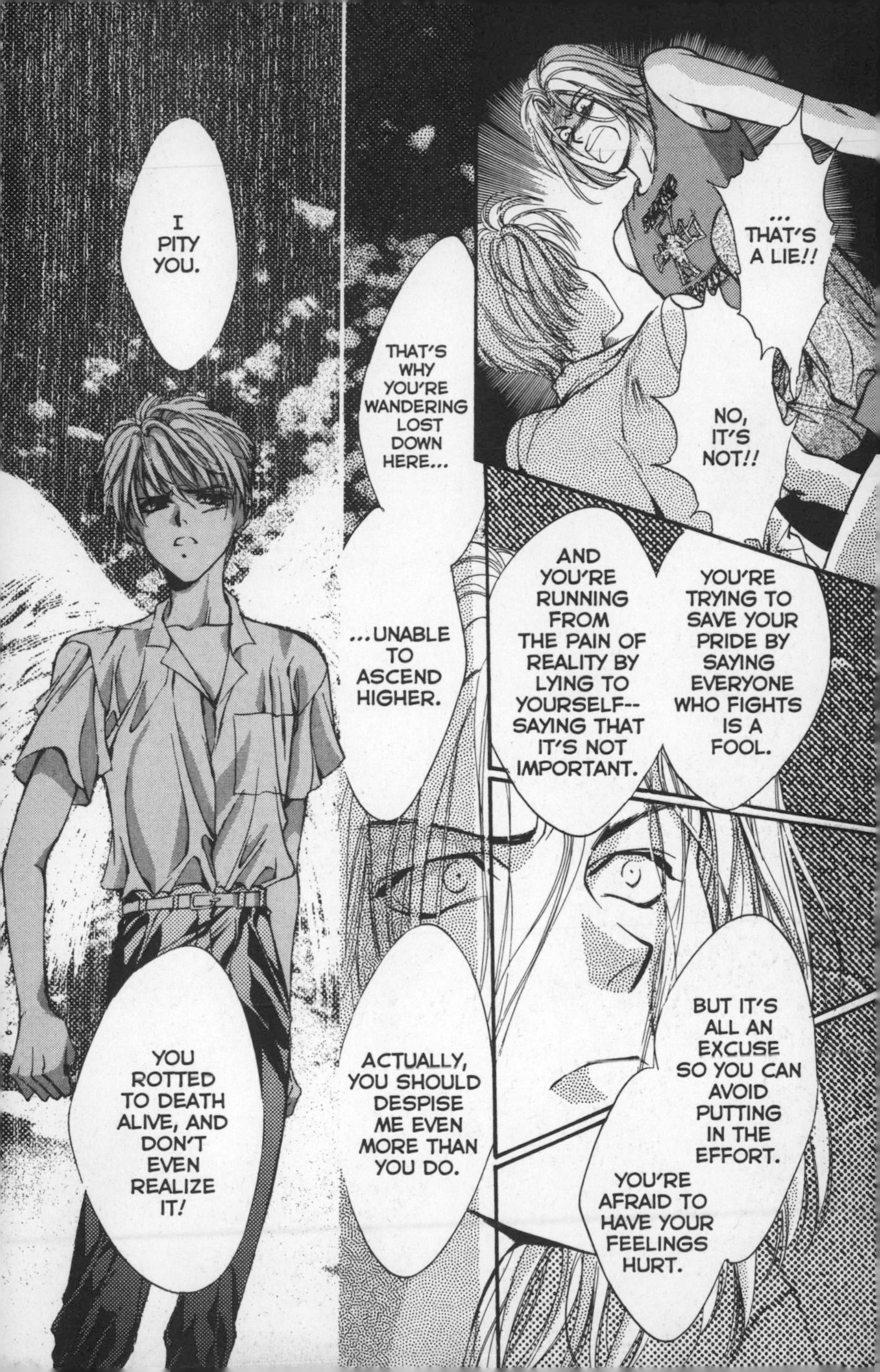
...THAT'S A LIE!!
NO, IT'S NOT!!
YOU'RE TRYING TO SAVE YOUR PRIDE BY SAYING EVERYONE WHO FIGHTS IS A FOOL.
AND YOU'RE RUNNING FROM THE PAIN OF REALITY BY LYING TO YOURSELF--SAYING THAT IT'S NOT IMPORTANT.
BUT IT'S ALL AN EXCUSE SO YOU CAN AVOID PUTTING IN THE EFFORT.
YOU'RE AFRAID TO HAVE YOUR FEELINGS HURT.
THAT'S WHY YOU'RE WANDERING LOST DOWN HERE...
...UNABLE TO ASCEND HIGHER.
ACTUALLY, YOU SHOULD DESPISE ME EVEN MORE THAN YOU DO.
I PITY YOU.
YOU ROTTED TO DEATH ALIVE, AND DON'T EVEN REALIZE IT!

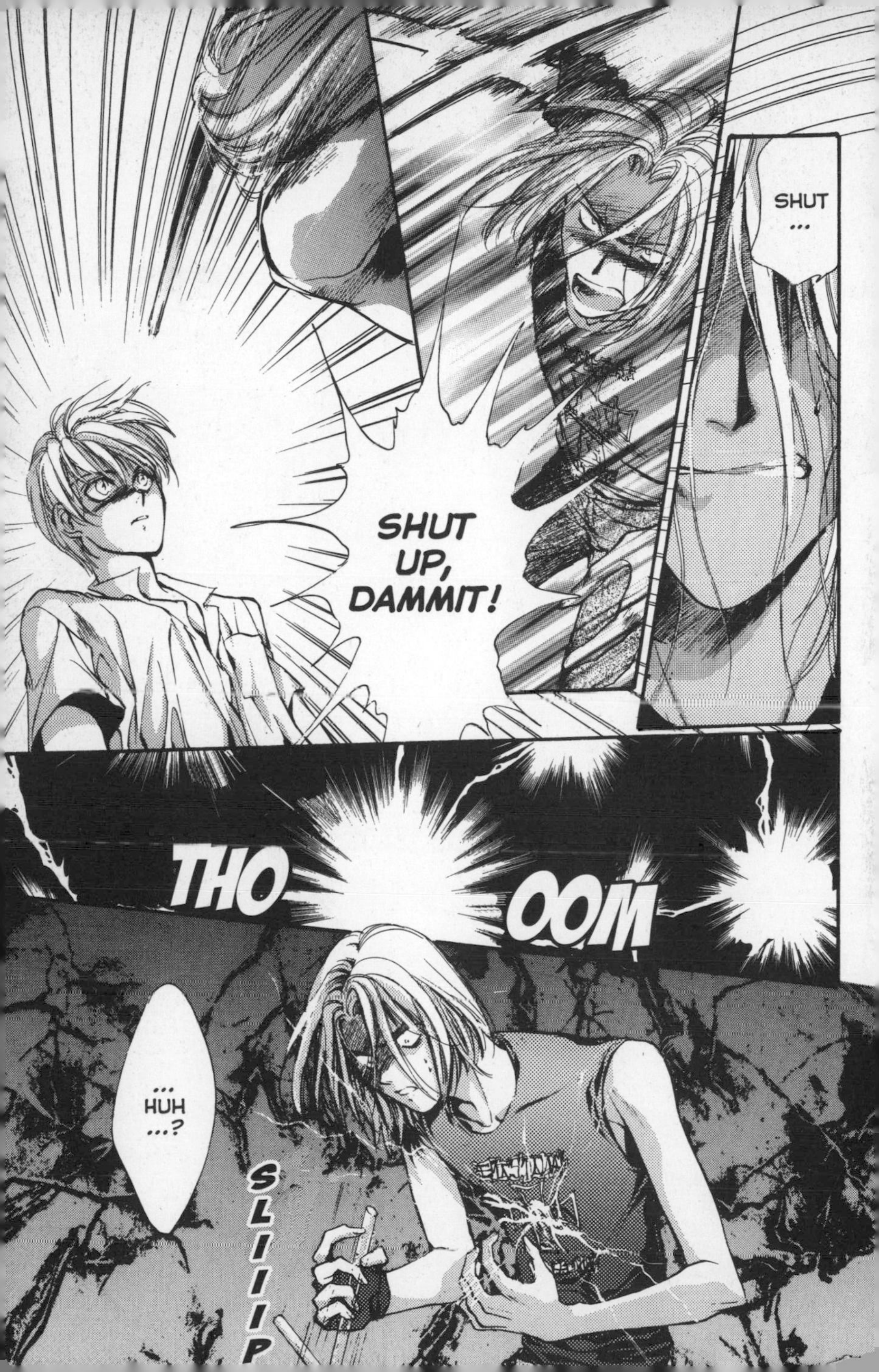
SHUT ...
SHUT UP, DAMMIT!
THO OOM
... HUH ...?
SLIIIIP

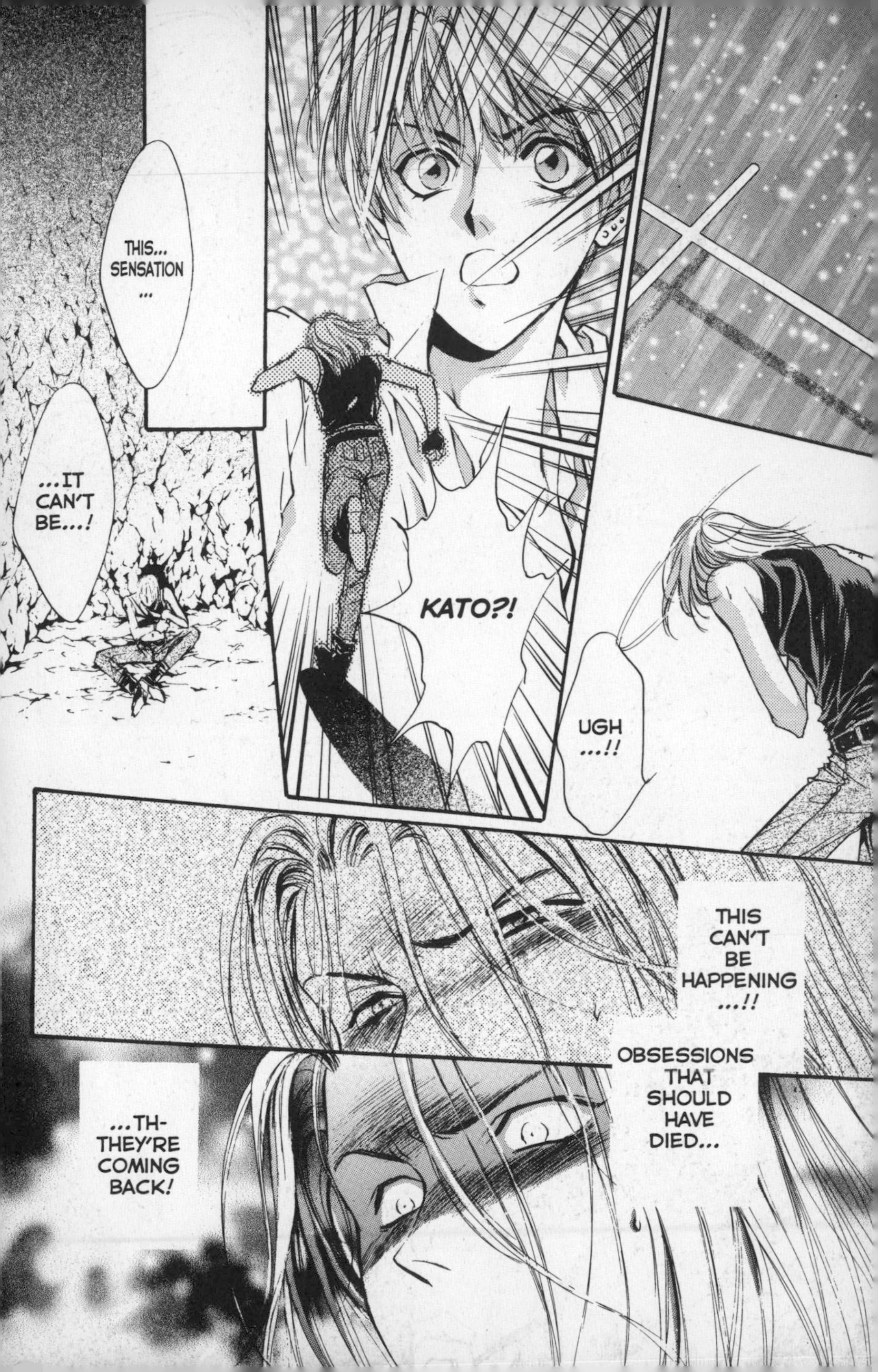
UGH ...!!
KATO?!
THIS... SENSATION ...
...IT CAN'T BE...!
THIS CAN'T BE HAPPENING ...!!
OBSESSIONS THAT SHOULD HAVE DIED...
...TH-THEY'RE COMING BACK!

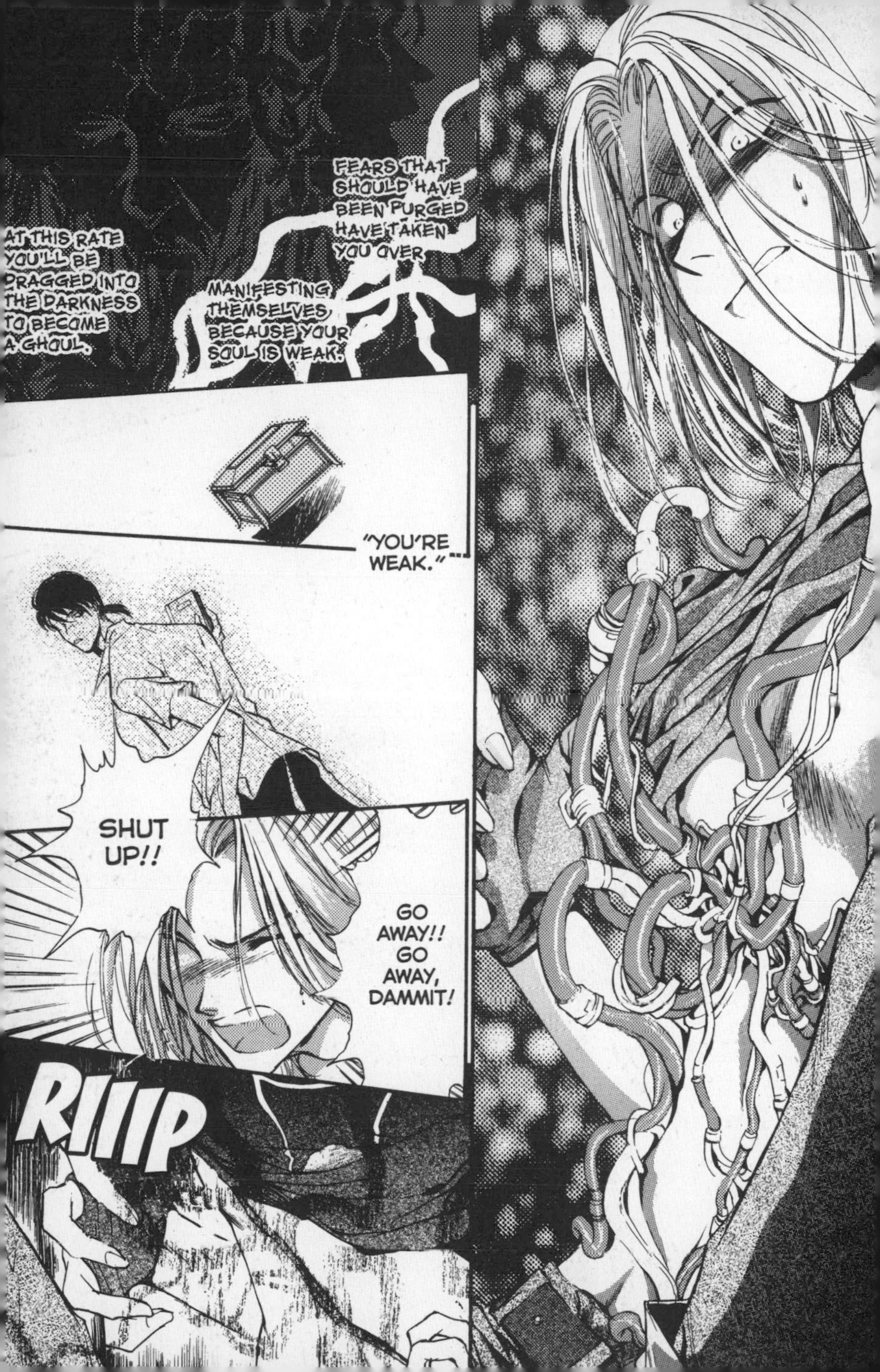
FEARS THAT SHOULD HAVE BEEN PURGED HAVE TAKEN YOU OVER
MANIFESTING THEMSELVES BECAUSE YOUR SOUL IS WEAK.
AT THIS RATE YOU'LL BE DRAGGED INTO THE DARKNESS TO BECOME A GHOUL.
"YOU'RE WEAK."
SHUT UP!!
GO AWAY!! GO AWAY, DAMMIT!
RIIP

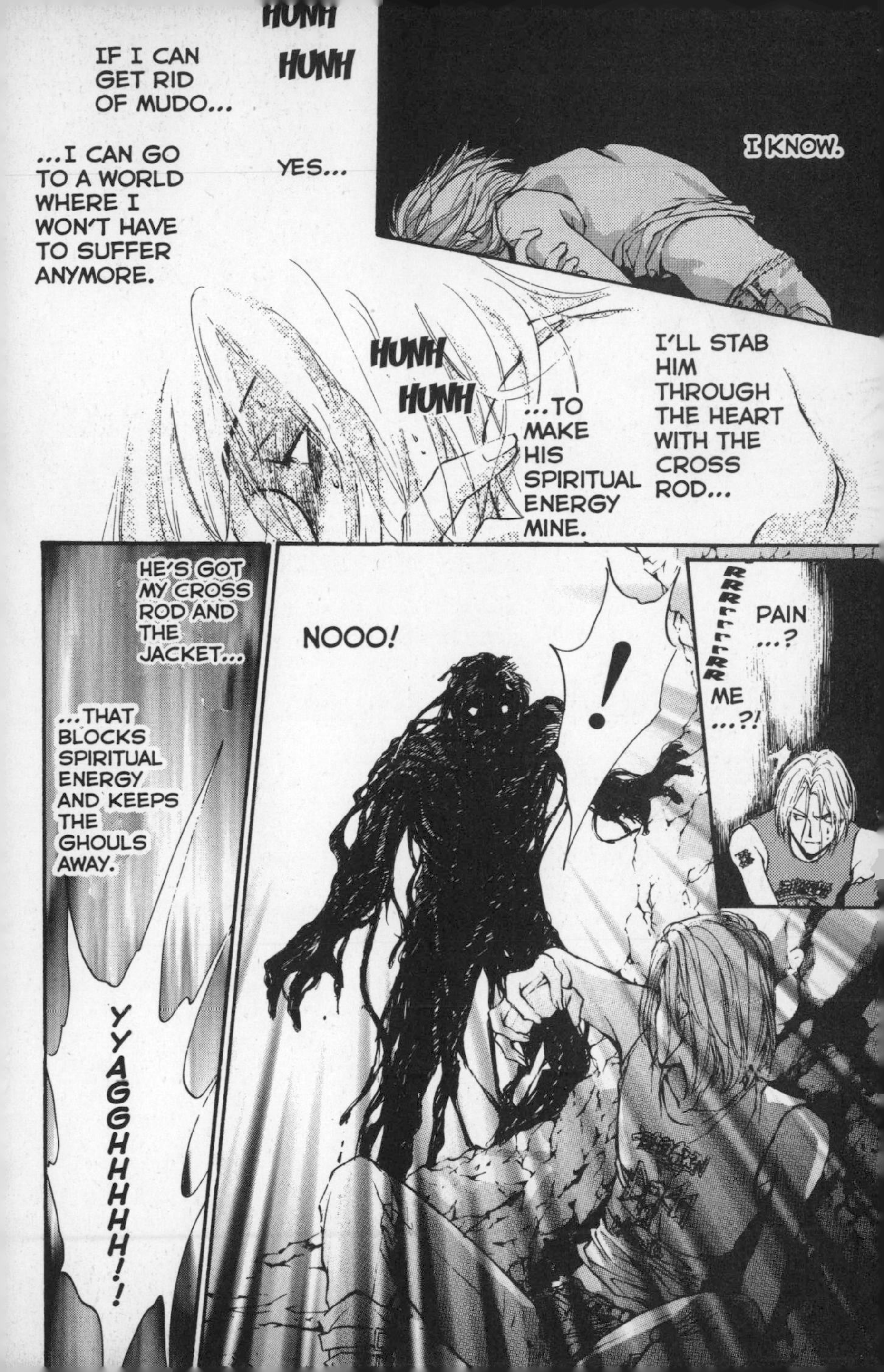
I KNOW.
HUNH
HUNH
IF I CAN GET RID OF MUDO...
...I CAN GO TO A WORLD WHERE I WON'T HAVE TO SUFFER ANYMORE.
YES...
I'LL STAB HIM THROUGH THE HEART WITH THE CROSS ROD...
...TO MAKE HIS SPIRITUAL ENERGY MINE.
HUNH
HUNH
RRRrrrrrRR
PAIN ...?
ME ...?!
!
NOOO!
HE'S GOT MY CROSS ROD AND THE JACKET...
...THAT BLOCKS SPIRITUAL ENERGY AND KEEPS THE GHOULS AWAY.
YYAGGHHHHHH!!!

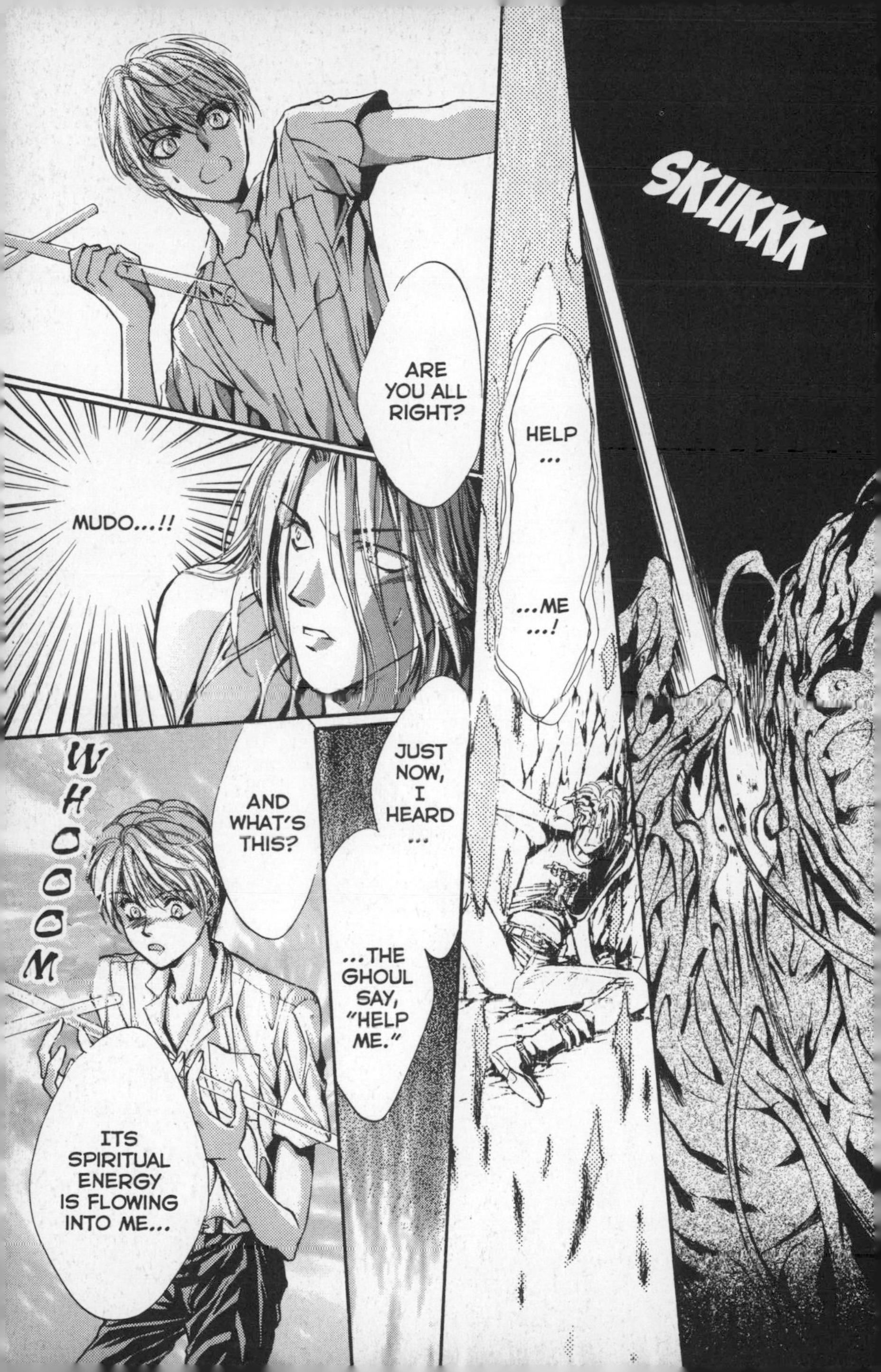
SKUKKK
HELP ...
...ME ...!
ARE YOU ALL RIGHT?
MUDO...!!
JUST NOW, I HEARD ...
...THE GHOUL SAY, "HELP ME."
AND WHAT'S THIS?
ITS SPIRITUAL ENERGY IS FLOWING INTO ME...
WHOOOOM

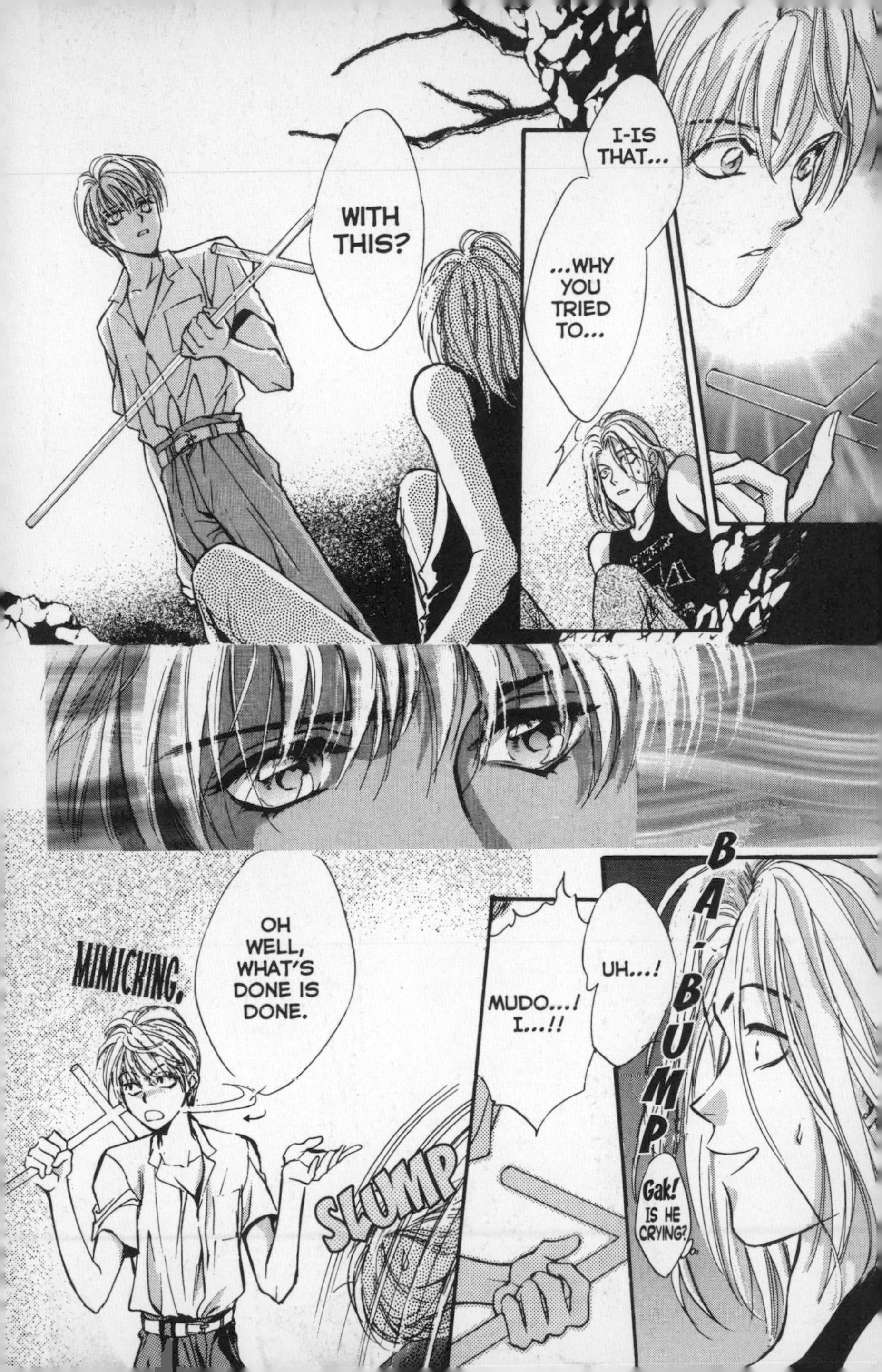
I-IS THAT...
...WHY YOU TRIED TO...
WITH THIS?
BA-BUMP
UH...!
MUDO...! I...!!
Gak! IS HE CRYING?
SLUMP
OH WELL, WHAT'S DONE IS DONE.
MIMICKING.

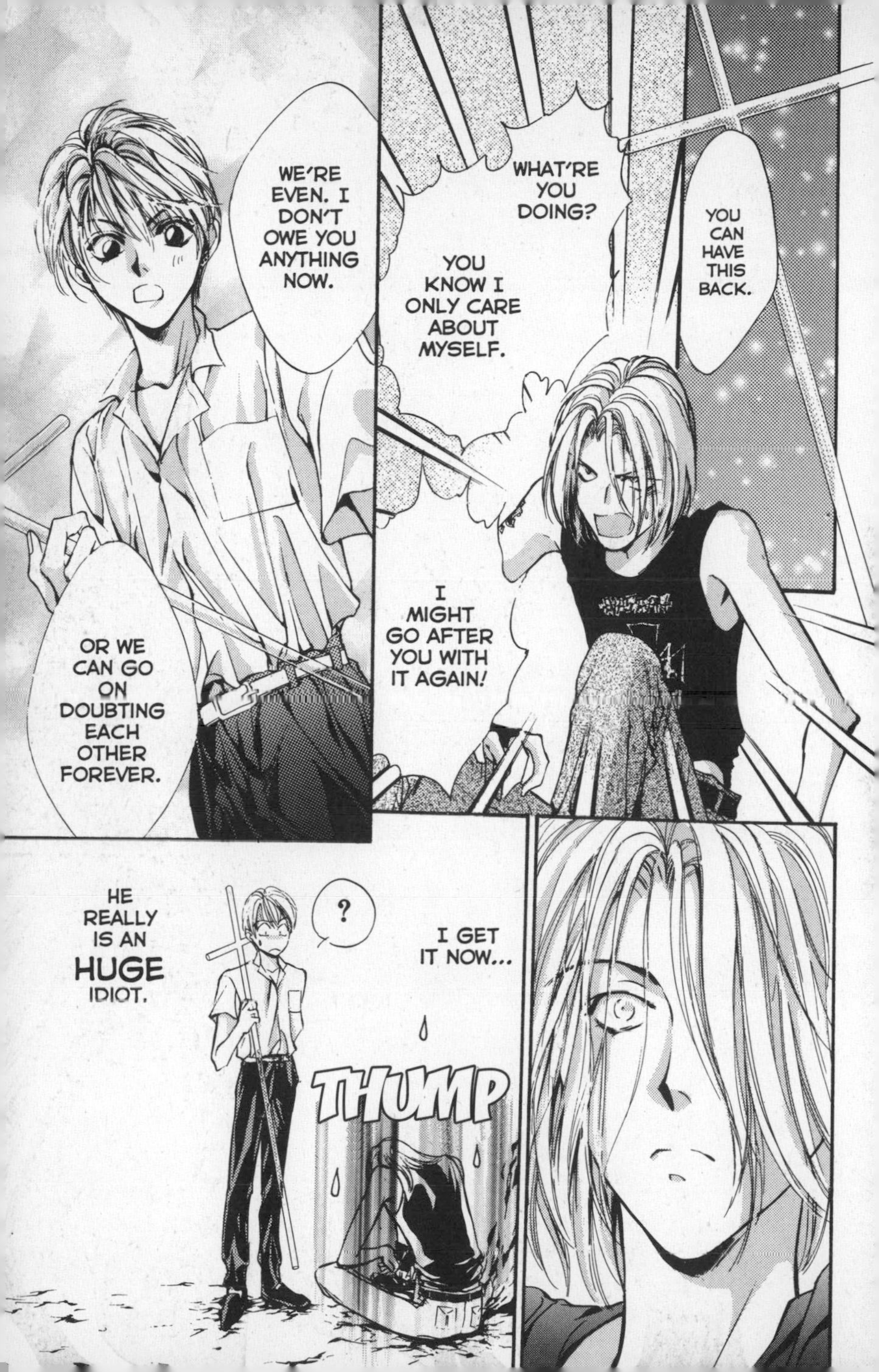
YOU CAN HAVE THIS BACK.
WHAT'RE YOU DOING?
YOU KNOW I ONLY CARE ABOUT MYSELF.
I MIGHT GO AFTER YOU WITH IT AGAIN!
WE'RE EVEN. I DON'T OWE YOU ANYTHING NOW.
OR WE CAN GO ON DOUBTING EACH OTHER FOREVER.
I GET IT NOW...
?
THUMP
HE REALLY IS AN HUGE IDIOT.

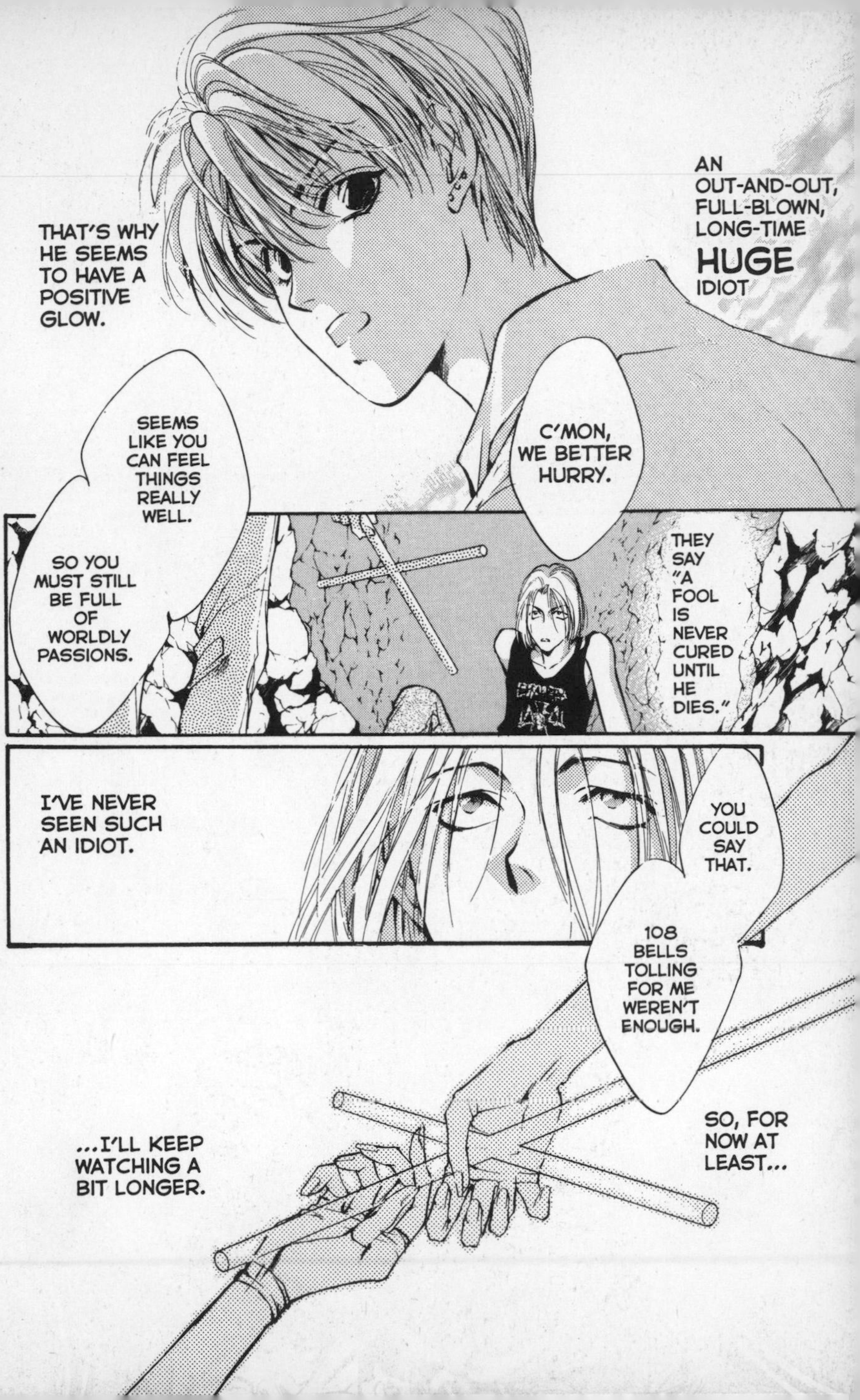
AN OUT-AND-OUT, FULL-BLOWN, LONG-TIME HUGE IDIOT
THAT'S WHY HE SEEMS TO HAVE A POSITIVE GLOW.
C'MON, WE BETTER HURRY.
SEEMS LIKE YOU CAN FEEL THINGS REALLY WELL.
THEY SAY "A FOOL IS NEVER CURED UNTIL HE DIES."
SO YOU MUST STILL BE FULL OF WORLDLY PASSIONS.
YOU COULD SAY THAT.
108 BELLS TOLLING FOR ME WEREN'T ENOUGH.
I'VE NEVER SEEN SUCH AN IDIOT.
SO, FOR NOW AT LEAST...
...I'LL KEEP WATCHING A BIT LONGER.

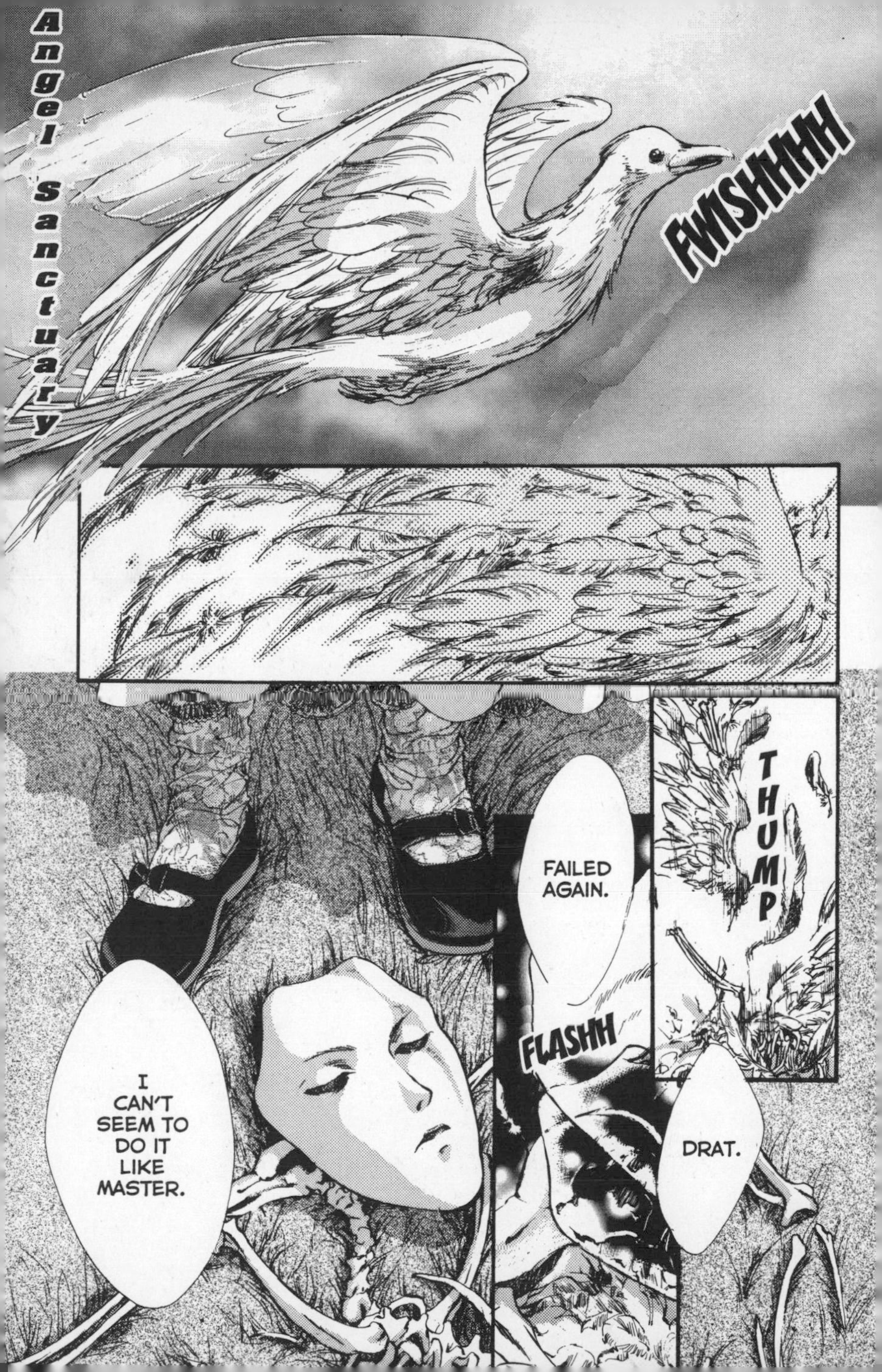
Angel Sanctuary
FWISHHHH
THUMP
FAILED AGAIN.
FLASHH
DRAT.
I CAN'T SEEM TO DO IT LIKE MASTER.

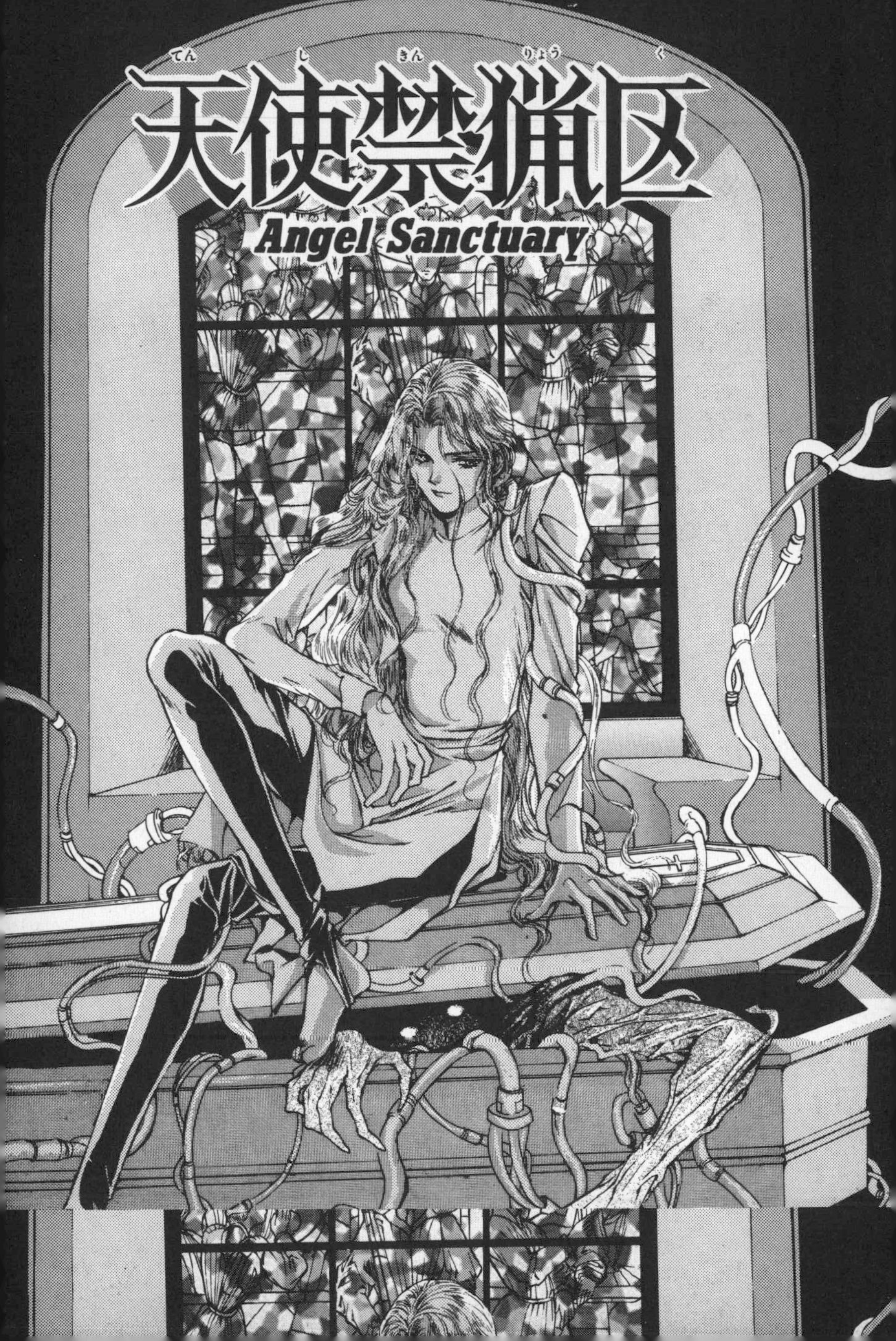
てんしきんりょうく
天使禁猟区
Angel Sanctuary

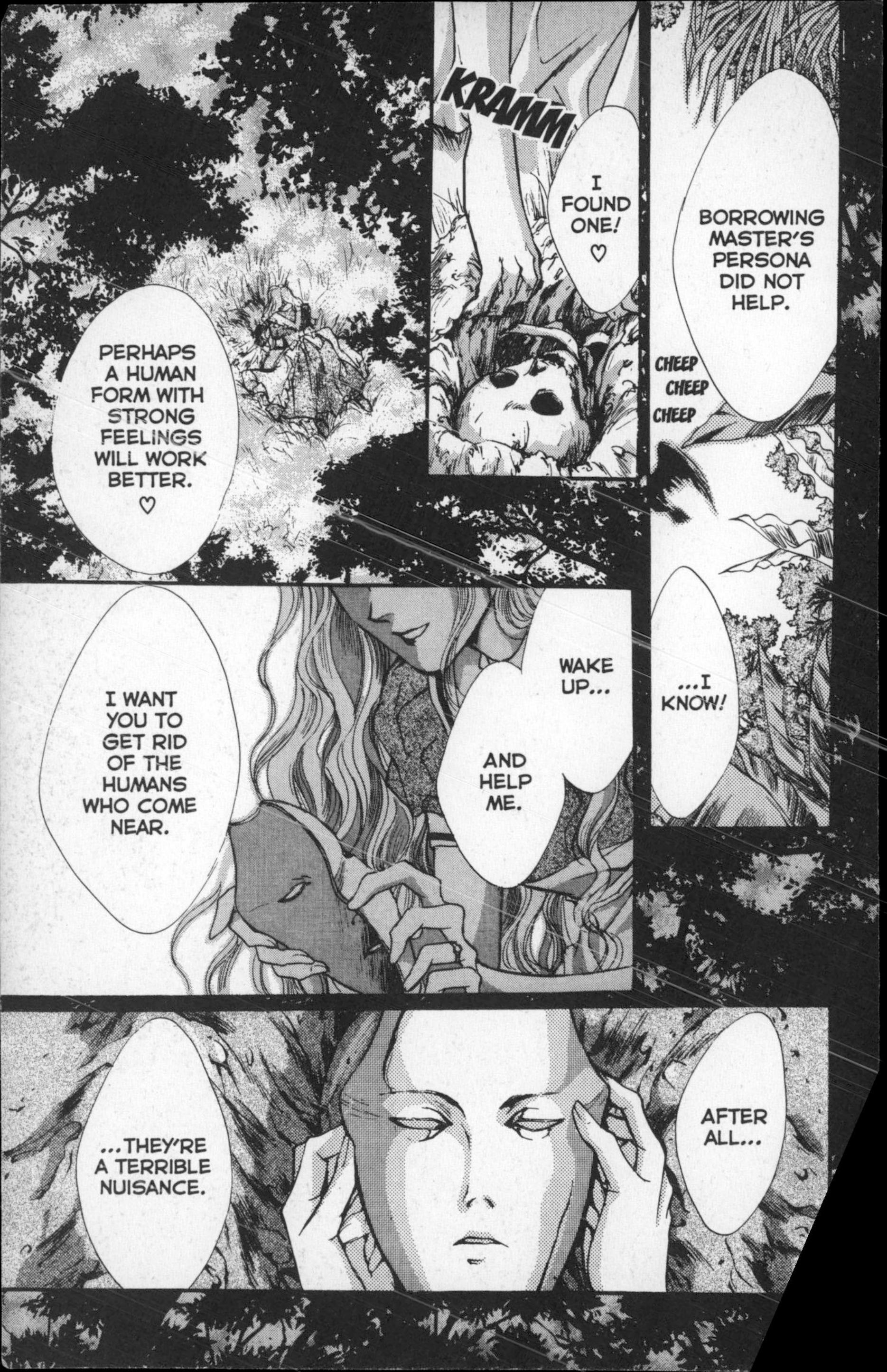
BORROWING MASTER'S PERSONA DID NOT HELP.
CHEEP
CHEEP
CHEEP
...I KNOW!
KRAMM
I FOUND ONE! ♡
PERHAPS A HUMAN FORM WITH STRONG FEELINGS WILL WORK BETTER. ♡
WAKE UP...
AND HELP ME.
I WANT YOU TO GET RID OF THE HUMANS WHO COME NEAR.
AFTER ALL...
...THEY'RE A TERRIBLE NUISANCE.

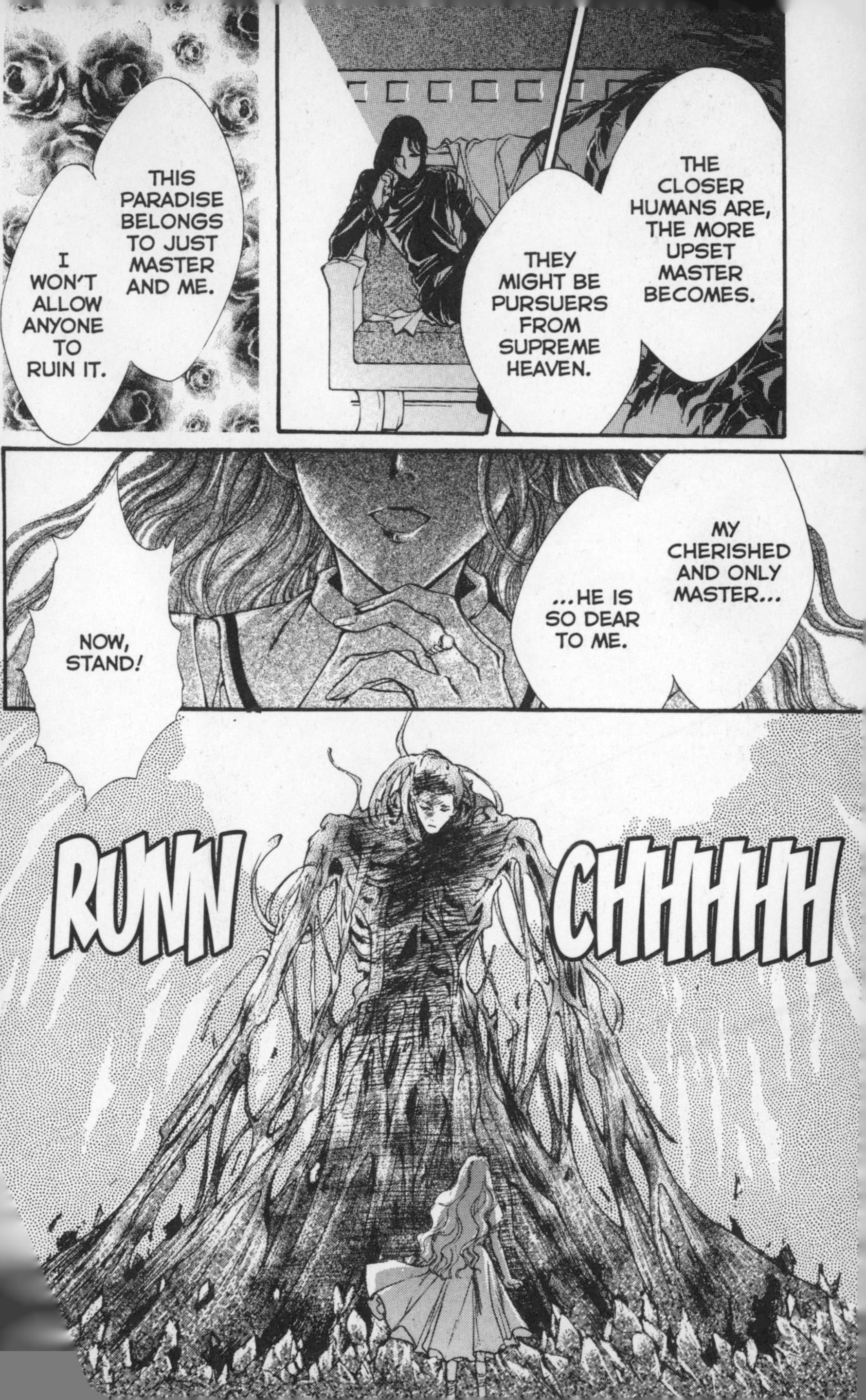
THE CLOSER HUMANS ARE, THE MORE UPSET MASTER BECOMES.
THEY MIGHT BE PURSUERS FROM SUPREME HEAVEN.
THIS PARADISE BELONGS TO JUST MASTER AND ME.
I WON'T ALLOW ANYONE TO RUIN IT.
MY CHERISHED AND ONLY MASTER...
...HE IS SO DEAR TO ME.
NOW, STAND!
RUNN
CHHHHHH

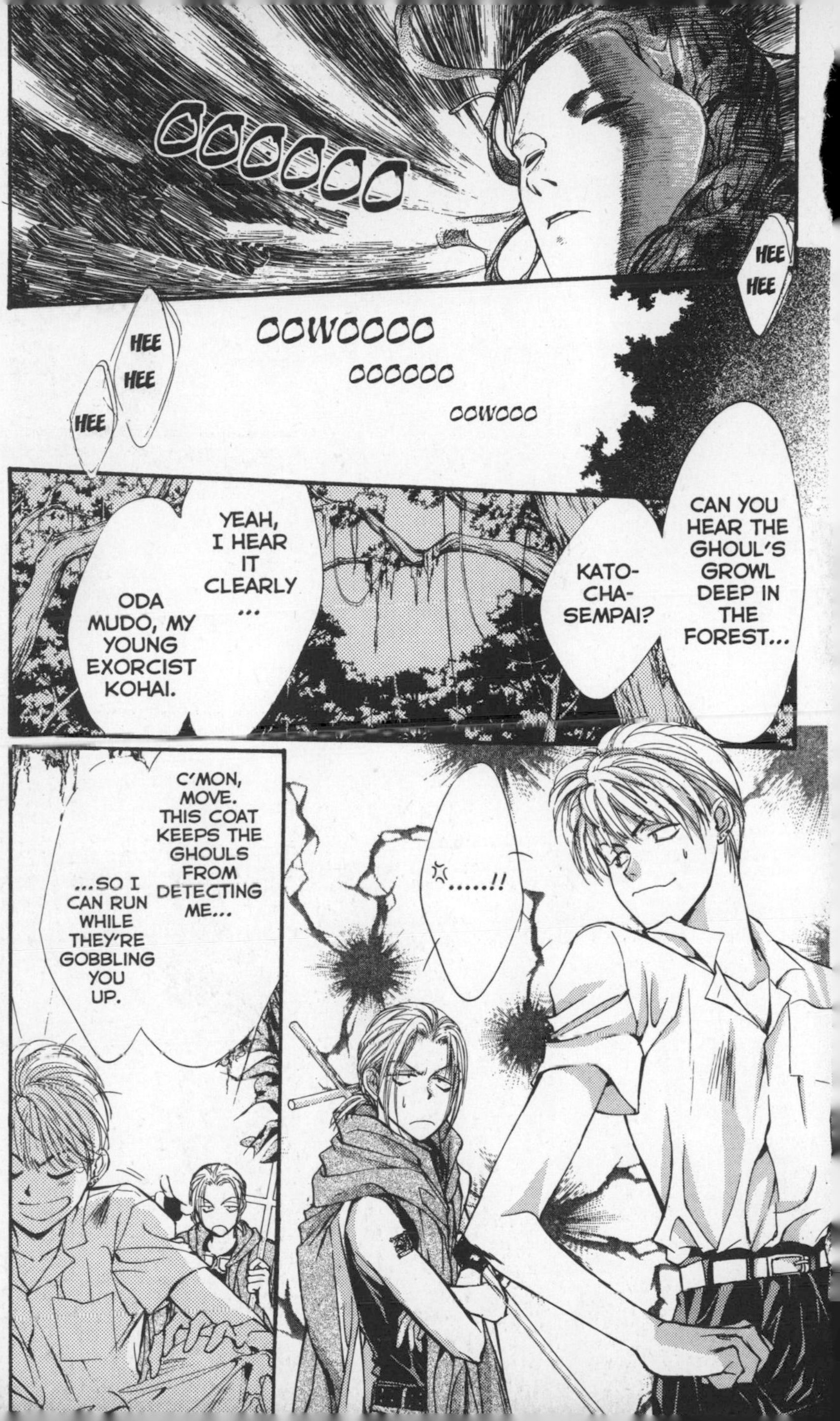
OOOOOO
HEE HEE
OOWOOOO
OOOOOO
OOWOOO
HEE HEE
HEE
CAN YOU HEAR THE GHOUL'S GROWL DEEP IN THE FOREST...
KATO-CHA-SEMPAI?
YEAH, I HEAR IT CLEARLY...
ODA MUDO, MY YOUNG EXORCIST KOHAI.
.....!!
C'MON, MOVE. THIS COAT KEEPS THE GHOULS FROM DETECTING ME...
...SO I CAN RUN WHILE THEY'RE GOBBLING YOU UP.

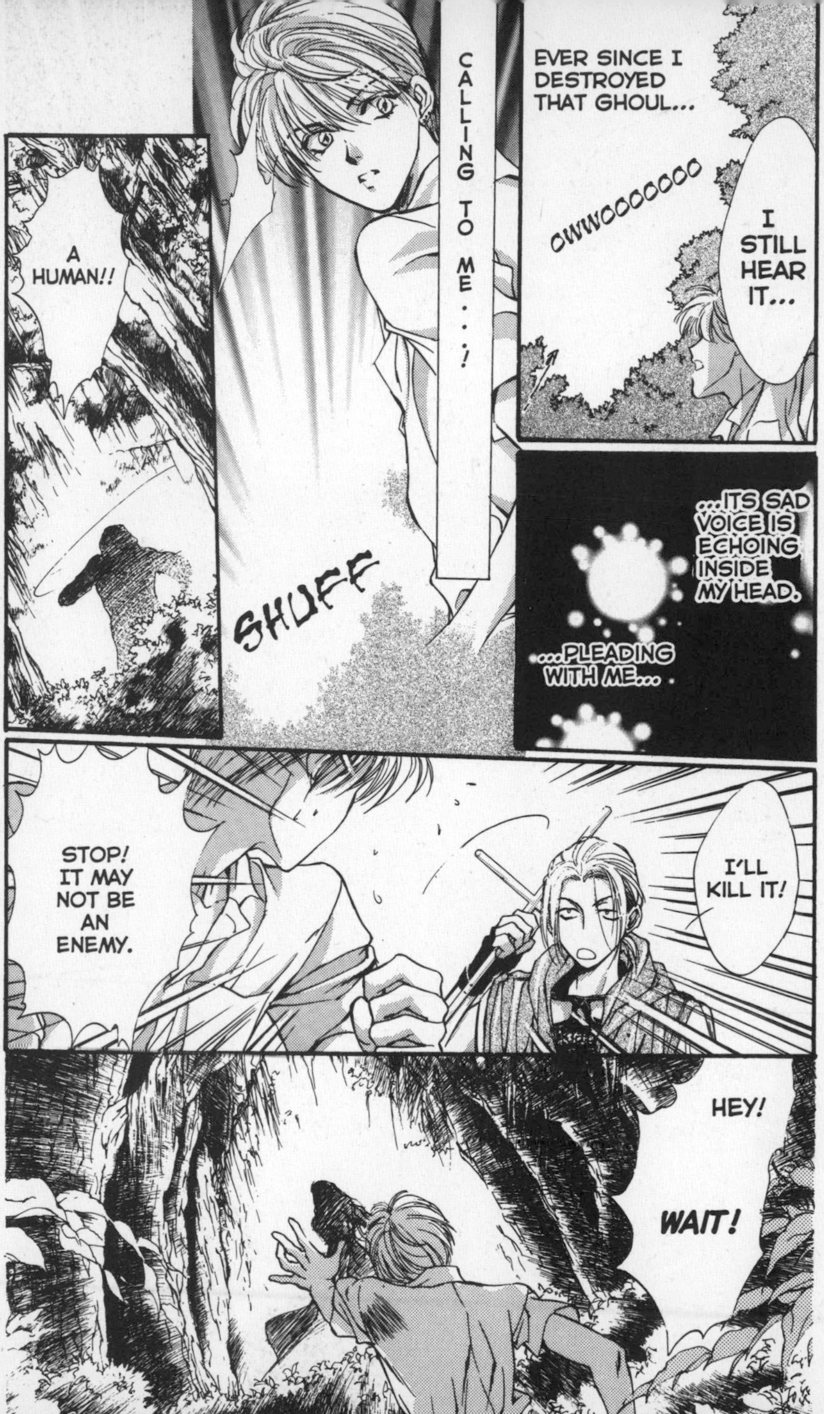
EVER SINCE I DESTROYED THAT GHOUL...
OWWOOOOOOOO
I STILL HEAR IT...
...ITS SAD VOICE IS ECHOING INSIDE MY HEAD.
...PLEADING WITH ME...
CALLING TO ME...!
SHUFF
A HUMAN!!
I'LL KILL IT!
STOP! IT MAY NOT BE AN ENEMY.
HEY!
WAIT!

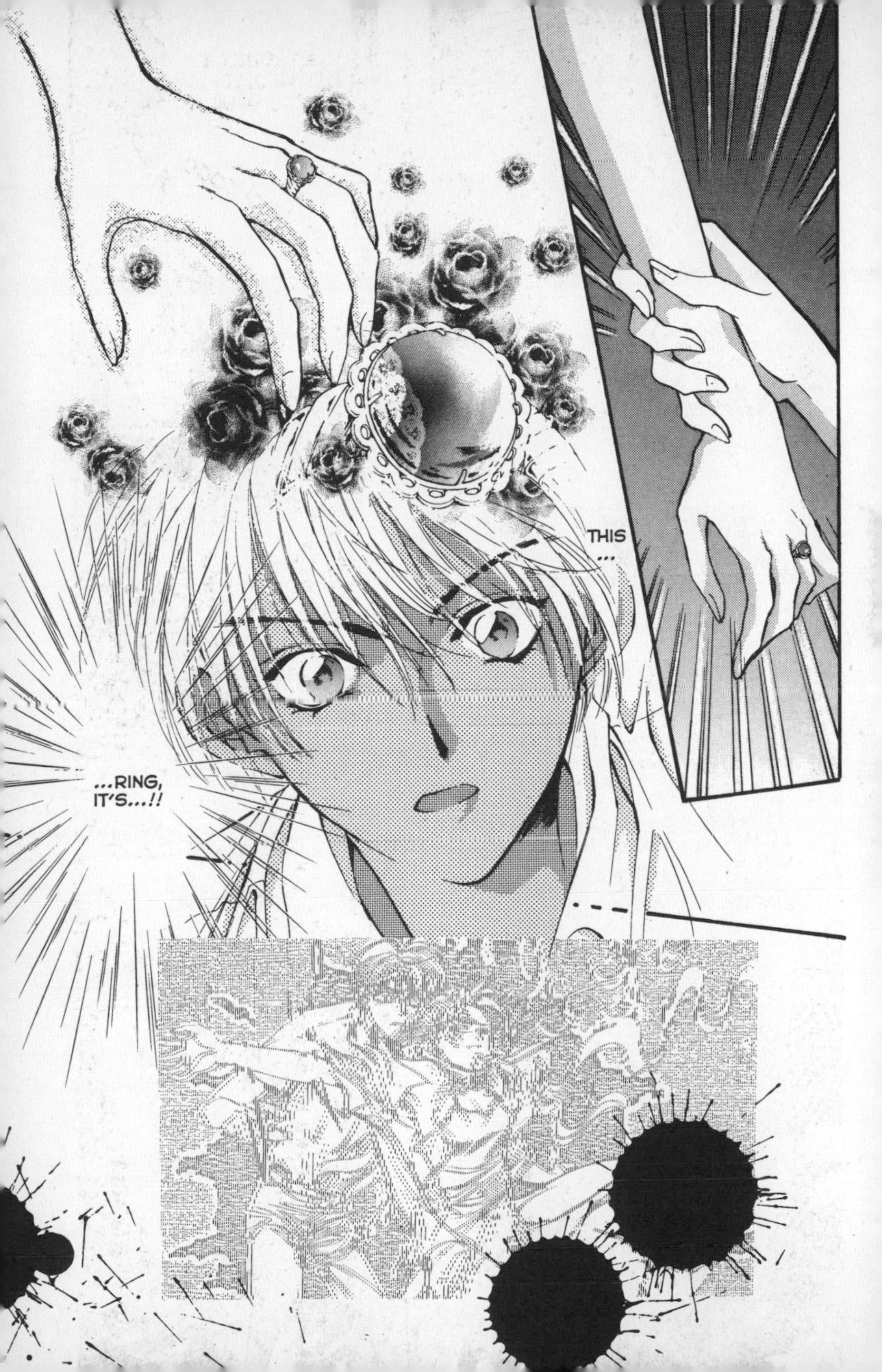
THIS ...
...RING, IT'S...!!

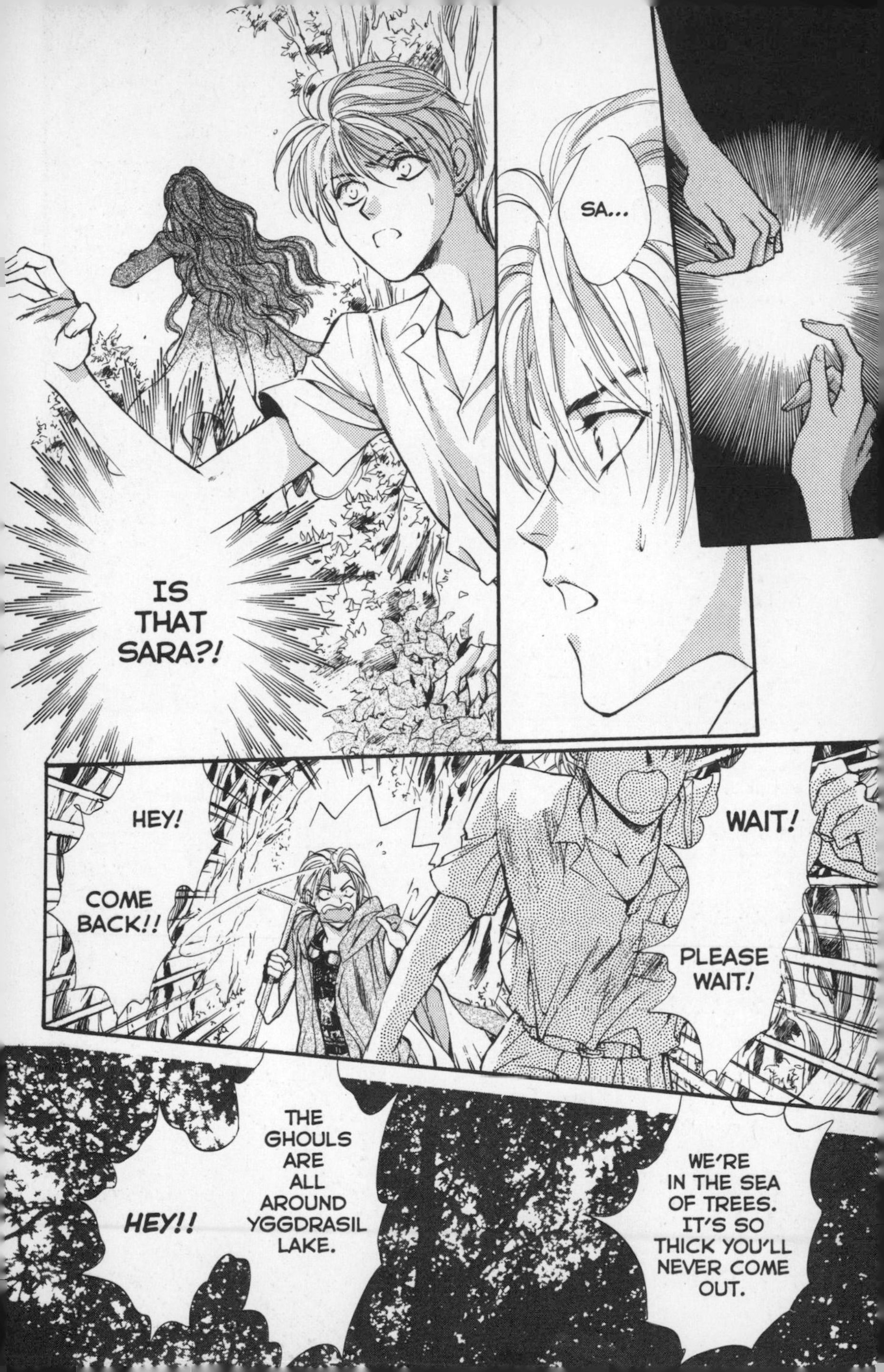
SA...
IS THAT SARA?!
WAIT!
PLEASE WAIT!
HEY!
COME BACK!!
WE'RE IN THE SEA OF TREES. IT'S SO THICK YOU'LL NEVER COME OUT.
THE GHOULS ARE ALL AROUND YGGDRASIL LAKE.
HEY!!

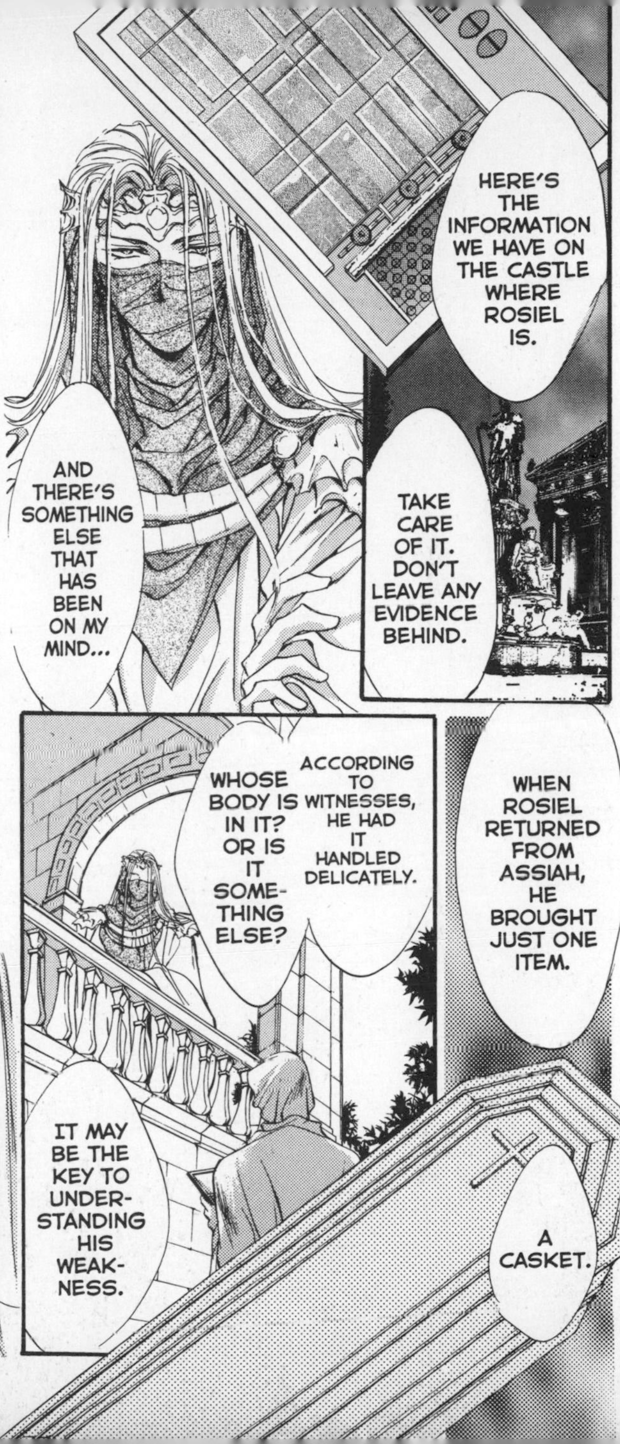
HERE'S THE INFORMATION WE HAVE ON THE CASTLE WHERE ROSIEL IS.
TAKE CARE OF IT. DON'T LEAVE ANY EVIDENCE BEHIND.
AND THERE'S SOMETHING ELSE THAT HAS BEEN ON MY MIND...
WHEN ROSIEL RETURNED FROM ASSIAH, HE BROUGHT JUST ONE ITEM.
A CASKET.
ACCORDING TO WITNESSES, HE HAD IT HANDLED DELICATELY.
WHOSE BODY IS IN IT? OR IS IT SOME-THING ELSE?
IT MAY BE THE KEY TO UNDER-STANDING HIS WEAK-NESS.

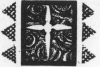

"Hades" is about to get moving. Since Katan is in that state, if you were relieved because you thought he was alive, your relief lasted only an instant. Some are still concerned for him. Hades has very few women, so it lacks feminine charm. I had fun drawing Metatron as a baby. The drawing coming up of him in the baby suit went over very well.
(Even R-kawa-sensei liked it!)
I liked the drawing of Meta-chan toddling out, but I also like the sometimes good, sometimes not-so-good relationships between Setsuna and Kato.
If they were on more equal terms, I feel they would have been the best of friends. They're always fighting, but after all is said and done, they're still together. How good is that? I'm looking forward to what comes next.
Maybe.

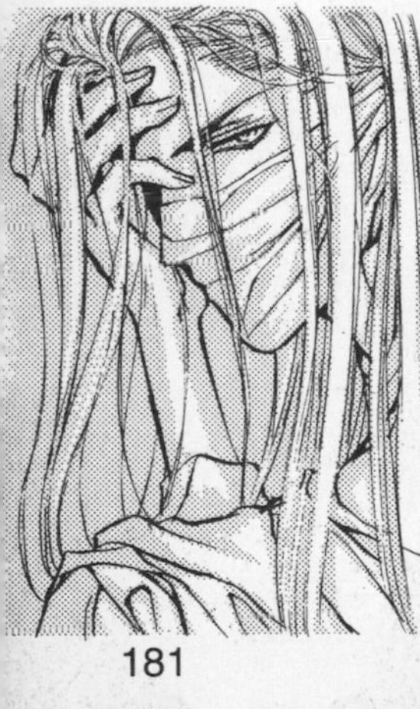

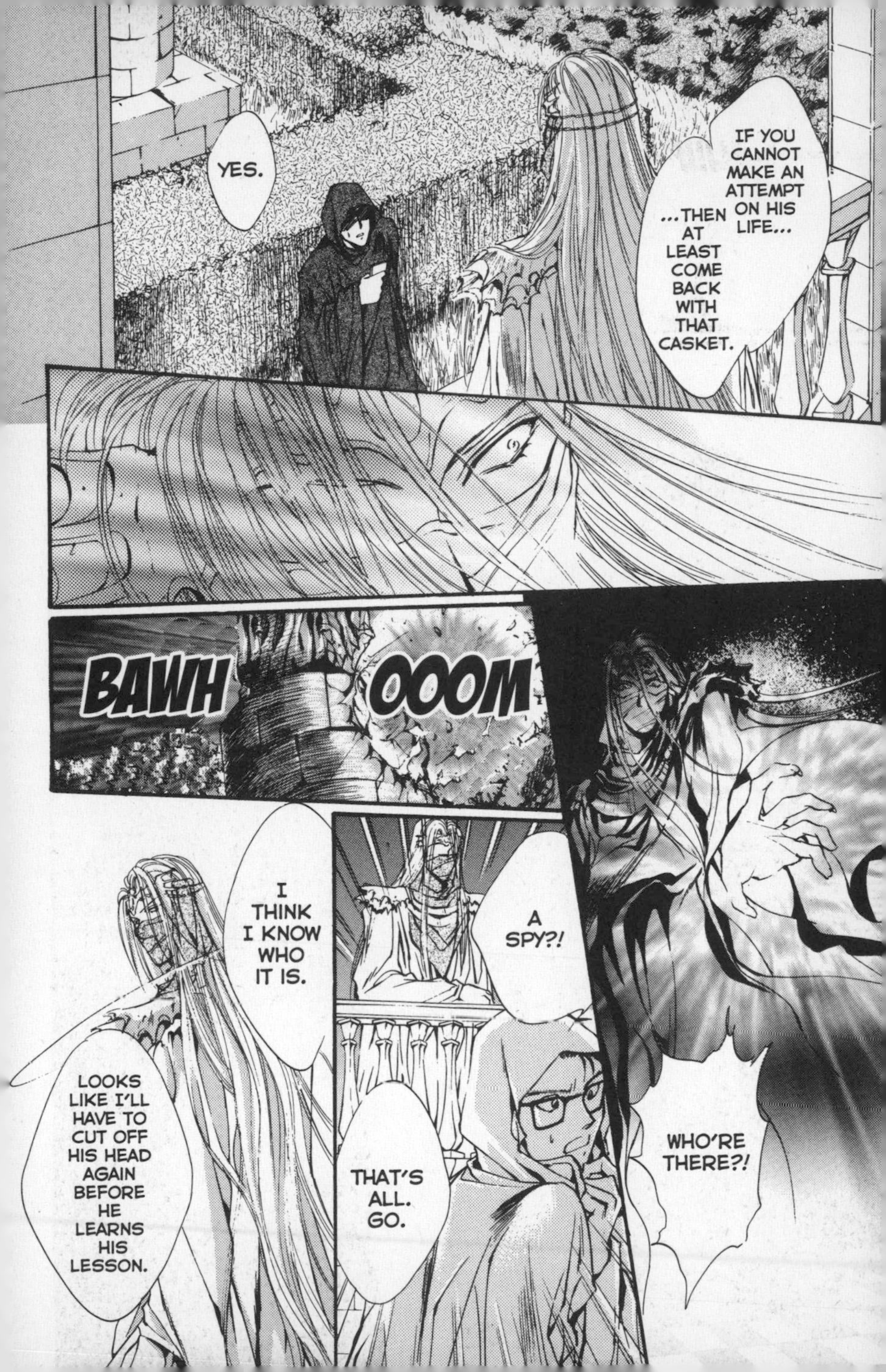
IF YOU CANNOT MAKE AN ATTEMPT ON HIS LIFE...
...THEN AT LEAST COME BACK WITH THAT CASKET.
YES.
WHO'RE THERE?!
BAWH OOOM
A SPY?!
THAT'S ALL. GO.
I THINK I KNOW WHO IT IS.
LOOKS LIKE I'LL HAVE TO CUT OFF HIS HEAD AGAIN BEFORE HE LEARNS HIS LESSON.

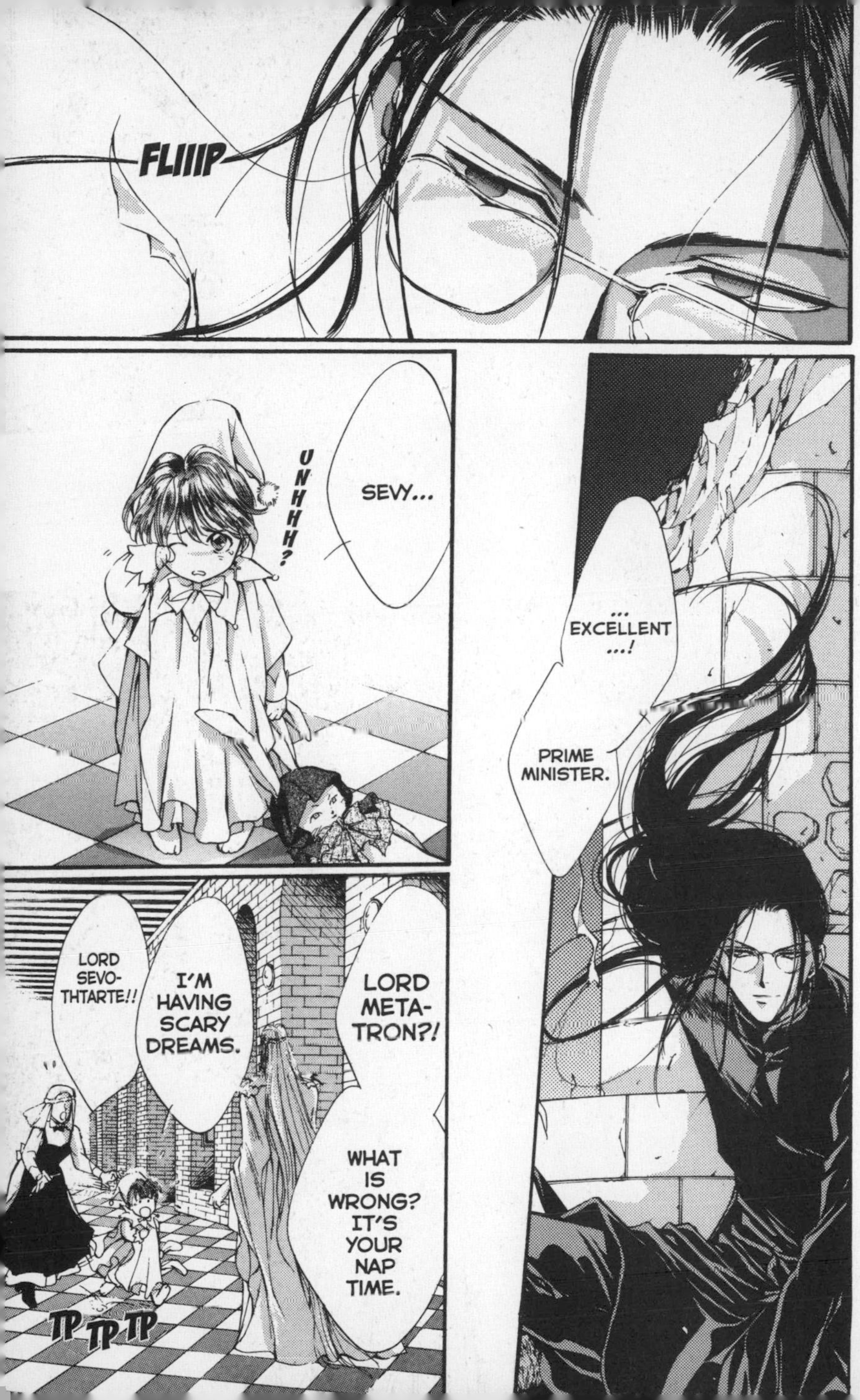
FLIIIP
...EXCELLENT...!
PRIME MINISTER.
SEVY...
UNHHHH?
LORD METATRON?!
WHAT IS WRONG? IT'S YOUR NAP TIME.
I'M HAVING SCARY DREAMS.
LORD SEVOTHTARTE!!
TP TP TP

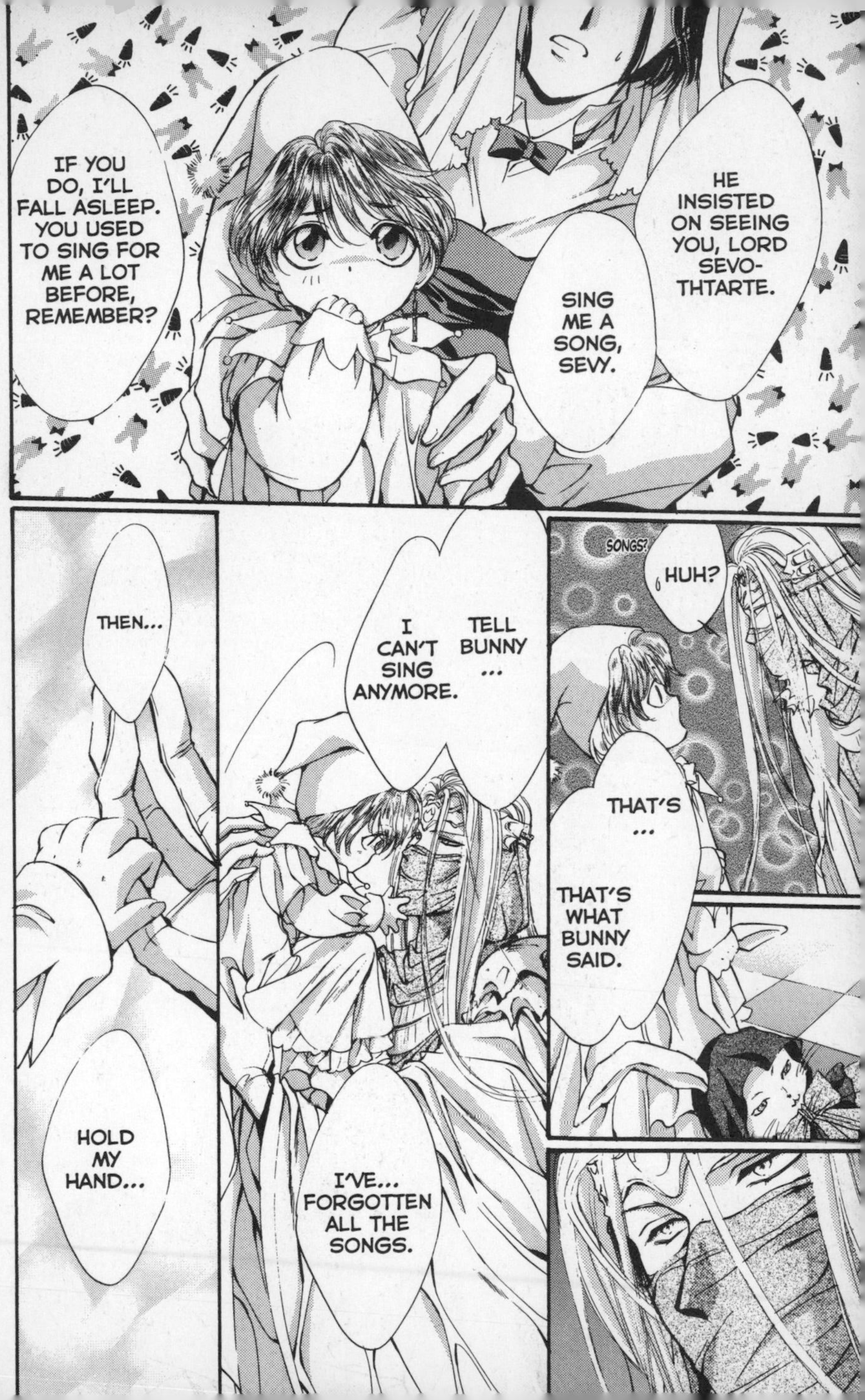
HE INSISTED ON SEEING YOU, LORD SEVO-THTARTE.
SING ME A SONG, SEVY.
IF YOU DO, I'LL FALL ASLEEP. YOU USED TO SING FOR ME A LOT BEFORE, REMEMBER?
SONGS?
HUH?
THAT'S ...
THAT'S WHAT BUNNY SAID.
TELL BUNNY ...
I CAN'T SING ANYMORE.
I'VE... FORGOTTEN ALL THE SONGS.
THEN...
HOLD MY HAND...

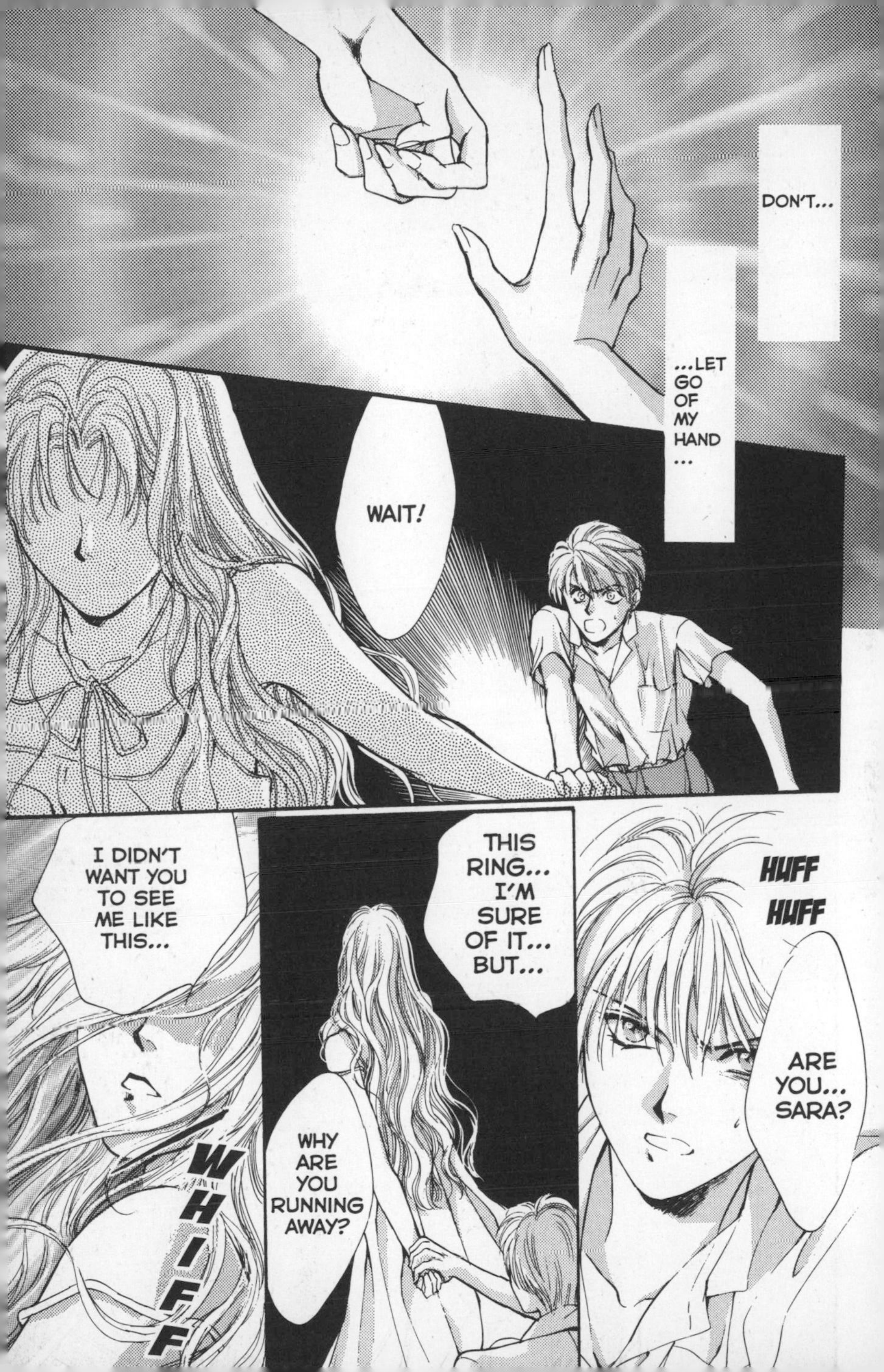
DON'T...
...LET GO OF MY HAND...
WAIT!
HUFF HUFF
ARE YOU... SARA?
THIS RING... I'M SURE OF IT... BUT...
WHY ARE YOU RUNNING AWAY?
I DIDN'T WANT YOU TO SEE ME LIKE THIS...
WHIFF

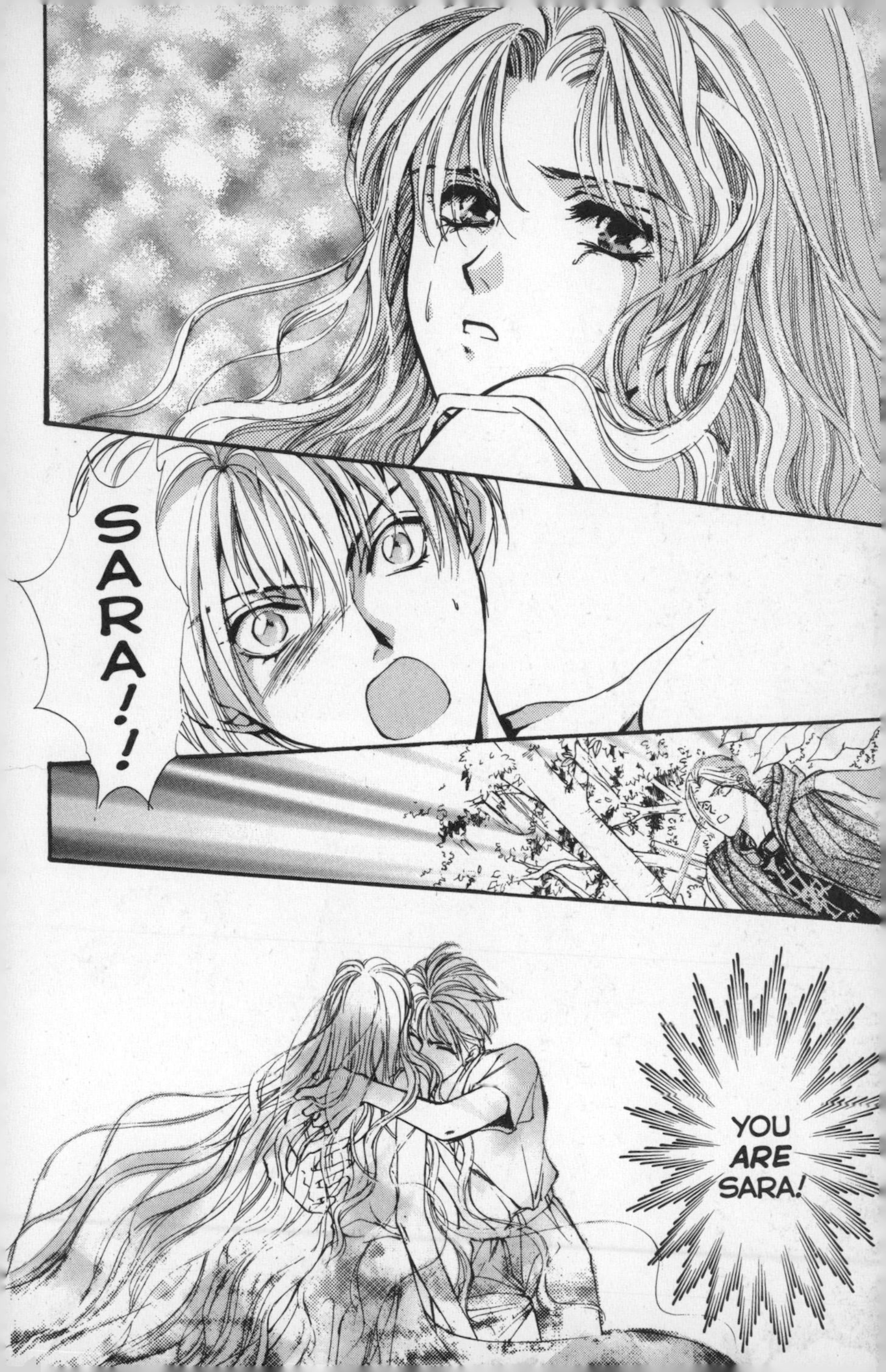
SARA!!!
YOU ARE SARA!

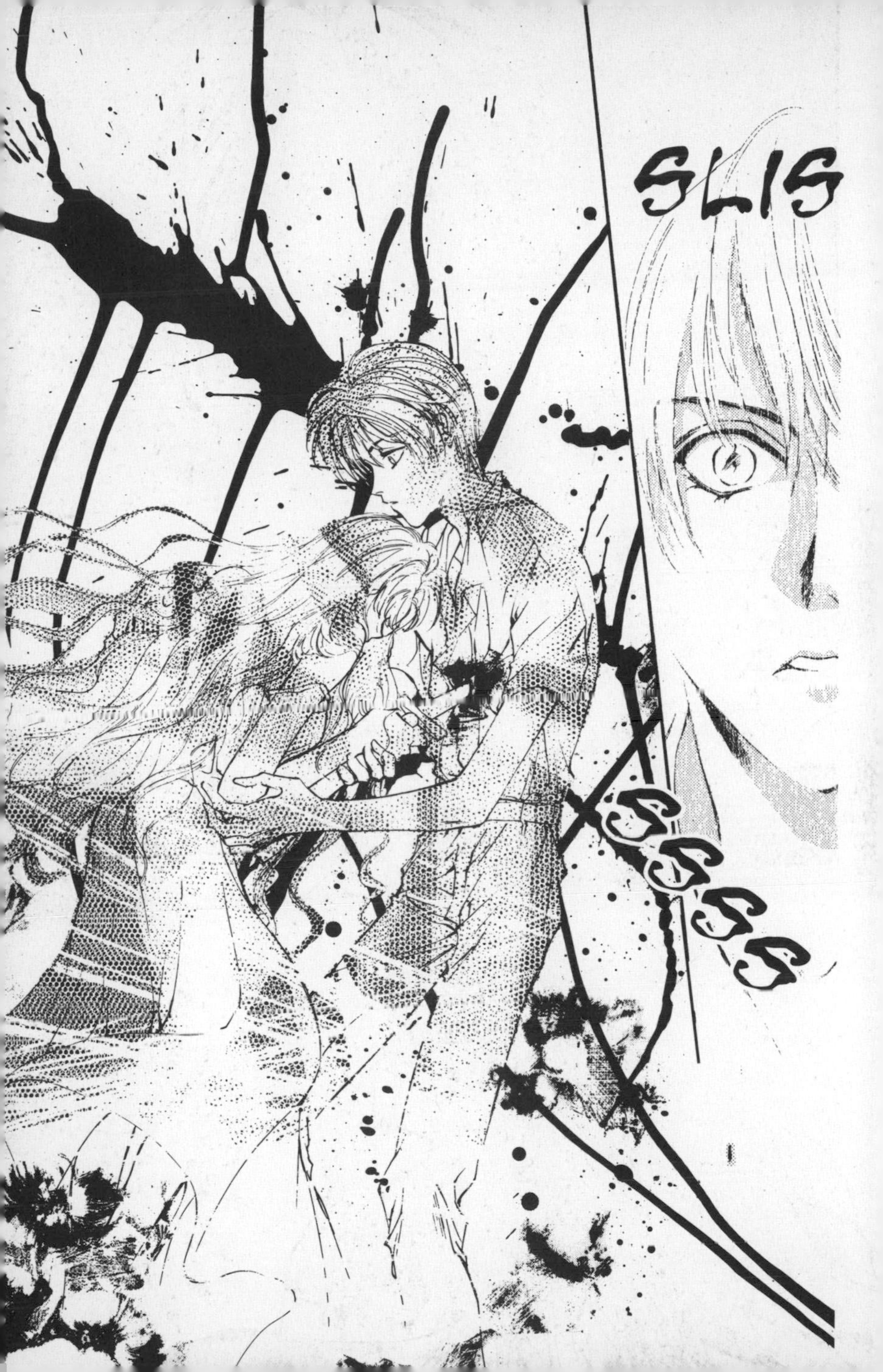
SLIS
SSSSS

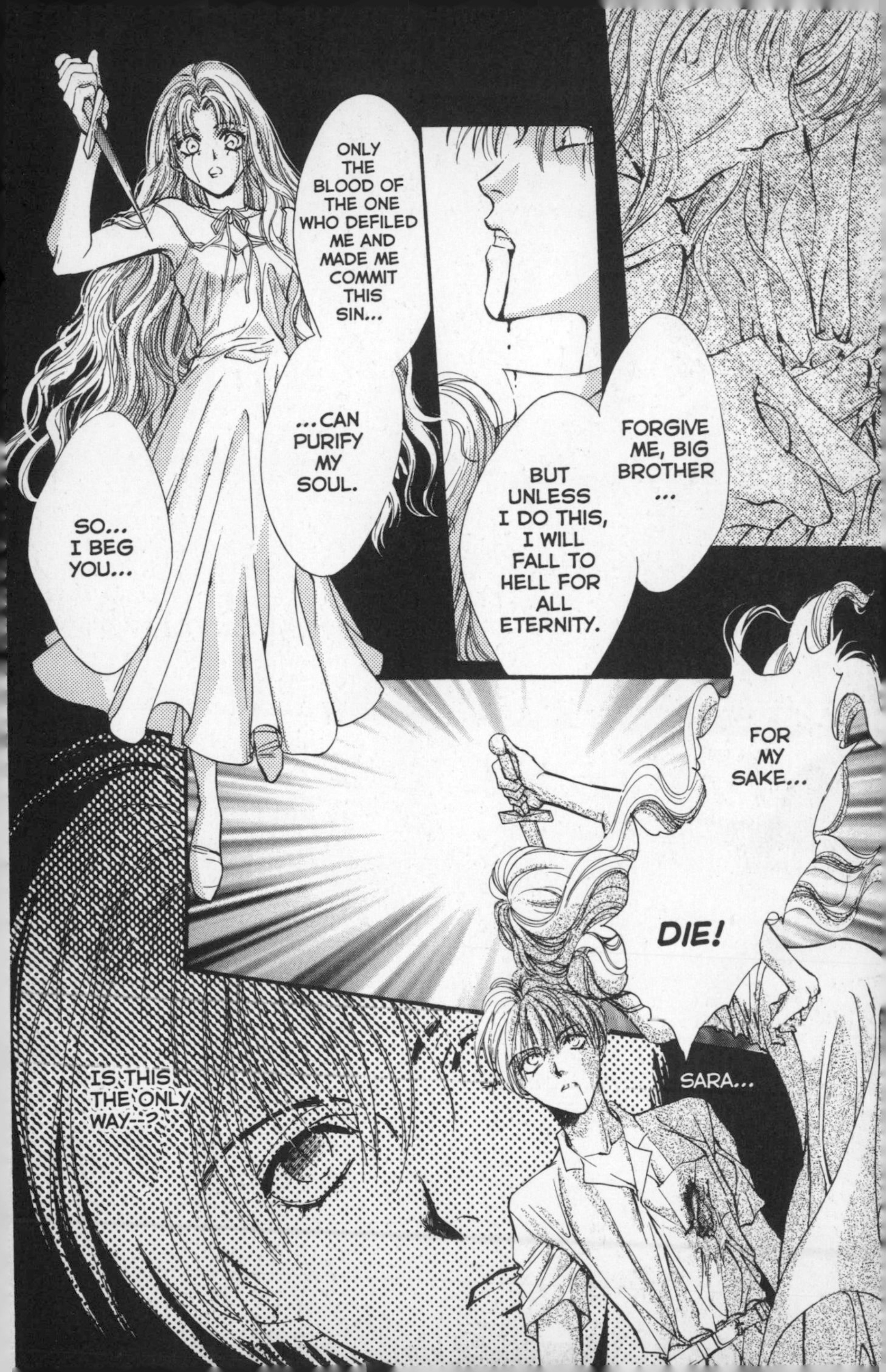
FORGIVE ME, BIG BROTHER ...
BUT UNLESS I DO THIS, I WILL FALL TO HELL FOR ALL ETERNITY.
ONLY THE BLOOD OF THE ONE WHO DEFILED ME AND MADE ME COMMIT THIS SIN...
...CAN PURIFY MY SOUL.
SO... I BEG YOU...
FOR MY SAKE...
DIE!
SARA...
IS THIS THE ONLY WAY--?

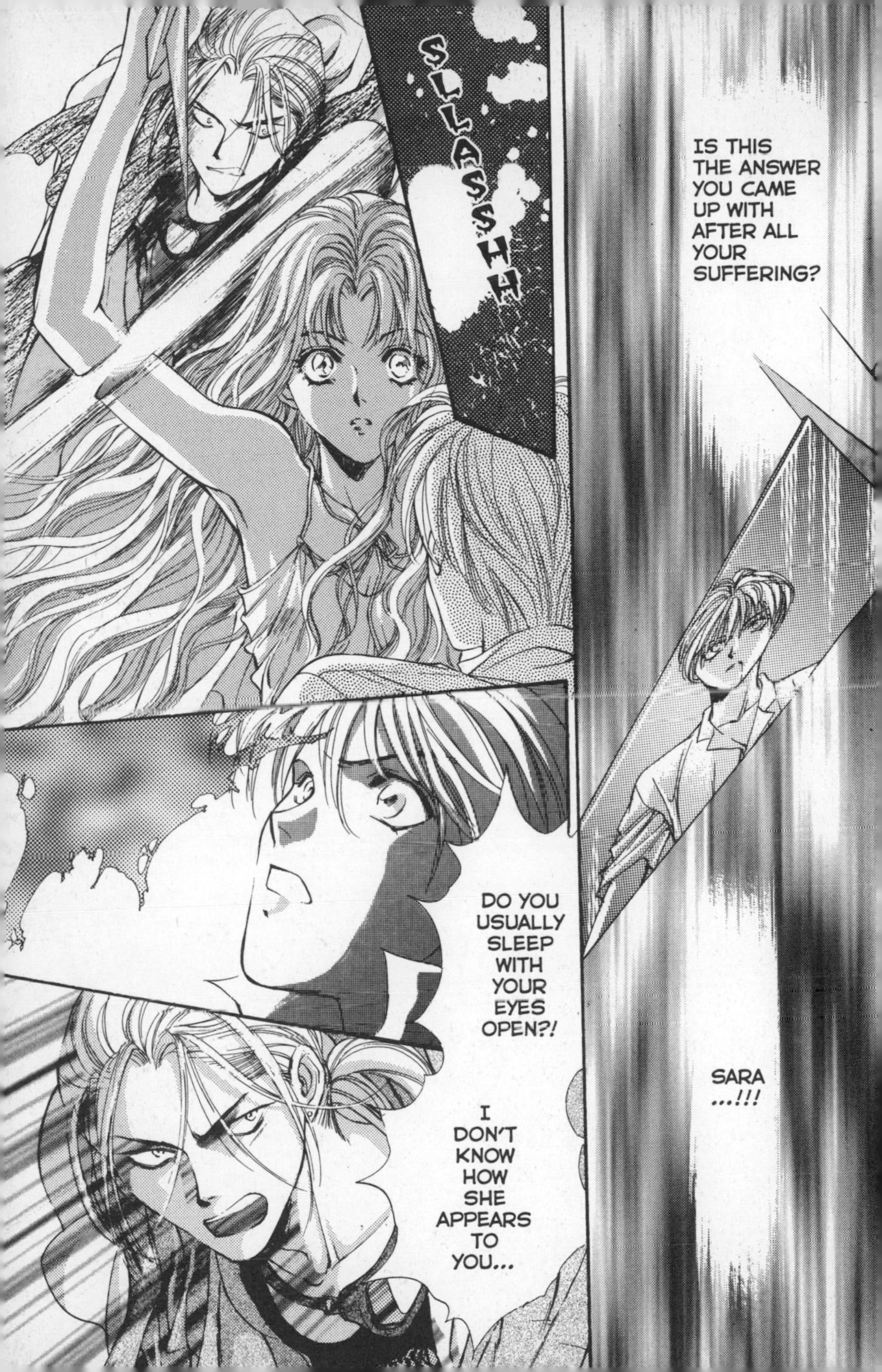
IS THIS THE ANSWER YOU CAME UP WITH AFTER ALL YOUR SUFFERING?
SARA ...!!!
SLLASSHH
DO YOU USUALLY SLEEP WITH YOUR EYES OPEN?!
I DON'T KNOW HOW SHE APPEARS TO YOU...

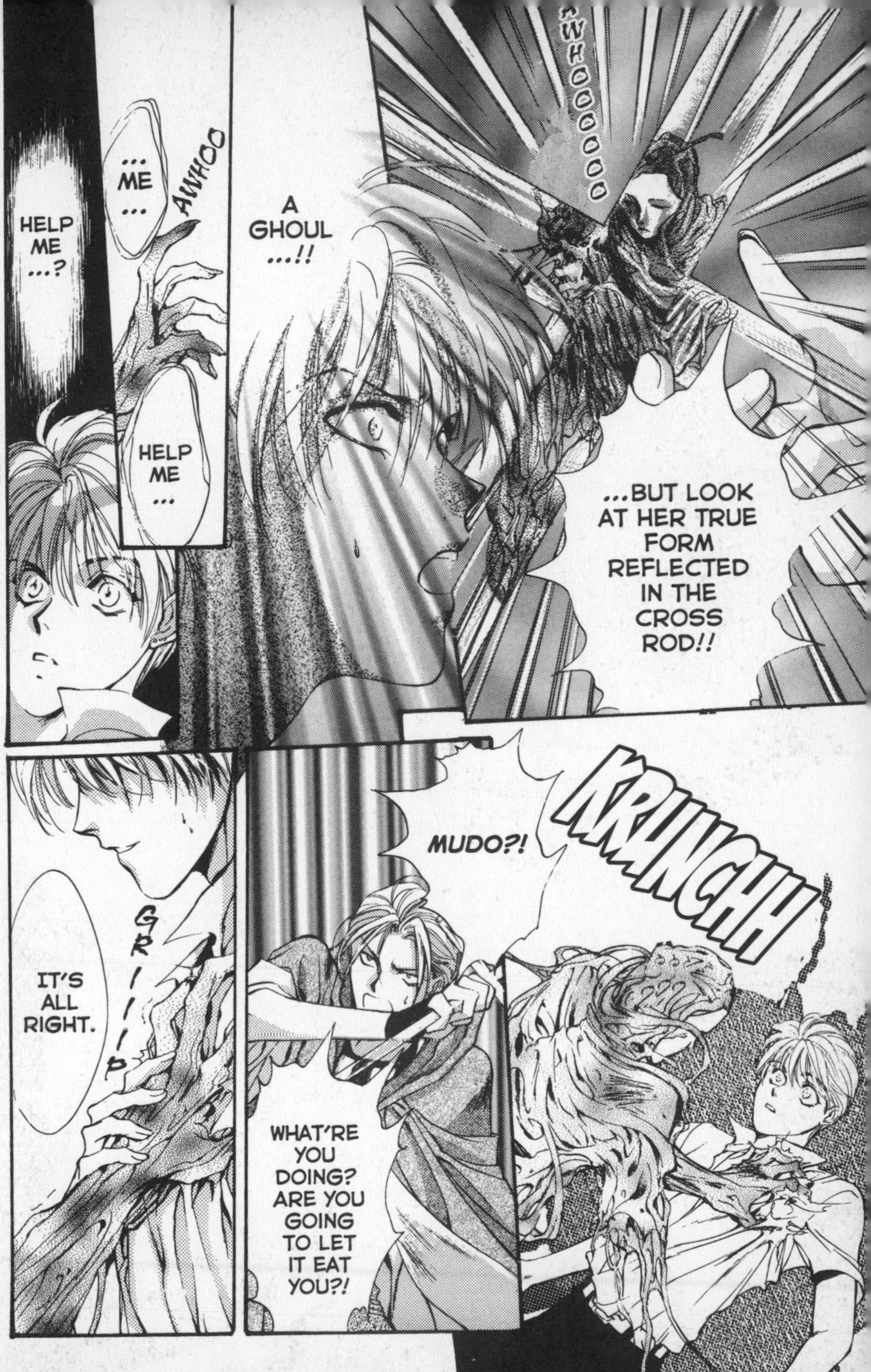
AWHOOOOOOOO
...BUT LOOK AT HER TRUE FORM REFLECTED IN THE CROSS ROD!!
A GHOUL ...!!
... ME ...
AWHOO
HELP ME ...?
HELP ME ...
KRUNCH
MUDO?!
WHAT'RE YOU DOING? ARE YOU GOING TO LET IT EAT YOU?!
GRIIIP
IT'S ALL RIGHT.

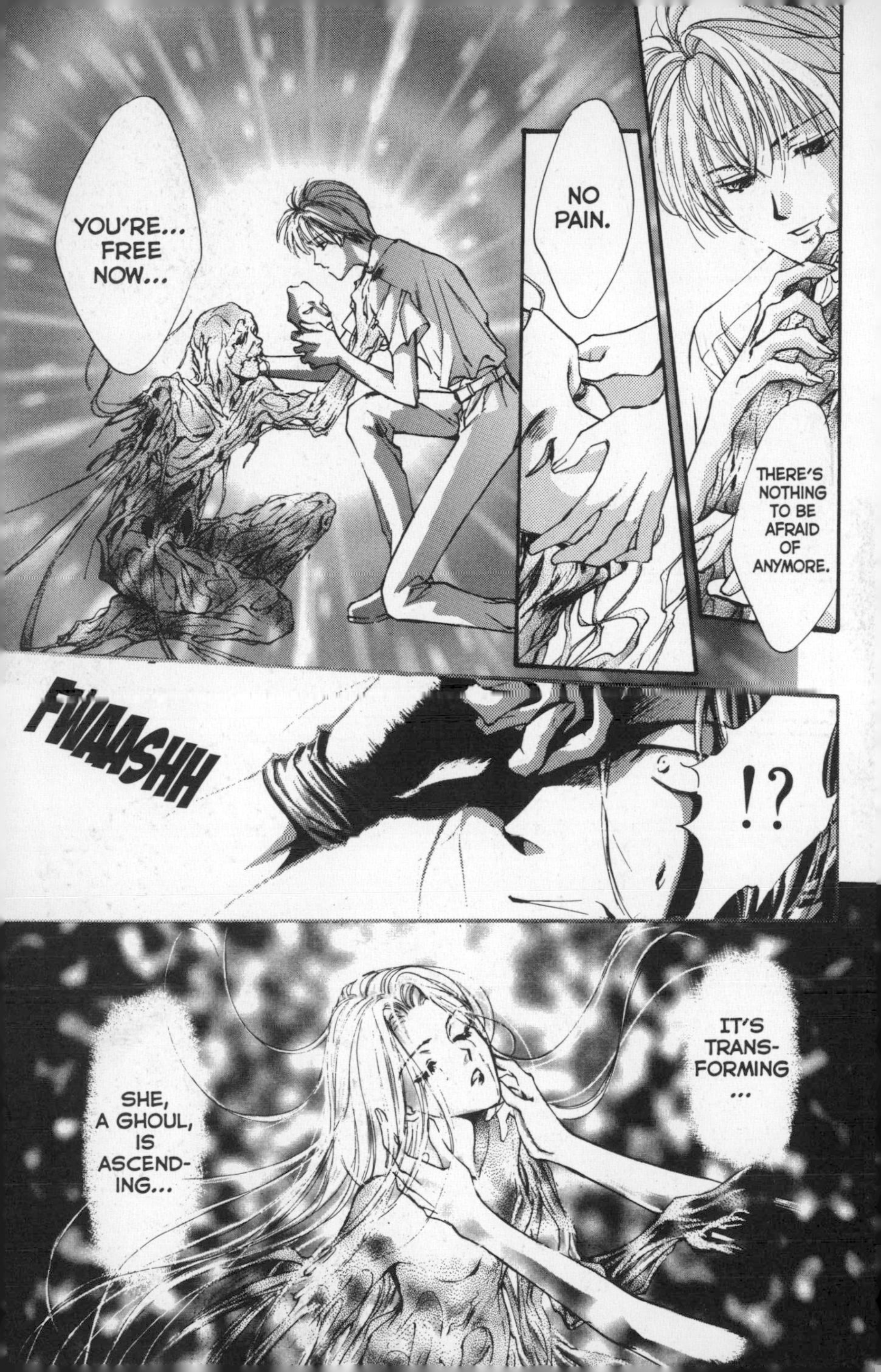
THERE'S NOTHING TO BE AFRAID OF ANYMORE.
NO PAIN.
YOU'RE... FREE NOW...
!?
FWAASHH
IT'S TRANS-FORMING...
SHE, A GHOUL, IS ASCEND-ING...

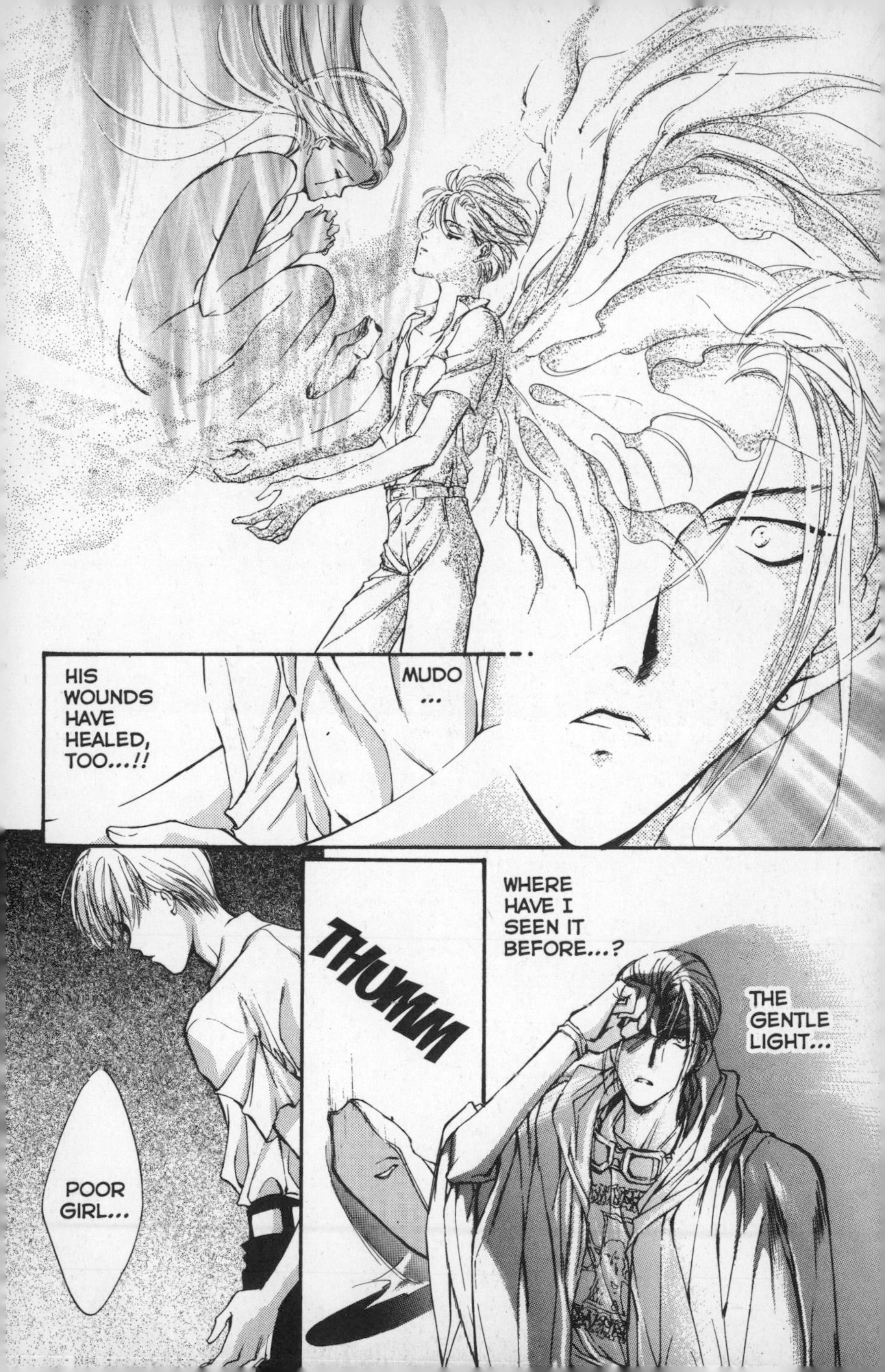
MUDO
...
HIS WOUNDS HAVE HEALED, TOO...!!
THE GENTLE LIGHT...
WHERE HAVE I SEEN IT BEFORE...?
THUMM
POOR GIRL...

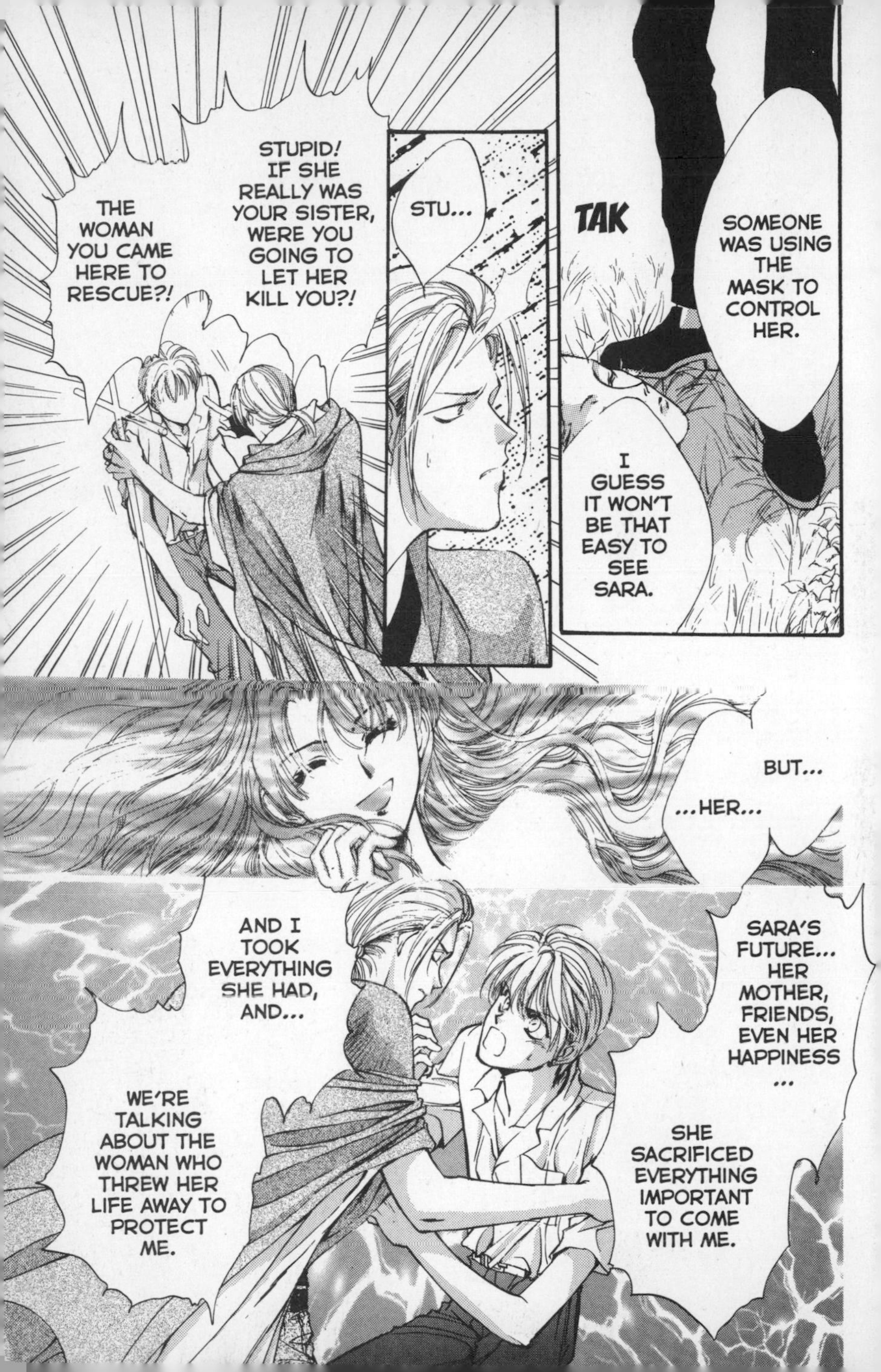
SOMEONE WAS USING THE MASK TO CONTROL HER.
TAK
I GUESS IT WON'T BE THAT EASY TO SEE SARA.
STU...
STUPID! IF SHE REALLY WAS YOUR SISTER, WERE YOU GOING TO LET HER KILL YOU?!
THE WOMAN YOU CAME HERE TO RESCUE?!
BUT...
...HER...
SARA'S FUTURE... HER MOTHER, FRIENDS, EVEN HER HAPPINESS ...
AND I TOOK EVERYTHING SHE HAD, AND...
SHE SACRIFICED EVERYTHING IMPORTANT TO COME WITH ME.
WE'RE TALKING ABOUT THE WOMAN WHO THREW HER LIFE AWAY TO PROTECT ME.

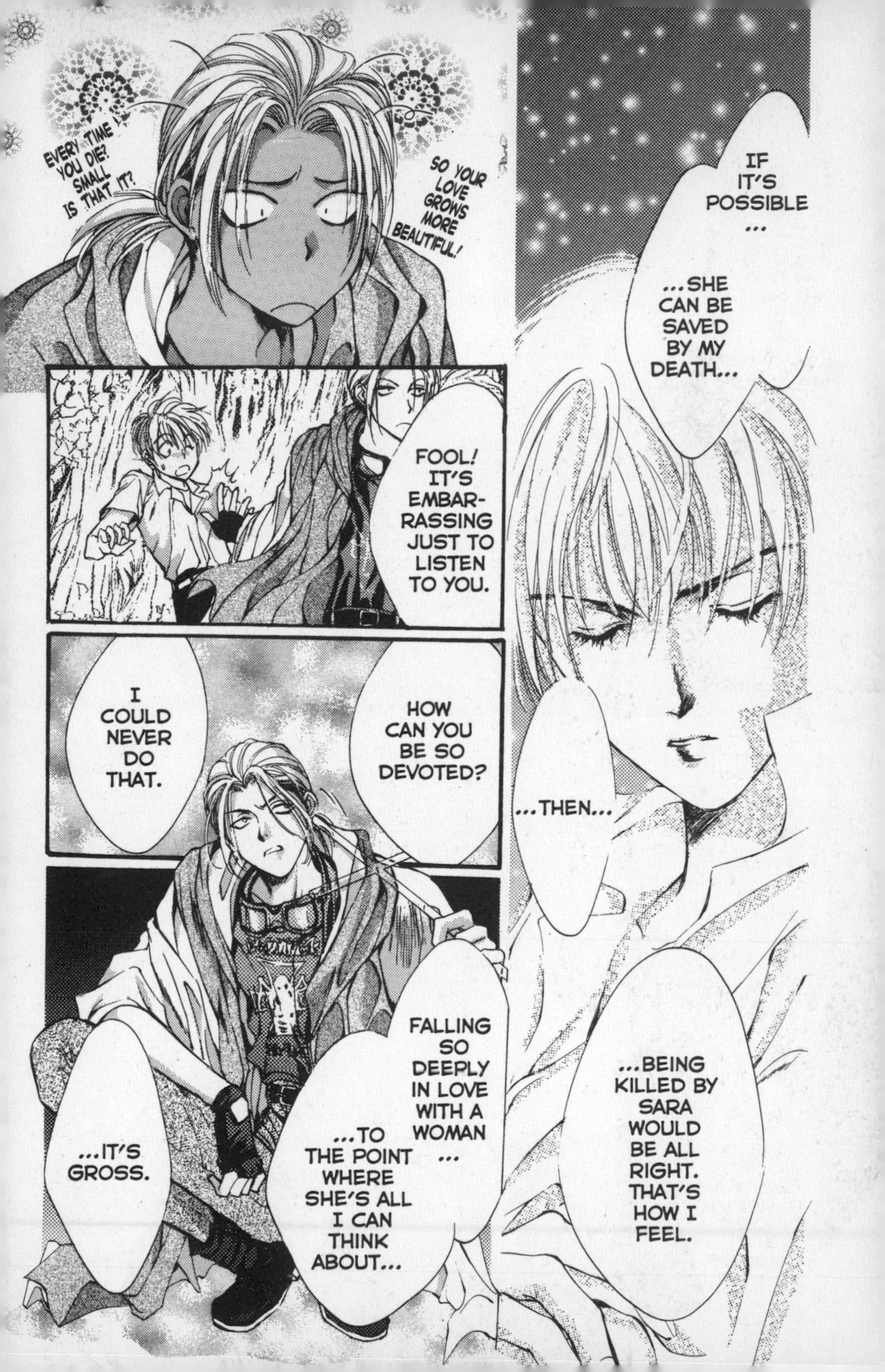
IF IT'S POSSIBLE...
...SHE CAN BE SAVED BY MY DEATH...
...THEN...
...BEING KILLED BY SARA WOULD BE ALL RIGHT. THAT'S HOW I FEEL.
SO YOUR LOVE GROWS MORE BEAUTIFUL!
EVERY TIME YOU DIE? SMALL IS THAT IT?
FOOL! IT'S EMBARRASSING JUST TO LISTEN TO YOU.
HOW CAN YOU BE SO DEVOTED?
I COULD NEVER DO THAT.
FALLING SO DEEPLY IN LOVE WITH A WOMAN...
...TO THE POINT WHERE SHE'S ALL I CAN THINK ABOUT...
...IT'S GROSS.

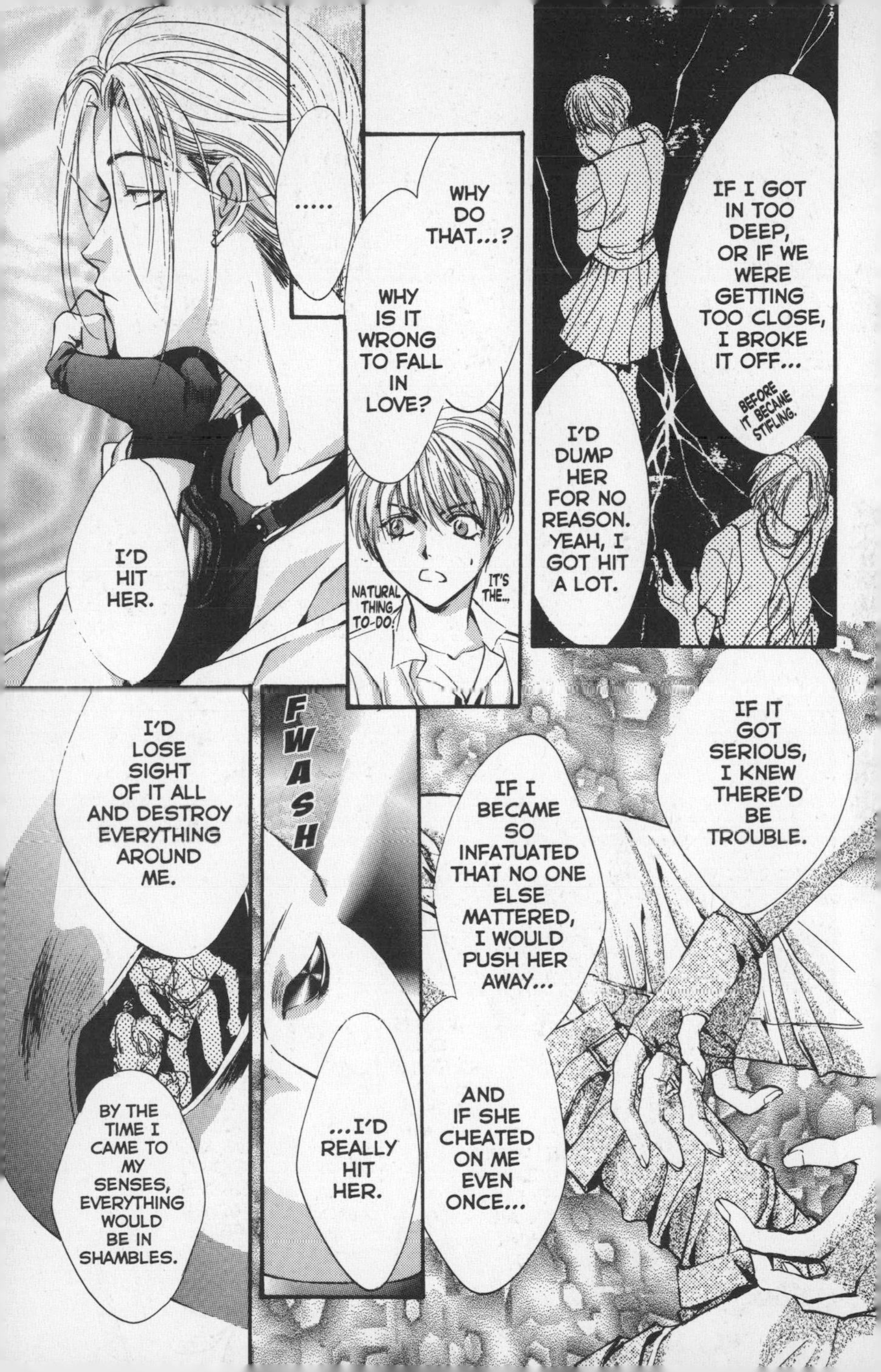
IF I GOT IN TOO DEEP, OR IF WE WERE GETTING TOO CLOSE, I BROKE IT OFF...
BEFORE IT BECAME STIFLING.
I'D DUMP HER FOR NO REASON. YEAH, I GOT HIT A LOT.
WHY DO THAT...?
WHY IS IT WRONG TO FALL IN LOVE?
IT'S THE...
NATURAL THING TO DO.
.....
I'D HIT HER.
IF IT GOT SERIOUS, I KNEW THERE'D BE TROUBLE.
IF I BECAME SO INFATUATED THAT NO ONE ELSE MATTERED, I WOULD PUSH HER AWAY...
AND IF SHE CHEATED ON ME EVEN ONCE...
FWASH
...I'D REALLY HIT HER.
I'D LOSE SIGHT OF IT ALL AND DESTROY EVERYTHING AROUND ME.
BY THE TIME I CAME TO MY SENSES, EVERYTHING WOULD BE IN SHAMBLES.

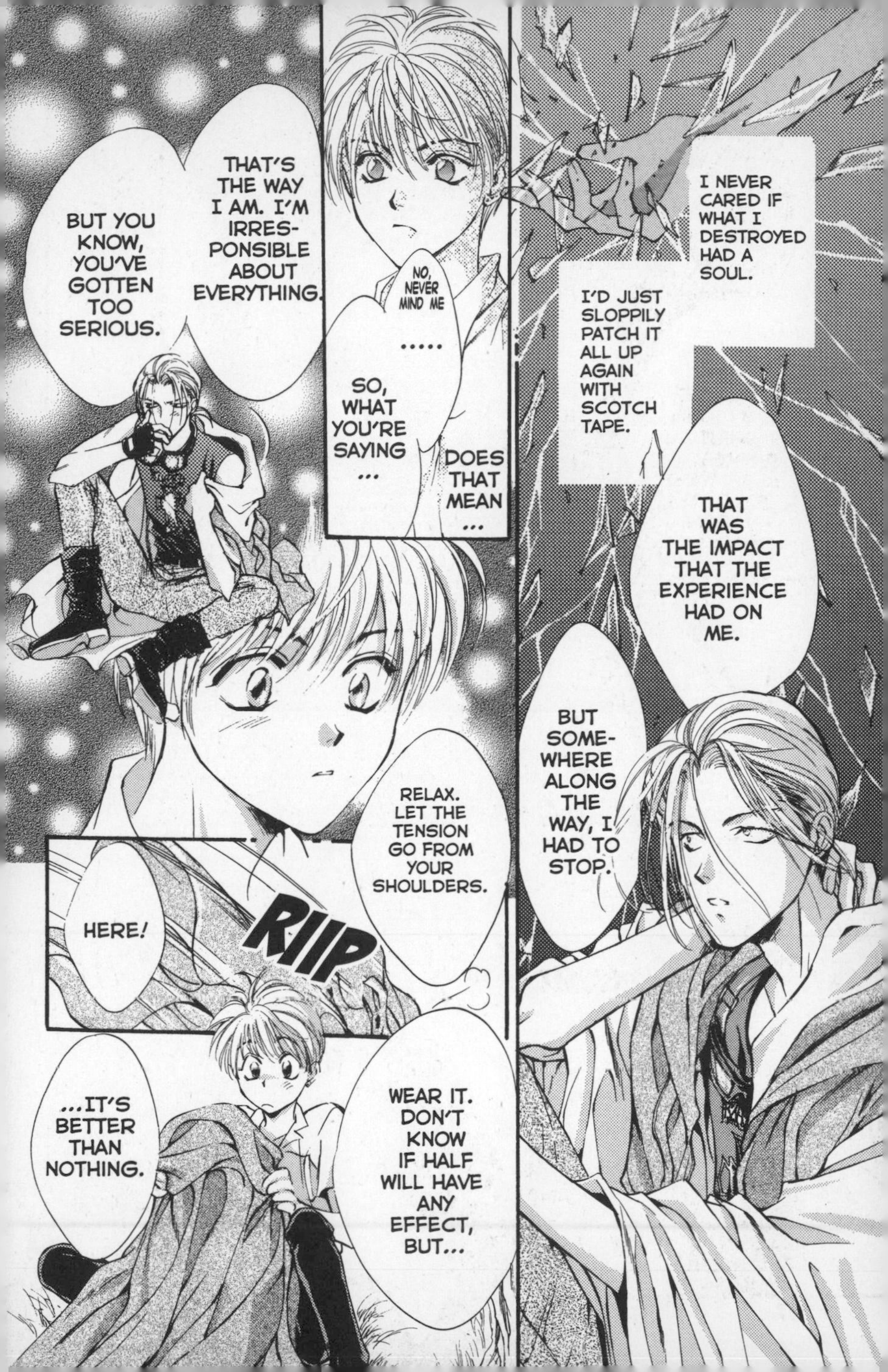
I NEVER CARED IF WHAT I DESTROYED HAD A SOUL.
I'D JUST SLOPPILY PATCH IT ALL UP AGAIN WITH SCOTCH TAPE.
THAT WAS THE IMPACT THAT THE EXPERIENCE HAD ON ME.
BUT SOMEWHERE ALONG THE WAY, I HAD TO STOP.
NO, NEVER MIND ME
......
SO, WHAT YOU'RE SAYING ...
DOES THAT MEAN ...
THAT'S THE WAY I AM. I'M IRRES-PONSIBLE ABOUT EVERYTHING.
BUT YOU KNOW, YOU'VE GOTTEN TOO SERIOUS.
RELAX. LET THE TENSION GO FROM YOUR SHOULDERS.
RIIP
HERE!
WEAR IT. DON'T KNOW IF HALF WILL HAVE ANY EFFECT, BUT...
...IT'S BETTER THAN NOTHING.

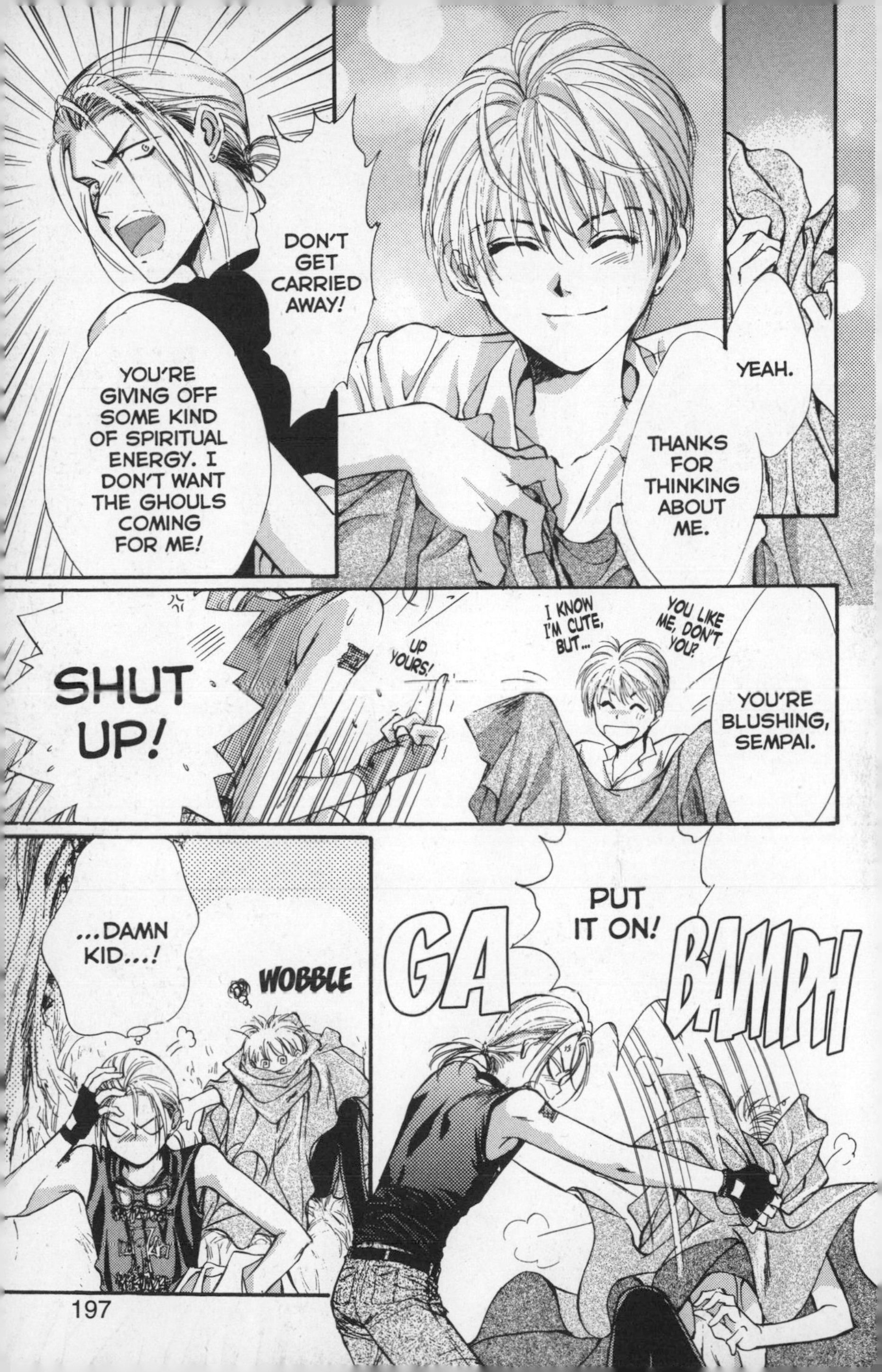
YEAH.
THANKS FOR THINKING ABOUT ME.
DON'T GET CARRIED AWAY!
YOU'RE GIVING OFF SOME KIND OF SPIRITUAL ENERGY. I DON'T WANT THE GHOULS COMING FOR ME!
YOU'RE BLUSHING, SEMPAI.
YOU LIKE ME, DON'T YOU?
I KNOW I'M CUTE, BUT...
UP YOURS!
SHUT UP!
PUT IT ON!
GA
BAMPH
WOBBLE
...DAMN KID...!

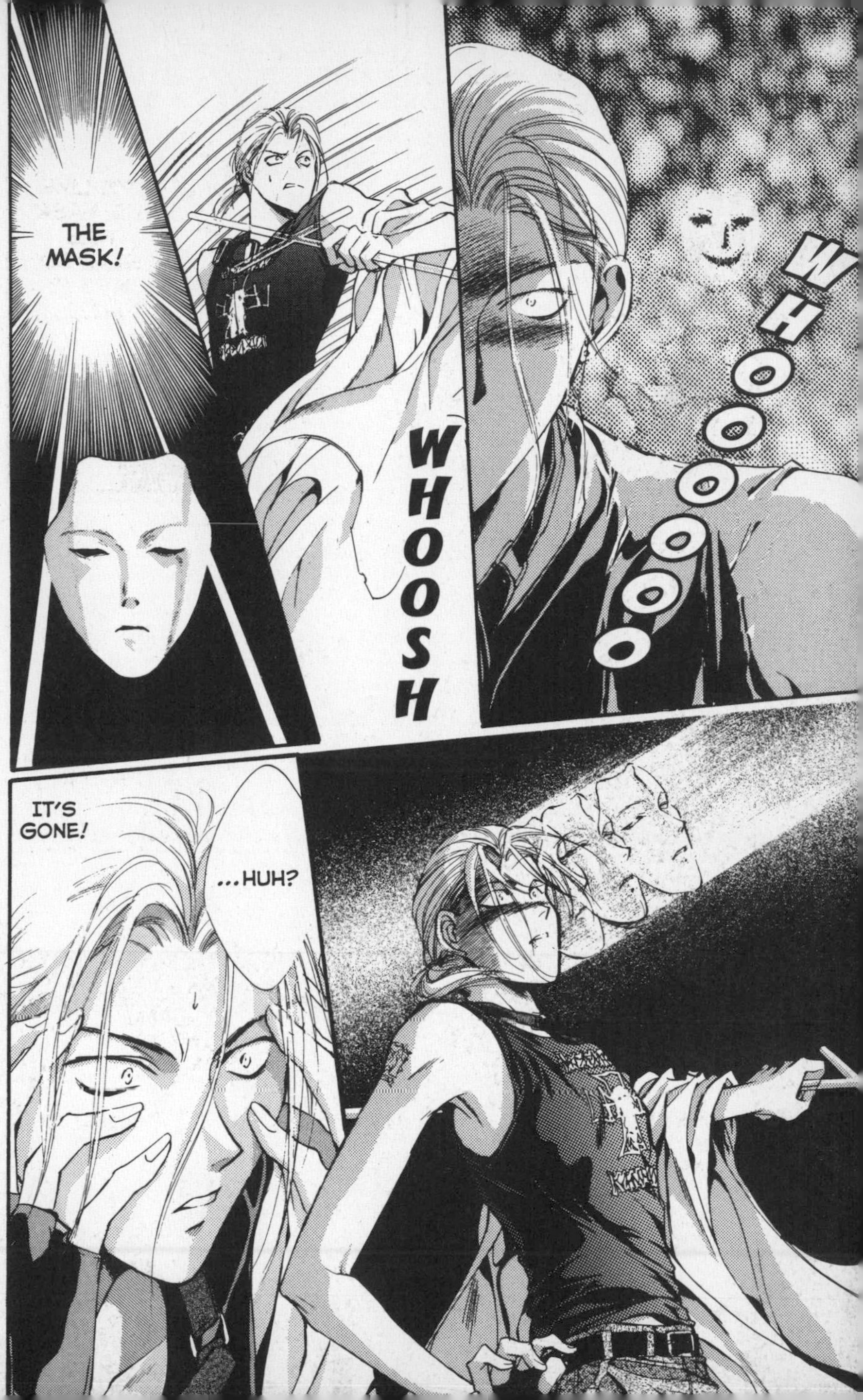
WHOOOOOO
WHOOOSH
THE MASK!
...HUH?
IT'S GONE!

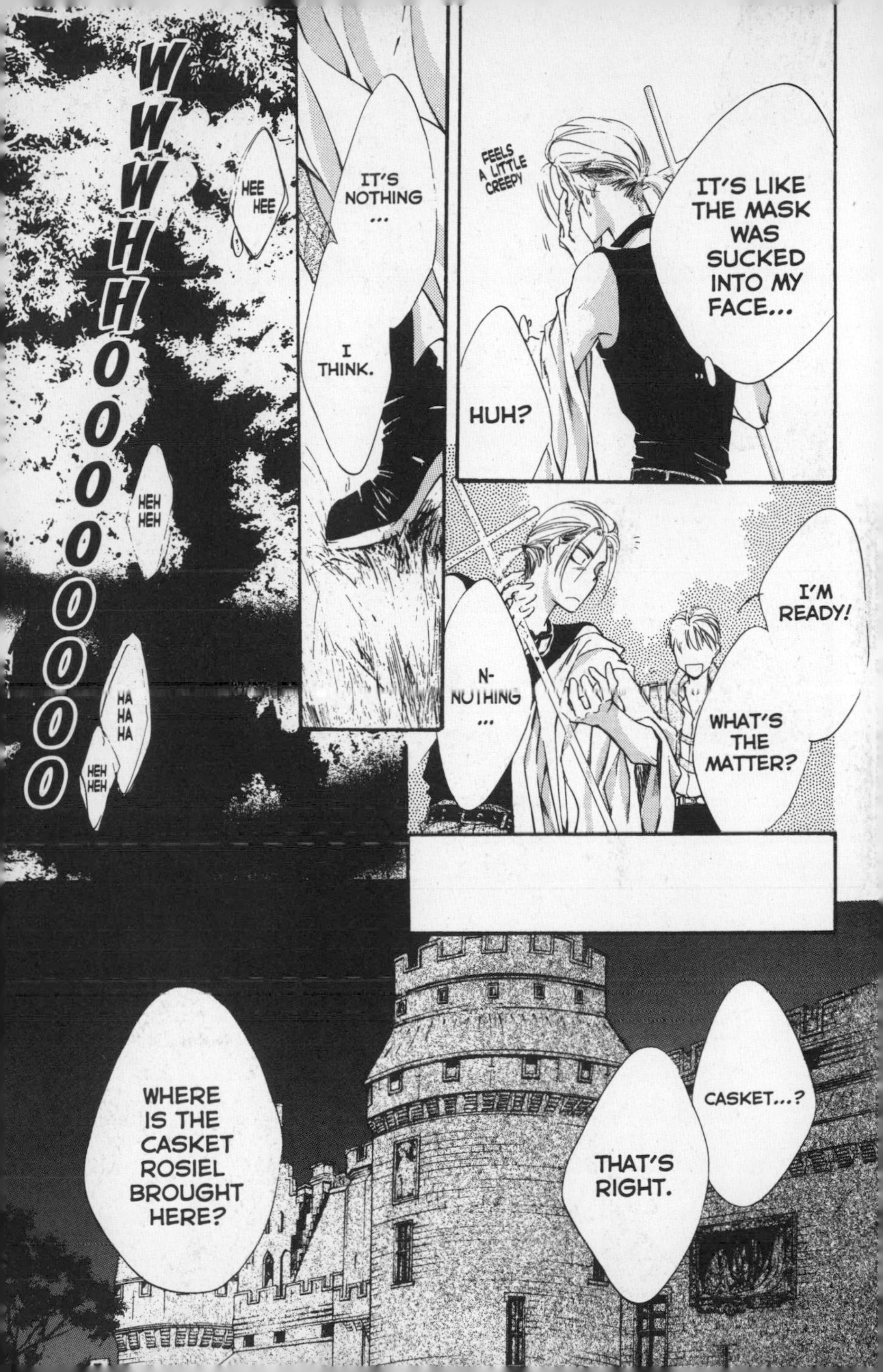
FEELS A LITTLE CREEPY
IT'S LIKE THE MASK WAS SUCKED INTO MY FACE...
HUH?
IT'S NOTHING...
I THINK.
I'M READY!
WHAT'S THE MATTER?
N-NOTHING...
WWWHHOOOOOOOOO
HEE HEE
HEH HEH
HA HA HA
HEH HEH
CASKET...?
THAT'S RIGHT.
WHERE IS THE CASKET ROSIEL BROUGHT HERE?

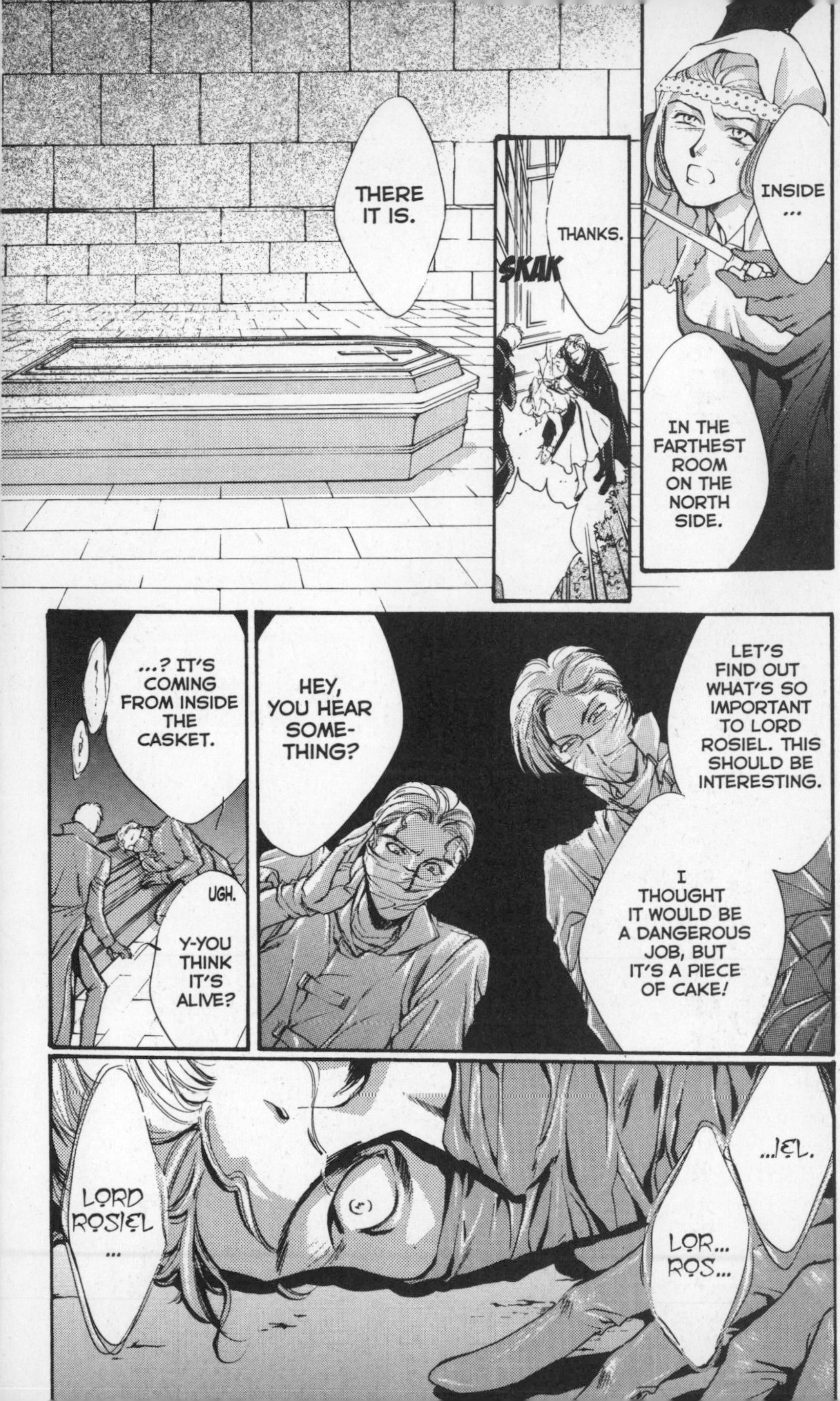
INSIDE ...
IN THE FARTHEST ROOM ON THE NORTH SIDE.
THANKS.
SKAK
THERE IT IS.
LET'S FIND OUT WHAT'S SO IMPORTANT TO LORD ROSIEL. THIS SHOULD BE INTERESTING.
I THOUGHT IT WOULD BE A DANGEROUS JOB, BUT IT'S A PIECE OF CAKE!
HEY, YOU HEAR SOME-THING?
...? IT'S COMING FROM INSIDE THE CASKET.
UGH.
Y-YOU THINK IT'S ALIVE?
...IEL.
LOR... ROS...
LORD ROSIEL ...

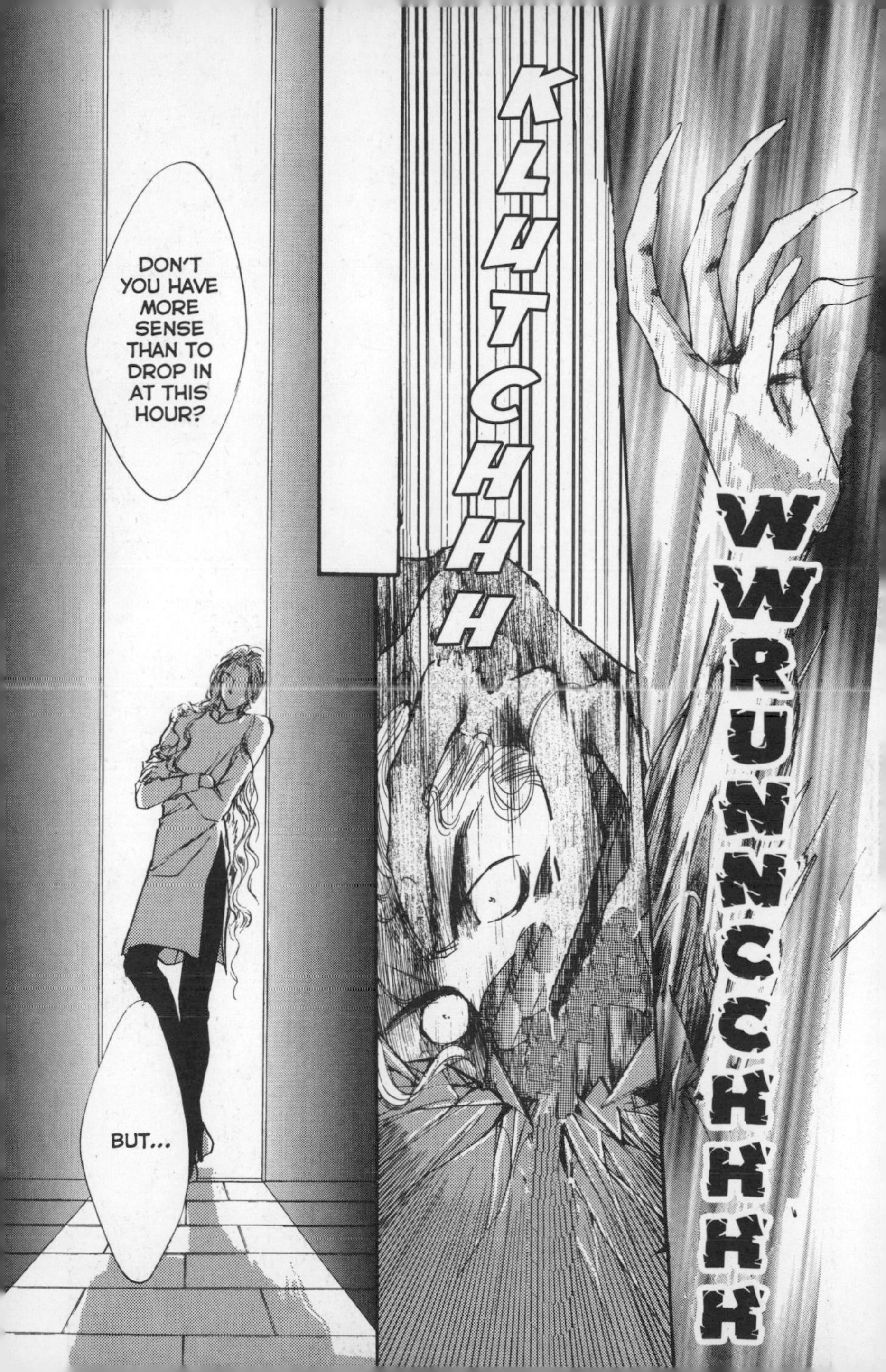
KLUTCHHHH
WWRUNNCCHHHH
DON'T YOU HAVE MORE SENSE THAN TO DROP IN AT THIS HOUR?
BUT...

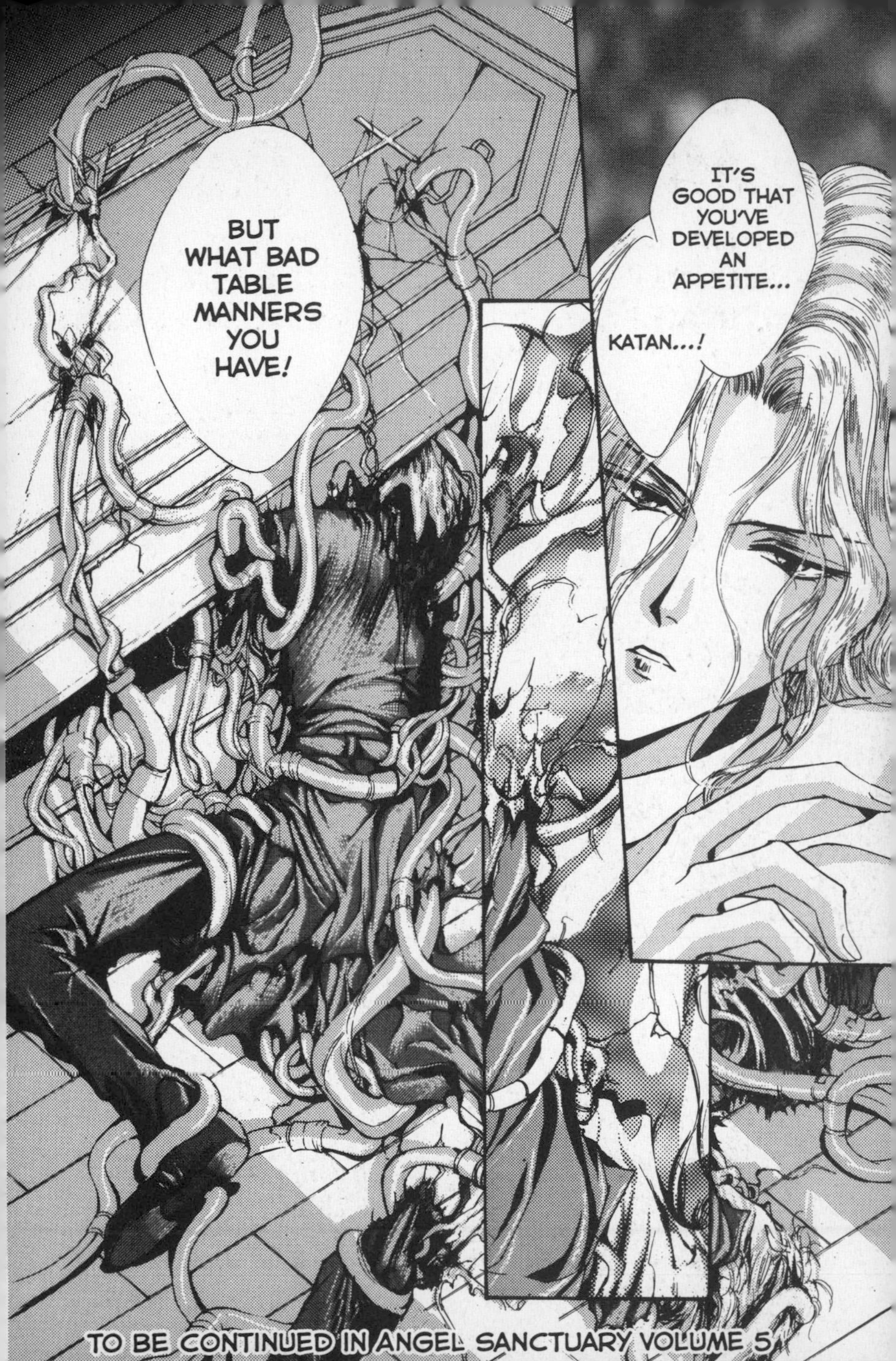
IT'S GOOD THAT YOU'VE DEVELOPED AN APPETITE...
KATAN...!
BUT WHAT BAD TABLE MANNERS YOU HAVE!
TO BE CONTINUED IN ANGEL SANCTUARY VOLUME 5

Who Knew There Was So Much Life in Death?

As a god of death, Tsuzuki has a lot to think about. First, he has to escort the dead to the afterlife, plus there's also endless bureaucracy to deal with. But despite the paperwork and budgetary concerns, death is big business... and business is good!

Descendants of Darkness

Start your graphic novel collection today!

Only $9.99!

shōjo

FRESH FROM JAPAN
日本最新

www.viz.com

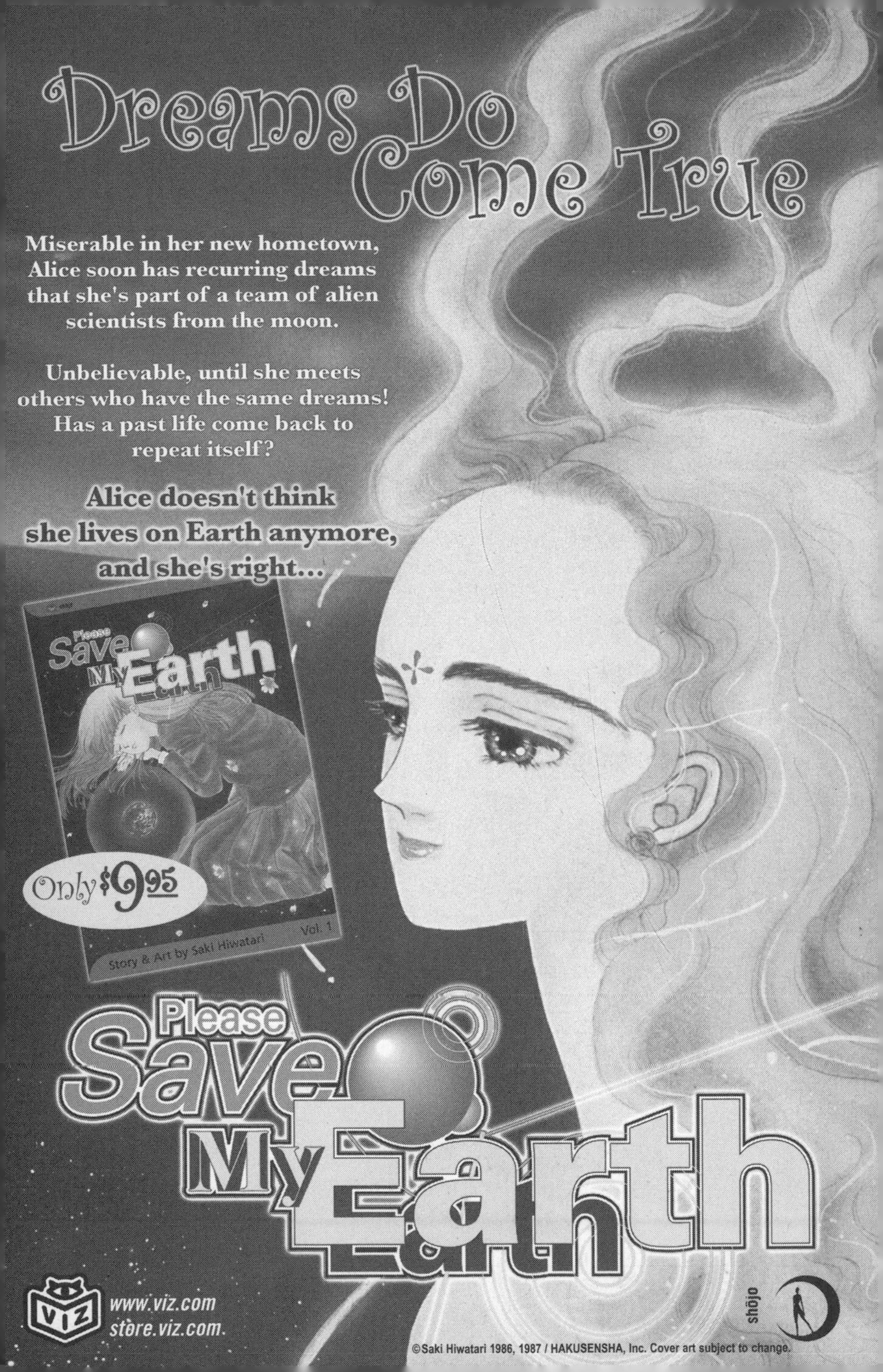
Dreams Do Come True
Miserable in her new hometown, Alice soon has recurring dreams that she's part of a team of alien scientists from the moon.
Unbelievable, until she meets others who have the same dreams! Has a past life come back to repeat itself?
Alice doesn't think she lives on Earth anymore, and she's right...
Please Save My Earth
Story & Art by Saki Hiwatari
Vol. 1
Only $9.95
Please Save My Earth
www.viz.com
store.viz.com.
shōjo
©Saki Hiwatari 1986, 1987 / HAKUSENSHA, Inc. Cover art subject to change.

COMPLETE OUR SURVEY AND LET US KNOW WHAT YOU THINK!

☐ Please do NOT send me information about VIZ products, news and events, special offers, or other information.

☐ Please do NOT send me information from VIZ's trusted business partners.

Name: _____

Address: _____

City:_____ State:_____ Zip:_____

E-mail: _____

☐ Male ☐ Female   Date of Birth (mm/dd/yyyy): ___ / ___ / ___ (Under 13? Parental consent required)

What race/ethnicity do you consider yourself? (please check one)

☐ Asian/Pacific Islander ☐ Black/African American ☐ Hispanic/Latino

☐ Native American/Alaskan Native ☐ White/Caucasian ☐ Other: _____

What VIZ product did you purchase? (check all that apply and indicate title purchased)

☐ DVD/VHS _____

☐ Graphic Novel_____

☐ Magazines _____

☐ Merchandise _____

Reason for purchase: (check all that apply)

☐ Special offer ☐ Favorite title ☐ Gift

☐ Recommendation ☐ Other_____

Where did you make your purchase? (please check one)

☐ Comic store ☐ Bookstore ☐ Mass/Grocery Store

☐ Newsstand ☐ Video/Video Game Store ☐ Other: _____

☐ Online (site: _____)

What other VIZ properties have you purchased/own? _____
_____

How many anime and/or manga titles have you purchased in the last year? How many were VIZ titles? (please check one from each column)

ANIME	MANGA	VIZ
☐ None	☐ None	☐ None
☐ 1-4	☐ 1-4	☐ 1-4
☐ 5-10	☐ 5-10	☐ 5-10
☐ 11+	☐ 11+	☐ 11+

I find the pricing of VIZ products to be: (please check one)

☐ Cheap   ☐ Reasonable   ☐ Expensive

What genre of manga and anime would you like to see from VIZ? (please check two)

☐ Adventure   ☐ Comic Strip   ☐ Science Fiction   ☐ Fighting

☐ Horror   ☐ Romance   ☐ Fantasy   ☐ Sports

What do you think of VIZ's new look?

☐ Love It   ☐ It's OK   ☐ Hate It   ☐ Didn't Notice   ☐ No Opinion

Which do you prefer? (please check one)

☐ Reading right-to-left

☐ Reading left-to-right

Which do you prefer? (please check one)

☐ Sound effects in English

☐ Sound effects in Japanese with English captions

☐ Sound effects in Japanese only with a glossary at the back

THANK YOU! Please send the completed form to:

NJW Research
42 Catharine St.
Poughkeepsie, NY 12601

All information provided will be used for internal purposes only. We promise not to sell or otherwise divulge your information.